Why Information Systems Fail:
A Case Study Approach

INFORMATION SYSTEMS SERIES

Consulting Editors:

D. E. AVISON BA, MSc, FBCS
Department of Accounting and Management Science
University of Southampton, Southampton, UK

G. FITZGERALD BA, MSc, MBCS
Oxford Institute of Information Management
Templeton College, Oxford, UK

This series of student texts covers a wide variety of topics relating to information systems. It is designed to fulfil the needs of the growing number of courses on, and interest in, computing and information systems which do not focus purely on the technological aspects, but seek to relate these to a business or organisational context.

INFORMATION SYSTEMS SERIES

Why Information Systems Fail: A Case Study Approach

CHRIS SAUER BA, PhD
Senior Research Fellow,
Fujitsu Centre for Managing Information Technology in Organisations,
Australian Graduate School of Management,
University of New South Wales, Australia

ALFRED WALLER LIMITED
HENLEY-ON-THAMES

Published by
Alfred Waller Ltd, Publishers
Orchards, Fawley, Henley-on-Thames
Oxfordshire RG9 6JF

First published 1993

Copyright © 1993 Chris Sauer

British Library Cataloguing-in-Publication Data
A catalogue record for this book is available from the British Library

ISBN: 1-872474-08-X

All rights reserved. No part of this publication may be reproduced, stored in a retrieval system, or transmitted in any form or by any means, electronic, mechanical, photocopying, recording and/or otherwise, without the prior written permission of the publishers. This book may not be lent, resold, hired out or otherwise disposed of by way of trade in any form of binding or cover other than in which it is published, without the prior consent of the publishers. This book is sold subject to the Standard Conditions of Sale of Net Books and may not be resold in the UK below the net price.

Produced for the publishers by
John Taylor Book Ventures
Hatfield, Herts

Made and printed in Great Britain
by Hollen Street Press Ltd, Berwick-upon-Tweed

Contents

Preface ix

1 Introduction 1
   1.1 Issues 1
   1.2 Approaches to Failure 2
   1.3 The Model of Information Systems Failure 4
   1.4 Outline 6
   1.5 Readership 7

2 The Information Systems Process 10
   2.1 Information Systems 10
   2.2 Project Organisations 11
   2.3 Information Systems as Innovations 12
   2.4 The Support Management Process 13
   2.5 The Information Systems Process 14
   2.6 Conclusion 16

3 The Nature of Failure 18
   3.1 Systems Failures and Information Systems Failures 18
   3.2 Changing Views on Information Systems Failure 21
   3.3 Concepts of Failure 22
   3.4 Critique of Expectation Failure 24
   3.5 An Alternative Account of Failure 26
   3.6 Discussion 30
   3.7 Conclusion 32

4 Understanding Organisations 34
   4.1 The Variety of Theories 35
   4.2 Decision-Making and Cognitive Limits 37
   4.3 Structure, Technical Process, Environment and History 42
   4.4 Power and Organisational Politics 47
   4.5 Conclusion 53

Contents

5		Model Overview	55
	5.1	The Triangle of Dependences	55
	5.2	The Project Organisation-System Relationship	58
	5.3	The System-Supporters Relationship	60
	5.4	The Supporters-Project Organisation Relationship	61
	5.5	The Model	61
	5.6	Flaws and Failures	63
	5.7	Summary	64
6		The Information Systems Innovation Process	66
	6.1	The Innovation Process	66
	6.2	Context, Problem-Solving, Solutions and Support	70
	6.3	Flaws in the Innovation Process	84
	6.4	Conclusion	87
7		Support for the Project Organisation	90
	7.1	Information Systems Evaluation	91
	7.2	The Nature of Evaluations	92
	7.3	Influences on Evaluations	95
	7.4	The Effect of Evaluations on Support	96
	7.5	The Flow of Support	99
	7.6	Influencing Support	103
	7.7	Conclusion	109
8		Innovation, Support and the Process of Failing	112
	8.1	Web Explanations	112
	8.2	The Power of the Project Organisation	114
	8.3	Management Strategies	120
	8.4	The Dynamics of the Information Systems Process	125
	8.5	Conclusion	131
9		The Case Study Approach	133
	9.1	The Value of Case Studies	133
	9.2	Research Method for the Mandata Study	134
	9.3	Conclusion	144
10		Mandata - a Case History	145
	10.1	Background	146
	10.2	Initiation - September 1970 to February 1974	159

Contents vii

10.3	The Initial Development - February 1974 to August 1976	180
10.4	Review and Revision - 1976	196
10.5	Reorientation and Consolidation - August 1976 to June 1980	199
10.6	The Decision to Scale Back - 1980	235
10.7	Towards a Minimum Viable System - June 1980 to April 1981	237
10.8	Termination	239
10.9	Epilogue	241

11	Analysis of Mandata		243
	11.1	Was Mandata a Failure?	243
	11.2	Why Did Mandata Fail?	245
	11.3	By What Process Did Mandata Come To Fail?	251
	11.4	What Options Were There For Alternative Management Strategies?	287
	11.5	Conclusion	290

12	Five Case Studies in Failure		291
	12.1	The USS Starship	291
	12.2	The Energy Conservation System	296
	12.3	The Retail Buyers' Planning System	300
	12.4	Swissair	303
	12.5	Fiscal Impact Analysis System	306
	12.6	Conclusion	312

13	Summary and Conclusions		315
	13.1	Summary	316
	13.2	The Inevitability of Failures	319
	13.3	Recommendations for Practice	322
	13.4	Recommendations for Research	329
	13.5	Finale	334

Bibliography 337

Glossary Of Terms Associated With The Mandata Case 349

Appendix 355

Index 361

Preface

My working life has been spent both as a practitioner - a systems analyst - and as an academic teacher and researcher. This book is the product of a combination of perplexity and curiosity which has accumulated over the years. Why, I have puzzled, is there such a gap between what is taught in most textbooks and the reality of information systems projects? How can it all look so straightforward in the books and yet be so complicated, even intractable, in real life? In view of this, I have asked myself, shouldn't we replace the romantic idealism of the textbooks with a more naturalistic depiction of the hard reality that lies in store for most students who graduate into the information systems profession? My firm belief that we certainly should be more realistic has served to motivate my pursuit of a suitable understanding which would satisfy my curiosity and exorcise my perplexity.

This book is intended to be relevant to academics in their research and teaching, and to be relevant to practitioners, not by producing recipes for success but by promoting understanding. It is a part of my argument that much problem-solving in information systems projects is ad hoc. For this to be successful, understanding is most important. Thus, while the construction of theory is a central part of this book, it is theory which speaks to the social, behavioural and political realities of everyday life in organisations.

A more general aim of the book is to engender a more realistic view of information systems. I want it to be publicly accepted that information systems are typically hard to develop and prone to fail. We laugh at computer jokes of the 'to err is human, to really foul things up you need a computer' variety because they are subversive. But the jokers have all along recognised truths which the technocratic establishment has refused to acknowledge, viz computer-based information systems do not always help people or organisations, and it is usually a risky project to build them. Once these facts are openly accepted we may hope for the growth of a more mature approach to the problems of the field.

In writing this book over a period of several years I have received generous support from very many individuals and organisations. I am grateful to the following for financial support: the Research Committee of the School of Social and Industrial Administration at Griffith University; the University Research Committee at Griffith; the InterState Travel Grant, Special Research Grant and Study Leave Funds at the University of Western Australia. Also for further support for study leave, I must thank the Department of Computer Science at the University of Western Australia. The Department of Computing at the Open University kindly accommodated me as a Visiting Research Fellow for seven months of 1989-1990. The Fujitsu Centre at the Australian Graduate School of Management has provided the facilities for putting the final touches to the manuscript.

Ian Oliver first put me on to the Mandata case study discussed in chapters 10 and 11. The research would never have got anywhere without the support of the Public Service Board and its partial successor, the Public Service Commission. As Chairman of the Public Service Board, Dr Peter Wilenski approved access to the file archive. Ron McDonald kindly sorted out office facilities for me, and Pam Rhodes found me files to study even when office moves prevented her finding files for the day to day operations of the Public Service Commission. Her help was quite outstanding. The Public Accounts Committee and its Secretariat under Michael Talberg were hospitable and helpful in the early stages of this research. The ACT branch of Australian Archives was helpful in the later stages.

In particular, thanks are due to the many people who worked on or were associated with Mandata and who agreed to talk to me. Many were kind enough to show me documents from their own private archives. Several have read and commented on the case narrative and my analysis of it. In view of the fact that some have intimated that they would prefer not to be personally identified I have chosen not to mention any of the Mandata people by name. My gratitude to them is nonetheless heartfelt.

I am pleased to acknowledge permissions received from various sources. These include Jossey-Bass Inc for permission to reproduce as Figure 8.1 in this book Figure 7, page 30, from Kraemer, K.L. et al, *Managing Information Systems: Change and Control in Organizational Computing*. I am also grateful to the American Association for Artificial Intelligence, Elsevier Science Publishers, S.B. Sloane, G.W. Dickson, M.A. Janson, W. Rudelius, S.W. Hartley, H. Buechi, and W.H. Dutton for permission to summarise in Chapter 12 works either written or published by them. In addition, various departments and agencies of the Australian Public Service have granted permission to reproduce quotations from copyright material; these include the Public Service Commission, the Australian Government Publishing Service, the Department of Prime Minister and Cabinet, the Department of Transport and Communications, and the Treasury. I am grateful to them all.

As the manuscript has gone through different incarnations a number of people have been kind enough to read and comment on parts. These include David Avison, Steve Little, Perry Morrison, Robert Wood, and Ray Zammuto. I have learnt much from suggestions by Lynne Markus about the presentation of case material.

On a more personal note, my parents have always provided a background level of encouragement and support for what I do. This has served as a wonderful psychological security blanket. Sadly my father has not lived to see this book published. Anne Wrightson has ungrudgingly given me enormous support. For her it has been at the cost of time we might have spent together. I hope that she will be able to cope with seeing some more of me in the future.

Chapter 1
Introduction

Pioneers of computing might be excused for having supposed that early failures were an aberration, that they were just part of a learning experience, and that with time and the development of the right technologies failures would be prevented entirely. Today, however, writers on computing continue to draw attention to an apparently high level of failure (Forester & Morrison 1990). The newspapers, both trade and popular, report troubled projects in a steady stream (*The Guardian* 1989, *Computer Weekly* 1989, *Computing (UK)* 1989a, 1989b, *Computing (Australia)* 1990a, 1990b, Henderson 1990, Sloane 1991, Arthur 1993, Kane & Whitebloom 1993) while information systems professionals confirm the view that, notwithstanding an academic and commercial marketplace awash with patent remedies, real live systems continue to be a source of problems. Thus, it is no longer excusable to suppose that information systems problems will evaporate. Failure is a continuing fact of life.

The costs of failure are various. Economically, there is the cost of wasted investment in equipment and labour. There is also the cost of missed opportunities when a system promises benefits but fails to provide them. Costs may also be incurred in terms of diminished client service, witness a headline in *The Guardian* in 1989 - '£7m computer *slowed issue of passports*'. There may be risks to the community in a variety of ways. The most obvious are in applications where outcomes are highly visible such as air traffic control. Less obvious, but also significant, are the risks inherent in computer-based financial transactions. On top of this, the impact of failure on job satisfaction for information systems professionals constitutes a little acknowledged cost. The fact of failure has also caused damage to the image of the information systems community. For all these reasons, then, failure is worth investigating, understanding, and, where possible, avoiding.

1.1 ISSUES

There are many different issues relating to information systems failure. Some are conceptual, others empirical, and yet others are normative. The foremost conceptual issue concerns the very nature of the subject itself. What, after all, is information systems failure? This is fundamental and is a prerequisite of any useful study of failure. It is addressed in chapter 3.

The empirical issues are various. Roughly, they divide into *cause* issues and *effect* issues. This book is chiefly concerned with cause issues. Effect issues such as what is the general level of failures, what impact do they have on the economy, on organisations, on individuals, and the like are given little consideration here.

The questions of interest in this book are:

(1)   What causes failure?
(2)   By what process does failure occur?
(3)   Are some failures unavoidable?

The issues for which normative answers are required are:

(4)   How can failure be avoided?
(5)   How can we make the best of impending failure?
(6)   How can we best learn from experience of failure?

This book does not aspire to give complete answers to these normative questions, though it does offer some suggestions in chapter 13. Rather, it focuses on the development and application of a theoretical model which provides answers to the empirical questions. In doing this, it provides a basis for addressing the normative questions in more depth. Unfortunately, developing detailed answers to these questions is beyond the scope of this book.

1.2 APPROACHES TO FAILURE

The approaches taken to failure in the past can be characterised along the lines of this empirical/normative divide. Practising information systems professionals and practically oriented researchers have taken the design of techniques and tools for building and maintaining information systems as the top priority. This is the normative approach. They have made rapid identifications of what they have perceived to be the most important problems in information systems and have endeavoured to develop the techniques and tools to

Introduction

overcome them. It has been something of a limitation of this approach that so many alternative but similar aids have been developed. It is therefore very difficult to determine which have proved successful and which have not. The fact that practitioners sometimes refuse to use proprietary methods or only use them in part suggests that they may, on occasion, be as much part of the problem as part of the solution.

Empirical researchers, motivated by the same desire to address failure, have sought to identify causes in a more rigorous way. The outcome of this effort has been patchy. There is an increasingly widespread acceptance that social and behavioural factors have been given too little attention (Lucas 1975, Boland & Hirschheim 1985), but this has not translated into a unified framework for understanding information systems failure.

A fault of both approaches has been that they have presumed that the causes of failure would be fairly simply identified either by casual inspection or by relatively simple factor analysis. This book challenges that assumption.

The approach recommended here is to give detailed attention to actual cases. Too often books offer case studies which are either fictions devised specially to demonstrate a particular point or they are carefully filtered so as to bring out some points at the expense of simply ignoring others. If instead we study whole cases, rejecting no part of them as obviously irrelevant, and if we are unwavering in our pursuit of answers to the questions *why* and *how*, then we shall come much closer to a realistic understanding of information systems failure.

The cost of this approach is complexity. Unpalatable though it may be to those who believe information systems work should be simple, we must accept that it is highly complex. The implication of this is that there are no simple models of information systems processes and no simple and generally applicable solutions to the problems that arise. Furthermore, there are no readily available theoretical models of even moderate complexity which can be applied forthwith to actual cases. Consequently, this book develops its own.

The virtue of the case study approach is that it gives first place to the realities of information systems processes. It allows that everybody's experience can be relevant. In taking advantage of this to understand case studies, the crucial thing is that that experience be ordered and organised in such a way as to give realistic answers to our questions. It is part of the aim of this book to provide just such a model.

1.3 THE MODEL OF INFORMATION SYSTEMS FAILURE

The model developed in this book is driven by the account of failure presented in chapter 3. According to this account an information system should only be dubbed a failure when development or operation ceases, leaving supporters dissatisfied with the extent to which the system has served their interests. It is a more forgiving view of failure than most. Where other writers accept events such as missed targets or user resistance as sufficient to define a system as a failure even though it may continue in development or operation, the view advanced in this book is that while a system continues to be the object of a project organisation's efforts it must be serving some interests and so has not failed. Consequently, we should be more conservative in our use of 'failure' than is sometimes the case at present. Underlying this account of failure is a view of information systems which tries to tread a middle path between the assumption that information systems are instruments of top management to the exclusion of the interests of all other parties, and the assumption that an information system should be able to serve all interests. Rather, information systems are seen as an organisational resource which serves some stakeholders but not others. This account privileges those who support a system but does not presume them always to be top management.

The model developed here is in the tradition of natural systems models (Scott 1981) which explain systems behaviour in terms of the goal of survival. Survival is achieved through acting on the environment so as to obtain necessary resources which in turn support the system's continued action. The model portrays information systems project organisations as pursuing their survival through their work on an information system which is intended to serve supporters well enough to yield the support needed for the project to survive.

The model focuses on the project organisation, the information system, and its supporters. For the purposes of analysis these three are arranged into a *triangle of dependences* in which the information system depends on the project organisation, the project organisation depends on its supporters, and the supporters depend on the information system. The triangle of dependences provides the dynamic necessary for understanding processes which end in failure. Put very roughly, support influences the likelihood of flaws while the occurrence of flaws influences the likelihood of support. These effects will on occasion combine to produce a positive feedback loop.

Introduction

However, the triangle is not a closed system. Exogenous factors affect the ways in which the dependence relationships are enacted. They provide a potential brake against runaway positive feedback. The exogenous factors constitute the *context*. They include cognitive limits, technical process, environment, organisational politics, structure, and history. Thus, if a system is underfunded because top management does not understand its strategic importance, the result will be a flawed system which will result in further problems for the project organisation for which it will have insufficient funds. The process will go from bad to worse unless there is some change to the context. One such change might be a company takeover, the introduction of new management, and the provision of a more satisfactory level of support.

The context is also the source of problems. For example, the environment might generate new legal requirements, or it might be the source of flawed software utilities. Project organisations manage their problems with a combination of systematic problem-solving mechanisms, ad hoc problem-solving, and support. Since some elements of the context will normally be beyond the control of the project organisation it will be quite normal for flaws to occur. Flaws are sub-optimal decisions that create consequential problems. Flaws can be coped with in a number of ways if there is sufficient support. If there is not, they will, over time, affect the way supporters evaluate a system. If the project organisation is not able to manage support, these negative evaluations will result in loss of support to the point where there is no longer sufficient support to sustain the project organisation's efforts. This, then, is an information systems failure.

In effect, this model characterises the task of the project organisation as twofold. There is the process of developing and operating the information system (the innovation process), and there is the process of managing support. Since support can vary as a result of contextual factors it is not sufficient to rely upon the quality of the information system alone to win all the necessary support. Equally though, it is not sufficient to do nothing but manage support, because without having information systems benefits to show, the project organisation will ultimately lose whatever room it has for managing support and with it the support it needs. Both innovation and support management processes will require attention from the project organisation.

Failure, according to this model, is the final outcome of a dual process in which support and systems outcomes interact to produce a situation where the project organisation is unable to sustain itself through the support available to it. Chapters 5 to 8 elaborate this model.

1.4 OUTLINE

This book can be thought of as dividing into four parts: introductory, model development, case study and conclusions. The introductory part consists of this chapter and the following three. Chapter 2 sets out some basic concepts and terminology of the information systems process. Chapter 3 explores the very nature of failure. It starts by exploring whether we have much to learn from some of the other literatures which deal with failure. It turns out that neither the general systems failures literature nor the information systems literature provides any satisfactory, ready-made, explanatory model. It is therefore necessary to start with certain fundamentals including the development of a new concept of failure. Chapter 4 reviews areas of the organisation theory literature and elicits a number of concepts which will prove useful in the model building that follows. In particular, it yields the contextual dimensions which are employed later.

The second part of the book is devoted to constructing and elaborating a model which can be used for explaining cases of failure. Chapter 5 is a brief overview of the model. Chapter 6 provides an analysis of the information systems innovation process. It characterises it as a staged process subject to a variety of constraints and contingencies whose source is the context. In addition, it demonstrates how the innovation process can be analysed in terms of the project organisation's problem-solving and the problems it faces. This demonstration also shows that it is normal for the information systems innovation process to be flawed. Chapter 7 analyses those factors that affect support, including both decisions about support and its actual provision. In this chapter, information systems evaluations receive some attention because of their influence on supporters. In discussing evaluations some of the ways by which the project organisation can influence support are discussed. Chapter 8 combines the analyses of the innovation and support management processes. It starts with an analysis of project organisation power. This provides the basis for understanding how much - more often, how little - power the project organisation has over its context and its supporters. It then

Introduction

discusses the main management strategies open to the project organisation. The remainder of the chapter presents an account of the process by which a system might come to fail in terms of the underlying dynamic of the exchange of system for support.

The third part centres on one large case history which illustrates the use of the model. Because the model is designed for wide applicability not all aspects of it are necessary in this particular case analysis. This case was developed through original research, so chapter 9 sets out the methodology. The case history is described in chapter 10 and analysed in chapter 11. Chapter 12 explores several different cases which have been published by other researchers. This chapter further illustrates the use of the model and highlights some of the limitations of existing analyses.

The last chapter is a part on its own. It summarises the main points and develops conclusions for practitioners and researchers. An explicit argument is presented to the effect that there are some circumstances under which failure is unavoidable, in the sense that it is beyond the capacity of the project organisation to prevent. This conclusion is made explicit because it seems to be rarely understood and even more rarely permitted to inform practical decision-making. A brief analysis of future prospects suggests that though the information systems milieu will not remain static, the changes which are likely to occur will counterbalance each other. The inescapable conclusion is that information systems will continue to fail for the foreseeable future.

1.5 READERSHIP

There is already a wealth of books devoted to the technical side of information systems processes. By contrast, this one is for readers who want to understand the social, behavioural, and political aspects of information systems. More than this, though, it is for readers who are ready to grasp the core fact that the technical aspect is crucial but indissociable from the social, behavioural, and political. These readers will include information systems professionals and their managers as well as students, and scholars.

Practitioners encounter a wide variety of behaviours every day including devious political manoeuvres, the indifference of alienated project staff, the resistance of users, the apparent lack of management support, and so on. One has only to listen to the informal analyses that practitioners offer when stimulated by a drink after work to understand that there are many who have an instinctive feel for the wider view of their situation. Yet at the same time many of these same people will steadfastly refuse to let these analyses inform their working decisions. This book is predicated on the view that not only should practical decisions be influenced by more than just technical matters, but that the health of information systems projects will benefit from a broad based understanding. This book puts forward the foundation for such breadth of understanding.

The case study approach is intended to both show how the explanatory model can be used and provide examples with which they may identify. To read cases which are resonant with familiar problems helps crystallise practical experience. The cases discussed here by no means cover the full spectrum of difficulties practitioners face. The literature and our understanding will benefit from a greater range of detailed case studies.

For the student of information systems studying at the advanced undergraduate, graduate, or postgraduate level, this book is intended to provide a foundation on which to base a sophisticated understanding of the problems encountered in information systems projects and in particular failure. For the student with prior practical experience, the formal model will prove the most valuable part of this book. For the student who has yet to engage in a first live project, the case study element will prove invaluable. Of course, nothing substitutes for experience, but examples drawn from real life do give some perspective to all those courses in development methods.

Scholars and researchers in the fields of information systems, systems failures, public administration, and organisational innovation should find something to stimulate them. It is to be hoped that this will in time feed back into the current work. The explanatory model will certainly benefit from extension and refinement as a result of critical review. Chapter 13 spells out a number of the challenges still to be met. The case presented in chapters 10 and 11 is sufficiently substantial to be of interest in its own right.

Finally, this book is also addressed to those who are not fellow travellers, so to speak. All too often a book like this is only of interest to those who are already largely persuaded of the rightness of the ideas it presents. However, this book has been written in the consciousness that there are many who still do not see the relevance of the social and behavioural factors in information systems projects. They prefer to put their faith in a technical fix, yet to be invented, which will transcend the messy human dimension. This is a pipe dream, and this book constitutes an argument against the plausibility of such a dream. If the book has a single moral for its reader, whoever she or he may be, it is that there are no simple solutions to the problems we encounter in information systems processes.

Chapter 2
The Information Systems Process

Information systems can be approached by way of a number of different perspectives. For the company accountant an information system may be just another investment; for the user manager it may be a solution to a persistent problem; for middle management it may be a control mechanism; for operational users it may be a threat to the quality of their working life; and for programmers it may be a technical artefact. Thus, among others, economic, task, organisational, human relations/labour process, and technical perspectives are applicable to information systems. These perspectives have a tendency to treat an information system as an object. For example, middle managers seek to ensure the smooth running of organisational processes, so they are likely to see information systems as objects that impart control. The problem with thinking of an information system as an object is that this object does not spring fully integrated into organisational processes. It has an organisational history the details of which will affect whom it serves and how well it does so.

In this book much emphasis is given to the fact that an information system is part of organisational processes that are extended over time. A system has to be initiated, developed, implemented, operated and maintained. It can change over time. It can fail at any point in these processes.

In this chapter the concept of the information systems process is introduced in terms of its dual character as an innovation process and as a support management process. The organisational entity which is the active subject in these processes is the information systems project organisation. From this perspective the outcome at any time of an information systems process will be a function of the problems the project organisation faces, its capabilities, and the support it can command.

2.1 INFORMATION SYSTEMS

The term 'information system' can denote any of a wide variety of systems. Here, it applies especially to those computer-based systems whose major inputs and outputs are information, and which serve to coordinate the work of many different organisational functions. Typically, this includes systems such as payroll, sales orders, inventory control, and personnel records.

Many information systems thus defined appear to be purely administrative in that they support back office administration. However, not all information systems are administrative in this sense. For information industries such as banking, travel, and insurance, information systems are part of the technical or operating core of organisations. For example, automatic teller machines provide a core banking service; likewise, airline reservation systems provide a core service for travel agents. The model presented in this book is intended to be applicable to both back office and core systems.

All systems start out as an idea. This idea, or *abstract system*, is a necessary part of the process by which information systems are developed prior to being operational. When they can be executed they have achieved *concrete form*. Abstract systems are important because they have the potential to be realised and thereby serve some organisational stakeholders. It is this potential that allows an information system in abstract form to act as a resource for the project organisation in the gathering of support. When thinking about information systems in process terms, it is important to remember that systems have a lengthy existence as little more than an abstract idea before ever they are implemented as a deliverable product.

2.2 PROJECT ORGANISATIONS

A project organisation is simply that group of people who at a particular point in time are occupied with the processes of initiating, developing, implementing, operating or maintaining a given system. Typically those people recognised by other organisational actors as chiefly responsible for these various processes constitute the project organisation. It is not easy to be precise about project organisation boundaries. Pfeffer and Salancik (1978) place organisational boundaries around those parties the organisation can control. This serves as a handy rule of thumb. Thus, users involved in development full-time may still not be part of the project organisation because they remain independent. On the other hand, a user liaison officer under the authority of the project manager will count as part of the project organisation despite residual affiliations with users. Even with a heuristic like this, there will still be difficulties on occasion, for example where developers are a sub-set of the users. Indeed, in some circumstances it may appear as if there is no project organisation. Usually, though, this will not be the case. Ultimately, defining the boundaries of the project organisation is a matter of analytic convenience.

Use of the term 'project organisation' is not meant to imply anything about its structuring - hierarchical, organic, matrix, what you will - the structure may even change over time. Neither does it imply that there will be a distinctive formal organisational unit, nor that its membership will remain the same. It is simply that the different individuals performing a particular innovation process at any given time will constitute the project organisation.

2.3 INFORMATION SYSTEMS AS INNOVATIONS

An information system will almost always involve some element of innovation. Usually, information systems will embody some new organisational procedures. The physical realisation of the system will often be new; it may involve new equipment and new software. Moreover, because office manuals, where they exist, are rarely entirely up to date or accurate, the apparently straightforward task of automating existing clerical procedures will require new work. In some cases, the degree of novelty in both the procedures automated and the method of automating will be very high. A system exhibiting none of these characteristics will be solely a technical redevelopment. Even this will involve rewriting the program code. Thus, information systems will usually be innovations, but they will vary in their degree of innovativeness.

The fact that an information system is an innovation is important on several counts. First, though there may be carefully specified designs, there is always uncertainty about what the final product will be. Second, there is uncertainty about how the process of constructing the product will turn out. Third, there is uncertainty about who precisely the final product will serve and how well it will serve them. These three points add up to the conclusion that it is inappropriate to fix determinate criteria for what an information systems process must achieve. The information systems innovation process is a flexible process in which all kinds of things can change without invalidating the process or the end product. In particular, the design can change for a number of reasons. The system's application might change because its environment changes; an alternative design may appear preferable; new stakeholders may see new opportunities for using the system; the project organisation may discover or gain access to a better technology. Over time, stakeholders' understanding of the system will change as more information becomes available about the system and the context in which it will operate. It makes sense to accept that a project organisation will adapt its behaviour to changing knowledge of its circumstances. Other stakeholders will do the same. Users will change their requirements as they come to understand their systems better. In some cases these adaptations and changes may be quite major. The original sponsor of a system might drop out believing it no longer in her best interests. That the project organisation will sometimes seek an alternative sponsor for a revised version of the original sponsor's system seems a reasonable response. Changed behaviour in the face of changed circumstances is to be expected.

Thus, an information system is an organisational resource the responsibility and control for which can shift over time. Different groups can be involved in the innovation process at different times, each trying to make it an effective resource for them. As interests and stakeholder groups change, so the characteristics of the system may be adjusted accordingly. To paraphrase Cohen, March and Olsen (1972), the information systems innovation process can be roughly characterised as users looking for systems to which to attach themselves, systems looking for problems they can solve, and project organisations looking for work. This captures the fluid nature of the information systems innovation process. A more detailed account will be given in chapter 6.

2.4 THE SUPPORT MANAGEMENT PROCESS

The innovation process is one part of the information systems process. The other part is the support management process. Support management is necessary because the project organisation rarely if ever commands sufficient support on its own. Support is necessary to permit the project organisation to carry out the innovation process.

What the project organisation needs is resources which fund innovation, access to those who control contingencies over which the project organisation itself has no control, and power-broking by those with the ability to influence other potential supporters.

Some support may be guaranteed at the start of a project, but much of it will have to be won during the course of the innovation process. The continued provision of resources needs to be justified because funding an information system is an uncertain investment. There may be no return on the investment if things go wrong. Moreover, there is bound to be uncertainty about fixing and power-broking because they will be required to handle events which have not been anticipated. The project organisation will often have to seek out the relevant support as it is needed.

It is important to note that this description of the support management process does not imply that all project organisations devote half their efforts or anything like it to managing support. Indeed, some may give little or no attention to this process. How much attention they should give it will depend upon the problems of the innovation process and the uncertainty of existing support. These are both matters which will be discussed further in later chapters.

2.5 THE INFORMATION SYSTEMS PROCESS

The information systems process as a whole incorporates both the innovation and the support management processes (see figure 2.1). Innovation is uncertain and may be beset by a variety of unexpected problems. Even a smooth running innovation requires resourcing. Unexpected problems may require other forms of support. While the project organisation is learning about what it can do and who wants what, supporters and potential supporters will be learning about the rewards they can hope for, and evaluating their investments.

There is considerable flexibility in both innovation and support management. A project organisation can adjust its objectives, it can shift its schedule, it can cut corners, it can favour some users or supporters rather than others. Indeed, it can revise its situation in many ways. If supporters are unhappy with a project they can either back out or they can pressurise the project organisation to meet their demands. Equally, if a project organisation fears it might lose support it can take the initiative and attempt to persuade or bribe its supporters with promises of a better return. As a precautionary measure, a project organisation can give time to maintaining support by keeping its supporters informed, or by giving them an opportunity to participate. It can even hedge its bets by seeking out alternative supporters.

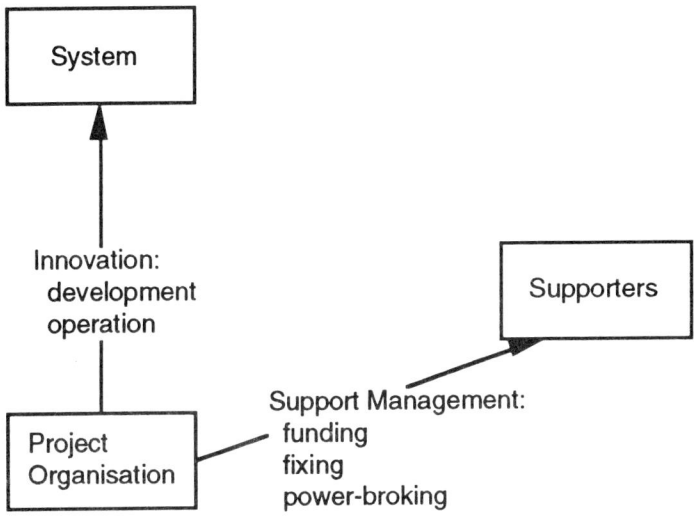

Figure 2.1. The information systems process as a dual process of innovation and support management

This flexible view of the information systems process stands in contrast to the traditional view in which at the start of any project objectives should be set, and constraints such as budget and schedule agreed, and in which failure is the failure to meet these standards. By contrast, the view proposed here is that deviations from what is agreed initially are to be expected in a process which is extended over time, often as much as several years, in which there are many uncertainties, and in which there is room for manoeuvre by both supporters and project organisation. Extending the characterisation of the information systems innovation process given in section 2.3, the information systems process as a whole can be thought of in terms of users looking for systems to which to attach themselves, systems looking for problems they can solve, supporters looking for investments, and project organisations looking for supporters. All of these component activities should be treated as legitimate or valid activities, so that the information systems process as a whole is seen as a natural response to extended uncertainty.

It must be emphasised that this characterisation of the information systems process as very fluid does not mean that project organisations are radically free to do just anything they choose. Project organisations are not free to change their activities in mid-process from, say, an accounting system for a hospital to a stock control system for its laundry. There will be constraints. Likewise supporters will usually not have unlimited support with which to seduce a project organisation. Supporters also work under constraints. Nonetheless, there will often be room for manoeuvre, and there is nothing wrong with project organisation and supporters alike making use of it.

2.6 CONCLUSION

The information systems process consists of two component processes - innovation and support management. They both permit room for manoeuvre by all the parties involved. The information systems process is therefore a fluid process in which the information system finally produced may vary considerably from its initial conception and where its supporters may have changed over its lifetime. This view of the information systems process will inform the concept of failure constructed in chapter 3.

Suggested Readings

1. Gorry, G.A. & Scott-Morton, M.S. (1971) A framework for management information systems, *Sloan Management Review*, Fall 1971, pp 55-70.

This paper was an early and influential attempt to place information systems in relation to their organisational setting. Much of its importance lies in its insistence on taking a decision-centred view of organisations. It was reprinted with a retrospective commentary by the authors in *Sloan Management Review*, Spring 1989, pp 49-61.

2. Markus, M.L. (1984) *Systems in Organizations: Bugs and Features*, Pitman, Marshfield, Mass.

This is a delightfully readable book. Chapters 2 and 3 present a taxonomy of information systems, indicating the likely organisational effects of the different types of system. It also contains interesting case study material.

3. Walton, R.E., (1989) *Up and Running: Integrating Information Technology and the Organization*, Harvard Business School Press, Boston, Massachusetts.

This book is also very readable. It treats information systems as innovations, and recognises the importance of support.

Chapter 3
The Nature Of Failure

There is no generally agreed account of the nature of failure. An answer is needed to the question, what situations, events or outcomes should count as characterising an information systems failure? This is a prerequisite of any further progress because it defines what is to be studied.

The purpose of this chapter is to construct a conceptualisation of information systems failure on which a descriptive framework may be based. Underlying the account that follows is the view that failures are best considered in terms of the process by which they come about. Failure is a failure of the information systems process. What counts is that the project organisation obtain sufficient support to enable it to continue to exist and to continue to service its information system. If it cannot manage this, then it is a failure. By contrast, more traditional approaches measure performance against such metrics as cost-benefit, user satisfaction, or schedules. These will generate useful evaluations but they do not constitute the very essence of failure.

This chapter starts by looking at what has been said about failure in a number of related fields to see what can be learned. This is followed by a brief review of what writers on information systems have typically made of failure. Four types of conceptual account of failure found in the literature are criticised. These criticisms are used as the basis for an alternative account.

Once the nature of failure has been clarified, it will be possible to develop a model in later chapters which will help us to understand failure in information systems processes.

3.1 SYSTEMS FAILURES AND INFORMATION SYSTEMS FAILURES

All kinds of technological and organisational systems suffer failure. Typically, each type of system is studied separately within its own field. While each field provides some interesting insights, all stop well short of providing any ready made theory of failure which could be applied to information systems.

There are various focuses of interest in both the popular and academic writings on failure: accidents, political/economic/financial failures, planning disasters, natural disasters, and information system failures. The general label, 'system failures', is sometimes taken to embrace all these different classes of failure (Bignell & Fortune 1984).

Accidents usually involve the breakdown of some system resulting in dysfunctional outcomes such as death, injury or damage to property. They are largely unintended, unanticipated discontinuities in system performance. Grand scale examples from recent years include the Chernobyl nuclear accident (Hawkes et al 1986, Hamman & Parrott 1987, Haynes & Bojcun 1988), the capsizing of the ferry, *Herald Of Free Enterprise* (a sadly ironic name for the boat in question), the Bhopal chemical process accident (Shrvastava 1987), and the *Challenger* space shuttle (Rogers 1986, Feynman 1988).

Politico-military failures cover a broad spectrum which includes failed military initiatives such as the US attempt to retrieve the hostages in Teheran, and the Bay of Pigs invasion, as well as political failures such as the Watergate cover up (for further examples and references see Janis (1987)). Economic/financial failures include such events as the October 1987 stock market crash and the more routine occurrences of corporate bankruptcies.

Planning disasters cover cases where a major physical planning process has been severely criticised in public and where its actual implementation has been undertaken in the face of major opposition and has not succeeded, or where the plan has had to be modified at substantial cost during the implementation process (Hall 1981). Hall's examples include the building of the Sydney Opera House which cost vastly more than originally proposed and which failed to meet the specifications for its main auditoria (though it did succeed outstandingly in becoming a symbol for Sydney). Another of Hall's examples is the Anglo-French Concorde which has found few buyers despite being technically very successful. It is worth noting that though these examples may have been planning disasters, they do not fall within the definition of failure to be developed here because they received the support necessary to implement them, and both still continue to operate.

Natural disasters include examples such as the 1989 San Francisco earthquake and the 1974 Darwin cyclone. Here it is the forces of nature which cause the damage. The interest in such cases often fixes on the failure of precautions such as earthquake reinforcement of physical structures or the failure of the information systems (not necessarily computer-based) by which warnings are issued and disseminated (Foster 1987). It is interesting to note that this latter is an increasingly common feature of discussions of all types of failure (Perrow 1984).

Recent studies of system failures exhibit a number of themes which provide some initial bearings for anybody interested in computer-based information systems failure. One strong theme is that failure, particularly in complex systems, is multicausal (eg Bignell & Fortune 1984). Those who take a general systems approach are especially likely to embrace this viewpoint.

Another theme is that minor failures are endemic in large, complex, tightly coupled systems, and that these will occasionally concatenate in unforeseen and unpredictable ways to generate a major accident or catastrophe (Perrow 1984, Reason 1987). In his analysis of the British accidents at Aberfan, Hixon and Summerland, Turner (1976) notes that the amount of information that can be attended to with scarce resources is considerably less than is required by the complexity of the situation. That there will be some accidents among such systems is therefore inherently unavoidable.

A further theme is the responsibility of designers as well as operators. There has in the past been a tendency to blame system operators such as control room staff, pilots and drivers, or maintenance staff for not acting in accordance with procedures, or for not diagnosing a problem quickly enough. In some recent public inquiries, investigations, and commentaries there has been an increasing recognition that operators cannot be expected to perform optimally when they are working in less than optimal circumstances. (Perrow (1984, p7) notes that the President's Commission into the Three Mile Island nuclear accident 'blamed everyone, but primarily the operators'!) In the stress of an emergency, the operators are even more in need of effective support systems, and these may be lacking as a result of design shortcomings or organisational exigencies. By similar reasoning it will be seen that designers too are human; and, like everyone else, they work in difficult organisational circumstances; therefore they will be unable to think of every eventuality. Failures, then, emerge from a complex interaction of factors including the human and technical components set in a social situation rather than resulting directly from the failure of a single human.

All these considerations are important and will inform the subsequent analysis of computer-based information systems failure. However, in themselves they do not constitute a complete framework for analysing systems failures. It is therefore necessary to examine information systems failure as a problem independent of other fields.

3.2 CHANGING VIEWS ON INFORMATION SYSTEMS FAILURE

In view of the apparently pervasive nature of information systems failure, the literature is surprisingly unilluminating on the topic. There has been a growing awareness of the different manifestations of failure, but our understanding of the nature and causes of failure still has some way to go. The specialist literature has slowly converged on a view that social and behavioural factors are more important aspects of information systems failures than the technical. A brief survey illustrates this progress.

There is no precise historical starting point to the literature of information systems failure; studies of management science implementations shade into studies of management information systems and information systems generally. Russell Ackoff's (1967) widely cited paper, *Management Misinformation Systems*, is perhaps as good a place to start as any. Its theme is that designers do not understand their context. Though Ackoff gives no evidence for his conclusions, his theme of the shortcomings of individuals in systems occupations was taken up by others. Dearden (1972) baldly blamed 'incompetent or ineffective people in charge of these systems'. Likewise Morgan and Soden (1973) saw the senior MIS executive as the prime determinant of success or failure.

However, even as these analyses were being published, alternative views were beginning to emerge. Argyris (1971), on the basis of studies of developer-user interaction, drew attention to the limitations of the interpersonal relations of the two parties and the likelihood that MIS would create conditions which would lead to executive resistance. Mason and Mitroff (1973) raised the issue of designing for individual differences among managers, although they did not directly link this to failure. They also included the type of the problem, the organisational context and the mode of presentation of information as relevant variables for study. Meanwhile Colton (1972), in surveys and interviews conducted in US police departments, discovered that it was not technical but behavioural and people oriented problems that hindered development there. He found that the main variables determining the difference between success and failure were top leadership, the extent of the gap between police and edp (electronic data processing) personnel, the establishment of development priorities, the quality of technical staff, and the emphasis on human-computer interaction.

Colton's view was echoed by Lucas (1975) who concluded that it was the fact that social and behavioural factors had been ignored that caused failures. This position has now been taken up by many students of the field to the point where Boland and Hirschheim (1985) see it as a research conclusion - effectively a consensus.

It is however a very limited conclusion. Baldly stated, it offers no suggestions for avoiding failure other than attending to the social and behavioural factors, advice which scarcely counts as practical. And, quite crucially for making further progress, it offers no coherent account of what constitutes information systems failure. The rest of this chapter is therefore devoted to the nature of failure while chapters 4 to 8 develop elements of a theoretical model for understanding failure in information systems processes.

3.3 CONCEPTS OF FAILURE

The best available platform from which to approach the concept of failure is a wide ranging review made by Lyytinen and Hirschheim (1987). Their analysis is a valuable starting point, but the concept of failure they develop is limited in certain respects. In order to develop a revised concept, it is therefore necessary to describe Lyytinen and Hirschheim's work and point out its limitations.

In discussing the question of what constitutes failure Lyytinen and Hirschheim abstract from the literature three distinct concepts: correspondence failure, process failure, and interaction failure.

Correspondence failure is a matter of failure to meet predefined design objectives. The system implemented does not correspond to what was required. This outcome has been common to many projects.

Process failure comes in two forms: failure to produce a system at all, and failure to produce it within reasonable budgetary and timescale constraints. A great many systems have encountered problems with budgets and schedules (Brooks 1975, Lehman 1979). Many others have been cancelled before being completed (eg Buechi 1982).

Interaction failure concerns levels of use and degrees of user satisfaction. It is not uncommon for systems which do reach implementation to fail to satisfy their users. Sometimes they are left totally unused, sometimes only partially (eg Miller 1983, Ince 1988, Sloane 1991). These are interaction failures.

Each of these three concepts is limited in that it takes no account of the forms of failure defined by the other concepts. Lyytinen and Hirschheim therefore propose a fourth concept of failure which they argue encompasses the others. They call their concept *expectation failure.* They define it as (Lyytinen & Hirschheim 1987, p263):

'inability of an IS [information system] to meet a specific stakeholder group's expectations'

The thrust of this definition is that failure hinges upon people not getting what they want out of an information system. Lyytinen and Hirschheim (p261) actually say that information systems failures 'signify a gap between some existing situation and a desired situation for members of a particular stakeholder group'.

Lyytinen and Hirschheim expand their account in a number of ways. They see it as being particularly relevant when the information systems process is viewed as one in which there are multiple interests, interests are fluid over time, and the satisfaction of those interests is the result of bargaining and negotiation, a view which is consistent with that advanced in the previous chapter of this book. The concept of expectation failure does not give preference to the interests of any particular group and so can in principle accommodate any kind of shortcoming in an information system. However, it is this very flexibility and scope that prove to limit its value.

3.4 CRITIQUE OF EXPECTATION FAILURE

In preparing to criticise expectation failure it must be made clear from the start that there is no objectively correct account of failure. Criticisms can only be justified in terms of a wider frame of reference which itself cannot be objectively right or wrong. Rather we may choose to accept or reject the frame of reference according to whatever values we hold.

'Failure' is an explicitly evaluative term. It implies a problematic and undesired situation. It is a natural response to wish to remedy it. Therefore it would be desirable to have an account of failure which indicates both where to look for the causes of failure and how to respond. It is in this respect that expectation failure is found wanting. In giving equal weight to all interests, the concept does not distinguish which inabilities to satisfy stakeholders' interests are most problematic to explain and which least so. Consequently, there are no indications as to which problems demand priority and what types of action might satisfy them.

Expectation failure is rooted in the apparently politically equitable stance of total pluralism. On this view, no interest is intrinsically worth more than any other. However, it does not follow from this that all discrepancies between stakeholder interests and outcomes are equally puzzling. This is the basis of three criticisms:

(1) Some expectations are more reasonable than others
(2) Expectation failure ignores intention
(3) Some stakeholders have greater capacities than others

Some expectations are more reasonable than others. Clearly, there are expectation failures where the expectation is on the face of it perfectly reasonable, such as failures to meet objectives, to satisfy user requirements, to be used, to meet the budget and/or schedule, and the like. But there are also others which are more peripheral. For example, expectation failure allows that I may be a stakeholder in a system by virtue of my status as an interested observer and commentator on the field of information systems. It is in my interest that systems be built according to the design principles I advocate so as to show off the virtue of my way of thinking, yet this does not make me a stakeholder in every information system. Or, more precisely, it does not make me a stakeholder whose values and interests should form a basis for ascribing failure.

Consider another example. Suppose that computer-based information systems had with almost no exception eliminated routine work, and deskilled or displaced clerical and manual workers, while at the same time they had increased productivity, effectiveness and profits. Had such been the case, the interests of routine workers would have been systematically ignored. Any expectations they might have had that computers would serve their interests would have been disappointed. Yet it would be stretching credulity to suggest that these systems would have been failures.

The purpose of these examples is to show that expectation failure encompasses just about any mismatch between the interests of any person or group and an information system. Attempts to exclude such counterexamples will only lead to undesirable exclusions as well. For example, to fall back on an appeal to *established* interests would be to exclude new found interests.

This problem is more pervasive. Not only does expectation failure apply to any situation in which anybody has an interest in a given information system, it appears also to apply to interests however unrealistic or ephemeral. If users wanted a system that would never produce incorrect output, the first bug would make it a failure.

The second criticism is that expectation failure ignores intention. Failure implies intent to avoid it. To describe a system as a failure in respect of interests that are not recognised and when the goal of satisfying those interests is not actively pursued is to miss the distinction which separates the problematic case where a stakeholder intends to further some interest but fails to do so from the far less problematic case where there is no such intention.

The third criticism is an extension of the second. Some stakeholders have greater capacities than others, yet expectation failure makes no reference to stakeholders' capacity to achieve their desired ends. Thus, clients of a powerful monopolist may have no say over information systems that the monopolist develops and with which they are obliged to interact. If information systems make life harder for the clients, it is surely significant that the clients could not have prevented the outcome. Expectation failure makes no acknowledgement of differential capacities to act in a given situation.

This last point is important because it motivates the approach outlined in the next section. Failure to achieve your own interests when you are powerful is very different from failure when you are powerless. The former is an intriguing problem. The latter hardly so.

The expectation failure concept permits a single information systems process to be studded with failures. Not to distinguish between those situations which are retrieved by the actions of the project organisation and its stakeholders and those which are not seems strange particularly when it is accepted that the information systems process is very flexible with stakeholders moving in and out of the process over time. Expectation failure does not respect the difference between the situation where a system is terminated and serves nobody and the situation where it serves some and not others. The latter is surely the normal state of affairs.

Despite its shortcomings, expectation failure has many virtues. It makes it explicit that failure is relative to interests which may reasonably differ among stakeholder groups. In focusing on this aspect, it makes it very clear that failure is an evaluation rather than a description. It also points out that the satisfaction of interests may vary in degree and over time. These are worthwhile advances in our understanding of failure. They delineate dimensions along which classifications may be usefully made. However, if we want to treat expectation failure as anything more than a basis for taxonomy, its shortcomings intrude.

Expectation failure permits the delineation of a boundary around a class of problems that all reasonably warrant serious investigation, viz cases where stakeholders do not get what they want out of a system. What it fails to provide is a concept that discriminates among more and less problematic situations.

3.5 AN ALTERNATIVE ACCOUNT OF FAILURE

Where expectation failure is too liberal a concept, the account which follows is more conservative in two respects: whose interests count for most, and the level of dissatisfaction that is required. These differences aside, it retains considerable flexibility with respect to recognising changing interests and conceptualising information systems as part of a complex web of social action. In this section an alternative account of information systems failure is outlined. This is followed by a discussion of its virtues and its limitations. The account is firmly based in a process view of information systems. A more detailed description of the process of information systems failure will be offered in chapter 8 based on the model developed in chapters 5 to 7.

To start, how should we think of information systems failure? Information systems are the product of a coalition of stakeholders, one of which takes the major part of developing, operating and maintaining the information system in question. This is the project organisation. It is able to carry out its work because of the support it receives from other stakeholders. This support is given because these other stakeholders expect or find that the system will or does serve their interests. The coalition is thus united by its interest in the information system. The project organisation performs its work in the interests of supporters in return for their support. Roughly speaking, when this exchange is no longer viable, the system fails.

The exchange between project organisation and supporters is important because the project organisation has the technical capabilities which are required for sustaining an information system while its supporters provide resources (eg materials, decisions, and power) without which the project organisation would be unable to exist and make progress. On the face of it, the project organisation and its supporters are the coalition with the best chance of making the system serve their interests. It surely is interestingly problematic if this coalition is unable to make the system work for it.

Failure finally and irreversibly occurs when the level of dissatisfaction with a system is such that there is no longer enough support to sustain it. The objective indicator is the cessation of all work whatsoever on the system. This means the termination of all development, maintenance, and operation. It is convenient to label this view *failure as termination* or *terminal failure* This state has been referred to elsewhere as project abandonment (termination in development) and system abandonment (termination in operation) (Ewusi-Mensah & Przasnyski 1991). Ewusi-Mensah and Przasnyski distinguish total, substantial, and partial abandonment. Termination, as it is used here, implies total abandonment. Substantial and partial abandonment are better seen as strategies available to a project organisation for retaining necessary support. The case history presented in chapter 10 provides instances of all three forms of abandonment.

Termination or abandonment is a necessary but not sufficient condition for failure. Where there is a large measure of agreement between project organisation and supporters that a system has been a good investment but that it no longer serves as a basis for their relationship then there is no need to talk in terms of failure. The changes to interests and to the system which occur over time will have done so at a rate acceptable to the parties concerned. It is for this reason that the account presented here makes reference to the level of dissatisfaction.

Dissatisfaction is not easily gauged. One way to estimate it is in terms of the level of criticism and its surrogates aimed at the system at the time of termination. In this context 'surrogates' means actions that evidence opposition to the system. For example, if a system is scrapped because managers do not use it, this may be taken as a surrogate for criticism. It clearly expresses their opposition and dissatisfaction. Another relevant indicator is if the terminated system is not replaced even though the organisational application it was designed to perform remains.

Failure as termination is distinctive in that it accepts expectation failures as a normal part of the information systems process. The occurrence of discrepancies between interests and outcomes is normal because of the inherent uncertainty of the innovation process. The innovation process is a process of discovering answers to the questions: what exactly the system will do, how it will do it, and what its effects will be. Different parties will have differing views about what the answers should be, and they will try to influence what answers are actually given. As the uncertainty is reduced, so new parties may become involved while earlier stakeholders may drop out depending upon their assessment of the degree to which the system will be instrumental to their goals. As such changes will be actively pursued by different stakeholder groups, it is inevitable that there will be dissatisfactions among stakeholders. Expectation failures are not interesting in their own right so much as for the causal linkages among them, and for their combinative effect. Terminal failure is the culmination of a process in which conditions build up to a point where the project organisation's relationship with its supporters breaks down irretrievably.

This is very much an ecological or natural systems view in which the information systems innovation process involves a search for a niche which provides the information system with enough support to continue to exist. Underlying this is the assumption that the project organisation whose task it is to develop, implement, and operate the system is concerned chiefly with assuring the continued existence of the system. This is not an unreasonable assumption. The premature termination of any system reflects badly on the project organisation. Avoidance of this is a means of assuring the project staff's own continued employment. Success or avoidance of failure may also lead to promotions, pay rises, and stimulating assignments. Furthermore, the close association of information systems professionals with their systems makes it very likely that they will experience a sense of pride in and responsibility for their system regardless of matters of employment or reward. It is therefore reasonable to conclude that project organisations aim to sustain the continued existence of their system.

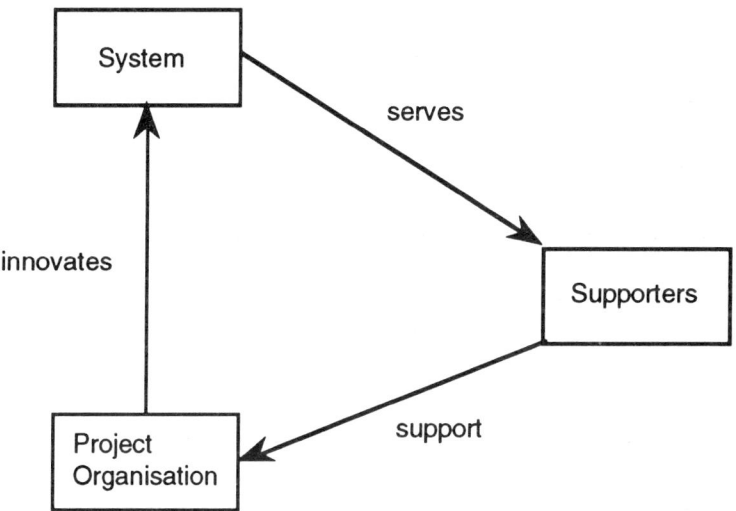

Figure 3.1. Triangle of dependences: system, supporters and project organisation

This account of failure focuses on the exchange relation between the project organisation and its supporters where the information system and support are the resources traded. The project organisation is heavily dependent on the provision of support in the form of material resources, help in coping with contingencies, and other exercises of power. The provision of this support will be dependent on the benefits supporters expect to obtain. Supporters will from time to time review their investment through the course of the systems innovation process. So, the information system requires the efforts and expertise of the project organisation to sustain it; the project organisation requires supporters' support; supporters require benefits from the information system. This yields a triangle of dependences (figure 3.1). In chapter 5, a number of contextually based qualifications will be introduced which will show that these dependences can be upset from any of a number of quarters. The process by which failure eventuates can start anywhere.

To summarise, systems can have all kinds of adverse outcomes yet not be described as failures. Systems can be delivered late, at inflated cost, with inadequate functionality, and may be largely unused, all without necessarily being failures. So long as the project organisation can command the resources and power to sustain its system, it will not be counted a failure because it is serving some organisational purposes.

3.6 DISCUSSION

In their classification of failure concepts, Lyytinen and Hirschheim (1987) subsumed failure as termination under process failures. Its seeming deficiency was to exclude the other types of failure. Here, the strategy has been to develop a view of the information systems process according to which correspondence, interaction and the other forms of process failure are not appropriately viewed as failures because they are all recoverable over time.

The concept of failure as termination has a number of advantages. First, it highlights the distinction between instances of expectation failure in the information systems innovation process and subsequent events and outcomes. It follows through the causal effects of expectation failures.

The second virtue is related. A process need not be judged a failure the moment it encounters unforeseen difficulties. Though the system may be performing below expectations, this may prove to be only temporary. Provision of further support may arrest or reverse the process of failing. For example, the OS/360 operating system project suffered a variety of problems over a long period but received continuing support from IBM. Brooks (1975) rightly views it as not a failure.

The third advantage of this conceptualisation of failure is that it gives direction. It targets a particular kind of phenomenon that is distinctly problematic - termination. It also directs us to the relationship between the project organisation and its supporters as a source of explanations and a focus for efforts aimed at avoiding failure.

Following on from the third point, this view of failure suggests some interesting insights. The premise that information systems are the product of an innovation process, and are to some extent instruments in search of organisational purposes and protectors, implies that the more innovative the system is intended to be, the greater the uncertainty, and hence the more likely that there will be a flux of potential supporters, with the project organisation seeking to balance its ability to sustain the system against the possibility of valued support. More political activity may be expected in cases where the system is particularly innovative. The project organisation will need to tailor its system to the requirements of those supporters it believes it can satisfy and who in turn can provide support. If it is unable to do this satisfactorily, the project organisation may actively seek out parties willing to support a system with the specific features it has the ability to construct and operate.

One problem of this account relates to its reliance on the public evaluations of the supporters who finally withdraw. Unfortunately, unlike reaching the end of a book, reaching the end of a system is not the end of the story for the organisation. An expression of dissatisfaction at termination may relate less to the system that has just been closed down and more to the pursuit of some further goals. For example, a supporter may refrain from criticism in the hope of obtaining preferential treatment from the information systems department in some future project. It is for this reason that behaviours other than just linguistic utterances are considered. Even so, the same problem may apply. Ultimately, 'failure' is a judgement, and expressions of dissatisfaction which impute failure may be part of a political game of wider dimensions. So, final perceptions of a system have to be viewed with caution.

A deliberate feature of the account of failure offered in this chapter is that it leaves open the possibility that some information systems cannot realistically satisfy the expectations set for them.

Information systems professionals may simply be unable to mobilise and retain the support necessary to meet their supporters' expectations. This should not be a surprise. Indeed, some writers are well aware of the difficulties of achieving satisfactory results. Markus (1984, p211) says of her approach, 'None of these recommendations is foolproof and none is especially easy . . . '. Lyytinen and Hirschheim (1987, p274) note of their concept of expectation failure, 'It also denies the availability of simple failure resolutions in all situations'. So we may ask, are some failures impossible to avoid?

Lyytinen and Hirschheim (1987, p301) conclude their review with the hope that 'future research will ultimately result in the demise of information systems failures'. Given their definition of failure, this implies that it will be possible to satisfy all interests in an information system. Even on the more conservative account presented here this seems an implausible prospect. Chapter 13 will pursue this conclusion.

3.7 CONCLUSION

In this chapter it has been argued that the systems failure literature yields a few useful, general insights but that information systems failures warrant separate study. The literature directed specifically to information systems failure has so far been quite limited in its value though there has been a discernible shift toward studying social, behavioural and organisational factors. Existing concepts of information systems failure have all proved to have shortcomings. A critical review has led to an account in which failure is seen as occurring when termination of a system leaves the system's supporters dissatisfied with the service they have received from it. The focus for study is the project organisation's relationship with its supporters. It emphasises survival of the project organisation and system. This account yields a focused conception which has direct implications for the questions we ask. It leads to the substantial question: why do information systems fail to serve their supporters sufficiently to obtain the support needed to sustain them?

The next four chapters are designed to provide a basis for a discussion of the process of failing which is given in chapter 8. Chapter 4 elicits from the organisation theory literature some working principles for applying to the analysis of the information systems innovation process and the behaviours of supporters. Chapter 5 returns to and expands upon the central exchange relationship between project organisation and supporters. Chapter 6 considers the difficulties that beset the information systems innovation process while chapter 7 looks at the problem of managing support. Chapter 8 attempts to put it all together in a thoroughgoing process perspective.

Suggested Readings

1. Department of Bignell, V. & Fortune, J. (1984) *Understanding Systems Failures*, Manchester University Press, Manchester.

This is a good starting place for understanding the variety of systems failures and their common elements.

2. Lucas, H.C. Jr (1975) *Why Information Systems Fail*, Columbia University Press, New York.

This book is close to being a classic. It is the earliest synthesis of knowledge about information systems failure. It emphasises the importance of social and behavioural factors in causing failure.

3. Lyytinen, K. & Hirschheim, R. (1987) Information systems failures: a survey and classification of the empirical literature, *Oxford Surveys in Information Technology*, Vol 4, 257-309.

A long paper, this survey covers an enormous range of literature.

4. Laudon, K.C. & Laudon, J.P. (1991) *Management Information Systems: a Contemporary Perspective*, Macmillan, New York.

For those wanting a succinct piece on the standard view of success and failure, chapter 19 fits the bill.

Chapter 4
Understanding Organisations

Computer-based information systems are built by organisational units for operation in organisational contexts with a view to obtaining organisational benefits. If we are to understand the development and operation of information systems we must understand how organisational factors enter into these processes, a conclusion already arrived at in the research literature about failure. This is not to ignore the technical side of information systems, rather it is to say that technical matters are to be subsumed under a broader framework - the organisational.

Life in organisations is not only more complicated than was supposed by early management and organisational thinkers, it is more complicated than is acknowledged by the folk theories of people working in organisations today. As Stamper (1973, p340) has put it, 'Commonsense is not an adequate guide to the anatomy of an organisation'. Indeed, one of the central problems of avoiding failure is knowing what to do in what context when even the best theories currently available are unable to provide reliable guidance. In this chapter I shall make the best I can of organisation theory to develop a model for applying to information systems processes. In fact, it will be a sub-model of the model for explaining failure which is outlined and elaborated in the following chapters.

Organisation theory concerns itself with explaining the behaviours of organisations and of the people and other organisations with which they interact. Organisation theorists have mostly sought generally applicable conclusions. They have had very little to say about the subject of interest here, the individual applications of computers to organisations, although during the last decade some writers have shown growing interest in the use of microchip technology in the manufacturing and service industries (Buchanan & Boddy 1983, Wilkinson 1983, Davis & Associates 1986, Child & Loveridge 1990).

The position adopted here is that the innovation and support management processes are both organisational processes and consequently require an organisational model to explain their outcomes. The organisational model focuses on problem-solving and decision-making and the factors which affect decisions and their effects. These factors count as the *organisational context.* The model proposed is therefore a contingency model in that it takes outcomes of decision-making to be contingent upon the actual contextual circumstances obtaining. The same decision will yield different outcomes in different circumstances.

This chapter describes six dimensions of context. These are cognitive, technical, environmental, structural, political and historical factors. Elements associated with these dimensions of context will help us understand why things go wrong in information systems processes. While it is the negative side of these dimensions that are of most interest here, it is always worth remembering that social structure is both constraining and enabling (Giddens 1984). This insight can be extended beyond social structures: the same factors that make life hard also make it easier than it might otherwise be. Thus, memory may be cognitively limiting, but at the same time it enables problem-solving.

Before proceeding to elaborate on the dimensions of context to be used in the rest of this book, it is worth giving some indication of theories which will not be considered, for there are too many to explore them all. So, section 4.1 addresses this matter. Section 4.2 points out the limits to organisational decision-making and indicates their relevance to the study of flawed organisational processes. In section 4.3 the role of organisational structure, history, technical process and environment is outlined. The ubiquitous political dimension is explored in section 4.4.

4.1 THE VARIETY OF THEORIES

Hirschheim (1985) has drawn the attention of information systems researchers to the variety of theories which might be applicable. In this book our attention will be confined to what might be called mainstream objective theories.

Burrell and Morgan (1979) classify theories on two axes: subjective-objective, and regulation-radical change. The theories to be discussed here are clearly at the objective end of the first axis, but hover on either side of the midpoint of the regulation-radical change axis. Thus Marxist and neo-Marxist class-based analyses will be left aside, as will what Burrell and Morgan (1979) classify as 'radical humanist' approaches such as existentialism. 'Interpretivist' theories which give prominence to actors' interpretations of situations will also be disregarded even though some information systems researchers are exploring them (eg Hirschheim 1985). Even within the mainstream, Classical Theory and the Human Relations ideas will be left aside though it is worth saying a word or two about them because they still have a considerable influence on management culture.

Classical Theory includes Taylor's (1947) scientific management, and the administrative theory of Fayol (1949) and others. Classical Theory has emphasised the design of work into rigidly formalised routines with a view to achieving clockwork performance. It is out of favour for a number of reasons. First, several studies have shown that there is no one best way of organising (Woodward 1965, Lawrence & Lorsch 1967). Second, Merton (1936), Selznick (1949) and Gouldner (1954) have all demonstrated that Classical Theory's preferred form, bureaucracy, exhibits serious dysfunctions. Third, writers such as Dalton (1959) have shown the limits of the formal structure as a description of organisational functioning. This has been sufficient to 'do for' Classical Theory in social scientific circles. Unfortunately it continues to have a pernicious effect elsewhere. Many hard-line technologists and computer scientists persist in believing that because they themselves deal with well-behaved mechanisms, organisations could be equally well-behaved if only they were engineered properly. The context described in the rest of this chapter shows why this view of organisations is profoundly misconceived.

The Human Relations school emerged in competition with Classical Theory because the latter appeared to ignore the human aspect of organisations. It has emphasised job satisfaction, motivation, morale and similar variables. Though in many respects well-intentioned, it too has been interested in developing an understanding of organisations which would allow them to be engineered more precisely. However, the Human Relations School has failed to demonstrate any relationship between its key variables, such as morale, and performance, and its very foundations have been formidably criticised (Carey 1967, Perrow 1979). It is an approach which offers little to the understanding of information systems.

By contrast with these earlier mainstream theories, an eclectic

4.2 DECISION-MAKING AND COGNITIVE LIMITS

There is a long line of development of the idea of organisations as decision-making systems from Simon (1957) through March and Simon (1958), Lindblom (1959), Cyert and March (1963), Thompson (1967), Galbraith (1973, 1977), Mintzberg (Mintzberg 1973, Mintzberg, Raisinghani & Théorêt 1976) to Cohen, March and Olsen (1972). It is a development which has introduced new complications over time as the inadequacy of earlier conceptions has become clear.

The model developed in chapters 5 to 8 and applied in chapters 10, 11, and 12 is directed at improving our understanding of decisions about information systems. The fact that these are organisational decisions permits us to take advantage of the insights offered by the decision-making perspective. Precisely because of its recognition of the variety of decision processes, the variety of non-rational influences, and the limits to decision-making, this perspective can be employed to help understand the difficulties of complex organisational processes such as information systems development and operation. It provides us with some insights into why organisational processes fail.

A brief review of this perspective is followed by an explanation of how these ideas help us understand the fallibility of organisational processes, a matter which has obvious bearing on information systems failure.

4.2.1 Organisational decision-making

In the first half of the twentieth century the most influential view of organisational decision-making was that of economists who took it as axiomatic that organisations make rational decisions based on perfect information. This was rejected by the Carnegie school (in particular, Simon 1957, March & Simon 1958) which drew attention to the psychological factors affecting decision-making. It focused on how people solve problems as a basis for making decisions. Its central insight was that human cognitive capacities are severely limited. They are rarely able to match the complexity of real world problems, so algorithms which generate optimal solutions are generally unavailable. Moreover, we rarely obtain perfect information. But, even where we do have perfect information and an algorithm, we may not have the computational resources to take advantage (Simon 1981). Problem-solving in organisations will rarely be a rational application of a known maximising algorithm to a base of perfect information. More often, problem-solvers satisfice which is to say that they adopt the first acceptable solution they find rather than searching for the best possible. The conclusion was that problem-solving, and so decision-making, occurs under bounded rationality - rationality limited by cognitive constraints.

According to March and Simon (1958) problem-solving consists of several phases: problem formulation, search for alternatives, evaluation of alternatives, and choice of preferred option. Each phase might be made up of smaller problem-solving processes. Instead of using maximising algorithms, problem-solvers employ heuristics (rules of thumb). For example, they suggested that problem-solvers would focus on variables over which they have some control in preference to those under the control of others.

Problem-solving and hence decision-making will vary in its form. At one extreme where a problem is well understood, it will be routinised into a performance programme. Each time the problem has to be solved, the individual worker will execute the pre-existing programme. Any decisions will be automatic as defined in the programme. Highly routinised organisational tasks such as taking telephone orders for a mail order firm will be like this.

At the other extreme, where there is a high degree of uncertainty associated with a problem, decision-making will be subject to problem-solving from scratch. This is the case with innovation. By definition, new problems will not have pre-existing programmes.

Decision-making theory under bounded rationality is appealing on first acquaintance. In particular, it seems obvious that organisations are nothing without humans, and this theory functions at the human level. Moreover, as March and Simon show, it can be applied at the supra-individual level of groups, committees, units and whole organisations.

Despite its seductive appearance the theory of decision-making under bounded rationality requires a number of elaborations if it is to capture the splendid pageantry of organisational life. As Lindblom (1959) argued, much of the time people just 'muddle through'. Braybrooke and Lindblom (1963) subsequently presented the strategy of disjointed incrementalism as an empirical description of certain kinds of decision-making. Disjointed incrementalism is a combination of adaptations employed to overcome the limits to our decision-making capacities. It includes such practices as considering only small shifts from the status quo rather than reviewing radical solutions, and adjusting ends to means as well as means to ends.

Cyert and March (1963) also found the theory wanting. They identified conflict of interests as a fundamental characteristic of organisations. According to their account, goals are established through bargaining among coalition members. There may be many inconsistent goals at any time. The organisation may even pursue inconsistent goals by only attending to a limited number at once. Moreover, they noted that search need not be rationally driven. Information may be acquired because the organisation is looking for alternatives, but it may also become available because alternatives are looking for an organisation.

Thompson (1967) extended this by proposing that there would be a dominant coalition which would be the most influential source of decisions. He noted that coalitions form for defensive reasons as well as because of conflict. Coalitions form as a means of increasing their members' power over some source of dependence. So power is significant for decision-making regardless of the perceived levels of conflict. Pettigrew (1973) provides a detailed exemplification of the political process involved in organisational decision-making.

Cohen, March and Olsen (1972) took an even more radical step away from the bounded rationality tradition. In a much cited passage they suggested (March 1988, p294) that some organisations are best seen as

> 'collections of choices looking for problems, issues and feelings looking for decision situations in which they might be aired, solutions looking for issues to which they might be an answer, and decision-makers looking for work'

Together they all rattle around in the 'garbage can' until propitious circumstances arise. Thus, rather than a problem being treated as a given, it is just as much a dependent part of the whole decision-making process as the solution. It has, of course, been commonplace in industry, especially in the computing field, to describe particular projects as solutions in search of a problem, a phenomenon sometimes known as technology-push, of which more will be said in later chapters. The view of the information systems process as a flexible process in which stakeholders and project organisation negotiate over what interests an information system will serve is influenced by this conception of organisational decision processes.

There are further influences on decision-making. That affective considerations enter into decision processes is only just beginning to be understood. Dean (1987) stresses the deep emotional involvement of managers in decisions relating to innovative projects. Research for the case study described in chapter 10 has provided evidence of high levels of emotional commitment in the problem-solving processes of an information systems development, with corresponding levels of distress when things went wrong. Even ten years on, one manager found it almost too painful to speak about the project.

The picture that emerges from this discussion is of organisations as decision-making systems where decision-making is bounded by human cognitive limits, disjointedly incremental, the object of political activity, subject to affective influence, and may depend on what chance has placed in the 'garbage can'. It is a complex picture.

4.2.2 Fallible decision-making

Once fully rational decision-making is seen to be untenable as an empirical account, the hope that organisational decision-making can be flawless is dashed. The limits to cognitive capacity necessitate the use of heuristics and heuristics are not algorithms for obtaining a right answer every time; they are rules of thumb which may or may not work. Consequently, the likelihood of flaws is built into organisational decision-making processes.

Taking the stages of decision-making one at a time, each one can be conceived as itself a fallible problem-solving process.

Starting with problem formulation, nothing guarantees that our selection of a problem is well made. If a particularly vociferous user clamours for attention, the project organisation may be inclined to see the problem as doing what the user wants rather than rectifying a deeper problem which underlies the user's complaints. In the search stage we may easily generate ineffective solutions. This is particularly so where the effect of a proposed solution is not readily testable, perhaps because its outcome would be expensive in time or resources to achieve. For example, the proposal to develop an expert system may be inappropriate, but this may not be possible to determine in advance. The evaluation stage involves assessing different possibilities according to the decision-maker's values. But, this will not be a simple, determinate process. For example, cost-benefit analyses may include some factors and not others. Are overheads such as heating and lighting to be included? What is the appropriate discount rate for a discounted cash flow? And, when all is said and done, it is still possible to make mistakes in the calculations, to omit important factors. So it remains quite possible that evaluations will be incorrect. When it comes to choice, the dimensions on which proposed solutions are evaluated may not be commensurable. If for this reason no total ordering of options is possible, the choice will be as much subject to heuristics as any other stage, and like all the other stages may be flawed.

Much the same point can be made about problem-solving in the organisational hierarchy. A top level decision will be implemented by many decisions at lower and lower levels. Regardless of the merits of the top level decision, those taken lower down the structure may fail to implement the top decision in any of the ways discussed in the previous paragraph.

The difficulty of effective decision-making will be exacerbated by other factors such as the political and the affective both of which add further dimensions to the problems faced and the behaviours involved in problem-solving processes.

To summarise, this section has reviewed the decision-making theory of organisation in order to draw out some of the richness of this conception. In particular, we have looked at the constraints on individual and organisational problem-solving which affect organisational decision-making. The basic message is that all organisational decision-making is constrained by *cognitive limits*. This applies to information systems project organisations as much as any other. In the next section four further dimensions of the context will be described. Finally, the political dimension will be introduced.

4.3 STRUCTURE, TECHNICAL PROCESS, ENVIRONMENT AND HISTORY

An organisation's context will influence both the problems it faces and the process by which it solves them. The problems will be shaped by the constraints which the organisation recognises, particularly those deriving from its environment. This process will be influenced by the organisation's own structure and by its problem-solving technology. Where unanticipated events occur which affect the problem and the problem-solving process we may call them *contingencies* (Thompson 1967). A constraint which is not recognised may be experienced as a contingency (Friedman 1989) by its actually impinging on the organisation. These considerations indicate that an organisation's *structure*, its technology or *technical process*, and its *environment* will all be significant elements of the context affecting its decision-making. In addition, though, it is worth taking account of *historical factors*.

Organisational structure will be discussed in the next subsection. Technology, to be referred to as technical process, and environment will be the subjects of sub-sections 4.3.2 and 4.3.3. History is discussed in section 4.3.4. Power and politics are discussed in section 4.4 not as a variable but as a fundamental condition of organisational life.

4.3.1 Structure

Classically, organisation theory has viewed structure in terms of design parameters such as job specialisation, behaviour formalisation, training and indoctrination, unit grouping, unit size, planning and control systems, liaison devices, vertical decentralisation, and horizontal decentralisation (Mintzberg 1979). These are by no means comprehensive or necessarily the most appropriate categories. However they are a useful starting point for considering how structure can affect information systems outcomes.

Organisational structure is important in two ways. When

Understanding Organisations

information systems project organisations are viewed as organisations in their own right it becomes apparent that structural arrangements will be relevant influences on organisational action and outcomes because that structure will affect problem-solving. For example, a high degree of behaviour formalisation in a project organisation may result in a failure to recognise contingent problems because no scanning occurs beyond that which has been formalised. When project organisations are viewed as sub-units of a larger whole, structure is important because it constitutes both an influence on problem-solving behaviours and a dimension of the problem the project faces. As an example of the former, a project organisation structurally distanced from top management may be constrained in the possible solutions available to it because it does not have access to the support it needs. The fact that existing structures define existing information flows in user areas shows that structure will constitute part of the system design problem for a project organisation.

In focusing on structure we are free to be more catholic in our choice of relevant structures than the organisational research literature which is based on statistical correlation of measures of variables. In fact, any established organisational practice may be viewed as a structural constraint.

4.3.2 Technical process

Several writers on organisations have emphasised the role of technology in affecting outcomes. Mintzberg (1979) following Hunt (1972) distinguishes the technical system from the technology. The technical system concerns the core operating processes as instantiated in the work organisation and its associated machinery, whereas technology concerns the knowledge and skills inherent in the technical system. The view of technology as machinery alone is now widely held to be inadequate. Hage (1987, p261) calls it 'the fallacy of misplaced concreteness'. Technology in the sense of knowledge and skills is here treated as a feature of the environment. The term 'technical process' is used rather than 'technical system' to avoid confusion with information systems usages.

Woodward (1965) identified three types of technical process: unit, batch and continuous production. Her research indicated that the technical process had a profound effect on the efficacy of the associated organisational structure. Perrow (1967, 1970) posited two dimensions of the technical process: the extent to which exceptions could be anticipated, which he called the routineness of the work, and the degree to which the technical problems could be analysed. Thompson (1967) distinguished three types of resource interdependence related to technical process - pooled, sequential and reciprocal interdependence - each of which would influence structure differently.

Table 4.1. Dimensions of the technical process

Dimensions	Relevance
unit production	each system must be treated separately
partly analysable	not possible to routinise the process
reciprocal interdependence	formalisation likely to inhibit innovation
complexity of software	software inherently prone to flaws
software medium	human difficulty with logic makes medium prone to flaws
construct levels mismatch	leads to inescapable complexity

Information systems typically involve unit production. They are not routine despite attempts to develop systematically applicable methods. (This point is developed further in chapter 6.) The technical problems are only partly analysable. For example, our ability to control complexity in programs is still more of an art than a science because we lack a practical theory of programs. The technical process requires reciprocal interdependence. Development methodologies are not so well developed that it is possible for information systems to be built in a sequentially dependent structure. Clearly, if a project organisation structure inhibits reciprocal interdependence it is to be expected that it will encounter difficulties. This would be likely to occur where structures are highly formalised and centralised (eg in an information systems development project this would lead to an overloaded project manager), or where there is limited job specialisation leading to cognitive problems in coping with the less routine parts of the job (eg a single programmer analyst developing a project involving many different technologies), or where there is greater specialisation but restricted coordinating mechanisms (eg many technical specialists working in geographically remote locations).

At a more detailed level, there are various other aspects of the technical process which will affect information systems outcomes. The most important are the inherently high level of complexity in software, the fact that the medium employs logical constructs which humans are not typically good at handling (Wason & Johnson-Laird 1972, Johnson-Laird 1983), the very abstract nature of the software medium, and the mismatch between the level of the primitive constructs with which programmers deal and the level of constructs by which organisational applications are typically described by users. All of these pose technical constraints on the problem-solving behaviour of information systems project organisations. Table 4.1 summarises the various dimensions of the technical process.

4.3.3 Environment

Burns and Stalker (1961) brought to general attention the role of the organisational environment. They distinguished only stable and dynamic environments, arguing the case for bureaucratic organisation in stable environments and more flexible, organic organisation in turbulent environments.

Thompson (1967) following Dill (1958) divided the task environment into four categories: customers, suppliers, competitors, and regulators, this last including government and unions. An organisation is then seen as having boundary spanning units which form a protective layer to buffer the productive core from the effects of a volatile environment. But, organisations do not just protect themselves from their environment; the organisation is now seen as an active interventionist in its environment (Perrow 1979).

More recently, there has been growing interest in an institutional environment whose relation to the organisation is less obviously rational than that of a task environment (Meyer & Rowan

1977, Scott 1987, Little 1990). Others have drawn attention to sedimented selection rules (Clegg 1979, Clegg & Dunkerley 1980). The common theme is that there are deeply embedded social structures or norms that may influence organisational activity even though they are not instrumental to any particular organisational task. Requiring that an apprentice printer study outmoded hot metal technology is an example of a constraint set by an institutional environment. For an information systems project organisation this amounts to much the same thing as saying that the organisational culture and its constituent sub-cultures function as a form of environmental constraint.

For the purposes of subsequent analysis, seven environmental components are distinguished. The first six are: customers, suppliers, competitors, regulators, representative/interest groups such as trade unions, and institutions or culture. The seventh is technology which, as was mentioned in the last section, means the knowledge content of technology rather than its physical attributes which are a matter for suppliers. All these components of the environment have the potential to affect the work of the information systems project organisation although not all will be salient in any given case.

4.3.4 History

In trying to make sense of organisational decision-making and action, history can be important. Past decisions and events may often become institutionalised in an organisation's structure, but not always. Single events are not structural. The memory of a past mistake does not have to be embedded in structure to influence future decisions.

Kling (1987) has noted the role of the history of commitments made in a given computing milieu in influencing subsequent events. For example, an abortive attempt to develop a particular type of application need not itself generate new structures yet it may have a crucial deterrent effect on future efforts.

History seems more obviously a constraint than a contingency, but different interpretations of the same events leave it open for history to be represented in different ways. Thus, history can come to affect a situation in unexpected ways. For example, past decisions can be inspected to find ways of interpreting them which will be consistent with current preferences. Promises of support are likely to be particularly susceptible to reinterpretation. It is therefore worth including history as both a constraint and a contingent source of uncertainty for organisational decision-making.

Not only is organisational decision-making constrained by cognitive limits, it is also subject to the influence of structure, technical process, environment, and history. All these contextual dimensions are relevant to understanding information systems processes. In chapters 6, 7 and 8 the features of the context will be used to help us understand the problems of information systems project organisations and their supporters.

It remains to discuss one further aspect of organisational life. This is the crucial matter of power and politics.

4.4 POWER AND ORGANISATIONAL POLITICS

So far the focus has been on the factors which influence organisational decision-making. It has been assumed that the value element could be taken for granted, that what was at stake was getting the organisation's job done. But, things are not so simple because as was noted earlier there may be multiple competing constituencies, each seeking its own advantage. This section now expands upon the role of power and politics in understanding and explaining organisational outcomes.

It is very tempting for the theoretically tidy minded to set up a contrast between different types of theory, particularly between theories which emphasise task orientation and those which emphasise political behaviours, and suppose that one must be superior. By contrast, Weick (1979) points out the systematic equivocality of organisational actions. We as humans make organisations what they are, and there is no requirement that we be consistent in this. We may alternate between giving primacy to the political and the task rational. Indeed, the same action may constitute both a rational solution to a task problem and a political response to a political problem. There can be no definitive answer as to which it really is. Both types of theory are valuable aids to understanding.

4.4.1 The nature of power

To start, it is worth trying to get clear what power is in order to be able to identify the organisational actions and events which this concept can help us understand and explain.

Power certainly involves some party or constituency having the capacity to obtain its own ends. Early conceptions of power saw resistance as an indication that power was being exercised (Dahl 1957). If the less powerful party was prepared to do what the more powerful wanted, then power was not exercised. Subsequently it has been argued that it is an exercise of power to prevent an issue reaching an arena in which it can be contested (Bachrach and Baratz 1970). Consequently, resistance is not an essential indicator. For example, Pettigrew's (1973) study shows how control of information flows can influence outcomes by preventing important issues being contested in key decision-making forums. Power can be even more subtle in that it may be possible to control the wants of others (Lukes 1974). More radical theorists see the very social structures by which we live as suffused with power (Clegg 1979).

For the purposes of this book it is not necessary to pursue the subtleties of various definitions. What we can conclude about power is that it involves the potential to influence others both positively by getting them to do things they would prefer not to do, or negatively by preventing them from contesting issues they might otherwise contest.

4.4.2 The sources of power

Organisational politics does not arise, as many think, solely because devious people pursue self-aggrandising policies. In fact, power emerges naturally from division of labour and the dependences that arise from it (Pfeffer 1981). Division of labour results in differences of interests. The need to integrate the products of these divisions and differences guarantees there will be dependence relations which will in turn form the basis from which power may be established and exercised.

Dependence is the basis of power (Emerson 1962). Asymmetric dependence differentiates power relations from exchange relations (Blau 1964). Pfeffer (1981) notes that there are two basic forms of dependence and hence power. First, there is *resource dependence* where some other party controls important resources. The main forms of such resources are monetary and material resources, information, and social legitimacy (Pfeffer & Salancik 1978). Second, there is *dependence on another for coping with important uncertainties* (that is, control of strategic contingencies) (Crozier 1964, Hickson et al 1971). In this book the capacity to cope with important uncertainties is treated simply as a type of resource, so that in general we can say that power accrues to those who control resources which are important to others.

There are various factors which affect the degree of dependence of one party on another. Pfeffer and Salancik (1978) identify three such factors. First is the importance of the resource to the party that lacks it. Second is the discretion of the party possessing the resource over its allocation. And third is the concentration of control over the resource. Thus if resource X is important to A, B has control over the allocation of X and B is the sole source of X, then B will have power over A through A's dependence on B for X. According to strategic contingencies theory, the effects of dependence on power will be qualified by the immediacy, substitutability, and pervasiveness of the valued service (Hickson et al 1971, Hinings et al 1974). Such qualifications not only help us to recognise the likely power relations obtaining in an organisational situation, they suggest ways in which dependent parties may act to reduce the power of the other party. For example, Blau (1964) notes that the dependent party can avoid dependence by providing a reciprocally desired resource or service, by finding alternatives, by coercing the provider, or by doing without the resource or service.

Pfeffer (1981) points out that both resource dependence and strategic contingencies views are static, and that in addition power can be derived from control of some part of a sequential decision process. Pfeffer identifies three sources of power to control decision processes: control of decision premises, control of considered alternatives, and control of information about the alternatives.

Pfeffer also notes three further relevant factors. First, he points out that the greater the consensus about values and goals within a subunit, the easier it will be to act coherently and effectively in a power struggle.

Table 4.2. Static bases of organisational power

Dependence	Resource/Service	Influences on Dependence
Control of resources	money	importance of resource to party lacking it
	materials	
	information	discretion of resource possessor over allocation of resource
	social legitimacy	concentration of control of resource
Control of services	strategic contingencies	immediacy
		substitutability
		pervasiveness

His second point is that what counts as central to an organisation's mission and consequently which are the most important resources and contingencies is a matter for negotiation and manoeuvre within the scope defined by certain established business constraints. Thus, for an information system it may be that a crucial activity is promoting an image which defines the system as central and hence empowers the project organisation. Who becomes important within the project organisation will then depend on the outcome of negotiations over the provision of appropriate image-making services.

Pfeffer's third point is that power requires the ability to exploit it. The more skilful players are at exercising power, the more potent their sources of power. Two factors are important in this. The one is structural position within the organisation. Clearly, hierarchical position will affect the ability to exercise power. The other factor is the individual's personal attributes such as articulateness, existing stature, skill at diagnosing situations, knowledge of the rules of the organisation's decision processes, and personal self-belief.

In all, the sources of a particular party's power will be

significantly dependent on pre-existing circumstances. The existing social structure will largely determine who has what degree of control over which resources. It will not be possible simply to decide to become powerful and achieve such a position immediately. Certainly, it is possible to make small adjustments in the power differential in a particular relationship, but it is rarely possible to make major changes quickly.

Power is a relational concept in the sense that it concerns the relations among multiple parties. The power differential associated with a given relationship will vary over time as the resource on which it is based becomes more or less important to the dependent party and as other relevant factors concerning the availability and control of the resource change. Power is not an absolute attribute that applies to all of a party's relationships.

Table 4.3. Dynamic bases of organisational power

Aids to Control of Decision Processes	Factors Affecting Exercise of Control
control of decision premises	consensus about values and goals
control of considered alternatives	ability to negotiate preferred goals
control of information about alternatives	political skills - structural position - personal attributes

Tables 4.2 and 4.3 summarise the factors that affect organisational power and its use. Having obtained a picture of what power is and how it is derived, there remains the question of its use in organisational politics.

4.4.3 The political process

The political perspective explains organisational outcomes in terms of exercises of power which themselves may have been preceded by actions intended to change the relative power of different parties. This is the political process.

Pfeffer (1981, ch5) discusses a number of political tactics. He suggests that there are three classes of tactic. Most important is the unobtrusive exercise of power. Second, is the gaining of legitimacy for the decisions that have been subject to influence. Third is the building of support for a favoured position. Within these three classes Pfeffer describes a number of specific tactics.

The selective use of objective criteria is a tactic for unobtrusively influencing which alternatives are discussed seriously in a given decision process and on what dimensions the alternatives are evaluated. The apparent objectivity of the criteria imparts legitimacy. The employment of external consultants works in a similar way. Controlling the agenda is another tactic. The objective of this class of tactic is to determine which issues are considered for decision and which are not allowed to surface. Pfeffer notes that factors such as the order in which issues are considered will influence what options are available to different parties.

Where it becomes necessary to build support for a particular organisational position or strategy other parties have to be involved. It may be appropriate to build a coalition either internally or externally. The basis for coalitions will usually be some common interests which both parties think they can pursue more effectively through joint action. The other common tactic for building support is coopting. This is important where the coopted party is either uninterested or actively opposed to the position for which support is sought. Pfeffer explains the efficacy of coopting as deriving from a number of sources. First, it exposes the coopted party to new information. Second, it brings to bear pressure to conform and with it pressure to justify uninterest or opposition. Third, by labelling the party as now a member of a particular constituency both that party and others will form new behavioural expectations. Finally, coopting gives the new member of the constituency a stake in its common interest. Committees, Pfeffer notes, serve as a vehicle for coopting interests as well as imparting legitimacy, and helping build support for decisions.

Chapter 7 will discuss the process of sustaining support for an information systems project organisation. The analysis employed there will make use of this catalogue of political tactics.

4.5 CONCLUSION

What we have discovered from organisation theory in this chapter is not so much *what* to think about information systems as *how* to think about them. The general approach to be taken in subsequent chapters is that decision-making and organisational performance can be understood in terms of the organisational context. The factors to be considered are cognitive limits, organisational structure, history, technical process, environment, and politics.

While any of these may affect an information systems situation at any time, following Kling (1980) it is reasonable to suppose that where there is a high level of uncertainty, as in a radically innovative system, there will be a substantial role for power and political analysis in explanation. This is because radical change threatens the established power relations of an organisation far more than minor change. By contrast, where a problem is relatively well understood, involving minor change, more established structures can be expected to be more important in explaining performance and outcomes. Here organisational structure and technical process may prove to be more salient. This perspective will be taken as a basic underpinning of the analyses that follow.

Suggested Readings

There are many good introductory texts on organisations.

1. Morgan, G. (1986) *Images of Organization*, Sage, Beverley Hills, Calif.

This provides an excellent introduction to the many different and fruitful ways by which people are able to understand aspects of organisations.

2. Mintzberg, H. (1979) *The Structuring of Organizations: A Synthesis of the Research*, Prentice-Hall, Englewood Cliffs, N.J.

An elegant resumé of the research findings which relate organisational context, structure, and performance.

3.   Weick, K.E. (1979) *The Social Psychology of Organizing*, Addison-Wesley, Reading, Mass.

Widely cited, Weick provides an alternative, almost subversive, view of organisations. Full of accessible insights.

4.   Pfeffer, J. (1981) *Power in Organizations*, Pitman, Marshfield, Mass.

A thorough account of the research findings on power and politics by one of the leading researchers in the field. Well written.

5.   Pfeffer, J. (1992) *Managing with Power: Politics and Influence in Organizations*, Harvard Business School Press, Boston Mass.

A more up to date offering from the author of 4 above. Highly readable with plenty of concrete examples.

6.   Cohen, M.D., March, J.G. & Olsen, J.P. (1972) A garbage can model of organizational choice, *Administrative Science Quarterly*, 17,1, March.

Proposes a fluid account of organisations. It can be seen to have influenced the model of the information systems process developed in this book.

Chapter 5
Model Overview

Failure as it is defined in this book is intimately linked to project organisation survival which is itself coupled to system survival. A project organisation's existence depends upon its having a system to build and operate. When support for the project organisation evaporates leaving dissatisfaction at the termination of the project, then the system can be said to have failed. The advantage of this approach to failure is that it captures a distinctive class of cases which are uncontroversially failures. It has the further benefit of suggesting particular aspects of the information systems process as central to the understanding of failure.

This chapter serves as a relatively short summary of the explanatory model developed in the succeeding three chapters. It is based upon the triangle of dependences introduced briefly in chapter 3.

The chapter starts with some background. It describes how each of the three relationships characterised by the triangle is problematic inasmuch as it will be influenced by a variety of exogenous factors. Some implications of the fact that the triangle is not a closed system will be discussed. Finally, the distinction between failures and flaws is introduced for subsequent use in understanding how failures come about.

5.1 THE TRIANGLE OF DEPENDENCES

Information systems exist to serve stakeholder interests. They require a variety of forms of support if they are to function at all. The information systems project organisation has a special role in getting a system to function. But support for carrying out this role will only be given if supporters' interests are served. So, there is a triangle of relationships as depicted in figure 3.1 and reproduced below as figure 5.1. Put simply, what it says is: an information system is fashioned through its project organisation's activities; the project organisation requires support; and supporters need a payback from the system. Problems in any of these three relationships will be the source of consequential difficulties for the other two, and unless the problems can be solved, this will lead ultimately to a total withdrawal of support and system failure. Of course, life is never so simple. Many qualifications are appropriate. This chapter indicates the nature of these qualifications.

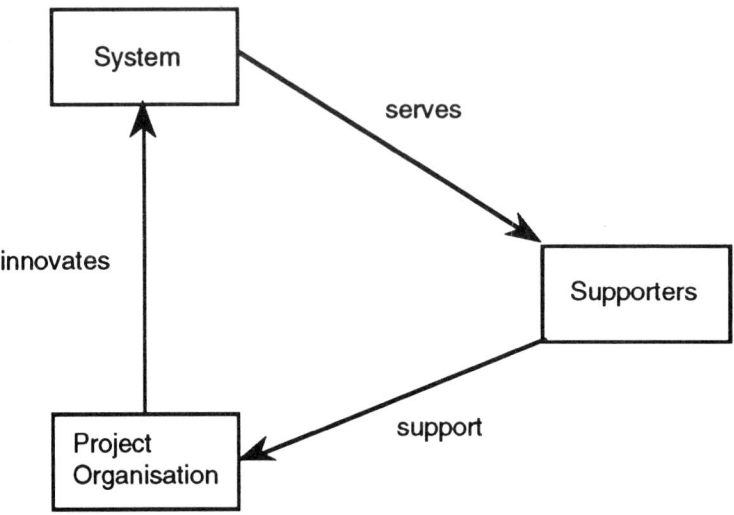

Figure 5.1. Triangle of dependences: system, supporters and project organisation

To expand the explanation of figure 5.1 it is first necessary to say something about the system, the project organisation, and supporters. Recapping from chapter 2 a project organisation is simply that group of people who at a particular point in time are occupied with the development, operation or maintenance of a given information system. An information system can have either an abstract or a concrete form. The important thing about an information system whatever its form is that it must serve some organisational stakeholders and thereby function as a resource for the project organisation in gathering support.

Who, then, are the supporters? Supporters are those who actually provide support. In chapter 4 a total of five types of resource on which an organisation may be dependent were identified: monetary resources, material resources, information, social legitimacy and control of strategic contingencies. For the analysis of information systems project organisations, particularly those which are part of larger organisations and are therefore subject to its rules, a slightly different categorisation is preferable. *Funders* provide finance, material resources such as buildings and people, and information where it is more like a capital resource than a consumable. *Fixers* manage strategic contingencies, control important decisions, and provide information with a shorter lifespan. *Power-brokers* have the power to influence funders, fixers and other power-brokers. Not a lot is known about how the social legitimacy of information systems is managed. It might be that it would be appropriate to have a fourth category called legitimators, but for the present purposes it is assumed that this is a function performed by funders and fixers in the process of providing support.

It is important to note that there are internal as well as external supporters. The members of the project organisation will receive inducements for their work, but if they withdraw their support for a project, this will have immediate effects on their system.

Sometimes a project organisation will negotiate for support from a stakeholder who has not previously been involved, or it will seek to regain support from a stakeholder who has previously withdrawn support. Strictly, neither stakeholder meets the definition of supporter given above. However, sometimes it is convenient to refer to them as supporters so long as the meaning is clear.

As indicated above, the triangle of dependences (figure 5.1) depicts three relationships which need elaboration. The crucial point to note is that the triangle is not a closed system. Each relationship is subject to a variety of exogenous factors which influence how it will affect the rest of the triangle. How well the project organisation conducts the innovation process depends on a variety of factors such as the extent to which the application is understood, the technical process employed, the rate of change of the technology, the quality of the information systems professionals and so on. Likewise, whether supporters decide to continue their support depends on factors such as how they perceive the system in relation to their interests, what alternative uses there are for their resources, and what external pressures there are on them to provide support. And, the actual support they provide may depend upon what they perceive to be needed and this may differ from what the project organisation wants or thinks it is getting.

Thus the triangle acts as a device for organising our thinking about the information systems process. It does not in itself offer any explanations. It provides a framework on to which an explanatory superstructure can be layered. This superstructure consists of more detailed accounts of the three relationships depicted in the triangle.

5.2 THE PROJECT ORGANISATION-SYSTEM RELATIONSHIP

The process by which a project organisation develops, maintains and operates an information system is widely acknowledged to be problematic. The purpose of this section is not so much to explore in detail the different ways in which the systems innovation process may be approached, but rather to use the conclusions of chapter 4 to show the sources of constraint and contingency for the project organisation in its relationship with its information system. Systems development and, to a lesser extent, operation and maintenance have been the subject of extensive discussion by writers in the field. Some of their ideas will be considered in the next chapter which addresses the project organisation-system relationship at far greater length.

The organisational context of an information systems process will create difficulties for the project organisation. The information system which it seeks to build and maintain will function in an organisational environment which is typically understood and partly controlled by those who are to operate it, interact with it, and use it. These parties, generically called users, are themselves subject to an intra- and extra-organisational environment which they have to manage. Environmental changes can affect the context into which the system is to fit, with consequent implications for the project organisation. Either the project organisation makes changes in order to adapt the system or its subsequent performance will be diminished. The environment is thus a source of constraints and contingencies which the project organisation will not necessarily be able to control. Moreover, cognitive limits suggest that the project organisation will not be able to predict or anticipate all relevant environmental change with the consequence that environmental contingencies will be experienced.

The technical process consists of designing the system, constructing it, and subsequently adapting it to change over time. Ideally, the environmental management task is completed satisfactorily so that the technical process can be carried out unhampered by intrusions from the environment. In practice, things are never so neat. But, even supposing they were, the technical process would not be a programmed procedure for problem-solving. Information systems are one-off developments which require some problem-solving from first principles. The complexity of the task far exceeds the current cognitive limits of individuals or organisations to control with precision. Consequently, there are reasons to suppose that even under ideal conditions the technical process would be a source of difficulty for the project organisation.

In addition, there are usually predefined organisational structures which constrain the project organisation. For example, a fixed hierarchy of decision may mean that user approval for the system design lies with an uninformed, or uninvolved manager. Or an historical decision may constrain the space of possible problem solutions.

The reality is complicated still further by organisational politics. Two types of politics are relevant. There is the politics of support where the resources needed are subject to contest by other stakeholders. This is the core of the two relationships which involve supporters. And, there is the politics of the system and the innovation process. The system itself may be a matter for contest among different organisational stakeholders (see Markus (1984) for an example). Or, the innovation process may be contested internally as for example when there is dispute about how to structure the programs in the system or by what strategy to implement it. Clearly, where users are significant supporters as is often the case, the two types of politics overlap. The differentiation is made to help simplify the analysis.

Thus, it can be seen that the organisational context will make the process of developing, maintaining and operating an information system problematic for the project organisation. It does not follow that given a certain level of support a project organisation can guarantee to achieve a certain quality of system. Other factors may intervene.

5.3 THE SYSTEM-SUPPORTERS RELATIONSHIP

What is important in this relationship is not that an information system should serve its supporters at any and every point in time, but that supporters judge it to serve them or be likely to serve them *at some time*. Thus, it is supporters' evaluations that are crucial. These evaluations will depend on far more factors than the actual value of the system to them. The context will play its part in various ways.

The cognitive problem is readily exemplified. The development phase of an information system is when most support is required, but it is also the time when outcomes are least certain. All the factors which potentially adversely affect the quality (in terms of supporters' interests) of the final system remain as uncertain for supporters as for the project organisation.

In addition, supporters may be subject to pressures from their environment. Alternative projects may compete for their support, or the interest the system was to serve for a supporter might cease to exist as a result of other changes. For example, a production planning system designed to smooth an assembly process in the face of erratic supply of components would cease to be relevant if the manufacturer obtained control of the supplier through a takeover.

The technical process by which systems are evaluated may also prove a source of variability in outcomes. There are many evaluation techniques, some of which are highly complex mathematically. Moreover, the task of data collection is likely to be uncertain, especially when it concerns a system that may yet not be fully designed.

Existing organisational structures may affect supporter evaluations. Structures will influence what information supporters receive about a system. Or, supporters may fail to see potential benefits or costs because they are unable to see beyond established practices.

Finally, there is the politics of evaluation. Because support is so important to the project organisation, and because other stakeholders may want that support or may not want the system, there is likely to be a significant political element to the evaluation of a system by supporters. Chapter 7 discusses this in some detail.

Thus, even if a project organisation were to develop a system exactly as it intended, it could not rely upon this being sufficient to guarantee continuing support because contextual factors affect decisions about support.

5.4 THE SUPPORTERS-PROJECT ORGANISATION RELATIONSHIP

The third side of the triangle of dependences concerns the relationship between the supporters and the project organisation. As figure 5.1 portrays it, the essence of this relationship is the flow of support to the project organisation. Once supporters have decided that the system is worth their support one might suppose this to be relatively unproblematic. However, there are some facets of even this relationship which are worth attention.

There are cognitive problems for the project organisation knowing in advance what support it needs. Moreover, it may draw incorrect conclusions from supporter behaviour about what support to expect. For example, supporters and project organisation may have different views about the timeframe over which support will be available.

Over time, changes in the environment may affect the value of promised support. An obvious example is the changing purchasing power of funds under conditions of wage inflation or exchange rate variation. The latter will be particularly important with respect to countries which import computing equipment.

Structural and political factors may also influence what support is actually delivered. If a fixer lacks access to or is deliberately excluded from appropriate decision-making arenas, then she may fail to deliver promised support.

So, like the other two sides of the triangle of dependences, the third may be affected by a variety of contextual influences.

5.5 THE MODEL

The triangle of dependences (figure 5.1) is not a statement of theory, but the basis of a model which is to be used as an analytical tool. It portions the focal situation, an information systems process, in a way that aids analysis. It does not say that if a system serves its supporters, then the project organisation will receive support and continue to build and maintain a system that will continue to serve its supporters and so on. The thrust of the previous three sections has been that other factors affect the outcomes of the relationships depicted by each side of the triangle. It is not a closed system. Of course, it is fundamental to the triangular representation that, other things being equal, a reduction in support will adversely affect the project organisation's ability to provide a system that will serve supporters, which will result in reduced support and so on. But, other things need not be equal. And it is this that gives all parties reason and room for manoeuvre.

In particular, the fact that the triangle is open to influence extends the range of tactics by which the project organisation can manage its support. It has more options at its disposal than just exchanging the system for support. It can attempt to influence supporter perceptions, interests, evaluations, and support decisions. It can do this directly with supporters or indirectly through third party power-brokers. Tactics for managing support will be discussed in chapter 7. In chapter 8, system building and support management will be viewed in process terms. The long-term costs of manipulating support by means other than the focal information system will be seen to result in less and less space for manoeuvre. In the long run a project organisation's system must serve its supporters or perish.

A triangular representation of the relationship between project organisation and its supporters is most appropriate because the information system is such a central aspect of it, and because it is so problematic for the project organisation to convert it from abstract to concrete, from idea to executable system. However, it is also worth viewing the project organisation-supporters relationship as a dyad so as to bring out the fact that the relationship works in both directions. The two parties may negotiate over the inducements each offers the other. The project organisation does not just receive support in return for the system it builds, it negotiates over what kind of system will yield continuing support. This negotiation will be mediated by pre-existing structures which may then serve to constrain the continuity of support.

The triangle of dependences, then, is designed to organise our thinking about the information systems process, in particular processes which lead to a terminal loss of support. It recognises both the importance and difficulties of information systems work and of the management of support. The distinction between

Model Overview

problems and terminal loss of support forms the basis for a further distinction between flaws and failures.

5.6 FLAWS AND FAILURES

Information systems are the product of a process which is open to flaws. And, every information system is flawed in some way. But, flaws are different from failure. *Flaws* are characteristics of both systems themselves and of the innovation process which are not desired by the project organisation, users, or supporters. In general, flaws may be corrected at a cost, or accepted at a cost.

The most obvious kind of system flaw is a bug. Bugs either stop a program running altogether, or they yield incorrect results. Usually we expect that bugs will be corrected, but if they are sufficiently infrequent and insignificant in their effects they may be allowed to remain. The cost is that they will recur on occasions. If they are corrected, the cost is the cost of their repair.

Another kind of flaw is the system characteristic which users find inconvenient or otherwise undesirable. Thus, a misleading statement of account may generate a high number of customer queries. Or, the design of on-line transactions may not be entirely compatible with user tasks so that several enquiry transactions may be required where one would be preferable. Once again, this kind of flaw may be corrected or borne - at a cost.

There may also be flaws in the innovation process. These arise from sub-optimal decisions about how to proceed. A particular technique may yield the desired result but at greater cost of time or other resources than had been anticipated. Or, it may yield one of the other kinds of flaw.

The point about flaws is that they are problems which occur in consequence of the events that make up the innovation process. Unless there is support available to cope with them they will have the effect of reducing the system's capacity to serve its supporters or of resulting in further flaws.

It is important to understand clearly that as it is used here the term 'flaw' is not intended judgementally. There is no normative standard against which innovation is being judged. Rather, flaws describe the perception of stakeholders that they face undesired situations which constitute problems for them as a result of the innovation process. 'Flaw' does not imply that the project organisation should have been able to avoid it.

Flaws relate to failures through their costs. Flaws are often discovered and dealt with before they have a substantial effect on the system. Design flaws are caught in walkthroughs. Bugs are caught in testing. The earlier they are caught, the less they cost to cope with. If a flaw goes uncorrected, it will ultimately affect the level of service provided by the system and will thereby affect supporters' decisions. On the other hand, the cost of correction will be a diminution of available support for other systems activities with the likelihood of consequential flaws. If a project organisation can persuade others to absorb the costs of a flaw, knock-on effects may be avoided.

Given the inevitability of flaws, what is important is who pays for them and what consequence this has. If flaws are willingly absorbed by users, then there may be no major consequences for the project organisation. Or, if supporters are prepared to fund the flaws, there may be no consequential cascade. On the other hand, if the project organisation has to pay for flaws, whether they are of its own making or not, then they will be damaging to its ability to carry out further work on the system.

No party can continue to soak up the costs of flaws forever. In the long run, they will start to tell on the level of support that is provided. When support dries up, the system fails. But, flaws alone do not cause failures. The many other factors that affect the relationships in the triangle of dependences combine to cause failure.

5.7 SUMMARY

The triangle of dependences depicted in figure 5.1 is a tool to aid analysis of the information systems process. Each relationship represented by a side of the triangle is subject to a variety of influences. These influences make some aspects of the process uncontrollable but at the same time they provide scope for managing other aspects. Under the standard organisational constraints and contingencies the information systems process will be flawed and will produced flawed systems. However, flaws alone do not constitute failure. Rather, it is the role of flaws in diminishing levels of support that links them to failure.

The next chapter will explore the difficulties of the

Model Overview 65

information systems innovation process. This will help show in more detail the sources of flaws. Chapter 7 focuses on supporters, the influences on their evaluation of an information system, and the problematic nature of support itself. Then chapter 8 pulls the analysis together in order to consider the dynamics of the process, in particular how support may be managed or lost.

Chapter 6
The Information Systems Innovation Process

Building and maintaining an information system is not a routine process even with the best methods and tools available. It is an innovation process and therefore necessarily involves uncertainty. One effect of this uncertainty is that flaws will occur.

This chapter focuses on just one side of the triangle of dependences - that representing the relationship of the project organisation to its information system. It shows how, within the structure provided by a stage model of the innovation process, the organisational context sets the parameters of the project organisation's problems and serves to constrain the performance of problem-solving. If the problem-solving methods adopted do not adequately address the context then the outcome will be flawed. The availability of support influences whether and how far the project organisation will be able to address the context. The result is a model which can be applied to actual information systems processes to explain why some flaws arise and why others are avoided. This sets the scene for a discussion of failure in terms of the other relationships depicted by the triangle of dependences. Chapter 7 discusses the provision of support and chapter 8 shows how flaws interact with the provision of support to produce failure.

Section 6.1 exploits both the organisation theory and information systems literatures to yield a stage model of the innovation process. Section 6.2 provides a model which links context, problem-solving, outcomes and support. This serves as a basis for explaining flaws. Section 6.3 shows how the model can be applied in combination with the stage model to explain why flaws occur in the innovation process despite the availability of a variety of systematic means of problem-solving. As a result, the occurrence of flaws is seen to be relatively normal.

6.1 THE INNOVATION PROCESS

The information systems innovation process is readily divisible into stages. This is convenient for analytical purposes because stages are identified in terms of typical objectives or problems. Moreover, as we shall see in section 6.3, there are many standard means of problem-solving and these can be matched to the stages and their problems to explore their likely efficacy. Where the match is not good, flaws will result.

6.1.1 The stages of innovation

The use of a stage model for describing information systems is common to both the information systems and the innovation literatures. For example, Davis and Olson (1985) use three main stages - definition, development, and installation and operation - broken into eleven sub-stages. Kwon and Zmud (1987) merge the two literatures to yield six stages - initiation, adoption, adaptation, acceptance, use, and incorporation. There is little real disagreement about the activities and processes that make up the innovation process, just different ways of presenting the stages. The model presented here is derived from both literatures and gives prominence to four main stages - initiation, development, implementation and operation - with various sub-stages also identified. In general, information systems writers have emphasised development and implementation while organisation theorists and management scientists have concentrated on initiation and implementation. The continuing operation and integration or incorporation into the host organisation has not rated much attention in any of the relevant literatures.

Information systems writers, where they have addressed initiation, have often argued for a corporate information technology plan with the assumption that this would drive system initiation. Where this has not been the case, two component activities have been recognised. Problem definition is one. The other is the proposal. The latter is supposed to establish the technical feasibility and economic viability of the project. It is normally expected that it will lead to an authoritative decision about the project's future.

Organisation theorists, being interested in the factors that influence innovation adoption, are more informative about initiation. The model presented here will include a sequence of four sub-stages starting with the detection of a performance gap, and proceeding to the formation of attitudes, the development of a proposal, and a decision process.

At a general level, Hage (1980) notes that initiation is the stage in which resources are mobilised to support major change. Others have useful things to say about the various sub-stages. First, the detection of a performance gap is not straightforward. It often may not occur until a problem is very serious because of factors such as complacency and conservatism (Child, Ganter & Kieser 1987). Second, the process of attitude formation may involve information dissemination to achieve 'softening' prior to a formal proposal for change (Dean 1987). Third, Dean notes the affective character of the proposal process. Once individuals have made commitments to a proposal, they back it with a strong emotional commitment which will be resistant to new information rather than being dispassionately open. Dean further observes that problems change in form as they rise through the hierarchy. At the lower levels technical issues are central. Toward the top they transform into financial issues. Fourth, there is the decision process. The decision taken at the end of initiation is referred to here as *the strategic decision*. Obtaining a strategic decision to proceed is the project organisation's task objective during initiation.

The second stage is development. It is commonplace in information systems to think of the development stage in terms of sub-stages. While these may include systems analysis, systems design, programming and testing, this book uses a higher level terminology to distinguish the development of an abstract system, or design, from the development of a concrete, executable system. The former sub-stage includes eliciting information and requirements from users, analysing them, and synthesising them into a design. Its objective is the abstract system. The latter sub-stage emphasises the transformation of representations of the abstract system into a concrete, executable form. Its objective is the concrete system. Where it is necessary to establish a project infrastructure in order to develop and run the concrete system there may be a third sub-stage. Where existing facilities are being used this will not be necessary. The objective of this sub-stage is to put in place the technical, material, and human infrastructure for the project.

'Implementation' has many different meanings in the literature (Friedman 1989). Here, it refers to the introduction of a new system into its operational and organisational context. It is the transition stage between development and operation. Implementation can be distinctly traumatic, for it is the time when flaws will make themselves felt and when operational user resistance may become apparent. Implementation is a hurdle which some projects do not surmount. Implementation's objective is to get the concrete system fully operational.

Table 6.1. Stages of the innovation process

Stage	Component Sub-Stage
Initiation	detection of performance gap
	formation of attitudes
	development of proposal
	strategic decision-making
Development	development of abstract system
	development of concrete system
	establishment of project infrastructure
Implementation	introduction of concrete system to operational and organisational context
Operation	operation, maintenance and enhancement

The operational stage encompasses system operation, maintenance, and enhancement. The project organisation is faced with providing a service with its information system. This includes routine operation, and necessitates repairing flaws as they emerge, and responding to a changing context. This may include coping with variations in requirements and other environmental contingencies such as problems with the supply of equipment or staff. The aim of this stage is not simply to provide whatever service the system was built to offer, but to maintain its continued integration into its organisational setting.

Though obvious to some, it is worth reminding readers that while it is possible to distinguish stages and sub-stages it is not unusual for them to overlap in the course of a project. For example, some parts of a system may be in operation while others are being implemented and yet others are being developed. This may easily result in a feedback loop through which information discovered in the course of operating one part of the system comes to affect the development of another part. Thus not only is there feedforward from one stage to the next, but there may also be feedback.

Viewing information systems as innovations and combining conclusions from the organisational and information systems literatures, the information systems innovation process can be partitioned into four stages - initiation, development, implementation, and operation (see table 6.1). These will be used in section 6.3 to assist the analysis of the occurrence of flaws.

6.2 CONTEXT, PROBLEM-SOLVING, SOLUTIONS AND SUPPORT

The aim of this section is to provide enough of a model of problem-solving in the innovation process to show how and why project organisations' systems get to be flawed and hence why project organisations are sometimes unable to sustain support. The underlying model is based on the relationships among context, problem-solving, solutions and support. The contextual dimensions employed here are derived from chapter 4. The model is shown in schematic form in figure 6.1.

The innovation process is the core of the model depicted in figure 5.1. As described in the previous section, it is a staged process in which each of the stages can be thought of as characterised by certain typical problems. At its most general, the problem in any stage is how to get from the current situation to the typical objective. For example, following the discussion in section 6.1, the problem for the development stage is how to get from the strategic decision to a concrete system. Where stages are broken into sub-stages the same method can be applied to characterising their problems. And further decomposition is possible.

The information systems field is strewn with means for solving the problems of the innovation process. They can be characterised as *problem-solving mechanisms*. They have been devised by researchers and practitioners who have sought to find standard ways of solving standard problems, of getting a project from typical starting situations to typical objectives. For some stages such as initiation there might be just the one problem-solving mechanism prescribed - the feasibility study. By contrast, for a stage such as development there are many mechanisms available for different sub-problems.

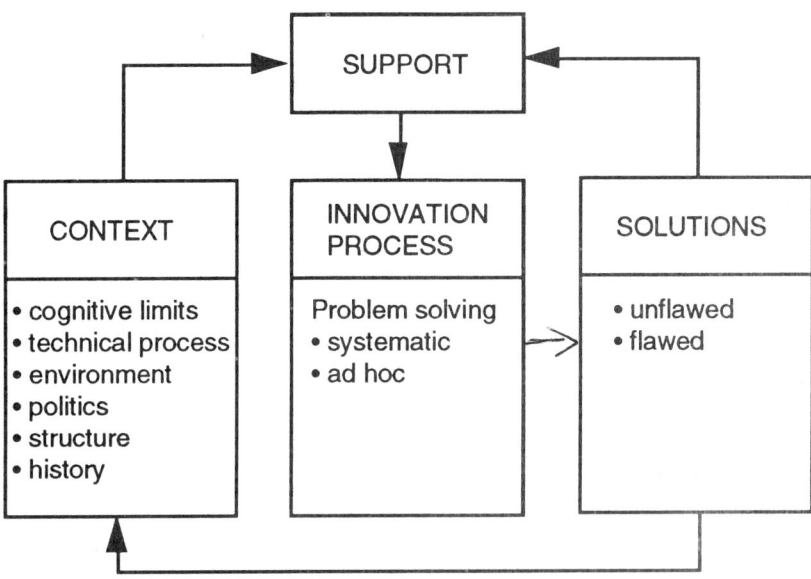

Figure 6.1. The relationships affecting problem-solving in the innovation process

Unfortunately, standard problem-solving mechanisms rely on the actual problems faced fitting the standard very neatly. In fact, problem-solving mechanisms often ignore the context. They neither consider the contextual influences on current situations and objectives, nor those which affect problem-solving itself. Yet the context is crucial in determining what needs to be done and what constraints there may be on achieving it. For example, eliciting user requirements might be regarded as a standard problem for which there are standard techniques including interviewing, observing, surveying by questionnaire, and documentary research. In addition, there are techniques for structuring the documentation of these requirements in graphical and narrative form. How effectively these techniques can be used will depend upon the way the context shapes the actual problem. If organisational structure prevents a systems analyst from reaching important users then there will be omissions in the requirements specification. If political frictions among users result in inconsistent requirements, the specification document will either misrepresent the requirements by ignoring some sub-set of them, or it will be faithful to this inconsistency and as a result the specification will not form an adequate basis from which to do further design. Thus context can significantly affect problem-solving. What appears to be a standard problem, eliciting user requirements, is in fact rendered far more individualistic or idiosyncratic by the context.

The point of the model developed in this section is to show how problem-solving in the innovation process has the outcomes it does. In particular, it tries to show that standard mechanisms will not always work because the problems to which they are applied are often defined in too general a way. When the context is factored in the problems appear far from standard.

In the rest of this section, the main components of the model shown in figure 6.1 are described more fully.

6.2.1 Context

The information systems context consists of six dimensions: cognitive limits, environment, technical process, structure, history, and politics. Context is important in a number of ways: it influences the starting situation for any problem-solving; it constrains the process of problem-solving; it affects the detailed objectives of problem-solving; and, it is a source of change or contingency. The different dimensions of the context will each have different effects.

In general, problem-solving mechanisms will not be able to address all the dimensions of the context at once. Thus, a mechanism for compensating for cognitive limits to human processing of complexity, say modular design, will not at the same time prevent the project organisation structure from creating barriers to communication among the information systems professionals developing different modules. Consequently, if a standard problem is in fact modified by some aspect of context which is not addressed by the problem-solving mechanism applied to it, then there will be aspects of the problem that will not be adequately addressed.

The dimensions of context were discussed in chapter 4. A few considerations specific to this model will be discussed below.

(1) Cognitive limits

Cognitive limits apply to any problem-solving (March & Simon 1958). Relevant limits include limits on memory, attention, logical skills, and conceptual understanding. Where problem-solving involves reciprocal interdependence (Thompson 1967), as information systems innovation does, there will be a need for communication. Consequently, limits to communication skills will be relevant. The fact that humans adopt heuristics to help them cope means that there can be no guarantees that problem-solving even under bounded rationality will be effective.

(2) Technical process

The technical process of information systems innovation embodies constraints in two ways. First, it includes underlying constraints deriving from the essential characteristics of computer-based systems. Second, it includes constraints contingent upon the particular technical process selected for a project.

The first essential characteristic of information systems is that they are automatically executable. Any system therefore has to have a final concrete form which respects the constraints of the configuration of hardware and software on which it is to run.

Second, the concrete system has to be totally prespecified, covering all anticipated eventualities. Therefore the abstract system has to be developed to cover a wide range of contingencies, some of which may not previously have been encountered.

Third, the low level of abstraction of most programming languages in comparison with organisational tasks implies high technical complexity. Complexity is a concept which is not well understood. All too often it appears to be used as a prophylactic against ignorance. Thompson (1967) emphasises interdependences. Perrow's (1984) view is that complex interactions involve unplanned, unfamiliar or unexpected sequences that are either not visible or not immediately comprehensible. Fetzer (1988) distinguishes two kinds of complexity: cumulative complexity arising from the incorporation of many smaller programs into a single larger one; and patchwork complexity arising from the complicated, peculiar, and ad hoc arrangement of smaller programs. Although all these aspects of complexity are relevant to understanding why flaws occur, what they share is a view of complexity as constituted in the interconnections among components. In information systems the connections among components are usually networks which include feedback loops. In these cases complexity is high.

These essential characteristics of the technical process influence the nature of the problems faced by a project organisation at all stages. They are likely to be particularly pertinent to the development, maintenance and enhancement tasks.

In addition, each innovation's technical process will impose contingent constraints. Thus, if particular techniques or particular methodologies are adopted then these will constitute constraints on the innovation process. If, for example, a detailed development methodology is adopted and rigorously applied, it will be a very strong constraint on the innovation process regardless of how effective the methodology's constituent techniques may be for the task in hand. But, even where a formal methodology is not applied, the solution to each problem defines the starting point for subsequent problems thereby constraining the innovation process.

Thus the technical process of any information systems innovation is a source of essential and contingent constraints both of which influence the problem-solving of the innovation process.

(3) Environment

The different components of the environment were identified in section 4.3.3. Figure 6.2 displays them while at the same time showing that influences on the innovation process may derive from a number of different societal levels. The layering of the environment can be illustrated with respect to regulators. Regulators may function at all levels: an international watchdog for transborder data flows; a national government audit office; a regional arm of a national data protection authority; an industry standards committee; and an organisation's internal auditor.

The environment is a source of constraints and contingencies. Customers or users are an important element of the environment. Their demands will usually influence what problems a project organisation faces. Changes to user demands will change its problems. Changes in user behaviour will significantly influence how effectively a project organisation can solve its problems. Other elements of the environment such as technology and equipment suppliers will be significant sources of problems where the technical infrastructure is important.

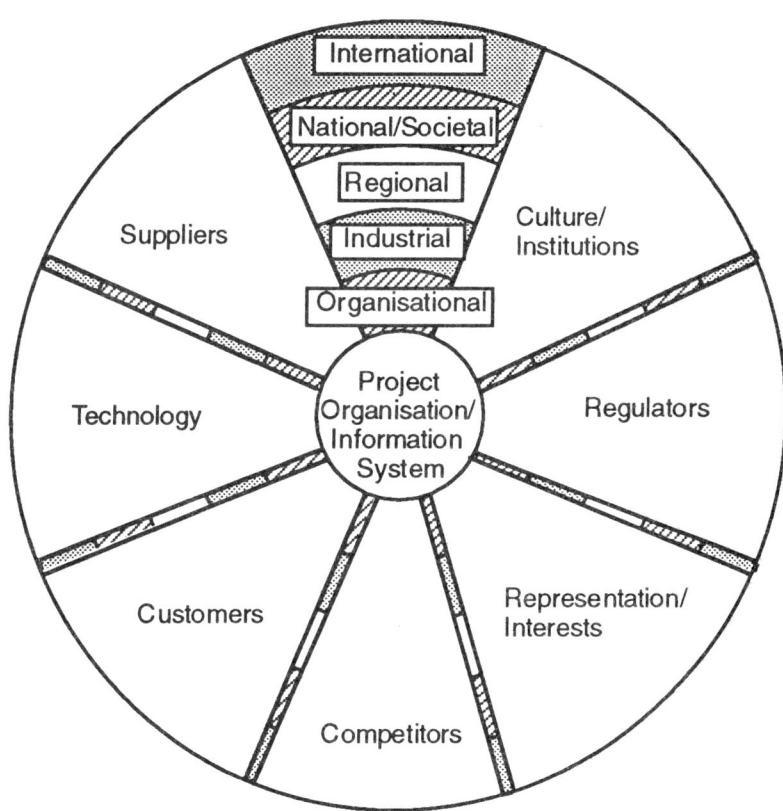

Figure 6.2. Elements of the environment

If a constraint is not recognised or there is a contingent change in the environment then there will be pressures to respond. For example, deregulation of an industry may open up opportunities for introducing new services in order to compete effectively with new entrants to the market. In the case of banking, this might include the introduction of new bank accounts which require interest to be calculated on daily balances where previously interest had not been payable.

It should be remembered that pressures do not directly *cause* change to computer systems. They are mediated by some form of explicit or implicit decision-making. In principle, no environmental change necessarily implies the need to change a computer system. Even laws can be ignored. In practice, some changes will be treated as so obviously demanding attention that they will be dealt with as if there were no alternative.

(4) Politics

There is something artificial about treating the political aspects of a project separately. Politics is not a separate task that can be managed by an apt division of labour and the employment of a specialist. It enters all aspects of organisational life. It will affect information systems innovation in any of three ways. First, within a project organisation the problem-solving mechanisms adopted may be subject to political contest, particularly where they are not formalised. Second, there may be political pressure from outside the project organisation as a result of the changes the information system is perceived to bring. The greater the anticipated effects of the system on the existing balance of organisational power, the more political the innovation process is likely to be (Markus & Pfeffer 1983). Third, apparently unrelated political conflicts in the environment may affect the shape of constraints and may generate contingencies. For example, competition among departments may result in changing system requirements.

Being pervasive, the political dimension may affect any problems and any problem-solving in the information systems innovation process. It has the effect of changing standard problems into non-standard and can reduce the efficacy of problem-solving mechanisms.

(5) Structure

Structure affects a project organisation both as an organisation in its own right and as a sub-unit of a host organisation. As an organisation in its own right, internal project organisation structures will influence problem-solving in the innovation process. For example, a standard technique such as a walkthrough may not be feasible if project structures inhibit meetings of the relevant participants. As a sub-unit, the structures of the host organisation will affect initiation and development by influencing how the project organisation communicates with its environment. They will affect problems of implementation and operation by defining constraints that the information system must respect.

(6) History

The past constrains the present and the future. The purpose of having a distinct category for history is to ensure that case-specific, one-off events are considered. Repeated actions and events become embedded in structure, but individual actions may otherwise be ignored. Particularly important here will be special agreements and commitments made by stakeholders which bear upon the information systems process. Thus, an earlier agreement not to attempt to automate a particular activity may fix a limit on what is considered for automation at a later date. The very existence of the agreement means that its appropriateness is not questioned. Thus, history will constitute a constraint on the innovation process by influencing the definition of the problems the project organisation faces. As this category relates to one-off conditions, it is only included in subsequent analyses where it is obviously appropriate.

To summarise this sub-section, the organisational context of information systems (table 6.2) influences the problems a project organisation faces and the problem-solving it performs. It renders apparently standard problems non-standard, and it constrains the application of apparently systematic problem-solving mechanisms.

6.2.2 Systematic and ad hoc problem-solving

The model depicted in figure 6.1 distinguishes two kinds of problem-solving: systematic and ad hoc. Problem-solving is systematic when it involves the programmed application of predefined steps. Ad hoc problem-solving involves devising problem-solving methods specially for the problem in hand. Information systems problem-solving mechanisms vary in the extent to which they are systematic. They are rarely defined so rigorously that they can be followed blindly like a computer program. Usually, how systematic they are depends upon the level of prior knowledge and training of the person who applies them.

Table 6.2. The elements of the organisational context

Elements of Context
1. Cognitive limits
2. Technical process
3. Environment
4. Politics
5. Structure
6. History

We can distinguish four kinds of problem-solving mechanism. There are approaches, techniques and tools (Avison & Fitzgerald 1988). In addition, there are organising devices. An approach emphasises a particular class of problem solution. For example, participation is an approach. A technique defines a procedure for solving a problem. Tools are usually artefacts which help the performance of problem-solving. Organising devices are ways of structuring a project organisation to enhance problem-solving.

An approach emphasises a particular class of problem solution. For example, participation and prototyping are approaches. So are structured, top-down methodologies. If an approach such as participation is used without the application of systematic techniques then it will require considerable intelligence. Indeed, it has been a complaint about radically participative approaches that they require highly skilled facilitators. They cannot be learnt by rote and followed blindly by drones. Other approaches such as the structured, top-down approach are defined in a lot of detail in methodologies. They can be applied as systematically as their component techniques.

There are many techniques available for use by information systems professionals. Among the best known are data flow diagramming, entity-relationship modelling, normalisation, and conceptual modelling. By comparison with a task such as eliciting requirements in the first place these techniques are relatively well-defined. They involve transforming an initial representation of some aspect of an information system into a more rigorous form. Nonetheless, it is quite obvious that all these techniques require a trained and intelligent development professional to use them. Even then, it is quite possible for the developer to produce a flawed new representation of the system.

A tool is an artefact, usually an automated software tool such as a fourth generation language or a screen formatter. In general, tools do not define how they are to be used, rather they provide a vehicle by which techniques and approaches may be implemented. How effectively they are used by developers is not something they determine. That depends on the developer.

Organising devices are designs for structuring a project organisation. Chief programmer teams (Baker 1972) and matrix structures (Galbraith 1973) are examples of organising devices. They are systematic to the extent that members of the project organisation observe the lines of authority and communication laid down in the design. Even then, there will be many interactions not specified by the organisation design. Formal structure charts do not tell the whole story in any organisation.

What this brief analysis of approaches, techniques, tools, and organising devices shows is that systematic problem-solving mechanisms for information systems innovation cannot be applied totally systematically. They rely in large measure on the intelligence, training, and experience of the information systems professionals who use them. Therefore, they cannot systematically avoid the introduction of flaws to the innovation process.

Ad hoc problem-solving will be applied in any of a number of circumstances. These include cases where there is no relevant mechanism known to the project organisation; where there are overriding constraints against the use of an appropriate mechanism; where an apparently appropriate mechanism appears not to be working; or where previous attempts at problem-solving have been unsuccessful. Newman and Rosenberg (1985) report a clear example of ad hoc problem-solving to overcome resistance to the use of a new stock system - the systems analyst burned all the old stock cards over a weekend.

The importance of ad hoc problem-solving is that it may be employed to avoid flaws notwithstanding a troublesome context. Thus, if a project organisation is so situated that it cannot apply a systematic mechanism, it may still be able to solve its problem ad hoc. Unfortunately, ad hoc problem-solving has to be thought out afresh each time it is required whereas systematic mechanisms avoid this cognitive burden.

6.2.3 Flawed and unflawed solutions

The outcomes of problem-solving in the innovation process will be either flawed or unflawed solutions. As was seen in section 5.6, flaws are undesired outcomes which have consequential costs for the project organisation whether they are repaired or allowed to persist. Flaws will occur when the problem-solving in the innovation process does not address the context adequately. There are five types of case. The first is where a standard mechanism has been inadequately applied to a standard problem. This was discussed in section 6.2.2 where it was shown that even systematic mechanisms leave room for human error. The second case is where a standard mechanism is not adequate to its problem. An example of this is the problem of managing technical complexity. No matter how carefully developers apply top-down methods, systems are frequently too complex for them to be sure that they have included correctly all the relevant interconnections. The third case is where a standard problem has been rendered non-standard by contextual circumstance. An example of this is where user training is applied as an implementation technique but where the users are politically opposed to the system. The training will not improve system acceptance. The fourth case is where ad hoc problem-solving has been inappropriately devised. For example, developers might adopt an ad hoc approach to evaluating tenders for a software package. If this does not include assessment of the suppliers' ability to stay in business it may lead to the purchase of a package from a company that then goes bankrupt. The fifth case is where the context changes post hoc. That is to say there is contextual change which renders earlier solutions inappropriate. If the old solutions are left unchanged, the system will be flawed.

This subsection has described five cases in which flaws are likely to arise. They are summarised in table 6.3. In the next section it will be seen that lack of support may also cause flaws.

Table 6.3. Five sources of flawed problem-solving

Problem Type	Problem-Solving Mechanism	Source of Flaws
standard	standard	appropriate mechanism inappropriately applied
standard	standard	inappropriate mechanism
non-standard	standard	mismatch between problem type and mechanism
non-standard	ad hoc	inappropriate mechanism
standard/non-standard	standard/ad hoc	contextual change causes appropriate problem-solving subsequently to be inappropriate

6.2.4 Support for problem-solving

The analysis so far has made a tacit assumption that support is normally unproblematic. In reality this is far from being true. Support is crucial to the effectiveness of problem-solving. Problem-solving must be resourced. It often requires fixers and power-brokers. In the absence of these, flaws will occur.

If resources are in short supply, problem-solving will suffer either because the most appropriate mechanisms cannot be used or because short-cuts must be taken. Here are some examples. Insufficient funding for requirements determination may result in the partial or total abandonment of requirements validation. This in turn is likely to result in incompletely specified requirements.

Insufficient resources for design may result in technical complexities being ignored. Too few programmers will mean some combination of incorrect programs, incomprehensible code and delays to the schedule.

Problem-solving also sometimes requires the efforts of fixers. For example, if organisational politics results in conflicting demands from users, a fixer will be required to make whatever changes are necessary to resolve the political situation. This could involve, for example, structural changes or changes to personnel.

Ad hoc problem-solving will need support to help it address the context if the project organisation lacks direct control itself. For example, if it has access to power over users either directly through a fixer or via a power-broker it may be able to influence users' demands so as to create a more stable environment under which to perform the innovation process.

The difference between systematic and ad hoc problem-solving is that with the former it is possible to estimate what resources will be required. It may also be possible to make some estimate of what level of fixing will be required. With ad hoc problem-solving the very fact of its being ad hoc suggests that it will not be possible to know in advance what will be needed.

To be effective and avoid flaws, both systematic and ad hoc problem-solving will need appropriate support. Even with support it may not be possible to satisfy the constraints that obtain. For example, no amount of future watching can confer the ability to make detailed and accurate predictions. Consequently, contingencies may occur necessitating more support or increasing the likelihood of flaws.

The conclusion of section 6.2.3 was that there were five cases where flaws would occur because problem-solving failed to address the context. It can now be seen that shortage of support brings with it further scope for the occurrence of flaws.

6.2.5 The feedback loops

Figure 6.1 includes feedback loops which are now described. First, as indicated by the triangle of dependences, the solutions or outcomes provided by the innovation process will affect the support available.

Second, outcomes will affect the context in that they create a new situation which contributes to the setting of new problems. Each change helps redefine the problem of the moment. In the case mentioned earlier in this chapter of the analyst burning the stock cards, his action changed the context by destroying the competing clerical system. If the clerks' resistance to the system was merely conservatism, the problem was probably largely solved by this action. If it was politically based resistance then the analyst's action may have only removed a political weapon without touching the root cause of the resistance. (It is perhaps worth noting here that feedback from outcomes to context is the basis of preemptive strategies. Thus, the practice of documenting a program at the time at which it is written is intended to reduce the cost of complexity and cognitive limits when the program subsequently has to be changed.)

The third feedback loop is that between context and support. The context will influence what support is available. This means that the project organisation will have limited scope for managing support. The implications of this point will be discussed further in chapter 8.

6.2.6 The accumulation of flaws

Flaws are rarely isolated lapses from grace. They are often interrelated, each new flaw compounding the effects of earlier ones. The feedback loops discussed in the previous sub-section provide the basis for an explanation.

First, if flaws reduce the available support, further flaws must be expected as a result of lack of resources or necessary fixing skills. Second, because flaws will affect the context, subsequent problems may be rendered non-standard, making them that much harder to address with standard mechanisms. Third, because flaws are not always recognised immediately, they may seed further consequential flaws. Fourth, the more work that is based on an unrecognised flaw, the more costly it will be to repair. This will be a drain on resources with the possibility of incurring further flaws as a result of short cuts. It should be clear therefore that unless a project organisation can deal with its flaws in a timely and effective manner these positive feedback effects may accelerate out of control.

The model described in this section can be best summed up as saying that if the project organisation cannot address the contextual sources of its problems within the limits of the problem-solving mechanisms and support available then flaws will result.

6.3 FLAWS IN THE INNOVATION PROCESS

So far this chapter has concentrated on showing that the innovation process divides into stages each of which addresses different problems, and that problem-solving whether or not it is systematic will easily give rise to flaws. The fact that flaws are a normal part of information systems innovation is not a point that is widely made. In this section this point is further emphasised through an examination of the different stages of the innovation process and through a discussion of the limits of two major strategies for managing problem-solving.

First, let us take the stages of information systems innovation starting with initiation. While there are a few systematic mechanisms designed to help with this stage including prior strategic planning and feasibility assessment, they suffer from the problem that there is inevitably a lot of uncertainty. At initiation, the project organisation cannot avoid the risk that the system it defines will address the wrong problem, or that it will be inappropriate to subsequent contextual circumstances. Assessment of the proposal may be only partial because of unavailability of information, and the strategic decision may alter the proposal in significant ways. If the proposal has political implications then the initiation stage may become very politically charged. The outcome of initiation will be a strategic decision about the information system to be built, but nothing can guarantee that that decision will not be flawed in the sense that it will set parameters for the project which are inappropriate and which have consequential adverse outcomes for the project organisation. For example, the strategic decision might approve development of a system which will be highly politically contentious, or it might require that the system interface with another particularly complex system. There are many ways in which initiation can have adverse effects on the innovation process.

The second stage is development. This has received more attention than any other in the information systems literature. In developing the abstract system, users will be a salient feature of the context, while in developing the concrete system the technical process will be more salient. There are many more or less systematic mechanisms addressing these two elements of the context for these two sub-stages. However, they usually only impart control over the context if the context is not hostile. For example, methods of eliciting information and user requirements will work reasonably well if users are willing and the requirements are not too extensive and complex. If users are resistant or unavailable, it may not be possible to apply methods at all. Equally, if the concrete system is very big and complex, there are no problem-solving mechanisms that will cope with these characteristics without there being some chance of flaws creeping in. There are, of course, many other ways in which the context can affect problem-solving in these two sub-stages, but even where there are mechanisms available, they will only be appropriate for a relatively benign set of contextual conditions.

It should be added that the sub-stage of development which involves constructing a project infrastructure is not so well served for problem-solving mechanisms. More of the problem-solving will be ad hoc. As ad hoc problem-solving imposes a heavy cognitive burden, this sub-stage will also be susceptible to flaws.

The third stage, implementation, is the transition between development and operation. Many of the problems to be solved will be installation specific. There might be existing procedures for some of these, say for the change from development to operational status. A few problems will be more common. For example, users will need to be trained for the new system. The crucial fact of implementation is that it is the time when decisions taken earlier are tested in operation. Uncertainties about user reaction to design decisions will be resolved into the certainty of either resistance or acceptance. And, unrecognised features of the context may reveal themselves. In general, there are few systematic mechanisms available for dealing with these kinds of problem. Problem-solving will often be ad hoc.

The fourth and final stage is operation. This includes keeping the system running under conditions of change. It involves managing flaws as they are detected, responding to a changing context, and doing whatever is necessary to provide a continuing service. Maintaining a service should be relatively straightforward, though if a system is badly flawed even day to day operation may be challenging, requiring ad hoc problem-solving. Otherwise, the project organisation's task is to respond to pressures for change. These are similar to the pressures arising during development except that during operation it is necessary to continue to provide an operational service, and the software structure of the concrete system is fixed. Repeated changes to software cause it to decay so that it becomes increasingly prone to flaws and hard to change. While a disciplined approach to maintenance and enhancement can help postpone the time when the decay is unmanageable, it cannot do so indefinitely. Indeed, program maintenance is inherently flawed because any change to software is likely to have consequential adverse effects on subsequent maintenance efforts. Moreover, there are no special problem-solving mechanisms for the operation stage. The fact that the problems of earlier stages cannot be solved with complete assurance of a flawless outcome translates directly to the operational stage. The occurrence of flaws is to be expected.

The aim of the first part of this section has been to show that flaws can occur at any and every stage of the innovation process. The problem-solving mechanisms available do not confer complete control over the contextual factors that affect problems. The aim of the second part of this section is to consider two strategies for dealing with problem-solving in the innovation process to show that they have no magical properties either. The two strategies are essentially strategies for selecting problem-solving mechanisms. The methodology strategy involves following a relatively fixed set of procedures and applying the prescribed mechanism at each stage. The toolkit strategy involves selecting a particular mechanism for a particular problem in a particular context (Benyon & Skidmore 1987).

Methodologies have several substantial virtues. First, they eliminate the cognitive burden of choosing techniques. Second, they set out the order in which work is to be done. Third, by identifying what has to be done they provide a basis for estimating the resource support needed and the time it will take to carry out the innovation process. Fourth, where they use consistent representational forms such as diagramming techniques they reduce the cognitive burden on developers solving problems and on users reading documentation. Against these points, methodologies are usually rigid; they may employ the wrong technique for a problem. They are often redundant, recommending activities which might be safely omitted. And, they rarely cover all aspects of the innovation process. While they have been strongly recommended to practitioners, methodologies are by no means universally used (Friedman 1989).

Toolkits attempt to avoid the vices of employing either wrong or unnecessary mechanisms by selecting specifically for the context. The disadvantages of this strategy are several. There are no reliable guidelines relating problem-solving mechanisms to the information systems context. The selection process is highly dependent on the knowledge, experience and skill of the individual information systems professional (Avison, Fitzgerald & Wood-Harper 1988). And, the mechanisms adopted will not necessarily articulate neatly the one on to the next.

Attempts to construct a contingency-based methodology which matches problem-solving to context (Wood-Harper, Antill & Avison 1985, Avison & Wood-Harper 1986, 1990) encounter the same basic difficulty of there not being knowledge adequate to specify what should be used when.

Ultimately, neither methodologies nor toolkits transcend the limits of their component problem-solving. This is to say that in the wrong circumstances any problem-solving mechanism can result in flaws.

6.4 CONCLUSION

In this chapter it has been argued that the information systems innovation process can be characterised as a staged process where problem-solving which does not address the contextual sources of problems will result in flaws. Though the systematic problem-solving mechanisms typically employed by project organisations will mostly address the problems they face, there is usually room for flaws to creep in. If the context deviates from that which is presumed by any particular mechanism then that mechanism will fail to solve the problem. This may lead to flaws but does not do so necessarily. There is always room for ad hoc problem-solving to address those elements of the context not satisfactorily managed by systematic means, but there can be no guarantee that this will not itself result in flaws. It is therefore reasonable to conclude that the occurrence of flaws will be a normal feature of the information systems innovation process.

This conclusion is reinforced by the fact that any shortage of support will increase the likelihood of incurring flaws. Flaws accumulate and persist if not recognised and repaired. Persistent flaws can cause new flaws to propagate. The longer they persist, the more they will cost to repair.

The general model explaining how flaws occur is applicable at every stage of the innovation process. General strategies such as methodologies and toolkits provide no magical solution to problem-solving.

The analysis presented in this chapter tries to restore some balance to our view of information systems. They are not developed and operated in a wholly routine fashion. There are many uncertainties. In a hostile context, the problem-solving mechanisms typically used will be of little value. It is entirely to be expected that project organisations will incur flaws. Yet, seemingly, few of those who design problem-solving mechanisms or who compose methodologies provide guidance as to what to do when things go wrong. It should therefore not come as a surprise if the correction of flaws is itself a source of further problems for the project organisation. More to the point, it should not come as a surprise when flaws lead to failure.

It is a central tenet of this discussion of information systems failure that flaws are normal. But, it is also central that the occurrence of flaws is alone not sufficient for failure. Flaws can be repaired. To repair them costs resources which may or may not be available. Not to repair them risks their affecting the continued provision of support. Chapter 7 gives an analysis of the factors affecting the provision of support while chapter 8 explores some of the ways in which flaws and support interact to produce failure thereby completing the elaboration of the model. Chapters 11 and 12 exemplify the model's use in the analysis of examples.

Suggested Readings

1. Davis, G.B. & Olson, M.H. (1985) *Management Information Systems: Conceptual Foundations, Structure, and Development*, McGraw-Hill, New York.

Chapter 18 discusses the different stages of the life cycle, or the innovation process as it is called here.

2. Walton, R.E., (1989) *Up and Running: Integrating Information Technology and the Organization*, Harvard Business School Press, Boston, Massachusetts.

As noted in an earlier chapter, Walton treats information systems as innovations.

3. Although the processes of problem-solving are widely discussed, nobody seems to discuss their costs. The soft systems literature has focused strongly on problem-solving. A useful reading from this perspective is

Checkland, P. & Scholes, J. (1990) *Soft Systems Methodology in Action*, Wiley, Chichester.

Chapter 7
Support For The Project Organisation

Project organisations develop and operate their information systems in return for various kinds of support. Where chapter 6 explored the difficulties associated with the information systems innovation process, this chapter examines the factors which affect the provision of support. Thus, chapter 6 expanded on the project organisation-system side of the triangle of dependences while this chapter concentrates on the other two sides, viz the system-supporters and supporters-project organisation sides.

The importance of supporters and support is well recognised. Many writers have emphasised the importance of top management support. However, just as understanding the innovation process is a complex matter, so too understanding the process by which support is provided is complex. First, the decision to provide support is subject to a great many influences, some associated with a wider context than that of the system alone. Second, the actual flow of support suffers from a variety of factors including ambiguity which may result in misunderstanding between project organisation and supporters as to what is to be provided.

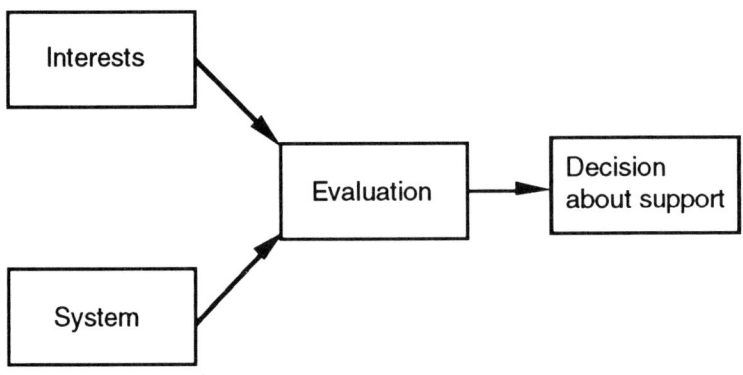

Figure 7.1. The role of evaluations

The central presumption of this chapter is that supporters evaluate information systems to determine whether they serve their

Support For The Project Organisation 91

interests, and on the basis of their evaluation decide what support to provide. Figure 7.1 illustrates this. How evaluations affect decision-making about support and the problematic nature of the flow of support forms the core of this chapter.

A review of some of the information systems evaluation literature is the starting point. This shows that although approaches to information systems evaluation are changing, there is very little discussion of how evaluations enter into the information systems process. Section 7.2 gives a brief analysis of the logical structure of evaluations. The influences on evaluations and their effects on support are discussed in sections 7.3 and 7.4. This leads into a consideration of the flow of support in section 7.5. The chapter concludes by considering some ways by which a project organisation can seek to influence the flow of support separate from its role in conducting the innovation process. The ideas advanced in this chapter will play a large part in the analysis in chapters 10 and 11.

7.1 INFORMATION SYSTEMS EVALUATION

Information systems evaluation is not confined to formal cost-benefit analyses. Contributors to the proceedings of the 1986 IFIP conference on information systems assessment (Bjørn-Andersen and Davis 1988) appear to have agreed that the literature has been unbalanced in its emphasis on the formal techniques for conducting evaluations. Several of the contributors to that conference offered more sophisticated conceptions of information systems evaluation, incorporating politics (Hirschheim & Smithson 1988) and context (Ginzberg & Zmud 1988, Davis & Hamann 1988). In general, though, most attention has been focused on prescribing how to carry out evaluations rather than analysing their role and effects (Srinivasan 1988).

The view advanced here is that any evaluation will be a political resource because it has the potential to serve some stakeholders better than others. A favourable evaluation will benefit the information systems project organisation while a negative evaluation will benefit opponents. This is because evaluations will either directly or indirectly influence decisions about support.

A distinction is often made between formative and summative

evaluations (Lyytinen & Hirschheim 1987, Ginzberg & Zmud 1988). According to these writers summative evaluations give merely evaluative information (viz the system is good/bad/indifferent) whereas formative evaluations give diagnostic information about how the evaluated situation came about. However, any evaluation, whether it is expressed summatively or formatively, is likely to have some effect on the information systems process and is in this sense formative. It is evaluations' formative effect on the provision of support that is given prominence here.

7.2 THE NATURE OF EVALUATIONS

Information systems evaluations can be quite varied. They are more than mere comparisons of system performance against management objectives. For one thing, many more parties than just management may evaluate an information system against their own interests. For another thing, there are many other factors than performance and objectives which can affect the outcomes of an evaluation process.

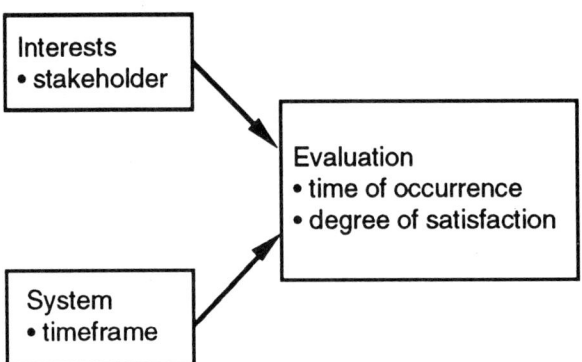

Figure 7.2. The structure of an evaluation

First, let us consider the structure of an evaluation. Zammuto (1984) has noted the crucial role of interests and time of occurrence in evaluation. An evaluation consists of a stakeholder's judgement as to how far a perceived situation pertaining to a given information system accords with a given set of interests. An evaluation will occur at some time. And, it will be relative to some timeframe. These essential ingredients are displayed in figure 7.2.

In any information systems process there will be a variety of stakeholders with differing interests. Consequently, any evaluation will be relative to a particular set of interests which may be shared by a number of individual stakeholders, a stakeholder group. An evaluation will be fixed according to the time at which it is made though it may relate to states of affairs situated in the past, present, or future. The notional scale of evaluations is continuous. An evaluative judgement is a matter of degree; it is not absolute. Thus, an evaluation expresses the evaluator's level of satisfaction at the time at which it is made but this need not be with respect to a current timeframe. For instance, a manager might be thoroughly dissatisfied with progress with an information systems development project judging it not to be in his current interests. Yet, he might nonetheless evaluate it favourably, judging it capable of serving his interests at some time in the future.

It is worth elaborating briefly on the nature of evaluation timeframes. Timeframes are not simply tenses - past, present, future. They are different length strips of time. There is no definitive period that counts as the present, neither does the past stretch infinitely backward, nor the future stretch infinitely forward (Giddens 1984). Different stakeholders may have differing orientations towards time (Little 1987) and hence may make their evaluations within different timeframes. The same stakeholder group may make different evaluations according to different timeframes. It is quite possible for a stakeholder to judge a system to be valuable to short term interests but potentially damaging in the longer term. Equally, the differing orientations of different groups will be a function of the interests at stake. For example, clerks who use an information system may see it in terms of its immediate effects on their work whereas managers may view the same system in terms of its effects on decision quality over several years. A later section will have more to say about the importance of timeframes for understanding the outcomes of decisions about supporting a project, and for appreciating the scope stakeholders have for negotiation and manoeuvre.

Evaluations can be expressed in any of a variety of forms. Different forms of expression can reveal or obscure an evaluation. How an evaluation affects events will depend in part on how actors interpret it. Unfortunately, interpretation is a dimension that cannot be fully explored here.

The most important aspect of the form of evaluations is that it has two parts - the judgemental and the informative. The judgemental aspect has already been discussed. The information accompanying an evaluation can be classified into three categories - descriptive, diagnostic, and prescriptive. *Descriptive information* will describe what aspects of a situation are unsatisfactory to the stakeholder. For example, management might be dissatisfied that its new system requires more staff than the old. *Diagnostic information* will give reasons why the unsatisfactory situation has arisen. For example, the diagnosis might be that extra effort results from more time being spent correcting errors in the data. *Prescriptive information* will indicate the conditions which will lead to future satisfaction of stakeholder interests. In effect, they specify what should be done. Thus, the conditional information might be that error correction activities be reduced. In the case study described in chapter 10 it was common for evaluations to carry prescriptive information.

There may be many facets to an evaluation. Figure 7.3 summarises the distinctions drawn in this section.

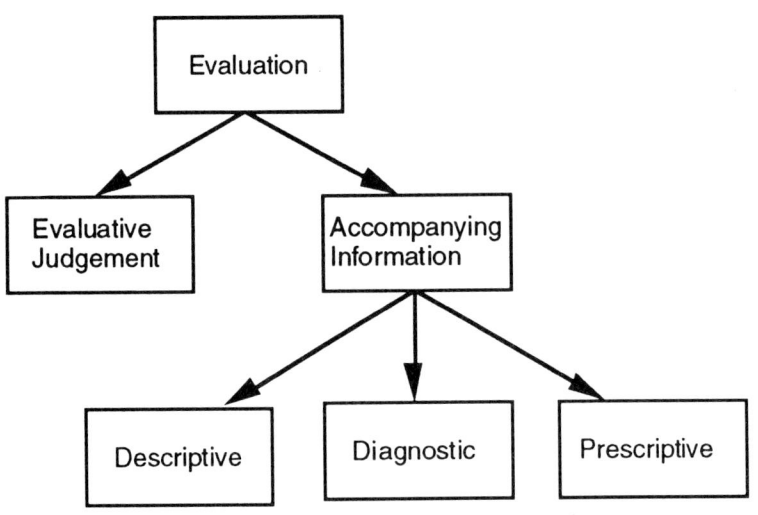

Figure 7.3. The elements of an expressed evaluation

Support For The Project Organisation 95

7.3 INFLUENCES ON EVALUATIONS

It is clear from the structure of evaluations that the outcomes of evaluation processes will depend on whose interests are the basis for the evaluation, on the evaluator's perceptions of the situation at the time of evaluation, and on the evaluation timeframe. In addition, the interests and perceptions of the situation will be mediated by the evaluation technique adopted and the sources of information used. Expectations about the likely effect of evaluations may also affect the outcome. Figure 7.4 depicts the influences on evaluation outcomes to be discussed below.

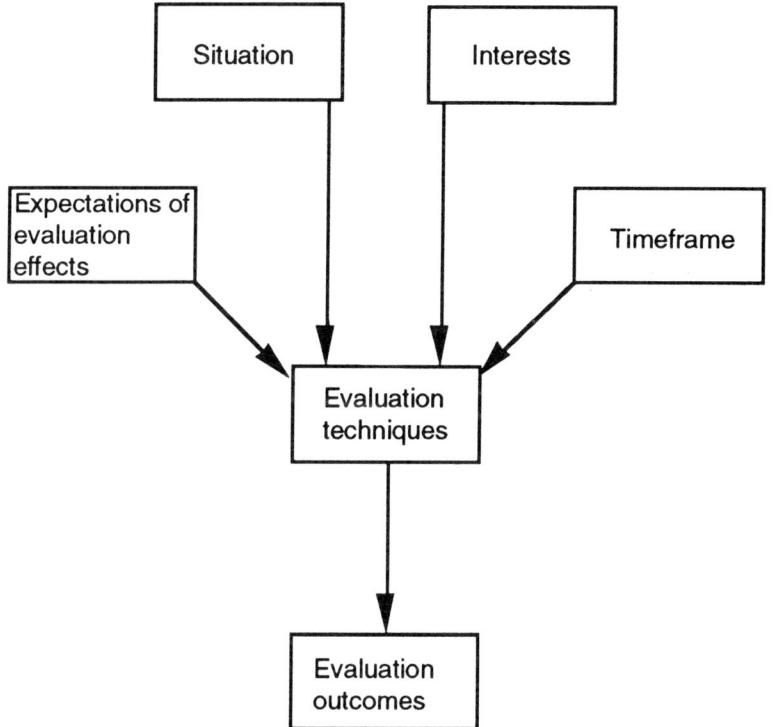

Figure 7.4. Influences on evaluation outcomes

In this model, the term 'situation' is taken to encompass both the focal situation being evaluated and the contextual situation within which an evaluation is performed. Thus perceptions of a situation will relate not only to the information systems situation, but also to the wider organisational situation with the possibilities it provides and the constraints it imposes. Which aspects of the focal and contextual situations are perceived will be influenced by the technique employed.

Most evaluation techniques are predicated on very limited assumptions which are rarely made explicit. This inevitably influences which interests are considered and which aspects of the situation are selected for evaluation.

Since interests are rarely publicly exposed in organisational life, most formal evaluation techniques concentrate on collecting and processing information to construct a picture of the situation under evaluation. The interests they respect are those widely considered legitimate in organisations, viz management's interests in such dimensions as efficiency, cost saving, profitability and competitive edge. Consequently, the picture of the situation is treated as if it were sufficient evaluation. For example, a financial cost-benefit analysis will rarely make explicit against whose financial interests the results should be compared though accompanying recommendations will usually make it easy to deduce.

A crucial part of any evaluation technique, whether it be formal or informal, is the evaluator's sources of information. An evaluator who is able to assess the current situation at first hand will avoid the influence of biases introduced when others mediate the flow of information. An evaluator who relies on users' perceptions will get a different picture from one who relies on the project organisation.

The other factor that will affect the outcome of an evaluation process is the evaluator's expectations about what influence the evaluation will have. If previous negative evaluations have appeared to make little impact on the conduct of the innovation process, an evaluator may choose to make a subsequent evaluation more forceful. By contrast, indications that a project organisation is sensitive to evaluations may result in more diplomatically expressed judgements and prescriptions.

7.4 THE EFFECT OF EVALUATIONS ON SUPPORT

It is not currently possible to say precisely how evaluations enter into supporters' decision-making. Here it is simply assumed that

Support For The Project Organisation

evaluations will directly influence supporters' decisions whether to support a project organisation, and that favourable evaluations will affect support positively, while unfavourable evaluations will have a negative effect.

Not only will an evaluation influence what a decision-maker does, it will also affect the organisational balance of power. A favourable evaluation is likely to enhance the power of a project organisation because it reinforces the dependence of stakeholders by making the information system appear less substitutable, while an unfavourable evaluation will reduce its power because it reduces stakeholders' dependence by making the system more substitutable. Consequently, evaluations will work directly by influencing decisions about support, and indirectly by shifting the underlying balance of power.

This straightforward connection between evaluations and supporters' decisions must be qualified in a number of ways. Two in particular are worth examining. First, there is the question of the linkage between evaluation and decision-making. Not all evaluations will carry the same weight with decision-makers. Second, there is the context of decision-making. There may be factors in supporters' context which will influence decision-making regardless of evaluations.

7.4.1 The link between evaluations and support

Not all evaluations will be as influential as each other. Much will depend on how tightly an evaluation is linked to decision processes. Three factors will influence this. One is who carries out the evaluation. The second is the structural relationship between evaluation and decision. The third is the timing of the evaluation.

Evaluations are not necessarily carried out by those who make decisions about support. There is nothing in the logic of evaluation that requires that the interests against which a situation is evaluated be those of the evaluator. Evaluations therefore may be made either for the evaluator's own decision-making or on behalf of another decision-maker. These alternatives are labelled *first party* and *third party* evaluations respectively.

First party evaluations can be expected to be directly influential because there is no gap between evaluator and decision-maker. But, where an evaluation is carried out by a third party there will be a gap. In this latter case, the characteristics and perceived importance of the evaluator will be significant. For example, the evaluator may be highly regarded for her expertise or may represent a powerful stakeholder. The other important factor will be the structural relationships between evaluation and decision-making. For example, if an evaluation is commissioned by top management in response to a perceived crisis, then it is likely that the reporting mechanism will be direct to top management who will make decisions about support. On the other hand, an evaluation by a policy committee may receive only scant attention from supporters.

An important source of third party evaluations is what may be termed institutional evaluators. Their interest in evaluating a system is not motivated by its particular benefits, but rather by their institutionalised role as evaluators. Thus, public auditors, press, internal auditors, data protection agencies, and specialist consultancies may have as a core activity the evaluation of information systems projects on behalf of others. By virtue of being institutionalised their reporting structure is likely to be well defined. The influence of such evaluators will then depend upon how tightly their evaluations are linked to decision processes and on how important they are perceived to be.

Timing will be another factor affecting how tightly evaluations link to decisions. Evaluations may be made at any time. The better synchronised they are to a decision process, the more effect they are likely to have. Evaluations made eighteen months before the next scheduled review of a project will have less impact than those made a month before the review.

7.4.2 Contextual factors

What a decision-maker does given a particular evaluation will depend upon the organisational context. Just as contextual factors affect the innovation process so too they affect decision-making about support.

Organisational structure and processes may set restrictions on how support decisions are approached and who is required to take part. The environment may introduce complicating factors, not least the possibility of better candidates for scarce resources. Cognitive factors may influence the way in which evaluations are understood in the decision process. Misinterpretations and misunderstandings, in whole or in part, may lead to ill-founded decisions. Prior commitments may impose restrictions on the extent to which support can be changed. For example, a contract with penalties for default will be a powerful deterrent against withdrawing promised support. Political factors will also play an important part in how evaluations affect support. For example, the political importance of other supporters may make it impossible for a decision-maker to renege on support for his own project, despite negative evaluations.

In concluding this section, two further points are to be noted. It is important to bear in mind that a decision to support a project need not be a decision to offer all possible support. Stakeholders may support some project activities and not others. Clearly an evaluation that gives weight to some characteristics as desirable and downplays others as undesirable is likely to result in support for the desirable only. However, such partial preferences may be overridden by political factors. It may be effective to withdraw all support in order to force a change in project policy.

It is also worth noting that evaluations can affect a more widely defined situation than the project in hand. Thus, senior management's judgement that a terminated project has been a failure will not affect that project any further, but it may significantly influence subsequent attempts to resurrect the project or to launch projects similar to it in the future.

To summarise, evaluations will affect decisions about support according to how favourable they are, how closely linked the evaluation is to the decision process, and how constraining the context is.

7.5 THE FLOW OF SUPPORT

The above discussion of the role of evaluations in decision-making about support constitutes an analysis of the second side of the triangle of dependences - the relation of system to supporters. The purpose of this section is to say a few words about the third side of the triangle which relates to the flow of support from supporters to the project organisation. The dependence of the project organisation on support so as to avoid flaws was discussed in section 6.2.4.

It is easy to assume that the flow of support is relatively unproblematic - if the project organisation provides a system that supporters evaluate favourably and decide to support, then the support will automatically become available to the project organisation. However, as was noted in chapter 5, there can be problems with support. These are now given some consideration.

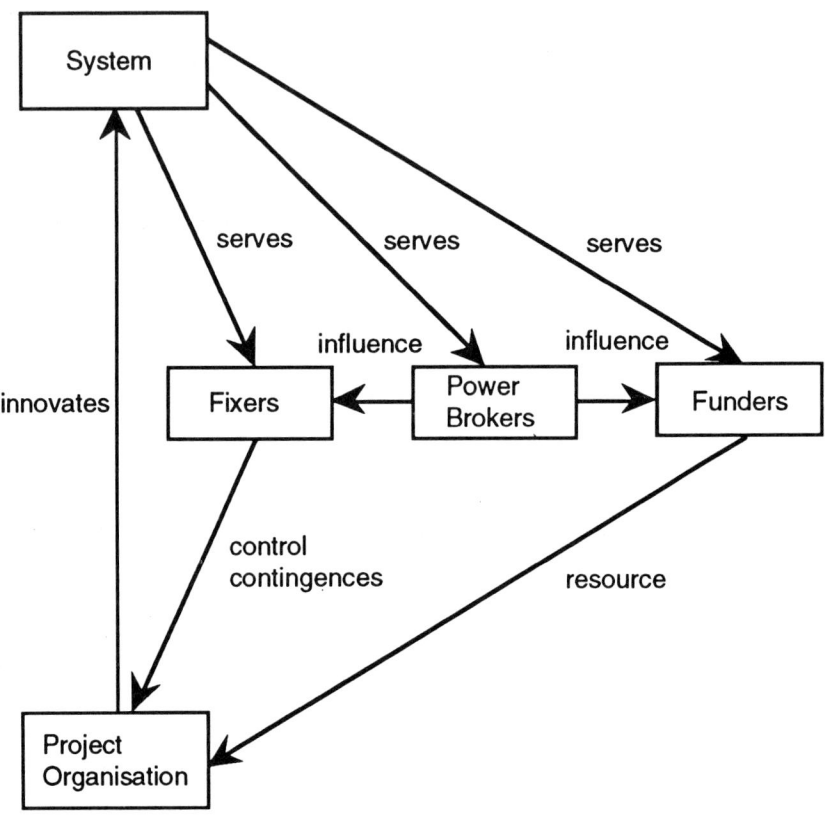

Figure 7.5. Expanded triangle of dependences

Support comes in various forms. It may be financial, or material - ie funding. It may involve control of constraints and contingencies - ie fixing. Or it may simply provide access to the power of another party - ie power-broking. The value of financial support is self-evident since it provides the means for a ready translation into other forms of support (Yuchtman & Seashore

1967). Material support may come in the form of supply of equipment, technical know-how, accommodation, staffing and the like. Fixing can also take many forms. It may relate to the power of some party to make relevant decisions about organisational practices, or to buffer the project organisation from external disturbances, or it may relate to the active and committed participation of the members of the project organisation itself. Finally, power-broking involves one party mediating with another on behalf of the project organisation. A supporter may seek to persuade some other constituency to provide one of the other forms of support to the project organisation, for example to lend it staff. Figure 7.5 extends the triangle of dependences to include funding, fixing, and power-broking.

What are the problems associated with flows of funding, fixing, and power-broking? In principle, funding would appear the least problematic, particularly financing. However, financing does not always consist of the unconditional transfer of funds to a project organisation. There may be conditions to be met and taeit assumptions of restrictions on the use of the funds. Even where the project organisation has a one-line budget to cover all its expenses, the likelihood is that there will be structural constraints on its use. There may be organisational policies about salary levels, or there may be preferential purchasing arrangements with particular equipment suppliers. Such constraints may or may not be recognised by the project organisation, and in some cases may not be appreciated by the funder either. If the project organisation is not aware of such constraints, funds will not represent the support that it supposes.

Financial funding will often be just one part of the resourcing of a project. Other resources may be seen as part of the infrastructure. For example, an information systems department may provide machine time to its project organisations without charge. The resourcing for a project may include this explicitly, but omit to make any provision for when machine time will be available. The project organisation may then find that it can only get access to the machine in the middle of the night. Or again, the central secretarial services facility may agree to provide a given number of clerks and secretaries, but if they are inexperienced or of poor quality, the effect will be of a lower level of resourcing.

Fixers will be either internal or external to the project organisation. Internal support will be less problematic for the project organisation. Though it may make misjudgements about the capabilities of project staff, project management will usually have greater direct control over them. It will therefore be better positioned to obtain from its own staff the support it requires. There will always be occasions where staff withdraw their support because the various inducements they receive are not deemed sufficient. However, the ambiguity as to what support is being offered will be less significant than for external support.

The need for the support of an external fixer will often not be recognised in advance. For example, a development may require existing organisational rules or practices to be changed perhaps because they are inconsistent or they are never properly applied, or because they are too costly to automate. When the rules are fully examined during development, the need for fixing emerges. The availability of a fixer is then subject to the circumstances of the moment. In general, a project organisation will not know in advance who it will require to carry out what fixing.

The other problem with fixers is that they may not be powerful enough to perform precisely the fixing required. Even where the need for fixing is recognised in advance, the fixer may find the problem more difficult than anticipated. There may be organisational constituencies which successfully resist the fixing.

The problematic nature of funding and fixing explains why it is important for a project organisation to have access to power-brokers who can influence those with control over funds and contingencies. The power-broker is an insurance against the uncertainties of other forms of support. When contingencies arise, the power-broker can be called upon to arrange suitable support. It is likely that an assumption that top management is always such a power-broker underlies the widely held belief in the importance of top management support for information systems developments.

There are also some general problems with the flow of support. It has already been noted that imprecision is one. This may take the form of insufficient detail, differing assumptions such as timeframes, ambiguous phrasing, and others.

Another problem is that it may be hard to recognise who is a supporter and who is not prior to calling for substantial assistance. Those who have verbally expressed support may, when faced with an explicit request, decline to meet it. Furthermore, the project organisation will not have explicit agreements with all its potential supporters. It will rely upon past experience and behavioural cues to guide it as to who will help when needed. On occasion, these will prove misleading.

A further problem is that even where a stakeholder agrees to provide support, if the stakeholder has sole control over the relevant source of support the project organisation may have to accept whatever priority the supporter gives to its provision. Thus, the timeframe in which support is provided may not be the timeframe within which the project organisation would like it.

The most significant general problem is that caused by the combination of the passage of time and the contexts of system and supporters. Thus, where support is arranged for some future time, changes to the system context may alter the requirement for support. Or, changes to the competing demands on supporters may affect their ability to provide the support agreed. Thus, because decisions about support are not synchronous with the requirement for it, project organisations sometimes find themselves short of what they require.

Problems with the flow of support have not received much attention from information systems researchers. It is likely therefore that this account is incomplete. However, it serves to illustrate some of the ways in which a project organisation may misunderstand, be misled, or be disappointed as to the support it will receive. And, this will affect its ability to manage the innovation process.

7.6 INFLUENCING SUPPORT

Just as a project organisation is not helpless in the face of the contextual constraints and contingencies affecting the innovation process, so too it can attempt to influence the support it receives, although not every project organisation does so. Some feel it improper or inappropriate in what they see as a purely technical activity. However, those project organisations that do attempt to influence support should not necessarily be interpreted as engaging in Machiavellian practices. In terms of the current model, the crucial thing is that support is essential to project survival. This will encourage political behaviours, and for some this will include tactics not normatively sanctioned.

A project organisation has two types of option for managing support. The one involves influencing evaluations. The better evaluations are, the greater the likelihood of sustaining support. The second option involves influencing the effects of evaluations. This is pertinent in the case of third party evaluations where there will be room for intervention between evaluation and decision. These two options are the subjects of the next two sub-sections, while the final sub-section considers the costs of influence attempts.

7.6.1 Influencing evaluations

The chief strategy for a project organisation wishing to influence evaluations is to manipulate those factors which affect evaluation outcomes, viz perceptions of the situation, interests, timeframes, time of the evaluation, techniques, information sources, and expectations about the effect of the evaluation. Practically, the most effective way of managing evaluations is to control information flows.

Traditionally, the acknowledged method of influencing stakeholders' perceptions of a system has been to 'build the right system and build it right'. On this view, evaluators can be trusted to make a fair evaluation based on a system's merits. However, once it is accepted that there will be multiple constituencies in any organisation, some with competing interests, this view can be seen to be at best only partially appropriate. Evaluations will be a variable political resource for the different constituencies. Merely building what the project organisation sees as a 'good' system will not be enough to guarantee favourable evaluations. The evaluator might see things differently.

The control of information flows is an important political resource (Pettigrew 1973). If a project organisation can control what information is available to whom it will be able to influence perceptions. Much will depend upon the organisational structures and the political relationships surrounding the project. In general, the ability to control information flows will vary across stages of the innovation process. The project organisation will have most control of information at the early stages of a project when very little has been made concrete or documented in any detail. It will have least control when the project has been implemented and the system's effects are immediate to the users. Nonetheless, at any stage, if some stakeholders are more satisfied than others it may be possible to ensure that an evaluator hears what the system does for those who are satisfied while filtering out the complaints of the dissatisfied.

One particular way a project organisation can influence perceptions is by promoting its organisation and methods as being advanced and of the right kind to ensure efficient delivery of its system. Formal tools suggest rigorous methods and strict control, both encouraging the belief that the project organisation will deliver the goods. This was used successfully in the Polaris missile development project (Sapolsky 1972). This is an instance of the more general point that in information systems situations rational facades can obscure from view political aspects of behaviour (Boland & Pondy 1983, Franz & Robey 1984).

Another way of influencing evaluations is to influence stakeholder interests. Interests will be at their most malleable when the stakeholder does not know for certain what he or she wants. The systems development process often involves the information systems professional helping form stakeholder interests by selectively informing and educating the user, and negotiating over system features. Other tactics, including cooption and coalition, were discussed in section 4.4.3. Both serve to draw outsiders into a project thereby shifting both their interests and their perceptions.

A project organisation may also try to influence the timeframe of stakeholder evaluations. The most obvious case where this is helpful is where delays in a project need to be offset. If stakeholders who will be disappointed by the delay can be persuaded to extend the timeframe of their evaluations, then it may be possible to avoid adverse effects on the continuity of support. Much the same will hold where operational problems arise and the system does not yield expected benefits. Probably the biggest stimulus to extending the timeframe of evaluation will be the sunk costs of the project. The project organisation may draw stakeholders' attention to this, and point to other projects that have initially been slow to yield benefits. A history of slow but steady progress in an information systems department's projects may also encourage stakeholders to trust to the future.

The outcome of an evaluation can be affected by the timing of its occurrence. Thus, for example, it will pay to delay formal evaluation processes until such time as sufficient progress has been achieved to ensure favourable outcomes. Meetings of potentially dissatisfied stakeholders may be delayed or even postponed indefinitely in order to avoid triggering unfavourable evaluations.

Techniques of evaluation are important in determining evaluation outcomes in that they filter interests and perceptions of the information systems innovation process. Where a project organisation performs self-evaluation for external consumption as is often the case with feasibility studies, it will be able to choose its techniques and the dimensions it will emphasise in the evaluation. Typically, a project organisation will try to stress benefits to its major user departments, for example faster service to customers, access to more information, lower cost per transaction and so on. At the same time it will gloss over other implications such as the need for some other departments to bear increased costs in the form of, say, a larger inventory or a greater volume of paperwork. Where an evaluation is conducted by another party such as a consultant, the project organisation may still be able to influence the techniques adopted by negotiating over the consultant's terms of reference.

Finally, it may be possible to influence an evaluator's conclusions by manipulating his expectations about the effect of any given evaluation. Thus, if the evaluator can be persuaded that negative comments about the innovation process might have a disproportionately adverse effect on support then he might be prevailed upon to hold back criticisms. Or again, if the evaluator can be made to believe that moderately worded criticisms will be sufficient to change the project organisation's practices then his evaluations may be phrased less strongly and be less likely to have an adverse effect on support.

It hardly needs to be said that the fact that there are a number of ways in which a project organisation can influence evaluations does not mean that they can all be applied in any single case, nor that where they are attempted they will be successful.

7.6.2 Influencing the effects of evaluations

Even if it is not possible to influence what evaluations are made, it may nonetheless be possible to influence what effects they have. The two main factors affecting the influence of evaluations on support are the linkage between the evaluation and the decision process, and the context of the decision process. Therefore, attempts to influence the effects of evaluations will be of one of two kinds. The first applies where evaluations are by a third party. In such cases, the project organisation may try to control what aspects of which evaluations are fed into decision processes. The second kind of influence attempt involves the contextual factors that bear upon the decision process.

(1) Controlling the link between evaluations and decisions

The aim of controlling who hears what is to ensure that supporters hear what the project organisation wants them to hear. A project organisation has a number of possible tactics open to it. Possibilities include influencing which evaluations are heard and how they are treated by decision-makers; what content is heard; and when and by whom evaluations are heard. Control of the organisational structures or processes that link evaluations to decisions will be a powerful means to implementing these various tactics.

On the general presumption that negative evaluations are undesirable because they will have a negative effect on support, project organisations will be advised to filter out negative evaluations wherever they can. If a project organisation believes that it is being unfairly criticised it may appeal to a higher authority to bring pressure to bear to silence the critics. *In extremis*, if it feels it has a legal case then litigation may be an alternative. Even if the case is subsequently withdrawn the threat of a law suit may have the effect of causing critics to mute their complaints. Litigation is most likely when a project organisation is contracted to another organisation rather than operating in-house. If it is not possible to filter out the negative then there are two options. One is to counter the negative with positive evaluations from different sources. The second is to undermine the credibility of the negative evaluations. For example, a project organisation might argue that a critic lacked the expertise to make a valid judgement, or that the evaluation technique had been improperly applied. In some cases, outright contradiction will be appropriate.

An alternative approach is to try to influence which aspects of an evaluation are given prominence. If some parts of an evaluation are more favourable than others it will be worth trying to focus attention on them rather than the less favourable. A number of tactics may be available. If a project organisation is responsible for writing the minutes for liaison and steering groups and formal review sessions, it may be able to control the emphasis accorded to different evaluations. In general, it will be valuable for a project organisation to control or substantially influence the wording of evaluations as they are transmitted to decision-makers.

Control of the dissemination of evaluations may be exercised along spatial and temporal dimensions. For example, control of the minutes of meetings at which evaluations are formally expressed may include control of the timing of their distribution and control of who will receive them. By managing the timing and location of meetings a project organisation may be able to prevent unfavourable evaluations surfacing in a decision-making arena. By arranging meetings inconveniently for critics and conveniently for supporters, the expression of evaluations may be controlled.

In general, where there is a gap between a third party evaluation and decisions about support we can say that any control a project organisation may gain over the structures and processes that mediate the flow of evaluations to the decision process will be most valuable. For example, the power to require that formal evaluations by institutional evaluators be presented first to the project organisation before transmission to decision-makers would be most desirable. Even if it could not change the evaluator's mind it would allow the project organisation to prepare itself better.

In trying to manage who hears which aspects of evaluations, it is possible to lose sight of the value of negative evaluations. Negative evaluations are often a warning signal, an early sign that future support might be at risk. So in trying to minimise any potentially damaging effects on its support from the expression and communication of unfavourable evaluations a project organisation risks not hearing criticisms. Thus, postponing meetings that might prove a focus for negative comment may backfire if the project organisation thereby fails to hear of shortcomings which it could repair.

(2) Controlling the context of the decision process

There are two aspects of the organisational context of decision processes about support which a project organisation may readily attempt to influence: structure and politics. It will usually be beyond a project organisation to have a significant impact on other aspects of the context.

The structure of the decision process itself will help define who will be involved in the decision, what processes will be followed, what other processes it will link to, and the like. For example, some project organisations have influence by virtue of having a say in the structure and procedures of their steering committees.

Political influence will be more direct. If a project organisation can call on power-brokers to influence other supporters or if it can itself apply leverage to decision-makers then it may be able to influence the outcome of decisions about support independently of any evaluations.

7.6.3 The costs of influence attempts

A project organisation cannot make influence attempt after influence attempt indiscriminately. There are three major costs to be considered. First, the more a tactic is repeated, the less weight it will carry as its purpose becomes more transparent. Second, the power to command favours is exhaustible. It is easier to persuade a supporter to give the first favour than the fifth. The third cost is that there is always a risk that an influence attempt will fail. The project organisation may lack the power to carry through its tactics. Circumstances may be unfavourable, stakeholders refractory.

The effect of a failed influence attempt will depend on how legitimate it is taken to be. Attempts to persuade through cooption, say, are usually regarded as legitimate even if rejected. Doctored minutes are less acceptable, and blatant lying still less so. If an influence attempt is seen to be illegitimately manipulative, the target stakeholders may respond even more negatively with stronger criticisms and less inclination to give their support.

Because influence attempts have these costs, a project organisation cannot persist with them *ad infinitum*. It is important to recognise that there are limits to a project organisation's ability to influence support.

7.7 CONCLUSION

This chapter started with the proposition that evaluations play a significant part in the determination of what support is available to a project. If an evaluation is favourable, the evaluator is more likely to proceed to support the project than if it is unfavourable. The relationship between project organisation and supporters is therefore shaped by evaluations. Tables 7.1a and b summarise the main points relating evaluations to support.

Table 7.1a. Summary of important evaluation concepts

Influences on Evaluations	Elements of Evaluations
Situation	Evaluative judgement
system	Accompanying information
context	descriptive
Interests	diagnostic
Techniques	prescriptive
Evaluator	
Feedback	
Timeframe	
Prior evaluations	

Table 7.1b. Summary of important evaluation concepts

Aspects of Evaluations Affecting Support	Approaches to Influencing Support
1st v 3rd party	Affect influences on evaluations
Form of expression	Influence effects of evaluations
Temporal pattern	control information flows
	control exogenous factors

Many characteristics of evaluations may affect the flow of support. Evaluations may be made at any time with reference to any stakeholder's interests over a variety of timeframes. First party evaluations will be tightly linked to support decisions, third party evaluations less so. But even where supporters have decided to provide support the project organisation may not get what it expects. A project organisation wishing to influence what support it receives may try to influence the factors affecting evaluations, and in the case of third party evaluations it may try to influence the effects they have on support decisions. Since negative evaluations can provide useful information to a project organisation, it is in its interest to hear the evaluations of all other stakeholders while influencing who else hears what when. However, there are costs associated with trying to influence evaluations.

This relatively neat analysis belies the organisational reality of complex transactions among many parties including the project organisation, funders, fixers and power-brokers. Chapter 8 takes the analysis closer to this reality through exploring the dynamics of the project organisation's struggle to carry out an information systems innovation process and sustain the support it needs to survive.

Suggested Readings

1. Bjørn-Andersen, N. & Davis, G.B. (eds) (1988) *Information Systems Assessment: Issues and Challenges, Proceedings of the IFIP WG 8.2 Working Conference on Information Systems Assessment,* Noordwijkerhout, The Netherlands, 27-29 August 1986, North-Holland, Amsterdam.

This collection of papers is a good starting point for exploring the issues associated with evaluating information systems.

2. Willcocks, L. (ed) (1993, forthcoming) *Information Systems Investments: Evaluation and Management,* Chapman and Hall, London.

Willcocks is a specialist on evaluation. This collection should give a more recent view.

Chapter 8
Innovation, Support And The Process Of Failing

The information systems process is not just a matter of finding out what users really want and developing a technical system to provide it. It consists of both an innovation process and a support management process. In the innovation process there are many uncertainties deriving from a variety of contextual sources. Even after a system has been developed, changing contextual circumstances can make the operational stage significantly problematic for a project organisation. In the support management process a project organisation needs to be able to sustain the support required to pursue the innovation process further. When it is no longer possible to continue the innovation process because there is too little support, the whole information systems process can be said to have failed. The purpose of this chapter is to combine the analyses of the innovation process (chapter 6) and the support management process (chapter 7) into a model which will serve to explain the process by which information systems fail.

This chapter starts with a brief discussion in section 8.1 of the web of interconnectedness that makes explanations of failure unavoidably complex. The importance of power in understanding the limits to project organisations' ability to control their own destiny is discussed in section 8.2. Section 8.3 considers the various management strategies that are open to project management. The chapter ends in section 8.4 with a discussion of the process by which a system, or project, comes to fail.

8.1 WEB EXPLANATIONS

Earlier chapters have drawn on both bounded rational and political analyses to provide the basis for a model for explaining how flaws arise in the innovation process and what factors influence decisions about support. Interactions among factors and the interrelationships among stakeholders have been largely ignored. In this chapter the intention is to bring the interconnectedness of the information systems process more into the foreground.

The model presented here is distinctly in the web tradition (Kling & Scacchi 1982, Kling 1987). According to Kling (1987) web models are distinguished in a number of ways. The following are particularly pertinent. They are committed to exploring the intertwining of relationships in the context of computing. The focal computing situation is at the centre of a production lattice of producers and consumers. In the case of the types of information system addressed here, the innovation process could be treated as the focal situation with the project organisation as primary producer and end users as primary consumers. The lattice spreads to include other stakeholders. Suppliers to the project organisation include consultants and vendors while consumers include all categories of user, clients of the users, and supporters.

The production lattice exists in a broader context which includes the remainder of the environment. Thus, the behaviour of all parties is subject to influences arising from relationships at some remove from the focal situation. The relationships, both within the production lattice and the context, and between them, form a complex web by which the focal situation is influenced.

The dynamic for the outcomes of relationships in the web is explained in resource dependence terms where the computing resource provides information processing and social symbolic benefits. A significant mode of action by which these outcomes are achieved is negotiation (see Strauss 1978). This interactionist perspective implies reciprocal causation according to which significant components of a situation are able to affect each other over time (see also Bandura 1986).

The effect of the triangle of dependences is to define three salient threads of the web of which an information system is part - the dependence of the system on the project organisation through the innovation process; the dependence of supporters on the system; and the dependence of the project organisation on its supporters. These three threads or relationships highlight the interdependence of a project organisation and its supporters as mediated by an information system. The production lattice and context provide the web of other relationships in which they are embedded. The interactions that occur within the information systems process can be explained by reference to these relationships.

Web models make it apparent that simple linear explanations

are misconceived because the relationships surrounding information systems processes and the dependences on which they are based are highly interconnected. While it easy to accept this in general terms, it is not so easy to feel satisfied with the resulting explanations. This is because they lack the clean edges of simpler analyses. Behaviour is a complex outcome of a complex situation. In terms of the model built around the triangle of dependences, the behaviour of a project organisation and its supporters is far more complicated in its origins than is suggested by the exchange of a system in return for support. Supporters do not adjust the support they give according to every development in the innovation process, neither do project organisations necessarily trim their ambitions because they find support to be lacking.

Web explanations are unavoidably complex. The moral is that for them to be enlightening and useful it is necessary to understand the information systems process and its context in considerable detail. A simplistic explanation easily leads to simplistic recommendations which fail to recognise the complexity and individuality of the situation, and are therefore either inapplicable or lead to undesirable consequences.

8.2 THE POWER OF THE PROJECT ORGANISATION

The power of a project organisation is important to its ability to obtain the support necessary to carry out the innovation process, and to avoid flaws by managing the innovation context or to cope with those flaws that do occur. A project organisation's power will derive from the extent to which other stakeholders depend on it. Clearly, this will be case specific. Nevertheless, some general comments can be made based on empirical studies and their outcomes.

It is often said that knowledge/information is power. It is therefore not surprising to find an *a priori* assumption on the part of many writers that information systems departments and by extension project organisations are relatively powerful. This view is sometimes reinforced by theoretical justifications. Thus, the resource dependence view sees computing technology as an organisationally scarce resource. Consequently, those who control access to it will have power relative to those who desire access (Pettigrew 1973, Markus & Bjørn-Andersen 1987).

Despite this prior assumption that information systems project organisations can be expected to be powerful, the evidence does not currently support it. The direct evidence derives from studies of information systems departments' power. The fact that so many information systems projects appear to run into trouble is further reason for doubting the power of project organisations.

Strategic contingencies theory (Hickson et al 1971, Hinings et al 1974) apparently provides a theoretical basis for the contention that project organisations will be powerful. According to this theory, management information systems will increase pervasiveness, ability to cope with uncertainty, and nonsubstitutability in user departments whose tasks are directly facilitated by the system used (Saunders 1981). It is an easy inference from such a theory to the supposition that information systems departments will themselves benefit by acquiring more power (Pedersen 1986a). Lucas (1984) hypothesises along just these lines. The same arguments apply to individual project organisations.

More directly, Bariff and Galbraith (1978) apply the strategic contingencies model to the information systems organisation and argue that it will be powerful by virtue of its high centrality, immediacy with respect to many classes of task, and its non-substitutability.

Both Lucas (1984) and Saunders and Scammell (1986) have tested the hypothesis that the information systems organisation is powerful, and found it largely unconfirmed when measured by the perceptions of users. Lucas notes that this finding is consistent with the complaint of information systems executives that they are rarely involved in top-level policy and decision-making. Also, information systems appear not to be a good background for progressing to top general management positions since few make this leap. Lucas explains his findings for the manufacturing companies he studied by reference to the lack of centrality of the information systems department, misperceptions, and historical lack of responsiveness by information systems departments. More generally, he suggests that information systems power is concealed through senior managers' lack of knowledge and understanding, and is reduced by their lack of regard for the information systems function, and their lack of involvement in it, and that this is sustained by past poor performance. Saunders and Scammell (1986) suggest that Lucas' explanations might be extended to include the political context. Thus, with many parties pursuing conflicting objectives or objectives with conflicting priorities, lack of power may be a reflection of lack of political skills on the part of information systems executives.

In fact, there are further reasons for concluding that project organisations will not typically be powerful. It is far from clear that information systems themselves confer power on their users in any systematic way. Studies in the Urbis programme at the University of California at Irvine have concluded that though information systems help consolidate the power of those who are already organisationally powerful, they do not empower the relatively powerless (Kraemer, Dutton & Northrop 1981). Pedersen (1986a, 1986b) argues that there is no simple relation between information systems use and the acquisition of power. Therefore an information systems department, and by extension a project organisation, is not a technological power-broker able to confer power on others as it wishes. Its lack of discretion in this respect has an obvious effect on its power.

The matter can be relatively simply put. During the development stage of the innovation process a project organisation will be more immediately dependent on its supporters than vice-versa. The project will not be able to proceed without a good measure of support whereas supporters will be continuing their activities while they await the system's completion. Supporters' control of resources and their ability to 'fix' organisational problems will be highly immediate for a project organisation whereas the system itself will be rather less so for supporters. Indeed, in many cases the information system will have a natural substitute in whatever procedures currently effect the organisational tasks for which the computer-based information system is intended. Consequently, during development the balance of power will lie with supporters who will be the less dependent party. Once a system has been implemented, there may be a real shift in the balance of power. However, if the system is functioning reasonably well, the project organisation is far less likely to need significant extra support. It may be more powerful, but it will have less use for its power. On the other hand, if the system is functioning poorly the project organisation will be under pressure to improve the situation. If supporters are now dependent on the new system the project organisation may find it has the power to demand the support needed to fix the problem. If not, it may be in a relatively weak position with a real risk that funding will be withdrawn completely.

		Locus of Managerial Control		
		IS Management	Departmental Management	Top Management
Type of Interest Served	Technical	SKILL	Service/Skill Mix	Strategic/Skill Mix
	Operational	Skill/Service Mix	SERVICE	Strategic/Service Mix
	Managerial	Skill/Strategic Mix	Service/Strategic Mix	STRATEGIC

Figure 8.1. States of computing management (Kraemer et al 1989, p30, copyright Jossey-Bass, reproduced by permission)

Analyses of a project organisation's relationships with its supporters give only a part of the picture. It is an integral part of the underlying web model that the relationships between and among supporters will be influenced by an array of factors, not all of which will be directly related to the information systems process, and which the project organisation will probably lack the position and resources to control. In other words, a project organisation may lack power because supporters are more dependent on another party than they are on the project organisation.

The foregoing discussion has shown that it cannot be taken for granted that all information systems departments and project organisations are powerful. When analysing the power of a project organisation it would be well to bear in mind these various factors that qualify the apparent dependence of stakeholders on the project organisation. That said, nonetheless some project organisations will wield very considerable power. In any particular case, a careful analysis of the project organisation's basis for power is called for.

A useful heuristic for deciding whether a project will have access to the support it needs can be derived from the theory of management states (Kraemer, King, Dunkle & Lane 1989). Using a three by three matrix, the theory identifies nine states of computing management. The two dimensions of the matrix are the locus of control over computing and the type of interest served by computing applications. This matching of control and interests makes the theory broadly consistent with the assumptions underlying the triangle of dependences. Figure 8.1 depicts the nine states. Three are congruent and may be expected to result in stability. When information systems management is in control and the interests served are technical, there is a congruent *skill state*. When departmental management is in control and the interest served by applications is departmental services, then there is a congruent *service state*. When top management controls computing and managerial interests are served, there is a congruent *strategic state*.

The theory, though not devised for the level of individual projects, is suggestive in the following way. If the interest served by a particular application is that of those who control computing then they, at least, are likely to support it. Thus, in the skill state, technically oriented applications are likely to receive direct support from information systems management. Equally, service applications will be supported in the service state, and managerially oriented systems will be supported by top management in the strategic state. Where an application is not congruent with the interests of those who control computing, it does not follow that support will never be forthcoming, but it is likely that it will be less readily supported. For example, if an assembly shop scheduling system is under construction but runs into difficulties, the project organisation has its best chance of access to the necessary power to provide funds and control contingencies if departmental management controls the information systems function. This is for two reasons. First, it will be more likely to receive the support of departmental management because they stand to gain from the system. Second, information systems management is more likely to exercise whatever power it has because it is directly controlled by departmental management. By contrast, if top management is in control and a technically oriented project runs aground, support will be less likely than if the application were strategically oriented. In such cases of incongruent management states, systems may be much more prone to failing than in congruent cases because they cannot obtain and retain the support. In the incongruent cases, support will be much more dependent on the contingencies of the situation, in particular the power and the political skills of the developers and their managers. Thus, the theory of management states provides something of an heuristic by which to make initial judgements as to the support a project organisation is likely to be able to obtain, in particular its access to effective power-broking.

The benefit of gaining an understanding of the project organisation's power with respect to other stakeholders is that it indicates what constraints and contingencies it can control and what support it can command. However, understanding the project organisation's ability to command support is not as simple as understanding a market transaction in which, for example, a customer hands a stallholder money in return for a bunch of asparagus. The market transaction is synchronous, both parties receiving immediate gratification. The exchange between project organisation and supporters is far more subtle. For one thing, the project organisation is rarely in a position to deliver benefits immediately. Supporters are similarly restricted sometimes. For another thing, because of the uncertainties of the innovation process and uncertainties associated with the flow of support, it will not be clear what the project organisation can offer nor what support will be provided. So neither party can be sure about what it is getting in return for its part of any bargain. Moreover, in negotiations there may be no explicit mention of inducements and costs. The project organisation may not mention the costs to the supporter of not providing the required support, and the supporter may not point out what effect it will have on the support available if the project organisation does not meet the supporter's demands. Thus, though the underlying exchange relation supplies the dynamic for the information systems process, it should not be expected that the interactions that enact this exchange will be like simple transactions in the vegetable market.

Having considered the problem of project organisation power, we are now in a position to consider what management strategies are open to a project organisation.

8.3 MANAGEMENT STRATEGIES

It is often thought that it is a prerequisite of successful innovation management that there be an idea champion (Schon 1967, Daft and Becker 1978), that is someone who is committed to the advancement of the innovation and attempts to push it through the various stages, sometimes in the face of considerable opposition. An idea champion is thus a kind of antidote to organisational conservatism, providing the momentum to keep a process going. However, an idea champion is not a substitute for a management strategy.

Table 8.1. Strategies for managing the information systems process

Strategies
1. Manage the innovation process
2. Manage resource and support decisions
3. Loosen the coupling between system and supporters
4. Combine strategies

The model developed in this book suggests four classes of strategy (see table 8.1). A project organisation can attempt to manage the innovation process through concentrating on the innovation process. In this strategy, the project organisation satisfies its supporters by constructing a system that is in their interests. A second strategy is to attempt to manage supporters' decisions independently of the extent to which the project actually serves them. This involves the application of some of the influence tactics discussed in chapter 7. The third option is to attempt to loosen the coupling between the system and its supporters. The fourth is to employ a combination.

8.3.1 Managing the innovation process

The information systems innovation process was described in chapter 6. A range of contextual factors was seen to influence progress. The conclusion was that flaws cannot always be avoided. Indeed, some level of flaws is normal. The essence of any strategy that emphasises management of the innovation process is to keep flaws to an absolute minimum and, where flaws inevitably intrude, to absorb their effects.

This is the strategy sanctioned in the normative literature. It largely presupposes that the necessary support is unproblematically available. Because of this it does not distinguish between what users want and what supporters want. Thus, to the extent that this strategy is predicated on keeping users happy it may fail to address the role of supporters. Shifts in support will then appear to be arbitrary, unmanageable contingencies. However, while it is true that the project organisation will not be able to control all the power relationships of which its supporters are part, if it makes no attempt to influence them it leaves itself open to losing support regardless of how effective the innovation process is. It is not uncommon for information systems professionals to take the attitude that it is not their job to try to manage support. The result is that they are more at risk of suffering morale sapping project terminations for what they would regard as no good reason than if they took a broader view of their role.

8.3.2 Managing the resource and support decisions

This management strategy consists of a project organisation influencing supporters by means which do not rely on its system speaking for itself. The rationale for this is that so long as the project organisation has the support to survive, even if the quality of its system is deteriorating, there remains the possibility that the system can be made good. Flaws can be rectified or absorbed given enough support. The support to survive provides funds and time for the continuing search for support. This is essentially a political strategy and as such is not normatively sanctioned.

Various tactics for influencing support were discussed in section 7.6. The project organisation's ability to implement these different tactics will vary with the circumstances. For example, if key supporters are end users, it will be impossible to hide from them the flaws they themselves discover in the system. On the other hand if supporters are not users, it may be possible to hide some flaws. The viability of changing organisational structures and practices so as better to control perceptions and preferences will depend very much on the political skills of senior members of the project organisation.

In the short term, a project organisation's ability to manage support will be dependent on its circumstances. In the medium term, it may attempt to enhance its bargaining power by attempting to influence the centrality, pervasiveness and non-substitutability of its information system. For example, if it can persuade users to abandon substitute systems, it will increase the importance of its own system and hence increase its power to command further support. This is a tactic which was attempted in the case described in chapter 10. Another tactic is to take on more functions so as to improve both centrality and pervasiveness. In the longer term, a project organisation may be able to effect changes which improve its position with respect to managing support. For example, if it has greater access to arenas in which resource decisions are made, it will be better able to influence them. However, where there is opposition there is no reason to expect that this will be achievable even in the long term. No matter how politically skilled information systems professionals may be, if they lack room for political manoeuvre, they will be unable to change the underlying structural circumstances that determine their ability to command support.

Thus, like managing the innovation process, the effectiveness of managing support cannot be guaranteed.

8.3.3 Loosening the coupling between system and supporters

The triangle of dependences implies a tight coupling between a system and the provision of support. Attempts to control the information received by supporters loosen this coupling by stealth. However, a more radical way of achieving this is to find supporters who are less interested in the system's performance. Thus, instead of relying on the control of strategic contingencies, a project organisation attempts to exploit the system's symbolic value (Feldman & March 1981) thereby reducing the importance of flaws. In pursuing this strategy a project organisation reduces its own dependence on existing supporters by finding substitute sources of support.

If alternative sources of support can be found, for example public funding agencies or private sponsors, they may be more interested in *being seen* to give support rather than in the outcome of their support. Thus, the actual performance of the innovation may be unimportant to external supporters, particularly if the system is not for their use. For example, a university library might obtain private sponsorship from industry for a new computerised catalogue. What the industrial company wants is good publicity and possibly research favours. It will have very limited interest in the degree to which the system serves its internal supporters and proponents. Kraemer et al (1989) cite examples from US local government of information systems departments which sought external funding from government agencies trying to encourage computerisation. Thus, where supporters are external to the organisation in which the system is to operate, the relation between project team and its supporters is far less tightly constrained by the outcome of the innovation process.

From the project organisation's point of view, this tactic has two advantages. First, it relieves it of total dependence on internal funders. Second, it also loosens its dependence on fixers because the effects of constraints and contingencies on the system are less important to the continuance of support.

However, this option is by no means always open. Even where it is, the external supporter may have *some* interest in the outcome of the innovation, for nobody wants the symbolic 'benefits' of being associated with an acknowledged white elephant. Thus, once again, the possibility of exercising influence or control over the provision of support is highly dependent on the project organisation's actual circumstances.

8.3.4 Combined strategies

The reality of most projects is that a combined strategy will be employed. In particular, the project organisation will try to manage its support as well as the innovation process. The differences among project strategies will be a matter of emphasis. In some cases managing support will be a relatively low priority compared with managing the innovation process, in others the reverse.

The combined strategy reflects the interaction of the innovation process and support. The innovation process needs support to help manage its context and thereby solve its problems.

If the project organisation needs more support, it may offer improved facilities as an incentive.

In some circumstances the whole project-support equation may be reassessed. In these cases, especially where it becomes clear that certain system functions are not realistically achievable or that the required level of support is not forthcoming, the project may be reduced in scale. Ewusi-Mensah and Przasnyski (1991) treat partial, substantial and total project abandonment as all forms of the same phenomenon of project abandonment. Here, partial and substantial abandonment are both treated as strategies for keeping a project alive. They are major strategies for redefining the exchange between project organisation and supporters.

8.3.5 Some limitations on strategies

The adoption of each of these strategies has its costs. While managing the innovation process to the exclusion of support leaves a project open to the vagaries of supporters, it is argued in this subsection that managing support distinct from the innovation process ultimately restricts the project organisation's room for manoeuvre to the point where the service the system provides becomes decisive.

Any project organisation needs basic resources to carry out its innovation process, topped up by funding, fixing, and power-broking to deal with contingent problems. Thus, support is constantly being consumed. Where the support consumed is from an existing reservoir such as a budget, the cost is merely the depletion of that budget. Where support is not pre-budgeted, persistent requests for supporter intervention may dispose supporters to evaluate the project negatively.

Any attempt to influence evaluations and the flow of support has a cost in terms of project resources. It has an opportunity cost of the effort lost to innovation. Any attempt to apply undue influence or devious tactics risks being exposed to general view, with sanctions being imposed in consequence.

Negotiating and manoeuvring for support also has its costs. The principal immediate cost is any concession the project organisation makes to its supporters. In the longer term, any concession or adaptive shift closes down future options reducing room for subsequent manoeuvre (Zammuto 1982). Zammuto argues that the effective organisation is a niche expander.

Innovation, Support, And The Process of Failing 125

Translating this to the terms of the current discussion, a project organisation will maintain its adaptability by satisfying as many supporters as possible, thereby maintaining the widest range of options possible. To have to make concessions in the pursuit of support closes off future options. For instance, once a project organisation negotiates an extended implementation deadline, that precise extension is no longer an option for dealing with future problems. Likewise, partial or substantial abandonment is unlikely ever to be reversed. The more adaptations the project organisation makes in order to maintain its support, the less room it has for subsequent manoeuvre.

Thus, even where a project organisation has the political wherewithal to manipulate support successfully, it will be unable to do so indefinitely independent of the performance of its system. The management of support is a strategy to complement the innovation process, not substitute for it. The more the project organisation manipulates and adapts, the more it will foreclose its strategic options. In the long run, if it is unable to produce a system that serves its supporters it will lose the support it needs to survive.

8.4 THE DYNAMICS OF THE INFORMATION SYSTEMS PROCESS

The analysis of the major relationships represented in the triangle of dependences has so far been relatively static. Yet, over time the bases for these relationships change, with consequential effects on the dynamics of the information systems process. Change to what is already a complex web makes it difficult to discern process dynamics which will be both detailed and generally applicable. The particulars of every case will be different. Nonetheless, the model presented in this book includes a core dynamic which helps organise analyses of the process by which information systems come to fail.

What the triangle of dependences suggests is that if a project organisation can convince supporters that its system will serve or is serving their interests sufficiently, then support will be forthcoming to maintain the innovation process. On the other hand, if supporters lose confidence in their investment so far as to withdraw or refuse support, then the innovation process will be adversely affected, further degrading the system outcomes on which supporters make their evaluations, leading to a downward spiral. A satisfactory balance of support for innovation may be disturbed by any of the contextual factors described in chapters 6 and 7. Equally though, the first hiccup in either the innovation or support management process will not necessarily lead to an unstoppable decline. There is room for manoeuvre to avoid or recover from innovation problems or a shortage of support.

Room for manoeuvre derives from the asynchronous nature of the exchange and from there being a measure of flexibility in the terms of the exchange. For example, though a project organisation may lack the support it wants, it may still have enough to continue working for a period during which it can try to retrieve problems in the innovation process or secure the support it needs. Whether it will be able to recover its position will depend on its power with respect to the innovation context and its power with respect to its supporters. Unless the project organisation possesses slack resources, any simple exchange of system features in return for support threatens to undermine some other aspect of the project affected by the change. The crucial requirement is that the project organisation control strategic contingencies for its supporters so that it can leverage further support when it needs it without incurring critical losses.

The effects of a shortage of support can be described as follows. A project organisation faces problems defined by its innovation context. These problems will be addressed by a combination of systematic mechanisms and ad hoc problem-solving. Both types of problem-solving require resources to perform, and both will on occasion require the support of fixers. A shortage of resources may be global with respect to the project, or problem specific. In the global case, the outcome will be either flawed problem-solving now or in the future; a project organisation can try to spread its resources evenly but thinly across the whole project or it can consume the resources it needs now and spread its resources even more thinly in the future. Inadequate resources will result in unsatisfactory outcomes one way or the other. Exactly where flaws occur will depend on how the resources are deployed. In the problem-specific case, if there is no compensation for the lack of resources then the outcome will be flawed. Fixers are usually required for particular problems such as resolving a disagreement between two users. If the problem cannot be resolved a project organisation faces the costs of trying to accommodate both sets of requirements. This may be costly and unnecessarily complex with the likelihood of resultant flaws.

Once flaws have been recognised, there are two options (see table 8.2). They can either be corrected or not. Correcting them costs yet further resources and possibly other support. Not correcting them results in one of two outcomes. The flaw can be accepted and any effects on users absorbed by them. For example, a report might be inadequately formatted, but operational users might agree to format it clerically for the manager who uses it for decision-making. The alternative is that the flaw is not absorbed and, in this example, the manager gets a report she cannot use to her satisfaction. The flaw generates a perception that the system is not serving the manager's interests. Over time, all three options might be applied to the same flaw. Initially nothing is done, then the flaw is absorbed temporarily, and finally it is corrected. This sequence might be the result of a deliberate tactic by the project organisation in its management of support, or it might be the natural outcome of a time lag in the flow of support.

Table 8.2. Options for dealing with flaws

Options	Outcomes
Project org corrects flaw	Support costs for project org, benefits to users
Project org does not correct flaw users absorb flaw	No resource cost for project org costs to users - application unaffected
users do not absorb flaw	no cost to users - application adversely affected

The complexity of most information systems means that the costs of leaving a flaw uncorrected may be significant because of consequential effects it might have on other parts of the system. Glasser (1981) notes the cumulative and combined effect of overlooking certain variables. She also quotes Schmitt and Kozar (1978) on the compounding of errors and omissions: 'a degenerative network of errors . . . that is difficult to escape once it is entered'. In general, we can expect flaws to propagate unless they are corrected. The more flaws in the innovation process, the more likely that support will decline and the process enter a downward spiral.

The support the project organisation has for managing the innovation process will come in a variety of ways. Common to all is the fact that support is an investment on the part of supporters. There is some risk that they will not receive the return they want. Support, then, is provided in advance of the returns it yields. In the case of resources such as finances, usually a budget will be made available for use by the project organisation over a period of time. The greater discretion it has over the budget, the more flexibility it will have in its problem-solving and its coping with flaws. The longer the period for which the budget is allocated, the longer the project organisation has in which to cope. The ability of the project organisation to influence budget size, timeframe and discretion will be a function of its power and negotiating skills with respect to funders.

In the case where the support required is fixing, there is less likely to be a reservoir to be tapped on demand. Rather, the project organisation will have to ask for it when it is needed. Once again, the project organisation's power and negotiating skills will be important to the outcome of the request.

Rather like requests for fixing, requests for power-broking will be somewhat ad hoc. The project organisation may have solicited support in advance from both power-brokers and fixers. In some instances, a request may be sufficient to elicit the support. In other instances, the matter will be subject to negotiation with the outcome depending on the power relations obtaining between the two parties.

Thus, the support the project organisation receives at any time will depend on the power it enjoys. If the balance of power favours the project organisation it may receive support without having to make concessions in return. On the other hand if the system is not sufficiently important to the supporter then the project organisation may have to offer special favours such as early implementation or extra system facilities, or it may have to reduce its demands. In the worst situation, support may be refused or withdrawn as the result of a request. It may be a trigger to an evaluation that the project is no longer worth supporting. However, the project organisation cannot know in advance the outcome of a request for assistance because it remains a matter of judgement as to what power it has with respect to which supporters.

The web perspective draws special attention to one particular way a project organisation or its individual members may attempt to build up and improve its access to support. Because a project organisation is embedded in a network of relationships, the more that potential and actual stakeholders are drawn into the project, made aware of its importance, asked for their requirements and generally coopted or included in the wider coalition of supporters, the more likely they will be to respond supportively if called upon. This practice is commonly referred to as *networking* and it permits a project organisation to build up credits for future use. It empowers by increasing perceptions of the centrality and pervasiveness of the project organisation's work.

The detailed characteristics of negotiations, bargains, and power plays are likely to vary across the different stages of the innovation process as both parties increase their knowledge of the constraints that face them. It was noted in chapter 6 that a significant part of the initiation stage relates to the garnering of support. A project organisation has its greatest flexibility to offer potential supporters whatever will induce them to provide support. Sub-stages such as attitude formation are specifically related to influencing interests and perceptions so as to obtain favourable evaluations.

Insofar as development involves the elaboration and refinement of the abstract system implicit in a strategic decision, a project organisation experiences greater constraints on its ability to tailor its system to supporters' demands during the development stage than at initiation. The constraints are not absolute but relative to other constraints such as budget and schedule. Thus, if a project organisation can do a deal which involves scrapping earlier work and replacing it by something more acceptable to a particular supporter, thereby gaining compensating support in terms of resources or extended schedules, then the deal will be worthwhile. Of course, in assessing such a deal a project organisation will have to bear in mind any losses to other supporters. The further a development has proceeded, the more fixed supporters' expectations are likely to be, the greater project organisation commitment will be, and the more expensive it will be to change the development. For these reasons, major deals between project organisation and supporters are likely to be less common as development advances.

However, as development advances, contingent problems are more likely to emerge. The unexpected has to be dealt with. Special funds may be required for a special piece of software; decisions may be needed to change entrenched practices; promotional support may be needed to maintain user commitment; and so on. Whether support is immediately forthcoming or whether supporters decide to reevaluate the project will depend on many factors. Where there is an evaluation process, the evaluator may seek to influence the project through the information that accompanies the evaluation. Support may be approved, but there may be a recommendation that the project organisation adopt a formal project control system. The project gets its support without actually agreeing to adopt project control. If it ignores the suggestion, it may risk subsequent support. As was noted earlier, the actual process by which exchanges occur is very different from a simple market transaction.

The implementation stage is the one at which operational user support is most likely to be crucial. Resistance can be terminal for a system. But, it works the other way too. If a system is discovered to be flawed, user support can serve to buffer the rest of the organisation from these flaws, thereby reducing the likelihood of other supporters perceiving the system negatively.

At the operational stage, if the system is well integrated, supporters will resource the project in return for continuing operational performance. Usually, there will be a budget to cover some level of system changes in maintenance and enhancement. Support beyond this may have to be negotiated, but at this stage the project organisation has least room for manoeuvre because the system is implemented. However, it will be less dependent on supporters because it will be seen to have done most of its job in getting the system implemented. Moreover, to the extent that the system has made users and supporters dependent on it, the balance of power may lie with the project organisation. If the system is not well integrated, there being various user demands for changes and improvements, then there may be considerable negotiation over support.

There is one final point to be made in this section. Supporters will sometimes be users and sometimes not. The difference can be crucial. If supporter interests are different from those of users, then a project organisation may create user dependence without creating supporter dependence. Thus, a user who is a supporter may be influenced easily enough because of the dependence, but the same will not apply to a supporter who is not a dependent user. It is for this reason that the model in this book emphasises the project organisation's relationship with its supporters rather than the more traditional project organisation-user relationship.

To summarise, this section has attempted to explain the dynamics of the information systems process in terms of the basic exchange relationship between project organisation and supporters. It has shown how the actual interactions between the parties are at some remove from simple market transactions. The asynchronous nature of the exchange relation gives the project organisation room for manoeuvre. The power relations of the various parties are central to the outcomes of the information systems process, and the basis of these relations varies over the course of the innovation process. Finally, it has been noted that power with respect to users and power with respect to supporters are distinctly different things.

8.5 CONCLUSION

The model expounded in this book emphasises the dual activities of innovation and support management. Previous chapters have explored some of the factors that affect these activities without relating them to each other. This chapter has sought to remedy this by describing the dynamics of the information systems process in terms of the interactions between project organisation and supporters, particularly the exchanges, dressed up in their various forms, that interweave around the triangle of dependences. It has argued the importance of power to project organisations and has shown that the actual power they are able to deploy depends upon the circumstances of any particular information systems process. Though there are different strategies available to project management, some mix will usually be employed. In the final analysis, the strategy of managing support needs to be accompanied by an innovation process able to satisfy its supporters' interests. The more a project adapts in order to survive, the more it cuts down its future options until it is unable to sustain the support it needs. In losing the support it needs a project finally fails.

The model outlined in chapter 5 has now been elaborated

sufficiently for it to be applied to actual cases. The next four chapters are devoted to this. Chapter 9 presents the research methodology for the case described in chapter 10 and analysed in chapter 11. Chapter 12 applies the model to some cases already published in the literature.

Suggested Readings

1. Kling, R. (1987) Defining the boundaries of computing across complex organizations, in Boland, R.J. & Hirschheim, R.A. (eds.) (1987) *Critical Issues in Information Systems Research*, Wiley, Chichester, pp 307-362.

Expounds and discusses the nature of web models.

2. Hickson, D.J., Hinings, C.R., Lee, C.A., Schneck, R.E. & Pennings, J.M. (1971) A strategic contingencies' theory of intraorganizational power, *Administrative Science Quarterly*, 216-229.

This is the original paper expounding the strategic contingencies theory of power.

3. Lucas, H.C. Jr (1984) Organizational power and the information services department, *Communications of the ACM*, 27, 1, January, 58-65.

A seminal paper which raised the problem of just how much power information systems do confer on their technical masters.

Chapter 9
The Case Study Approach

Case studies are excellent for helping understand information systems failure because failure is a complex phenomenon of which we are still largely ignorant. This point is expanded in the first section of this chapter. In the second section, the research methods used on the case described and analysed in the following two chapters are set out.

9.1 THE VALUE OF CASE STUDIES

There are many types of case study. The type considered here might perhaps be better termed the *case history*, that is the detailed historical description and analysis of actual information systems processes. In the current state of our knowledge case histories will be a major aid to our understanding of failure in a number of ways.

First, unless researchers publish reports of information systems processes which trace decisions through to their outcomes, the actual experience of failure will remain the only route to knowledge about it. Case histories can provide experience at second hand by showing what actions in what circumstances will lead to undesired outcomes, to the loss of support, and to failure. Second, the actual experience of conducting a systematic and rigorous case study brings home the complexities of the information systems process. In conducting a detailed case study the complex social and political web in which computing developments are undertaken becomes salient. Third, information systems failure is far from being well understood. Case studies help define what is problematic; they help generate ideas about cause-effect chains; and they stimulate our thinking about practical solutions given the constraining effects of an organisational context.

Detailed case descriptions and analyses help counter simplistic analyses and solutions. It is pointless to advocate the application of techniques which cannot be used for political reasons. Seeing how context constrains a project organisation will help in this respect.

Not just any case study will be valuable. A two paragraph account of a two year project is unlikely to encompass enough of the facts to illuminate its final outcome. An account based on a single source of information will inevitably risk being biased. A good case study needs to have been well researched. However, assuming that it has been conducted systematically and rigorously a case study of failure may be valuable in some or all of the following ways:

(1) Raising problems about the phenomenon of failure
(2) Stimulating theories of the causes of failure
(3) Stimulating theories of the cause-effect chains which lead to failure
(4) Stimulating the development of problem-solving mechanisms

These are all benefits which are most likely to accrue to the researcher who conducts the study. For those who read them, case studies have other advantages:

(1) They illustrate theories and models of failure
(2) They exemplify the application of those theories and models
(3) They show the processes by which failure occurs
(4) They are a surrogate for costly experience

The description and analysis of the Mandata case that follows is intended to provide readers with the benefits listed above. The cases presented in chapter 12 are taken from the literature. They serve to illustrate and test the model of failure presented in this book. They help indicate areas where further work is necessary.

9.2 RESEARCH METHOD FOR THE MANDATA STUDY

Case research is often subject to methodological objections. A common class of objection relates to the actual execution and reporting of studies. In the information systems field Benbasat, Goldstein and Mead (1987) have found much to criticise: research designs are not explained in any detail, sometimes not at all; choice of site goes unmentioned; and data collection may only be mentioned in passing with no explicit description of the techniques used. While the actual research methods employed will always be

The Case Study Approach

open to criticism, there is no excuse for not reporting what they were. Therefore this section gives a description of the research design, broadly following the guidelines of Yin (1989). This is followed by an explanation of how the research was carried out, together with details of the database produced.

9.2.1 Research design

This research was stimulated by a desire to understand the causal processes in cases of information systems failure. Initially, the study was expected to produce a descriptive answer to the question: *how do the commonly accepted causes of information systems failure, such as lack of top management support, come to have their effects?* This was predicated on the assumption that the causes of failure are clear and relatively unproblematic.

An early exploration of a discrete body of data (held by the Public Accounts Committee of the Australian Parliament) rapidly showed that this was not so. The public record did not give sufficient information to know what had happened. Even the most informative public analysis of the project (JCPA 1979) left many questions unanswered. For example, the Public Accounts Committee's report was critical that a full statement of objectives had not been developed, but it gave no clue as to why no such statement had been produced. A further study was therefore necessary.

The design of any case research study can be divided into five components (Yin 1989):

(1) the study's questions
(2) its propositions
(3) its units of analysis
(4) the logic linking data to the propositions
(5) the criteria for interpreting the data

Each component of the design will be considered in turn.

(1) The study's questions

The first question was fundamental in determining what was to be explained. It asked:

Chapter 9

(A) Was Mandata a failure?

Clearly, a negative answer to this question would lead to a rather different set of questions than an affirmative. In the event, according to the conceptualisation of failure derived in chapter 2 Mandata proved to be a failure. Two questions automatically followed. Of these two, the first sought explanation. It was a *why* question:

(B) Why did Mandata fail? What were the causes of its failure?

The second question following the conclusion that Mandata was a failure was frankly more exploratory. It sought to use the model constructed in chapters 5 to 8 to reveal by what process Mandata came to fail:

(C) By what process did Mandata come to fail?

In view of the emphasis placed upon support and support management it seemed worth exploring the options that were open to Mandata project management:

(D) What options were there for alternative support management strategies?

Finally, there was the question of whether the project as a whole could have been any different. There is always a trivial, determinist sense in which, if you allow no change to the antecedents of an action, it is determined that the action could have been no different. However, where the focus of attention is the project organisation, and you ask what options there were available that might have led to significantly different outcomes at any major decision point, and what constraints there were on taking up these options, then it can become somewhat clearer as to whether, realistically, decisions and events might have been different. It is, of course, fearsomely difficult to determine where a major alternative decision would have led if taken. Nonetheless, it is always worth exploring the question whether a project was an unavoidable failure?

(E) Could the Mandata project have avoided failure?

Of these five questions, (A) to (D) will be addressed explicitly in chapter 11 while (E) will be discussed in the context of a more general argument in chapter 13.

(2) Propositions

By propositions, Yin (1989) means the presuppositions of a study. In this case, the presuppositions are derived from organisation theory and information systems research. These have been combined in chapters 4-8 to provide a model for understanding the information systems process. Principally, it directs us toward the contextual constraints and contingencies that affected Mandata and the problems of support.

(3) Unit of analysis

The unit of analysis defines the boundaries of the case research. In doing this it helps set the place of the current effort among past and future research. The interest here lies not so much in isolating static factors that were fatal to the project, but more in understanding the ebb and flow of the whole process. In this case, therefore, the unit of analysis is the project incorporating the whole information systems process from initiation to termination.

(4) Linking data and propositions

Yin (1989) notes that research has typically been sketchy in its descriptions of the logic linking data to a study's propositions. This is not surprising because it is extremely hard to make these links in a sufficiently rigorous way. Chapter 10 provides an exposition of the data in accordance with the model developed earlier. It has been made detailed so that it will be apparent that the selection of data is not merely idiosyncratic, and that its ordering is consistent with the propositions of the model.

(5) Criteria for interpreting the findings

The point of requiring criteria for interpreting findings is to avoid rabbit-out-of-a-hat conclusions. There needs to be some systematic way of relating the data and the interpretations placed on them. Once again Yin (1989) notes that it is problematic to meet this requirement. Normally, though, a reader will make some assessments as to the coherence of an interpretation and its apparent relation to the data.

In the Mandata case, the author applied the tests of asking what other options there were, whether they were available, and what the outcome would have been if an alternative had been pursued. Discussion of the constraints on alternatives is offered in an attempt to demonstrate the coherence of the study's findings.

9.2.2 Choice of site

The Mandata case was chosen partly from lack of alternatives. Actual instances of failure, though they are sometimes written up in the press, are not widely advertised. Organisations are not keen to support what they fear may be critical investigations. Organisational politics may dictate that it would be better to let sleeping dogs lie. It is not easy to find a variety of sites from which to choose.

Nonetheless, Mandata had a number of virtues that would have made it desirable even in the face of alternatives. First, the public record includes several reports on the project by parliamentary committees and the Australian Auditor-General as well as numerous press items. Second, the Australian Public Service maintains voluminous files including memoranda, minutes, technical documentation, reports and so forth, many of which were identifiably annotated by the people who read them at the time they were current. Third, there is an informal network among present and past officers of the Australian Public Service which eases the process of tracing key personnel. Fourth, Mandata was a big project which had been through all stages of system development and maintenance including hardware acquisition, software acquisition, and contract and in-house software production. In this respect it was a very rich source of data.

Perhaps the least attractive characteristic of the case is its age.

It would be very easy to suppose that somehow what happened then could not happen now, and that therefore it is irrelevant to modern concerns. However, using terminology pitched at a relatively high level of abstraction allows us to see the generalities rather than the singularities. This strategy also permits us to avoid the criticism that because the technology is no longer extant the case is out of date. (In fact, in this case, like so many others, the hardware and software technology were less influential in the project's outcome than other contextual factors.)

The age of the case has also meant that it has had to be studied in retrospect. Unless we are prepared to study live cases until we happen across a failure, it will always be necessary to study failures after the event. This is a mixed blessing. Field work on the Mandata case started four years after the project finally closed down. At this stage the worst of the personal and political fallout had settled. By then, people were prepared to talk. On the other hand memories fade, and it becomes the harder to distinguish institutionalised perceptions from the reality. To have relied exclusively on interviews would have been too risky. The file record provided an invaluable cross check.

The final reason for choosing Mandata was that it was so well known. It was the biggest and best known case of its kind in Australia. This made it a special case (Yin 1989), of interest in its own right. Immediately after Mandata's closure Hoyle and Wettenhall (1981: 311) noted that, 'There is no doubt that the history of the project would make a fascinating case study'. Chapters 10 and 11 show this to be so.

Mohr (1985) has emphasised the importance of indicating how typical a given site is. There are several dimensions on which Mandata might be thought to be atypical. On examination we shall see that these do not detract from the value of the study.

The matter of the case's age has already been mentioned. A second reason for considering Mandata atypical might be that it was developed in the context of public administration where the norms are different from those of private business. While it is true that there are some differences in practices and culture, many large bureaucratic companies function very like public sector organisations. But even if there were critical differences, public sector computing is extensive. If Mandata were only typical of this sector it is still a very worthwhile domain about which to generalise.

Another distinctive feature of Mandata was that it was a large project. It might be argued that many of its problems would not arise in smaller cases. Size clearly exacerbates some problems, but it is doubtful that all the problems of Mandata could be put down to size. And again, there are plenty of large projects to which conclusions regarding Mandata might be transferable.

The above points are intended to show that Mandata was not so distinctive as to negate its value as a case study. What makes Mandata typical of many projects and therefore a valuable example is its very limited capacity to control the sources of its problems.

9.2.3 The research process

The case research was carried out by the author in two phases. The first was a pilot study which involved two one week sessions in Canberra in 1985, reading the files of the Public Accounts Committee to ascertain whether there was much to be uncovered that had not emerged in the reports of that Committee.

The second phase commenced in 1986 and continued in periods of one, two, and three weeks until the end of 1988. The total time spent in the field over this period was about eighteen weeks. This phase included detailed study of the Public Service Board's own files associated with Mandata, and a series of interviews with a mixture of major and minor players in the project history and one or two relative outsiders.

Permission to study the Board's Mandata files was granted by its then chairman, Dr Peter Wilenski. These were read either at the Board's own office, or at Australian Archives (some files had already been deposited with the official archive). Access to files marked confidential was variable, apparently depending on who actually provided the files. At Australian Archives, for example, all confidential files were vetted. Virtually everything requested was provided except for the odd file that had been misindexed, mislaid, or consumed by the silverfish and other bibliovores that inhabit dark and dusty shelves. It would have been easy to tell if anything had been removed from a file because folios were always marked sequentially.

The index of files provided by the Board contained 2002 distinct files. In addition, some pamphlet boxes containing reports and manuals which were only partly indexed were found by chance. The files contained memoranda and letters, minute notes,

The Case Study Approach

handwritten working notes, newspaper cuttings, progress reports, fault reports, advertising material for equipment and software, submissions to the Board, cost-benefit analyses, staffing reports, job descriptions, briefings for external scrutineers, training film scripts, design documents, manuals, indeed just about any document that one could imagine.

It would have been impossible to read all the files in detail. A sampling strategy was adopted. The strategy was to start with the files associated with the main committees and working parties so as to obtain fairly rapidly a basic chronology as well as gaining access to the most important documents that were made public to user departments. The files associated with the external scrutiny of the project were examined on the ground that the Public Accounts Committee and the Auditor-General would have been provided with a number of significant documents in the process of their investigations. Likewise, two consultants' reports. In addition, files associated with major studies such as the feasibility study and the 1978 impact study were carefully examined. Some files relating to each stage of the project were also studied. Thus, it was appropriate to look at files related to the tender process in 1974, and those related to implementation of Mandata from 1977. Many files contained working notes or early drafts of documents that were to reappear elsewhere.

Typical classes of files not studied in detail included various staff appointment files, files relating to peripheral system activities such as the use of the mainframe to provide a bureau service to departments, many of the files relating to Mandata machine operations, installation details for the state based Mandata cells and the like. These were sampled to see what kind of information they provided so as to make some estimate of their worth. The voluminous committee papers and MPO background briefings provided a cross check on what in these files was worth examining.

In total, 444 items (files or unindexed items discovered in pamphlet boxes) were noted. (A single file could easily consist of a hundred or more sheets.) The full archive probably amounts to 50 shelf metres of which about a quarter was examined. While it would have been possible to read on and to acquire a more detailed understanding of the project, in the last two or three weeks diminishing marginal returns set in. More and more, files contained material encountered previously (the files were both wonderfully and frustratingly redundant).

There were some difficulties in pursuing a systematic approach to the file research: the titles of some files were misleading; it was not possible to tell how many subsequent drafts there were of any given document; and some documents were very elusive.

From the public record, all the relevant reports of the Public Accounts Committee and the Auditor-General, and the Board's official responses were studied. In most cases, the press reports were constructed from press releases, statements to parliament, and the public reports. They offered little or nothing of real novelty. Their importance lay more in their persistent repetition of the scrutineers' criticisms.

Interviews were conducted throughout this period whenever and wherever planning and serendipity dictated. Initially, a contact at the Board put the author in touch with two or three individuals who had been involved with Mandata at various different stages, mostly at a senior level. They in turn made introductions to others. Not every introduction led to an interview because contact information was not always current.

In total 24 people were interviewed, including the idea champions who launched the project and its subsequent directors. Most had been members of the Mandata project organisation at some time though two were users, three were from other parts of the Public Service Board and three connected with the scrutiny process. A number of other people contributed comments and ideas in casual conversation.

The interviews were entirely open ended. Notes were taken and written up immediately afterward, rather than being tape recorded and transcribed. This encouraged openness leading to a richer picture of the project. Interviews varied in length from around forty minutes to nearly a whole day. By far the majority lasted between two and three hours. A copy of the interview notes was sent to each interviewee for comment. This permitted expansion, correction, and elaboration. A reply was not always received. Where there were matters outstanding or not understood, these were raised in the covering letter to the interviewee sent with the notes.

The interviewees had been employed on the project at different if overlapping times. They had a variety of posts, and consequently had distinctly different experiences and perceptions. Most interviews tried to elicit their route into, through and out of the project as well as their experiences during their stay in it. Almost everybody was keen to offer explanatory hypotheses, and this led to fruitful interchanges in which both the interviewer and the interviewee were able to exchange ideas and swap counter-evidence.

In all cases several years had elapsed between each interviewee's last involvement with the project and the interview. Nevertheless, feelings still ran quite high. There was a degree of bitterness displayed by several against the Public Service as a whole, against the Public Service Board in particular, against users, and against other individuals. The animosities, the disappointed expectations, and the jealousies provided some insight into what must have been an intensely political situation. They also served as a warning against taking information at face value.

One advantage of conducting the file research and the interviews in parallel was that not only could disparities in data from different sources be identified by triangulation, but they could also be resolved through questioning and directed file research. Thus, though interviews may have yielded distortions, the file record helped counteract this.

Subsequently, drafts of chapters 10 and 11 were sent to six interviewees. Two provided very detailed responses. A third made several useful comments. The others signified that they had no major objections to raise.

The analysis and interpretation of the data has been iterative as drafts have been generated and subjected to criticism, checked against the research database, and revised again. As Yin (1989) has indicated, we are not well equipped with tools for conducting analysis and interpretation systematically. It is left to the reader to judge how well this case study has been conducted and how valuable its analysis is.

9.2.4 The research database

The research process has resulted in the collection and construction of a database. This consists of the following:

(1) Published documents including parliamentary reports, and extracts from Public Service Board and Auditor-General's annual reports

(2) File notes (200-220,000 words)
(3) Handwritten interview notes, typed reports of interviews, letters of comment from interviewees
(4) Photocopies of selected file documents including the feasibility study report, a consultancy report, and various technical documents
(5) Chronology of nearly 1400 dates extracted from the above documents
(6) Detailed comments on an earlier draft of chapters 10 and 11 from two interviewees

9.3 CONCLUSION

Case studies of information systems failure are of particular value because of our relative ignorance of the phenomenon. They help the researcher in stimulating ideas, and they are valuable to the reader in a variety of ways.

Case studies can be subject to a wide range of criticisms. The justice or otherwise of criticisms of the conduct of such studies can be best determined if the research methods are fully reported. The details of the research process by which the Mandata study was carried out are given in section 9.2. Its substantive outcome, the case description and analysis, are presented in chapters 10 and 11.

Suggested Readings

1. Yin, R.K. (1989) *Case Study Research: Design and Methods*, Sage, Newbury Park.

A first class account of how to conduct case studies by a leading expert.

2. Benbasat, I., Goldstein, D.K. & Mead, M., (1987) The case research strategy in studies of information systems, *MIS Quarterly*, September.

A critical account of the use of case studies in the information systems research field. Gives the reader good cause to be cautious about conclusions drawn from information systems cases.

Chapter 10
Mandata - A Case History

Mandata was conceived as a system to automate personnel and establishments record processing for the whole of the Australian Public Service. It was to maintain a central database of records which would be accessible from offices in every state via an on-line network. It was also to provide a management information service. Furthermore, its originators intended it to stand as a technical model for similar systems in other areas of the Public Service.

The project was initiated in 1970, and finally abandoned in 1981. In the period between it went through one major metamorphosis and one lesser revision. It cost in the order of A$30 million and left user departments no better served than when it started. For those departments which had finally abandoned their establishment record cards, termination left them having to rebuild some of the basic resources of the task.

The project's progress can be divided into five phases. The period to February 1974 was devoted to initiation activities. From then until August 1976 the project concentrated on establishing its organisation, developing a technical infrastructure, and developing the application. In August 1976 there was a strategic reorientation of the project amounting to an abandonment of the original conception. It was replaced by an approach expected to yield shorter term benefits. This phase lasted until June 1980 when it was decided to scale back the project's ambitions still further. From then until April 1981 a last effort was made to give the project a firm footing. On 30 April 1981, it was announced in federal parliament that the project was to be terminated. It had a final six months in which to complete a decommissioning phase. More detailed chronological tables will be provided as appropriate throughout this chapter. A chronology for the whole project is provided in the Appendix. A glossary of terms is provided at the end of the book.

Mandata is something of an enigma. Its proponents were able to rally enough support to enable it to be actively pursued for more than ten years. It produced an operational system that some departments used for four years. Yet, it was a *cause célèbre* in

Public Service circles for those four years and longer. It suffered an extended barrage of both formal and informal criticism from public and private sources. The general impression is that it was a dismal failure. Yet, many of those closest to it in 1981 share the view that the system in its scaled back form had overcome the worst of its substantive problems and that its termination was a mistake. It is impossible now to say whether this assessment is correct or whether the system would have continued to be the object of criticism as a result of chronic flaws and limited support. What is clear is that having experienced several periods of intense criticism and realignment of objectives, the project could no longer command the support it needed to subsist in the politico-economic context in which it found itself.

This chapter provides a narrative in preparation for the analysis in the next chapter. It sets out the main events of the five phases of the Mandata project along with descriptions of the two major decisions to change project strategy. It starts by giving some necessary background.

10.1 BACKGROUND

This section provides some background information to assist the reader in understanding the subsequent account of Mandata. It starts with brief sketches of the Australian Public Service and the Public Service Board which was the host organisation within which the Mandata development was to take place. This is followed by an outline of the nature of the personnel and establishments application. The last part of this section consists of a brief survey of the history of computing in the Public Service, and a short historical background to the Mandata project itself.

10.1.1 The Australian Public Service

Australia is a federation of six states - New South Wales, Queensland, South Australia, Tasmania, Victoria, and Western Australia - and two territories - the Northern Territory and the Australian Capital Territory - (see figure 10.1). The states are responsible for a range of activities and services including law and order, local industrial development, primary and secondary education and many other local activities, while the federal government is responsible for defence, foreign affairs, international trade and other issues of national importance. There are two main sources of political decision-making: there are the state governments accountable to state parliaments and the federal government accountable to the nationally elected parliament.

Figure 10.1. The states of Australia

There are separate public service organisations for each of the states, while the Australian Public Service (APS) provides administration at the federal level. The Australian Public Service works according to the British model provided by the Westminster system of government. Departments and statutory authorities are responsible to a minister who is responsible to the Parliament. (The term 'department' will be used throughout this case study to refer to ministerial departments and other government agencies.) The permanent administrative head of a department or authority is a full-time public servant who provides continuity through changes of minister and changes of government. Departments and authorities are often divided into divisions, branches and sections. The efficiency of the administration is checked by the Auditor-General who is accountable to Parliament. Other administrative matters may be examined by parliamentary committees such as the Public Accounts Committee.

The Australian Public Service has its headquarters at the seat of government, Canberra, and has outlying offices wherever appropriate in state capitals and regional centres. In this respect, its structure mirrors the topology of distributed computer systems linked centrally. As a result, for applications such as employment, social security, statistics, defence, and personnel and establishment management, nationwide computer networks have obvious appeal.

The structure of the Service is bureaucratic in the Weberian sense of the word. Throughout the period of this case study, departments remained strongly hierarchical and formal in their communications. This sometimes manifested itself in slow decision-making. Decisions and communications would pass through every level until they reached their destination. Memoranda, or minutes as they are known, were often directed to a senior officer with a list of all other officers through whom they were to pass. Communication with another department would involve a junior officer writing a minute to be signed by a more senior officer for despatch to an equally senior officer in the other department. It would be marked for the attention of a more junior officer who could act upon its contents. While keeping everyone informed, this practice slowed communication and decision processes. Even within a department a large proportion of business would be formally documented by minutes or file notes. Frequently, these minutes and notes would appear on half a dozen different files.

In contrast to popular caricatures, the public servants and ex-public servants the author interviewed had obviously been committed to Mandata. Many worked extremely long hours for long periods at a time. The author was told of exceptions, people with chronic personal problems or their own agendas, but such exceptions are not unusual in any moderate sized organisation. For different reasons at different times individuals would lose heart, but most of the time most staff appear to have been prepared to work hard to make Mandata succeed.

Obtaining sufficient staff with significant professional experience was more difficult. The labour market for skilled and experienced computer personnel has always been relatively tight, there being strong competition for a limited pool of labour. This helped ensure that there would always be some background level of staff turnover. At times of rapid expansion, problems associated with staffing made themselves felt more acutely. They derived less from individual and cultural reasons and more from the Public Service's limited ability to attract skilled and experienced staff in a tight labour market.

10.1.2 The Public Service Board

The Australian Public Service is governed by the Public Service Act 1922 and statutory amendments to it. The Public Service Board was the authority that oversaw the continued validity of the Act's terms and which negotiated and authorised changes to staff conditions and entitlements. It was the authority that employed all Commonwealth public servants. It was responsible for matters of policy with respect to personnel, establishments and industrial relations. It provided staff development and training. It also advised departments on procedures to be used for administering personnel and establishments information.

As the body responsible for approving changes to establishment posts, the Board was in a very powerful position with respect to all other departments. It could delay, block, or expedite plans for expansion. It was also responsible for setting staff ceilings above which existing posts could not be filled. It also had quite strong statutory powers though in practice they were rarely if ever used (Wiltshire 1974). Being so powerful, it was disliked and resented by public servants in other departments and by Labor politicians (Juddery 1974). Both groups saw it as hindering their efforts to provide services to the public. The Board itself had no direct contact with the Australian public. Its clientele was exclusively the Australian Public Service. Wiltshire (1974) notes a structural reason for conflict between the Board and departments. The Board and permanent heads had significantly overlapping responsibilities for ensuring the efficiency and effectiveness of departments.

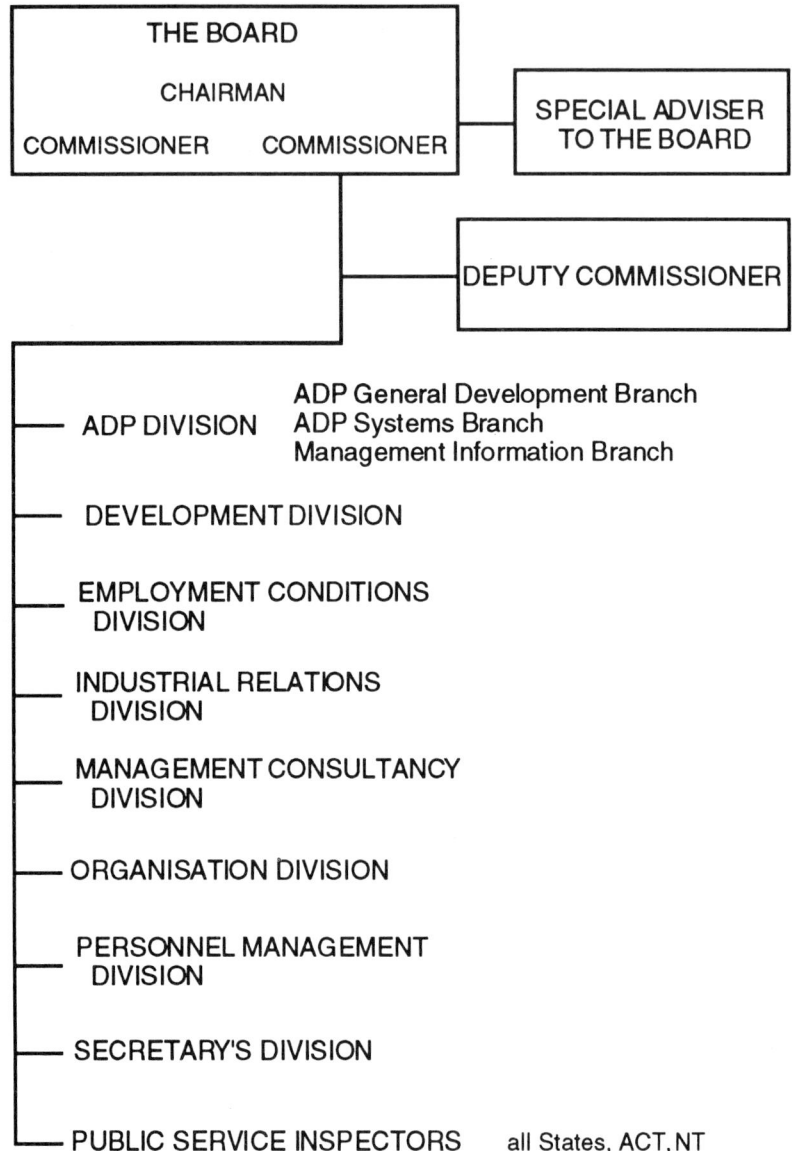

Figure 10.2. The structure and functions of the Public Service Board 1974

The Public Service Board's structure (see figure 10.2) consisted of a Chairman and two Commissioners who formed the Board and who made all the policy decisions. There was a secretary to the Board, a Deputy Commissioner and a number of divisions with separate responsibilities. There were also outposts in each state and the Northern Territory: the offices of the Public Service Inspectors. Much of the Public Service Board was traditionally oriented to policy work. Its staff would write papers for discussion which, when thoroughly reviewed and revised, would be submitted to the Board for consideration and decision. Most of the Public Service Board's office was not familiar with the practice of technological developments.

The exception was the Management Services Division whose responsibilities included both automatic data processing (adp) policy and its operational systems. The Board's statistical records were maintained on two computer systems. One was called the Continuous Record of Personnel (CRP). CRP took input from all departments and produced for Parliament annual analyses of permanent Public Service employees. CRP stored both current and historical data. The other system was an establishments system which recorded details of all permanent and temporary posts. It was simpler than CRP, lacking any historical data. Compared with Mandata which was to be orders of magnitude bigger and more complex, even CRP was a relatively small and simple system.

The difference between the Management Services Division and other divisions in their familiarity with technological developments, in particular adp, indicates some degree of cultural difference. It is therefore not surprising that other areas of the Public Service Board were not always active in supporting the project.

10.1.3 The personnel and establishments task

The Board managed the structure of the Public Service by controlling establishments. In part, it did this by formulating the criteria by which requests for new establishment positions could be judged, and by determining what new positions were permissible according to these guidelines. It left to the departments the day to day tasks of personnel management. For example, departments kept their own records and made decisions to grant or refuse leave requests. There was, therefore, a division of responsibilities. The Board had *de jure* responsibility for all aspects of personnel and establishments. It exercised its authority by issuing guidelines to departments. *De facto*, the departments took responsibility for how they operated Board guidelines. This meant that departments sometimes exercised a discretion that was not strictly theirs. For instance, in difficult personal circumstances an officer might be granted leave prior to having earned the entitlement thereby creating a negative leave balance. This was outside Board policy, but it was a necessary practical expedient which could be effected by departments because of this division of responsibility.

The application that Mandata automated was the personnel and establishments record-keeping function carried out by departments. This function consisted of two core elements, the person and the position. It is necessary to maintain information about both elements. For a position, it is important to know at what grade it is established, into which organisation it fits, to whom its occupant reports, and so forth. For each individual, personal information is needed such as full name, home address, qualifications, past experience, salary, leave balance, and others.

Most large departmental offices had their own personnel section which maintained personal details on a series of Standard Personnel Record (SPR) cards designed by the Public Service Board. The daily activity for personnel clerks included answering enquiries about leave balances and effecting changes to them, setting up new cards for new staff, transferring information when an officer moved department, recording promotions and salary increments, recording changes of name, and, not least, correcting previous errors. At regular intervals departments would submit returns to the Board so that it could keep its Continuous Record of Personnel up to date.

Establishment data were also recorded on cards. Beyond a minimum of data needed to complete statutory returns to the Public Service Board, there were considerable variations in the records kept by departments.

Despite the *apparent* simplicity of personnel record-keeping in the Public Service, there were significant complications. The clerical task was both demanding and responsible, but was difficult to staff satisfactorily. Over the years the rules relating to personnel matters had built up, often accumulating incrementally with new rulings partly modifying older ones. Understanding all the rules appropriate to staffing was a substantial task for a supervisor, the more so for subordinates. To give some idea of the size of the problem, there were more than two hundred different types of leave. Since many of them were interrelated, it could be quite taxing to apply the rules correctly.

Being a routine job, personnel clerks were low graded. Advertisements therefore did not attract good applicants. Yet, in fact their job was responsible. Mistakes in leave balances cost the Public Service in terms of unentitled leave taken, and more directly because untaken recreation leave was payable in cash to officers resigning. Unentitled days meant extra cash. Mistakes tended to work against the employer because individuals would be more likely to draw attention to mistakes against them than those in their favour. Over many years the Auditor-General had complained about the poor quality of record-keeping and its cost to the Service.

The situation was compounded by the fact that personnel sections often did not have a full quota of staff or had staff that were inexperienced. High turnover made this a recurrent problem - in one personnel section whose establishment was 36 there were 37 staff changes in a period of eighteen months in the mid-1970s. Being low graded, the job was mostly attractive to a transient work force. Any ambitious clerks would attempt to find promotion elsewhere. Consequently, it was very difficult to retain experienced staff. The high turnover was exacerbated by the protracted learning period before new clerks became fully effective.

Some sample figures will indicate the scale of the personnel and establishments record-keeping task. Including the Post Office with its 150,000 staff, the APS employed 300,000 people (JCPA 1979). There were estimated to be 1860 staff dedicated to maintaining the Standard Personnel Records. They were spread over 400 different centres. In addition, there would have been other staff in small country centres, part occupied on these and other personnel functions.

A computerised personnel and establishments system had the potential to reduce the staffing problems, and to improve the quality of the records. It would also speed the transfer of records among departments. Furthermore, a centralised computer record would enable Service-wide manpower planning. In the light of benefits such as these, automation of the record-keeping task must have looked very desirable.

10.1.4 Computing in the Australian Public Service

Computing in the Australian Public Service dates back to 1955 when a computer was first installed in the government's Weapons Research Establishment (JCPA 1978a). (See Chronology 10.1 for a list of significant events.) During 1958-9 the Commonwealth Bureau of Census and Statistics investigated the uses of computing in similar departments in the USA, Canada and Britain. Since the late nineteenth century when the US census had provided the inspiration and first application for Hollerith's tabulating machines (Campbell-Kelly 1990), censuses had grown increasingly complex to process. The first customer to take delivery of the UNIVAC in 1951 was the US Bureau of Census (Office of Charles and Ray Eames 1990). It is therefore no surprise that the Commonwealth Bureau was among the first to see benefits in applying computers to their problems.

Chronology 10.1. Early years of computing in the Australian Public Service

Date	Event
1955	First APS computer installed in Weapons Research Establishment
1958-59	Bureau of Census and Statistics investigates use of computing
1960	IDC on ADP established
1962	Dept of Defence buys first administrative computer
1964	CSIRO Division of Computing Research buys computer
1964-65	Bureau of Census and Statistics buys computers

The 1960s was a decade of learning about automatic data processing for the Australian Public Service. Various exploratory studies were established followed by more detailed feasibility studies. The Department of Defence bought the first computer for public service administrative functions in 1962. This was followed by purchases by the Commonwealth Scientific and Industrial Research Organisation (CSIRO Division of Computing Research in 1964 (JCPA 1978a) and a series of purchases by the Bureau of Census and Statistics in 1964-5 (JCPA 1966). Computing bureau services were established to support early systems for departments which could not justify a whole machine to themselves. Programmer-in-training courses were introduced by the Bureau of Census and Statistics to teach the arcane skills of programming (JCPA 1966).

Departments entering the field of automatic data processing included Treasury, the Superannuation and Retirement Benefits Boards, Health, Taxation, and Defence. Their systems, like most others around the world in that period, were beset by difficulties. The Auditor-General's Office, which was to be such a scourge for Mandata in the late 1970s, was generally sympathetic and understanding about those systems upon which its investigative eye fell (eg Auditor-General 1964).

Computer-based information systems did not immediately smother the public administration in a blanket of rationalised automatic procedures. Certainly, there was ample opportunity for proponents of the technology to pursue their interest, but those who felt queasy at the prospect of being made redundant by a player piano technology could nonetheless fairly safely continue to ignore computers. Proponents could see there was scope for expansion within the Service during the 1970s, but much of the public administration was to continue largely unaffected by the new technology.

Computing in the APS was strongly influenced by the Inter-Departmental Committee on Automatic Data Processing (IDC on ADP). The IDC's members were drawn from the Public Service Board which took the chair, Treasury, Defence, the Postmaster-General's Department, and the Division of Computing Research at CSIRO. The administrative and adp technical support was provided by the Board. The Board's power to establish itself so strategically derived from its statutory duty to, 'devise means for effecting economies and promoting efficiency in the management and working of departments' (Public Service Act section 17, quoted in JCPA 1978a). It also derived from an astutely arranged agreement with the Commonwealth purchasing authorities in September 1960 by which the latter would not act on acquisitions without prior approval by the IDC. The Board's adp experts therefore became very influential. Thus, the Public Accounts Committee (JCPA 1978a, p18) concluded that

'from the early days of computer acquisition in the Australian

Government the Public Service Board and the IDC on ADP have significantly influenced the extent and direction of computer development both through their advice and persuasion and through their de facto power to control purchasing of computers.'

10.1.5 Background to Mandata

Through the 1950s, 1960s and into the 1970s the adp area of the Public Service Board grew in organisational standing from being a section of the Organisation and Methods (O&M) branch to being a separate branch and finally a division in its own right. Of those who came to work for the Board in adp one had designed, written and implemented the Public Service's very first administrative computer system. Others were quite aware of the possibilities adp offered.

Organisationally the adp staff were well supported by their immediate superior in the hierarchy. Not only did he foster a climate in which ideas could be developed, he provided an effective conduit to support at higher levels.

The ideas that were to underlie Mandata evolved among the Board's adp staff. Right from the start there was an awareness of the special potential of adp if data communications could be made viable. To this end, in 1964 the Board's staff carried out experiments which proved successful. Throughout the period they kept themselves informed of overseas developments though these were rarely if ever significantly in advance of their own thinking. Even by international standards Mandata was an innovative idea.

In fact there were a number of different strands to the overall concept. One was the development of an architecture that would support decentralised access to a centralised database. This included many component ideas about protocols, security, privacy and the like. There was the application of this architecture to the personnel and establishments task. A single system for a task performed by all departments would avoid the duplication of effort which had led the US Comptroller-General to criticise the US armed forces for their multiple payroll developments. And, there was a more general concern to establish some standards for data communication in the Australian Public Service in order to avoid the problems of inconsistent protocols, a problem graphically illustrated by the transport problems that arise from railway lines with different gauges. (More detail of the concept is provided in section 10.2.1.)

The technical objective was to build what was called a software framework which was to feature a central database which would be secure and controlled for privacy. There would also be transaction handling software. Standard terminal units would be the remote points of input and access, with a communication network to carry the traffic in either direction. In the 1960s and well into the 1970s these were not facilities that computer vendors offered. They would have to be designed and built themselves. The broad design principles for this were formulated by the Board's staff during the 1960s.

The principles for the application looked clear cut. The Public Service Board had rules for how records were supposed to be kept. As indicated in section 10.1.3, departments had to maintain information on two types of entity - positions and people. The core structure of the Australian Public Service is defined by the positions established, their grade, their organisational locus, and their duties. The work of the Service is carried out by people who may fill many different posts in the course of their career. In addition to current information about each person employed, historical details of an officer's service are necessary for applying the various rules such as those concerning entitlement to salary increments. In order to be sure who is in which post, personnel and establishments data need to be linked.

The clerical method of linking records involves maintaining two sets of records with a certain amount of redundancy. Data such as name, grade and post are recorded both on the personnel record and on the establishment position record. Naturally this results in duplication of effort because if a person leaves to take up another position, both the personnel record and the establishment record need to be amended. As a result, it is easy for the records to get out of step.

Early adp designs for this task were constrained by the limitations of sequential file organisation. There would be one file for personnel data and one for establishments. It was very difficult to maintain the links between person and position without having to read each file more than once. The problem was that if you processed the personnel file first you might amend a record to promote an officer into a new position, but then when the establishment file was read you might find that the post had not been vacated by the previous officer, so that then in order to avoid having the two files inconsistent you had to return to the personnel record on the other file and revoke the promotion transaction. On the other hand, if you processed the establishment file first, you would have the same problem in reverse. Consequently, a technical solution involving a single database which could be checked for consistency at the time of processing each transaction looked appealingly elegant.

Thus evolved the 'Mandata concept'. Its proponents recognised that the hardware and software technology itself would change in time, but as best they could see the logical organisation of the storage of data and of the processing could last for as long as the Public Service itself.

As was noted in the previous section, from 1960 onward the Board's adp staff were structurally well positioned to observe developments throughout the Public Service and to influence them through the IDC on ADP. However, some departments were disinclined to respect the Board's reviews of proposals because they felt that it lacked the experience to back its recommendations. Successful implementation of Mandata would have neutralised this criticism.

The Board's staff clearly had experience both with its own systems and in other departments. At the same time there were very few people anywhere with experience of systems of Mandata's magnitude. If the project was to be advanced, the task of building an establishment of appropriate staff would be significant.

Because of the limited size of the Board's existing adp operations it did not have its own computer or a pre-existing operations and development structure. This, too, was a major task ahead.

In summary, by the late 1960s the Board had working on its adp staff some adventurous and innovative thinkers. The structure within which they worked provided supportive conditions in which their ideas could be developed and brought to maturity. The Board's role with respect to personnel matters presented an application which was ideally suited to the evolving technical architecture. But, Mandata would need considerable resourcing and support if it was to get from concept to implementation.

10.2 INITIATION - SEPTEMBER 1970 TO FEBRUARY 1974

The outstanding feature of the initiation phase was the obstacle course of an approval process which had to be negotiated. It involved formulating and revising a detailed proposal, undergoing external review, consulting departments, and getting successfully through several decision processes. It took from September 1970 to February 1974.

Much of the drive to obtain the appropriate approvals came from two or three of the Board's adp staff who had jointly developed the central ideas of Mandata. They bore many of the characteristics typical of idea champions. They had the energy, drive and enthusiasm to promote Mandata and to get it into an arena where it could be evaluated and approved by those with the power to support it.

10.2.1 The Feasibility Study

It is not clear when the idea of Mandata was first articulated. A common adp based personnel system for departments was on the agenda as early as 1963 (Public Service Board 1964). In 1970 a formal approach was made to the Chairman and Commissioners who established a working party consisting of two representatives each of its ADP Development and Project Services Branches and an officer of the Treasury. This group started work in September 1970. Their remit was to determine the feasibility of a Service-wide, computer-based personnel and establishments system. They submitted an initial report to the Board in January 1971, provisionally concluding that the proposed system was both feasible and cost-effective. The Board approved further study to be focused on perceived difficulties.

The full 200 page feasibility study report was completed in November 1971. It was a substantial piece of work. It not only proffered a high level system design, it also outlined a suitable technical strategy. It covered the level of the equipment and software to be purchased and their configuration into an operational system. Accountability and data protection issues were addressed in considerable detail. It even gave detail of batch control methods. Drawing on the ideas already developed by the

Board's adp staff, many of the proposals and recommendations constituted major innovations.

The report addressed substantial design policy issues and attempted to set criteria for their solution. In so doing it attempted to reduce potential uncertainties both about the scope of the application and the technology to be employed. For example, the high complexity of the rules applying to some small special categories of staff was acknowledged and provision made for omitting them from automatic processing. Likewise a proposal was presented for the division of responsibilities among the Public Service Board, Treasury and Superannuation Board.

Cognitive limits constrain both the writers and readers of any report of this nature. As argued in chapter 6 it is in the nature of the technical process of information systems innovation that taking an abstract system idea and realising it as an implemented concrete system is not a deterministic process that can be totally anticipated in advance. For example, in outlining the applicant area of the database no indication was given as to whether personal information would be recorded once for each applicant with the possibility of recording against those personal details multiple applications over a period of time. There were of course many similar issues for which, understandably, no resolution was suggested.

It is a fine art to estimate accurately under conditions of uncertainty, witness the many projects that exceed their budgets and deadlines. In 1971 it would have been very hard to anticipate the enormity of the task. Consequently, the feasibility study underestimated the range of tasks and volume of work involved in Mandata. For example, no mention was made of the magnitude of the organisational task of establishing and managing a project organisation. Though this was not desirable, it was not critical either. Projects often overcome low estimates if they can command the support they need at a later stage.

For the purposes of winning support to proceed with the project, the feasibility report served well. It gave a fair indication of the nature of the proposal, estimated the costs and benefits, and offered a schedule which included a clear indication of what else needed to be done to obtain the broad-based support necessary prior to a submission to Cabinet for funding.

Mandata - A Case History 161

10.2.1.1 System outline - the database

The feasibility study report was a detailed articulation of the Mandata concept and of how it was to be made operational. At the heart of the system was to be a large database containing all the relevant information about both personnel and establishments. Figure 10.3 summarises the categories of information the report expected would be stored.

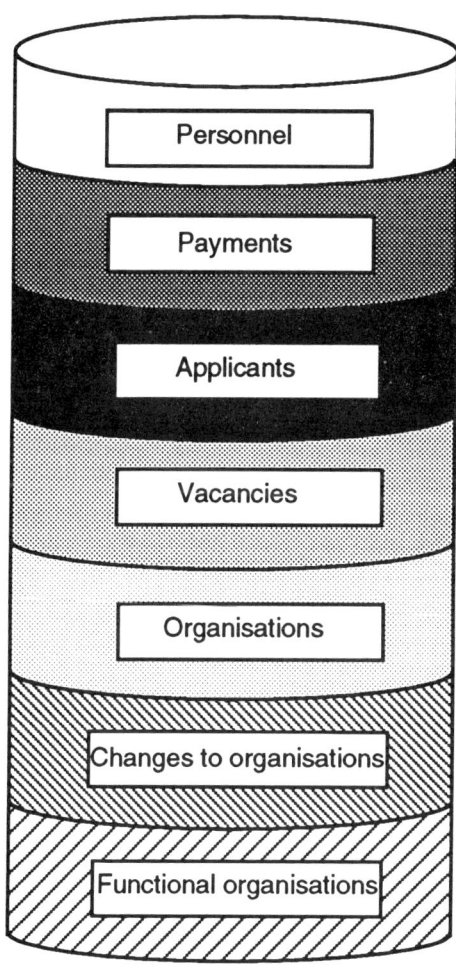

Figure 10.3. Proposed Mandata database areas

Two areas of the database were to be devoted to data on existing officers of the Service. The first of these concerned non-financial details. It included personnel history giving details of present and past appointments, whether the appointment was substantive, provisional, or acting; it covered formal qualifications as well as performance on various aptitude and proficiency tests; entitlements and balances for all types of leave, recreation or sick, approved or unapproved; miscellaneous data such as personal honours, emergency medical data and information about official and private overseas visits; and finally there were the standard identification details such as name and number, sex and date of birth. The second area reserved for personal data concerned the financial aspects of employment. It included current and historical salaries, allowances and ad hoc payments.

A further database area was to be established for recording data about applicants for Public Service employment. This would include data concerning the medical examination and entry exam in addition to basic identification details. Parallel to the applicants themselves were the positions for which they would be applying. This was more complex than merely recording the position and linking it to the applicants and to the position details. It required data on the selection process and on appeals against selection decisions. (In the Australian Public Service at this time appointments were made provisionally until the conclusion of an appeal period. If there was an appeal against the appointment, there would be an inquiry. Until the inquiry settled the matter the appointee could not be confirmed as substantive occupant of the position.)

For each position, descriptions and detailed duty statements were to be held in the organisations area of the database. Here would be stored information about existing organisation locations and plans for changes; status and history of administrative units such as ministerial departments; the structure of those units, their status, history and functions; and the established positions for those structures. A further area was to consist of data about proposed changes to existing structures. This area would have been of most use to those divisions of the Board's own offices that dealt with organisations and structures than to departments. It is indicative of Mandata's potential to serve the interests of other parts of the Board. For whatever reason, they appear not to have recognised the opportunity it presented. Had they been more supportive they would have provided another path through which to influence the decisions that most radically affected Mandata later.

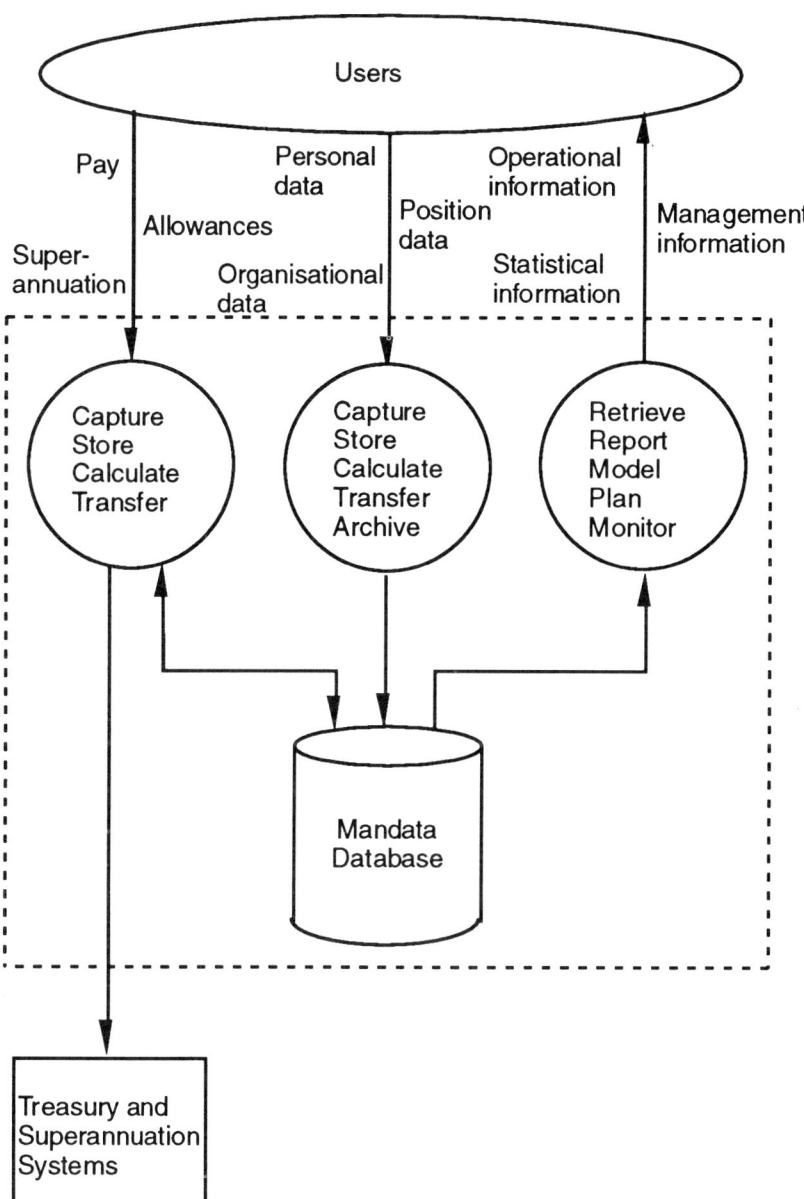

Figure 10.4. Functional diagram of the proposed Mandata system

The final database area concerned functional organisations. For example, there might be projects organised out of established positions to carry out some particular function such as to manage the clean-up of a disaster, to develop a computer system, or to build a new art gallery. Thus a functional organisation could be constructed orthogonal to an established structure. With a view to facilitating manpower planning, an area of the database was set aside to record the details of such organisations.

In addition, there were to be various reference tables which would provide commonly required information without having to record it on every individual record. The most important of these was the Designation/Salary reference. For each position designation such as Examiner of Patents Class 1 or Clerk Class 5 there would be position specific data detailing any restrictions on occupancy, the applicable salary ranges and eligibility for various taxable and non-taxable allowances.

The relations among the different parts of the database were complex because of the complexity of the Public Service rules that the database would be expected to support.

10.2.1.2 System outline - functions

The system was to serve three main functions. The first was to facilitate basic record-keeping practices. The second was to support the automation of payments on the basis of recorded position data. The third was to provide management information. What made the proposal radical was the way in which the data were to be maintained and used. The broader administrative system was to be rationalised. It would achieve administrative efficiency by replacing the existing patchwork of operational procedures and would provide an opportunity for abandoning ad hoc methods of manpower planning in favour of more formal methods. Figure 10.4 summarises the system's proposed functions.

The record system that Mandata was intended to replace was based upon Standard Personnel Record cards which had been introduced to all departments in the early 1950s. However these only covered personal data, not establishments. Establishment data were also recorded on cards, but beyond the bare minimum needed to complete statutory returns to the Public Service Board what was recorded varied from department to department. The clerical activities included basic transcription tasks to write in new details arising from appointments, promotions or transfers. There would be calculations of leave balances, and of payment details. In many cases, these required entitlements to be checked prior to the performance of the arithmetic. Naturally there were files to be filed, queries to be answered, and records to be transferred or archived. Whenever a new pay increase was agreed, all the records would need to be changed *en masse*. The record-keeping task was inevitably error prone by virtue of its being carried out by humans within a complex of circumstances that promoted errors from ignorance, inexperience, and pressure.

The benefits of automated record-keeping were obvious. Salary increases could surely be changed in a single computer update. Leave balances could be calculated automatically. Records could be transferred, not physically by mail, but electronically within the database.

The second main function of the system was to service financial systems. Direct transfer of personnel information from which entitlements could be determined by the Treasury and the Superannuation Board systems promised faster payment with fewer errors. This link was also perceived to have the advantage of providing a strong motive for operational users to maintain the data accurately. Lack of this motive was one reason why the existing statistical data on the Continuous Record of Personnel system was not kept to a high level of accuracy.

The system's third major function was to provide management information. The Board's existing statistical system, the Continuous Record of Personnel, would be replaced, by a system with a more comprehensive coverage. This would include categories ignored by CRP such as temporary public servants and those employed by the Service but exempt from the terms of the Public Service Act. The outputs produced would be substantially more accurate and up to date than previously when, because the data were not used for operational transactions, there was no incentive for departments to regularly prepare accurate inputs. Moreover, it would then be possible to carry out sensible manpower planning. The type of process envisaged was to scan the database to determine the profile of staff retiring over the next five years so as to inform decisions about what sort of staff to employ over the same period or what sorts of training to emphasise. Very different, and even more valuable to the Board, would have been the capacity to work out the cost of different bargaining points in pay negotiations. Or again, following the Canadian public service's system, Data Stream, career development patterns might be elicited from the system.

The extent to which the personnel process was to be automated is best understood from the three levels of adp 'penetration' identified. The first level was simple record-keeping. The proposal was that there would no longer be a need for any SPR cards, any functional statements, organisation charts, or duty statements, and apart from a few items such as medical reports, no other personnel establishment or manning records.

The second level of penetration added an order of complexity to the system. It removed from clerks much of the responsibility for applying rules. This level concerned entitlement assessment in areas relating to salary, payments and leave. The feasibility report noted that only processes which were repetitive and where the entitlement assessment was easily programmed were worth including, but it then asserted that the proportion of cases that were too complex for automation was relatively small. With the exception of initial determination of salary level on appointment or promotion, virtually all other payment details were to be computed by the system, including increments, higher duties allowances, qualifications allowances, functional allowances, district and travelling allowances, leave balances, and penalty payments such as overtime.

The third level of penetration was referred to as Computer Aided Decisions and Procedures. It was intended that the system would generate reports to aid management in standard control and planning functions. It would also report on exceptions needing management attention. The example given was of a report of positions remaining unfilled for more than six months. At this third level, the system would also manage some of the more complex and lengthy administrative processes such as appointment and promotion where there were several stages such as position falling vacant, advertisement, application, selection, gazettal of provisional appointment, appeal and substantive appointment. Within each stage there would be many further processes. The proposal was that the system would keep track of progress on the sequence of events and automatically initiate action or warn of the need to act. For example, gazettal could be automatic on completion of selection, and, in the absence of appeal, on termination of the appeal period.

Where the second level of penetration was designed to remove from clerical staff the difficult process of interpretation of the rules, the third level would relieve them of control of work processes. These changes combined with the mass change facility for automatically re-recording all salaries as a result of a national wage decision were designed to reduce the volume of clerical work substantially.

10.2.1.3 Mode of operation

The system would be operated by clerks using visual display terminals within personnel sections in locations across Australia to enquire about the status of an individual's record as needed. A 5 to 10 second response was envisaged, no longer than it might take to look up the record in the card file. Record creations and updates were to be entered from hard copy forms via terminals. Batches would be sent to a state based minicomputer for any validation that did not require access to the database so as to trap errors as early as possible. From there, batches would be sent to the central mainframe for updating as soon as capacity became available. Clerks making changes would be able to handle many errors without any state-to-Canberra line time or Canberra mainframe time being wasted. Interrogations requiring selection of subsets of the database populations would be batched and held at the mainframe for processing after business hours. Figure 10.5 shows the proposed system configuration.

At the mainframe, batches would be controlled and the transactions checked against the database for consistency. They would be processed by the application programs, and reports returned to the clerks via terminal printers and a line printer. Reports were to be of two kinds: validation and update reports which advised of action taken or needed on the transactions submitted, and consequential action reports which indicated further actions implied by the transaction just executed. Usually these would be relatively small reports and would be down loaded to the terminal printers. The line printers were intended for large print jobs such as staff listings as well as ad hoc interrogations. They would be stationed one per state capital in the office of the Public Service Inspector, the Public Service Board's outlying office.

168   *Chapter 10*

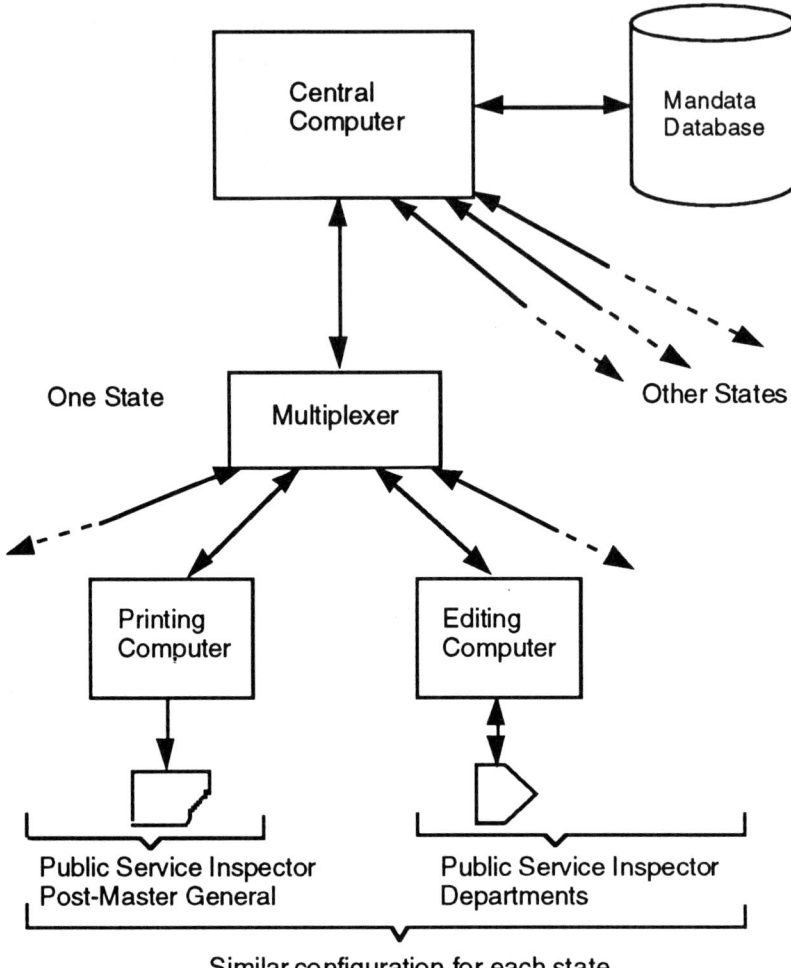

Figure 10.5. Proposed system configuration (adapted from Appendix 2 of the Feasibility Study Report, November 1971)

10.2.1.4 Cost-benefit

The report outlined costs and benefits (table 10.1), and proposed an implementation schedule. The main identified benefit was to be reductions in clerical staff numbers. The net saving was estimated to be 744 fewer clerks needed under Mandata than under the existing system by 1984. Allowing for expansion of the Service, this was to be an overall reduction of 25%. In view of the extensive automation outlined above, this does not sound an over ambitious estimate. In total, taking no account of the benefits to management from its ability to plan and manage staff resources, the system was estimated to save $62.1 million over a 10 year life to 1984. Had the system actually done what it was intended to it is very possible that these figures would have been exceeded as later estimates found further possible benefits.

Table 10.1. Summary of cost-benefit estimates for the period 1972-1984 (Extracted from Appendix 23 of the Feasibility Study Report, November 1971)

COSTS			SAVINGS	
site	250		staff	60,928
h/ware, s/ware	6,775		equipment	1,157
development	1,993			
implementation	1,280			
Total Capital		10,298		
special accommodation	240			
h/ware maintenance	3,103			
data entry	5,282			
data communications	3,329			
consumables	631			
staff	9,616			
Total Operational		22,201		
TOTAL COST		32,499	TOTAL SAVINGS	62,085
TOTAL COST DISCOUNTED*		25,501		
TOTAL SAVINGS DISCOUNTED*				41,166
TOTAL NET GAIN DISCOUNTED				15,665

(Figures in $A,000s, including 3% pa compounded for inflation)
* Discount rate of 8% pa applied

The costs were a different matter. These came in at $A32.5 million divided into capital costs for equipment and systems software, operating costs, development costs, and implementation costs. Applications development costs were estimated at 100 man years. In addition 50 man years of subject-matter effort was calculated for design work. (The term 'subject matter' covered much of what would normally be regarded as the domain of systems analysis: user relations, requirement specification, application advice, user documentation, implementation and training.) It is likely that, as with so many developments, even if progress had been smooth these costs would have been exceeded, for by mid-1977 154 man years had been expended on development and at that stage a further 238 were planned.

Chronology 10.2. Key events in the approval process

Date	Event
Sep 70	Feasibility study commences
Jan 71	Initial feasibility study report presented
Nov 71	Full report completed
Feb 72	Board considers report
Apr 72	Report circulated to departments
Apr 72	IDC on ADP's comments requested
Jul 72	Board asks staff associations for comments
Jul 72	Consultants review the feasibility study
Sep 72	Consultants support feasibility study findings
Oct 72	Treasury backs Mandata
Oct 72	IDC sub-committee established to review feasibility
Mar 73	Revised feasibility study approved by Board
May 73	IDC on ADP endorses Mandata
Dec 73	Board approves submission to Cabinet for funds
Jan 74	Committee of Officials approves submission
Feb 74	Cabinet approves funding

Admittedly these higher costs include work that would not have been necessary under the feasibility study's proposal but the disparity is sufficiently large to suggest that the original figures were an underestimate. In the event it turned out not to matter. An increase in the systems development costs by a factor of three would not have reduced the favourable benefit to cost ratio below 1.0, so it is unlikely that a more realistic estimate would have resulted in the project being refused support initially. Moreover, as it was unable to obtain even the staffing levels outlined in later proposals, it seems unlikely that a higher estimate would have made any difference at this stage.

10.2.2 The decision process

It took over two years from completion of the feasibility study to the formal decision to proceed. Chronology 10.2 details the key events. Departments and staff representatives had to be consulted, external consultants reviewed the feasibility study, and approval had to be gained from the Board, the IDC on ADP, the Committee of Officials, and Cabinet. In the process the feasibility study had to be revised to take account of changes arising from the passage of time.

10.2.2.1 Approval in principle

Typical of the many creeping delays that bedevilled the project throughout, the feasibility study report was completed in November 1971 but it was not considered by the Board itself until February 1972. Within the hierarchical structure of the Board the adp staff had no means of imposing their preferred schedule.

The Board provisionally approved proceeding according to the schedule set out in the report. The schedule of consultation suggested in the report was designed to meet most of the uncertainties the Board might feel. This involved submitting the report to the IDC on ADP, and circulating it to departments and statutory authorities for comment. The schedule was for the Board to reconsider its verdict in June 1972 in the light of comments received.

10.2.2.2 Consultation

The schedule assumed that the report would be circulated in February. In the event it was not circulated until 17th April, with comments requested by 12th May. To have met this schedule the report would have had to reach the appropriate officers in departments immediately and to have been acted upon as a matter of urgency. In fact, departmental heads would have had to decide to whom to distribute the report, and those who received it would themselves have had to decide who else under them should see it. Clearly, at the very least, adp management, where it existed, would be interested as would personnel staff management. Their views would need to be co-ordinated and drafted, the draft discussed, redrafted and transmitted back to the Permanent Head for consideration and signature. Any internal disagreement would have needed to be resolved before a departmental view could be formulated. It was unlikely that this would be achieved in three weeks by people with already full workloads. It is therefore not surprising that the schedule was missed by many departments.

The responses were mixed. Some came quickly, others like the Department of Trade and Industry did not reply until late November. Ironically the Auditor-General's Office which was to be such a bane for the project in later years was among the first to express its qualified approval.

The Director-General of the Post Office also responded promptly, outlining his department's concerns. In particular, he mentioned a recent feasibility study within the Post Office for a similar though less extensive system which had returned operating costs one fifth those expected by Mandata. He expressed doubts that the complexity and advanced nature of the concepts being employed could be matched by the existing state of technology and knowledge. He pursued the point by emphasising likely staff shortages which would make such an innovative project even less achievable. With apparent prescience he commented,

> 'In our experience, the development of an organisation of the size envisaged would take many years before producing a worthwhile output.'

In the event, this was to prove a serious difficulty for the Mandata project because it had to find staff, and then to establish many of its own work structures, processes, and conditions as well as trying to develop a system to justify its own existence.

The Director-General of the Post Office also predicted difficulty in coordinating the requirements of so many disparate departments, pointing to overseas experience to support his point.

To what extent this last might have proved a problem is hard to say because the project was reoriented in such a way that users' involvement in specifying requirements became unnecessary.

Objections to Mandata from the Post Office would have been worrying because, as employer of half the proposed population to be covered, its involvement was very important though not absolutely crucial to the cost saving calculations. More directly powerful, though, was the Treasury without whose support there would be no money for the development. Treasury did not reply until 30th June. Its response was hesitant and circumlocutory,

> 'Having regard to the overall scale and implications of the proposal and its essentially tentative stage of development, I feel compelled to affirm the view previously offered that a scheme of this magnitude needs to be more fully developed in systems terms and its economic viability and general performance tested by some type of pilot study before there is an ultimate commitment of resources to the total project. Only in this way can there be any assurance that the pay off will be worth the outlay.'

There were two problems with this response for those who wished to pursue Mandata. First, Treasury needed to be persuaded of Mandata's value. Second, it was suggesting a pilot study. It appears that what was being suggested was some kind of partial prototype that would demonstrably prove the system's worth. In view of the nature of the Mandata proposal it is not easy to see how anything substantially worthwhile could have been achieved without incurring considerable cost and delaying schedules. How much of the network would need to be established? Would a working version of all the software be required? If not, which would be the critical ones to develop? From the point of view of advancing the initiation stage, the delays involved in the pilot study strategy would have given the major potential supporters time in which they might have changed their minds. In fact, given the way national economic and political events turned out, had it been delayed there would have had significantly less chance of Mandata's being funded.

In addition, the Department of Taxation expressed its reservations based on its own assessment that it would not enjoy any cost savings. Though the Board's staff attempted to rebut

Taxation's arguments, Taxation remained unpersuaded. As it is not a particularly powerful department, Taxation's opposition was unlikely to affect the outcome of the subsequent decision-making.

10.2.2.3 The consultants' review and Board approval

To assure themselves of the viability of Mandata, the Public Service Board commissioned an independent review of the feasibility study. This was undertaken between July and September 1972 by a team from a leading consultancy. At a meeting on 28th September the consulting team presented its findings to senior Board staff including the chairman. It supported the cost-benefit findings encouragingly. It endorsed the proposal for a phased implementation. In addition it made several recommendations concerning specifying clearly the functional requirements of the application, using formal project management and control techniques, and abandoning the software framework on the ground that much the same facilities could now be acquired on the open market.

The consultants' endorsement included a comment that even if the savings were overestimated by a factor of two there would still be a favourable benefit to cost ratio. This served to put the Post Office's objections in perspective. Even without the Post Office's participation the project was cost justified.

In reviewing the feasibility study the consultants were to all intents performing a third party evaluation on behalf of the Board. Having been commissioned by the Board, the outcome was bound to be tightly linked to subsequent decisions whether to support the project. The fact that one of the consultants had himself held a senior and influential role in Public Service adp in earlier years would have added weight to the findings. It is worth noting that though this evaluation was coupled to the Board's decision-making there was no structural link to tie the accompanying recommendations to subsequent progress. There was no requirement to follow them. The significance of this is not that had they been followed the project would have succeeded since none of them addressed nor could address the economic conditions that eventuated and the constraints these placed on funding. Rather, its significance lies in the fact that the Public Accounts Committee was later able to use this as a basis for criticising the project, criticisms

Mandata - A Case History 175

which helped politically foreclose options which required further funding.

By 4th October further results of a pilot exercise in the Department of Supply to establish clerical savings became available. They confirmed the earlier findings. Then on 12th October Treasury advised the Board that its earlier remarks should not be construed as reluctance to proceed with Mandata. But for the IDC's approval the way was now clear to proceed. The ADP Departmental Systems Branch undertook a revision of the feasibility study report for submission to the Board with the comments of departmental Heads. This was received and approved on 6th March 1973. Permission was granted to proceed with preparation of a submission to the Committee of Officials on ADP which was required to approve adp projects relative to government priorities. This was the essential precursor to Cabinet approval.

The March decision effectively gave Mandata some formal status in that the Board also made its first allocation of establishment positions to the project. The initiation stage was now yielding substantial support.

10.2.2.4 Review by the IDC on ADP

The Secretary of the Public Service Board wrote to the IDC on ADP on 14th April 1972 asking for the committee's comments on the feasibility study report. The IDC appointed a sub-committee in October and eventually endorsed the proposal on the last day of May 1973 (JCPA 1979).

Compared with the feasibility study's nominal date for comment by the IDC of June 1972, the IDC's approval came a year late. The exact reason it took so long is not obvious. It is possible that there was disagreement within the committee as to the value of the project, but had there been evidence for this it might have been expected that the Board would use it in its response to later criticism of the IDC by the Public Accounts Committee to the effect that it had failed to play any role in preventing Mandata's problems. No such defence was offered (JCPA 1980).

It is worth stressing that consideration by the IDC was a crucial part of the project approval mechanism. Without it, funding would not be approved (JCPA 1978b). However its role appears not to have been properly understood for it later emerged that virtually all

176   Chapter 10

of the IDC's discussion of Mandata had concerned the equipment acquisition (JCPA 1979). It had according to its normal practice abstracted from the total proposal just the technical issues. The implication of the Public Accounts Committee's criticism is that this was not widely understood and that its endorsement was seen as encompassing all aspects of the project. If the Public Accounts Committee was correct in this then it illustrates how ambiguity in expressions of support can favour a project. This contrasts with a later example in which ambiguity worked against the Mandata project organisation.

10.2.3 Consulting the staff

An important and time consuming activity which was not part of the main decision process involved consulting the rank and file public servants whose records were to be stored on the system. Consultation commenced in July 1972 when the Secretary of the Board wrote to all the staff associations, ie the Public Service unions, notifying them of the Board's approval in principle of Mandata and asking for their comments. Mandata raised some very sensitive issues for staff. Its proposed benefits in terms of staff savings were benefits to management but not to staff whose jobs might be lost. Would there be any redundancies? Would staff be forcibly redeployed? Would there be retraining? Moreover, there were implications for all staff. Who would have access to the data recorded? Could staff in Veterans Affairs be sure that nobody at Civil Aviation could access their record? There were even more subtle concerns. What if management used the interrogation facilities to list staff who were persistently absent on sick leave on Mondays? A new level of management surveillance and control of staff would be possible. The Board, being the Public Service employer and negotiator of pay and conditions, understood the importance of consulting and defusing staff concerns in advance.

Initially the staff associations offered little response. Information pamphlets were produced and distributed to all public servants. In August 1973 a formal consultative forum, the Mandata Consultative Group (MCG), was initiated. The chief staff concern was that there should be no retrenchments. The Board issued a prompt reassurance. Soon after this, there was a struggle over the role of MCG and staff consultation processes for Mandata.

Substantive staff welfare issues were replaced by procedural issues. Most likely this was a continuation of the wider and continuing struggle between employer and staff associations.

Staff resistance could have wrecked Mandata from the outset. In the event no major problems emerged. From this point of view, the Board's staff managed the consultative process very successfully, but at a cost of time and effort that could not easily be spared.

10.2.4. Reorganisation and expansion

In February 1972 the head of the Management Services Division who had previously fostered and supported Mandata retired. A new ADP Division was created with two branches, the ADP Departmental Systems Branch and the ADP General Development Branch. (Figures 10.6 and 10.7 show the structures before and after February 1972.) The head of the new division was first and foremost an administrator. His role was to oversee two branches within only one of which was there any responsibility for Mandata at this stage. He did not have his predecessor's enthusiasm for Mandata. He took a non-interventionist approach, providing little or no management control. The position was very important. It had the potential to give access to senior management. A more active supporter in this gatekeeper role might have solicited greater support when it was needed once the project was under development.

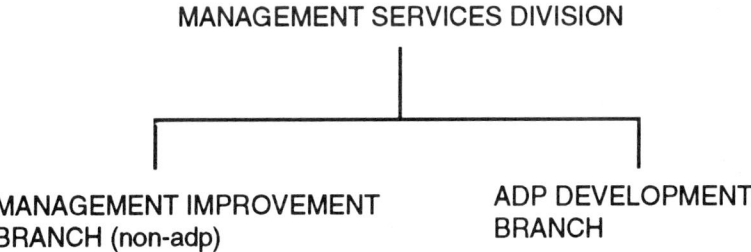

Figure 10.6. The Management Services Division prior to February 1972

As well as being responsible for advancing the Mandata proposal the ADP Departmental Systems Branch reviewed equipment proposals from other departments. The ADP General

178   *Chapter 10*

Development Branch serviced the IDC on ADP, oversaw Service-wide training and standards, and supervised computing bureau arrangements.

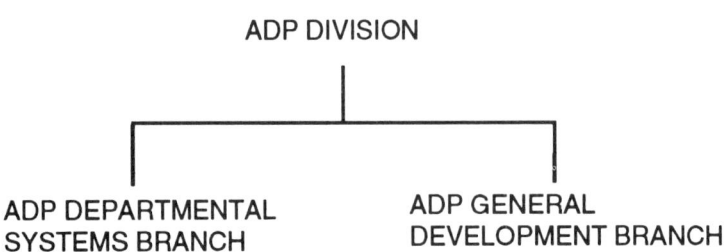

Figure 10.7. The new ADP Division after February 1972

As part of the preparation for Mandata, there were inter-organisational problems to be solved. In mid-1973 the Public Service Board, Treasury and Superannuation Board Liaison Committee was set up to tackle the problems of the proposed linking of Mandata with the Treasury and Superannuation computer systems. Quite fundamental issues such as establishing a unique identifier to be used across all systems required resolution. This particular problem was solved most promptly. A numbering system was designed, agreed and implemented within the year. The Treasury's new payroll system was already well advanced in its design. It was expected that their requirements would be frozen by the end of the year, well in advance of Mandata. This was regarded as in some ways an advantage because it meant that the Treasury system would be proven by the time Mandata was implemented. At the same time, the Post Office and the Superannuation Board were developing new systems. Further sub-committees were spawned to take the burden of finding acceptable solutions to the problems of standardising the means of communication between the different systems. They met regularly over the following two years, though, as events turned out, there never was any linking of the personnel and payments systems. It is, of course, in the nature of innovations that there will be uncertainty about what is needed. Sometimes it will be unavoidable that work is completed but not used.

In March 1973, the Board agreed that 28 positions should be credited to Mandata for the July 1973 to June 1974 financial year. This was a substantial increase over the existing team size. The tightness of the labour market has already been noted. There was a general acceptance at the time that it would not be possible to find sufficient experienced staff within Australia and that the UK was the best likely source. Though it was possible to bring staff in from abroad, competition from other parts of the Service and the private sector was always going to make it hard to retain a durable core of skilled and experienced staff. Keeping numbers topped up proved a chronic problem. Indeed the situation was worse than this because other Australian Public Service departments had recently recruited in the UK almost immediately before the Board's 1973 recruitment campaign.

Throughout the year work continued on aspects of the requirements, both applications and technical. The various papers prepared such as 'Preliminary Identification of Requirements - Mandata - Information System on Organisations', and 'Mandata - Transaction Processing to Facilitate Subject Matter and Population Security' are characterised by a considerable amount of complexity and unresolved difficulty. For example, a communication from another division of the Board revealed that there were no restrictions to what relationships might be required in an organisational structure. On the topic of transaction processing and security, another officer noted, 'The level of speculation required for work in the above areas has risen to a point where current decisions could be rendered useless by subsequent discoveries'. While, as I have noted before, system development is not a deterministic process all such uncertainties require effort in the form of communication and negotiation to resolve. If that effort were to be unavailable it would seriously hamper progress.

10.2.5 Final approval

By the end of 1973, the feasibility study had been revised and a submission to Cabinet completed. The submission was considered by the Board on 11th December. It was claimed that it was delayed pending expressions of support from staff councils. Only the Council of Commonwealth Public Service Organisations had so far provided this but similar affirmations were expected from the other councils. The submission then received the attentions of the Committee of Officials on ADP whose task it was to assess computing proposals in the light of government priorities. The

Board's timing was excellent coming immediately after three modest proposals from other departments and preceding proposals for $5 million and $6 million from the Bureaus of Meteorology and Statistics respectively. The Committee concluded that, 'the proposal is cost-effective and on that basis alone that it would represent a worthwhile investment of public funds'. The proposal received approval from the Federal Cabinet on 26th February. This was an explicit go-ahead for the expenditure of $7.18 million on equipment and system software.

The initiation stage for Mandata was largely concerned with passing through an extensive decision process in order to win the formal support necessary to secure funding. This it did successfully though somewhat more slowly than planned.

There are two points worth noting here. The Cabinet decision had been based on a full proposal for the project including all its costs, but it only explicitly approved the equipment and system software funding. Mandata staff took this as approval for all other costs outlined in the proposal since there would have been no point in approving equipment expenditure unless the other costs were also acceptable. This had not proved a difficulty before. But the fact that such approval, if there, was only implicit was, in this case, to prove a barrier to obtaining the support expected. The possibility of more than one interpretation of an expression of support such as the Cabinet's decision illustrates the problematic nature of the provision of support.

The second point is that against the original feasibility study schedule the project had slipped by some eighteen months. It was no longer the current schedule, but this was not sufficient to prevent the Public Accounts Committee much later from making criticisms as if the feasibility study were the agreed baseline. It is not clear how this possibility could have been anticipated or avoided. Rather it suggests that almost any information can be employed as a basis for criticism.

10.3 THE INITIAL DEVELOPMENT - FEBRUARY 1974 TO AUGUST 1976

The task confronting the project staff immediately after the final authorisation was daunting. They had to acquire, find accommodation for, and install a computer network across a continent; design, and write or commission the network software; design, and write or commission a database management system; develop a query language for the database; develop, implement, and operate a complex and advanced personnel and establishments system; and, not least, they had to build an organisation that could achieve all this.

This initial development period was characterised by an emphasis on the technical problems. Progress was hampered by various unanticipated contingencies. A decline in staff confidence in the project led to open criticism. The Board then made an intervention which was to totally change the nature of the project.

10.3.1 Organisation of the project

In order to handle both the application system and the technical infrastructure there was a reorganisation within the ADP Division. The new ADP Systems Development Branch was given responsibility for the technical development of Mandata. The Management Information Branch was to deal with user related or subject-matter issues, though MIB was also to include the Board's statistical section which was a sizable responsibility in itself and was to prove a significant distraction from Mandata. The ADP General Development Branch now serviced the IDC, reviewed departmental proposals, and dealt with policy and training.

10.3.2 Calling for tenders

Cabinet approval triggered an intensive effort to prepare tender specifications. The standard method of acquisition was through tenders issued by the Australian Government Supply and Tender Board (AGSTB) and contracts subsequently let through the same agency. This arrangement had the virtue of making available to any department the contractual expertise of AGSTB, but at the cost of adding to the chain of communication. The process involved inviting suppliers to submit a detailed proposal for how they could meet the requirements expressed in the specifications, and at what cost. These would be lodged unopened at AGSTB pending the deadline for submissions. A choice would be made on the basis of cost and quality. The process was designed to be fair to suppliers and to reduce the risk of government officials favouring particular suppliers. Occasionally a certificate could be issued to release a department from its obligation to call for tenders on the ground that it was inexpedient to do so. Ironically, one of the accepted reasons for pleading inexpediency was the tender process itself which could take so long that it would be expedient to short circuit it (JCPA 1978a). Mandata, however, used the standard process. Chronology 10.3 lists the main events in the process from Cabinet approval to machine acceptance.

Chronology 10.3. From the Cabinet decision to computer acceptance

Date	Event
Feb 74	Cabinet approves Mandata equipment funding
Mar 74	Board announces equipment funding
May-Jul 74	Meetings to define tender specifications
Aug 74	IDC on ADP approves tender specifications
Aug 74	Call for tenders
Nov 74	Tenders close
Feb 75	Tender evaluations completed
Mar 75	IDC on ADP endorses equipment selection
Apr 75	Letter of intent to terminal supplier
Jun 75	Letter of intent to mainframe supplier
Jun 75	Letter of intent to minicomputer supplier
Dec 75	First minicomputers delivered and accepted
Feb 76	Mainframe delivered
Sep 76	Mainframe accepted

In the event the whole tender process through evaluation and selection of suppliers ran very smoothly. Preparation of the tender documents took five and a half months instead of the two envisaged in the feasibility report schedule. Nobody looking at the detail of the specifications would quibble with that time. There were three volumes. The first contained specifications for the central computer unit (ccu) and software, including both standard products and special requirements; the second included specifications for the network's data concentrator units (dcu) and software (the dcus' function was to serve as multiplexers); and the third covered the state based minicomputers (mcu), their software requirements, and the terminals. Prior involvement in IDC work overseeing the acquisition of equipment by other departments appears to have resulted in thorough specifications. On 15 August the tender documents were issued.

Immediately teams were organised ready to evaluate the tenders as soon as the November closing date was passed. Project Evaluation and Review Technique (PERT) networks were drawn up. Film Australia was approached to make a film about Mandata for showing to Public Service staff. A proposal for a requirements specification was prepared and an overseas tour undertaken to investigate user issues in public service adp personnel systems.

Prospective tenderers meanwhile demanded attention. They needed a thorough understanding of the board's requirements in order to maximise their chances of winning orders. So there were lengthy discussions with Mandata staff. Between late August and late October, ADP Systems Branch staff met suppliers a total of 27 times. These meetings were very time consuming. On average there would be 6 Board staff involved in the meetings, each lasting approximately two hours. Allowing for preparation time and time for writing and agreeing detailed minutes at two hours per person per meeting, this amounts to 648 hours of effort. To put it a different way, over that two month period the work related to the meetings would, on these conservative assumptions, have taken up three out of the eight working weeks for each of six people.

Following the closure of tenders on 7th November, evaluation took place in three phases. The tenders were checked against specifications and the complete tally of costs made explicit. This was followed by a second, deeper assessment of the tender to clarify any residual doubts. Finally, the features and costs of each tender were tabulated and draft evaluations produced. This staged approach applied to all main items of equipment and was carried out by three teams. By 17th February 1975 the evaluation reports were ready for consideration by the IDC.

The recommendation that the IDC considered was for separate suppliers for the mainframe and minicomputers. The latter would act in two different capacities, some as data concentrators, some as local nodes for data entry and receipt of output. The local sites would operate with Australian Public Service standard terminals. These were to be built from scratch by a third manufacturer. The IDC lent qualified support for this configuration conditional upon its being satisfied that the manufacturers would provide the necessary technical support. This was particularly important in the case of the mainframe because it was a brand new model. There would be uncertainties about its performance and the manufacturer would be the sole source of troubleshooting. Because of the IDC's arrangement with AGSTB it would not have been possible to proceed with the acquisition without the Committee's unqualified support. It is interesting to observe the IDC requiring that attention be given to managing support from suppliers. In order to meet the IDC's condition two of the Board's adp staff flew to the US to obtain commitments from the manufacturers' top executives. How worthwhile the trip was is hard to say. What can be observed is that notwithstanding the manufacturers' expressions of support there was to be one occasion when the Board tried very hard to retain the services of a database specialist on loan from the mainframe manufacturer. She was recalled to the US nonetheless. Thus we have yet another example of how difficult it is to judge what support will be forthcoming until it is needed.

Once letters of intent had been issued to the main suppliers in June 1975 (JCPA 1979) a number of further tasks stood in need of attention. One was to specify in detail the special purpose software including the Processing Framework. Another was to arrange the sites for the equipment both in Canberra and in state capitals. There were many further details concerning design strategies to be worked out. And, there remained the continuing problem of staffing.

10.3.3 Configuring the technical infrastructure

The contracts for software production (special software, as it was called) were awarded to the companies supplying the mainframe and minicomputer hardware. The minicomputer company was to write communications software, transaction processing software for the minis, and a validation utility for data entry. The mainframe supplier had the core of the Processing Framework including the database management software and the query language, the Mandata Interrogation Package (MIP).

The project team to write the communications software was assembled rapidly. By mid-April 1975 schedules were being prepared. By contrast the other contractor encountered delays. Its project manager did not fly in from the US until July. The comparison of these two sub-projects is interesting in its own right since both had assured the Board's staff of their support yet other factors affected its provision.

The minicomputer company's project manager was experienced in working with the Public Service. He built up his team and insisted they have good accommodation separate from the Board's staff. His team was isolated from any hint of change in specifications by being physically and managerially buffered from the Board. Senior technical staff would emerge from their offices for progress meetings, returning immediately afterwards to their isolation. It was a shrewdly low key performance which resulted in software that the manufacturer was subsequently keen to market.

The other supplier had a more difficult time. The project manager had three teams working on the Processing Framework and a database interrogation system, MIP. It had not been possible to specify the software in detail until the successful equipment suppliers were known because until then it could not be known what facilities they would provide as standard. So the specification of software requirements became a central task for the adp technical staff. The contractors lacked familiarity with the Public Service and with the technical strategy being developed. As this was still an innovative strategy, achieving this familiarisation took longer than had been anticipated. Because it was crucial to the success of the whole project that its technical core be correct, this was a critical task. The conditions were therefore not ideal for the swift articulation of the specifications for the Processing Framework. Tensions emerged at what some saw as a lack of firm decisions from which progress could be made. In an effort to combat these difficulties joint Public Service Board/contractor teams were established in the hope that this would improve communication and speed decision-making. It had the result of reducing tensions and eventually led to a product being specified and built. Those close to the project offer mixed reports of the quality of the products. Certainly, the Processing Framework did not operate flawlessly as we shall see later (section 10.5.2.6). How far these flaws derived from the design, from changes in the environment or from its style of use is an open question. Clearly it worked well enough to support operational systems.

The difference between the experiences with the two contractors can be seen to derive in part from the different levels of experience of the teams involved. Experience on the part of the one supplier made it easier to organise the contract work and provide the Board's staff with the support needed to get the job done. Also, the Processing Framework was the technical heart of the project. It was complex and innovative. Its quality was crucial. The communications software though equally crucial to the distributed architecture of the system was less complex. The minicomputer software was self-contained. Thus for reasons associated with the nature of the contracts and the particular circumstances, the one contractor was better positioned to buffer itself than the other.

At the same time as the special software specifications were being organised other staff within the ADP Systems Development Branch and within the Management Information Branch were preparing a series of design related documents on topics such as the operational environment, project control, a data dictionary, a language specification for the interrogation language, security, an organisational model for implementation in the database, standards and procedures for the Management Information Branch, and many more. Between April and December 1975 nearly 40 such documents, often major papers, were produced, all requiring discussion and revision. This was no small effort.

It is particularly noticeable that many of these papers were concerned with the organisation of the development process itself rather than contributing directly to the development of the project. This was a major burden for the Mandata project and bore out the earlier comment from the Post Office to the effect that simply developing the organisation for Mandata was a major undertaking. Data processing organisations depend upon a very heavy investment not only in technology and staff but also in constructing work procedures. The Mandata plans appear not to have recognised the extent to which this would be a continuing process.

This left little time available for systems analysis of the application system and preparation of design specifications. Part of the problem was the urgency of the special software projects, part the need to build a development organisation, and partly a shortage of staff.

10.3.4 Staffing

Mandata was never adequately staffed by the standards of the resource estimates it proposed, as figure 10.8 demonstrates. In March 1973 Mandata was credited with 28 positions for the July 1973 to June 1974 financial year. In June 1974 it still only had 22 of them. In August 1974 the project was advised that instead of 51 new staff for the 1974-75 year only 46 were approved. By December, the actual staff numbers had increased to 39, just under half the 79 required.

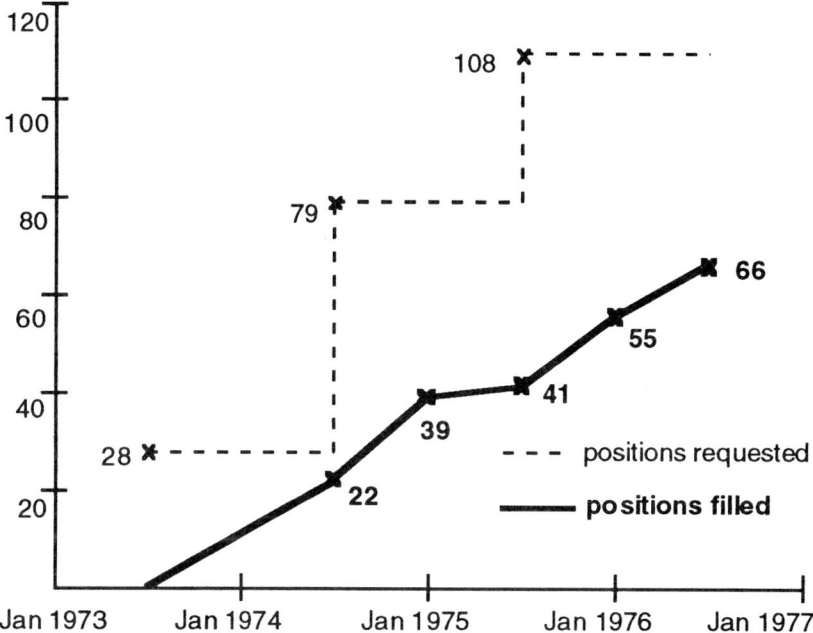

Figure 10.8. Staff numbers requested against positions filled

The attempt to rectify this over the following year makes sorry reading. In order to improve recruiting, a proposal was put forward for reorganising the ADP Systems Branch which included reclassifying programming staff as Computer Systems Officers (CSOs). The proposal went to the Board Secretary's division in early October 1974. It took until March of 1975 for the obstacles to be cleared and the Chairman to approve the reclassifications and redesignations involved. In the meantime, no appointments were made until the matter was settled. Within a fortnight of the Chairman's approval advertisements appeared.

At the same time though, the Board's Departmental Structures

Division expressed its opposition to the proposed reorganisation on the ground that it contravened existing Board policies regarding the CSO structure profile of departments. If the Board were to follow its own policy it would result in appointments only at the most junior level, CSO1, rather than at a mixture of more senior levels. This was an example of where the project organisation could have done with support rather than opposition from its colleagues in the Board. It was noted earlier that the potential benefits of Mandata to other areas of the Board were not recognised by them. In this case we can see that the asynchronous nature of the exchange of support in return for benefits can adversely affect what support is available and create contingent difficulties. The project overcame the problem but it would have been better off not having to expend the effort.

This problem resolved, interviews for CSO2s and 3s followed in late May and early June. By 11th June, 5 CSO3 appointments had been recommended. On 3rd July, 10 CSO2s were also recommended. At this stage Treasury approval and endorsement of the establishment of the positions by Executive Council was still lacking. By 4th September this hurdle had been surmounted, but in the process four of the ten people recommended for CSO2 positions had withdrawn. By 11th September 1975 the net result was that of 29 positions requested in early October the previous year, all 29 had been approved in principle by the Board, but only 14 had EXCO approval. In terms of actual people in post, the Branch had been augmented by 2 officers with a third due to arrive the following week. By the end of 1975 this total of new staff had reached 11. For the ADP Systems Branch whose technical work was critical, in 1975/6 it had a monthly average staffing of 32 as compared with the 74 officers that had been requested in earlier estimates. For the previous year the figures were 24 as against 62 requested.

The position was no less severe after the change of government at the end of 1975. The Prime Minister made it clear that it would be hard to obtain any new staff: 'Unless there are very good arguments to the contrary, the Permanent Head should terminate further processing of all current proposals . . . '. Even proposals already approved would be halted.

In May 1976 the head of the ADP Division drew to the Board's attention that the project was still severely understaffed, outlining the relation between staffing and project progress in a series of four possible options. The position was sufficiently acute that the last of these options was to abandon the project altogether and run the equipment on a service bureau basis.

The problem lying behind the staffing difficulties was the national economic situation which had resulted in severe restrictions being placed on Public Service expenditure. The Cabinet decision had appeared to sanction all the funding the project had asked for. Arguments to this effect were put to the Board in June 1974. Under changed economic circumstances the project organisation had insufficient leverage to prevent funding from being withheld or delayed. It lacked an enthusiastic advocate at a sufficiently senior level to have access to the Board and persuade it of the need for a continuing high level of support. Structurally it had no means of access to a higher authority, viz Cabinet, except through the Board itself. It took time for events to occur which would eventually lead to the Board's reconsidering its position with respect to Mandata.

10.3.5 Accommodation for the mainframe

The agency controlling space for the Public Service was the National Capital Development Commission (NCDC). It contracted building and works to the Department of Housing and Construction, and site fitting to the Department of Services and Property. (The names and responsibilities of the departments and agencies concerned with site and accommodation problems changed during the 1970s. I shall adhere to the names given here.) This division of responsibilities sometimes resulted in disagreements as to who should bear which costs. In the case of Mandata, a significant dispute arose.

Chronology 10.4 outlines the major events in the process of finding suitable accommodation for the Mandata computer. The 1971 feasibility report included no mention of siting for the computer because it was not a critical issue at that stage. By September 1972 a first stab was made at specifying accommodation requirements for the equipment. These evolved further during 1973. In September 1974, the Board suggested that the Trade building then under construction might serve its needs. This would have been very close to the Board's main office. Two months later NCDC ruled this out on the ground that they could not delay construction and fitting pending more detailed specification of site requirements by the Board.

Chronology 10.4. The process of finding accommodation for the central computer

Date	Event
Sep 72	First draft accommodation specifications for equipment
Jan 73	NCDC complains to Treasury about inadequate consideration of site costs
Aug 74	NCDC complains to IDC
Sep 74	Board suggests use of Trade offices
Oct 74	NCDC complains to IDC about late notifications for Mandata
Nov 74	NCDC rules out Trade building at Mandata site
Jan 75	Anzac Park West discussed as Mandata site
Apr 75	All parties agree on Anzac Park West
Jun 75	NCDC warns Board of financial problems with site alteration
Aug 75	NCDC advises of site preparation delay
Aug 75	NCDC and Board agree to interim site for Mandata in Trade building
Nov 75	NCDC stops work on Anzac Park West
Feb 76	Work completed on Trade site
Jun 76	Anzac Park West project officially cancelled

By mid-1975, when it was possible to make more accurate specifications because the exact configuration was known, the accommodation requirements were becoming more demanding. On 22nd April 1975 NCDC agreed to site the Mandata computer in offices called Anzac Park West. A likely installation date was set for 9th February 1976. The position changed dramatically on 4th August when NCDC announced at a site preparation meeting that in order to avoid any expenditure in that financial year as a result of cuts to its funding, it would not be able to start work on Anzac Park West until April 1976. Each side blamed the other. NCDC felt the Board should have supported it in its bid for special funding for Mandata. The Board felt that NCDC should have seen the cuts coming and organised itself accordingly. The Cabinet approval of its equipment funding had been in the knowledge of the site preparation costs and so the Board felt it was the construction authority's responsibility to manage the funding. The Board clearly felt aggrieved. The Commission likewise.

The background against which NCDC's decision was made helps explain the matter. The Board had been evasive in its specification of its requirements. It requested changes as it learnt more about its equipment's requirements. Whether fairly or not, the Public Accounts Committee later found it to have been ignorant of good site development practice (JCPA 1979). Furthermore, the Board was closely identified with the IDC on ADP to whom NCDC had written twice in 1974 complaining that computer acquisition decisions were taken without due consideration of siting implications. The IDC had done no more than acknowledge NCDC's complaint. So the situation was that with the increasing number of computer acquisitions NCDC was beginning to lose patience with a procedure which systematically gave low priority to its interests.

How far it would have helped if the IDC had paid more attention to the NCDC is hard to say. Had there not been the imposition of economic restrictions it is doubtful that Mandata would have incurred more than a handful of curses from NCDC. However, national economic and political policies dictated restraint. The likely bill for Mandata's siting was claimed by NCDC to be in excess of a million dollars. In the circumstances Mandata must have seemed to the Commission a very likely candidate for cost savings.

On 14th August, a week after NCDC's announcement, the Board's staff accepted a short term compromise. A new site in the Trade building which they had previously rejected as too small would be fitted out as a temporary home for the mainframe. Anzac Park West would remain its ultimate destination.

This remained the expectation until 26th November when NCDC renounced its commitment to refitting Anzac Park West. Its claim that it had wasted a lot of time doing work that was 'abortive' gives evidence of the tensions in the relationship. Various problems were mentioned including changed requirements and more immediately the fact that Anzac Park West had not been vacated by its tenants, the Department of Manufacturing Industry (DMI). Moreover, they showed no sign of going. This assertion was rejected by the Department of Services and Property, but at the same time this department was unable to say exactly when the space would be vacant. As ever the problem was not simple. In the first place the DMI had agreed to move out, but as this was a favour to Services and Property not the reverse DMI did not see it as its responsibility to find itself new offices. With a shortage of government premises of about 190,000 square feet finding new accommodation was not a simple matter. This was exacerbated by the austerity measures which placed tight restrictions on leasing new premises. Clearly where so many parties are involved it is impossible to expect that they will all treat their part of the transaction as having the same degree of importance. It was a structural constraint of the Public Service system that a project organisation could not have control over its own site preparation process, and that those who did would have different agendas.

The interim solution was by no means satisfactory. It omitted such basic facilities as toilets, leaving the Board to negotiate access to the nearby Department of Overseas Trade's washrooms. Nonetheless it promised a home for the mainframe for the short term and, as it turned out, provided it for the life of the project. By 1st February 1976 the site was ready. It was time for a new set of unanticipated problems to emerge.

10.3.6 Installing and accepting the mainframe

In the mid-1970s mainframe computers were mostly rather more sensitive than they are today. They required a closely controlled environment. In addition, given the relatively higher cost of hardware then, it was crucial for customers to assure themselves that the configuration they had bought was up to specification. In the case of Mandata, the mainframe was a brand new model, configured to the Board's requirements. There was no guarantee that it would function effectively from the start.

Delivery of the mainframe took place on Sunday 1st February after which it was necessary for the supplier to set the machine up and to test it to acceptance levels. On 11th March an officer reported that the computer room had reached a temperature of 25°C and appeared to be rising. The central processing unit's (cpu) recommended operating temperature was 21.5° to 23.5°. Moreover, one processor had 'gone down' overnight, and the air conditioning maintenance staff seemed not to be doing very much. The supplier contacted the Board to say that apart from some trivial activity on peripherals no further work could be done on the mainframe configuration without risking serious damage. The message was sent by telex signalling that the manufacturer was protecting itself against any contractual dispute. The pressure was on for the project organisation to get the computer room environment stabilised.

The troubles continued with the mainframe suffering a number of circuit board blow-outs. In early May, the machine room environment was still unstable. With the equipment powered up there would be a temperature of 17° below the floor while the console level read 25°. There were also unacceptable temperature drops occurring across single units. The cause was not understood. The response was to install a larger air conditioning fan. By early June the new larger fan had made some improvement. Nonetheless problems remained until further tests disclosed that some of the air flows were in fact blowing in the wrong direction and another fan was installed.

As if this were not bad enough, the acceptance of the machine was delayed further by problems with the power supply. Although an uninterrupted power supply had been planned, it had not been possible to obtain funding for it for the temporary site. In April, there were nine interruptions to the power supply. This not only slowed progress, but also risked damage to hardware components which were susceptible to sudden variations in voltage.

Though the mainframe was subsequently accepted, it was always to require considerable attention from the manufacturer. When Mandata was eventually an operational system, if Canberra suffered a lightning storm at night, the overnight update suite would invariably not be completed because the power supply had been interrupted. Whether problems with the machine lay in its manufacture is impossible to say for its environment was never entirely sound.

10.3.7 Developing the application system

Progress with automating the personnel and establishments system was slower than planned. Responsibility for the subject matter and user relations lay with the Management Information Branch (MIB). It had one section which undertook user requirements and another which was responsible for the implementation, user training, and documentation. To carry out its design responsibilities the branch needed to liaise with the ADP Systems Branch.

The first efforts to get user requirements specified commenced in 1974. A structure for the definition/specification of user requirements was put forward as part of one volume of the Codes of Practice under which Mandata was to be developed. In September 1974, an InterBranch Committee on Applications Definition was established. Also in 1974 the Mandata Consultative Committee (MCC) was established to facilitate liaison and consultation with personnel management in user departments.

In late February 1975 MIB produced a sample Mandata activity specification. The branch was trying to develop documentation standards for describing the activities Mandata was to cover. The sample was a 28 page specification for substantive, actual and provisional staff movements. Its sender acknowledged that it required further work but went on to note that he had no idea of what major design strategies would be employed and hence might be making assumptions that would not be valid. This reference to the uncertainty MIB staff felt about major design strategies is indicative of the dependence of MIB upon ADP Systems in relation to design. But ADP Systems was short staffed and totally absorbed by its technical problems throughout 1975, an allocation of priorities which the head of MIB supported. The constraint this placed on progress with the application led to frustration among some staff.

The main document prepared by the section dealing with user requirements was Document Number 23 (also known as Paper 23). This was entitled Strategic Plan - Activities in Phase 1 Mandata. Two drafts appeared in 1975 with further drafts still being prepared in mid 1976. Seminars for the Public Service Board, the Public Service Inspectors and departmental users were scheduled for September 1976. These were aimed at obtaining approval of the Mandata applications strategy. In the event the seminars were overshadowed by the announcement of a new strategy. Even had the departments accepted what was proposed, there would still have been a long way to go before an applications system was produced. Paper 23 in its relatively mature incarnation (draft 3.2 of 23rd July 1976) effectively specified the systems boundaries indicating where Mandata processes would be triggered and where they would interface with manual procedures. The 69 page appendix, detailing events and processes, indicated where an event would be recorded,

Mandata - A Case History 195

and when an enquiry transaction would be required, but it did not detail what information would be needed and what processing would be required. There was some way to go before a specification of requirements could be prepared. As an indication of the state of progress, by May 1976 it was estimated that even were the Board to approve significant increases in project staffing (in the order of 100 over two years), the earliest that a full implementation of the first phase could be achieved would be January 1978.

Not only was there a debilitating shortage of staff, but the situation was further exacerbated by the head of MIB being directed to give his highest priority to the statistical demands of the Royal Commission on Australian Government Administration. This was a clear sign of where the Public Service Board's priorities lay.

All this was against a background of the withdrawal of the major potential user from any involvement in the project. The Post Office had never been enthusiastic. In 1974 it became an independent authority with its services divided between Australia Post and Telecom. In January 1975 they both decided against involvement with Mandata and in so doing reduced the staff record base from a prospective 300,000 to 150,000. Though it was not desirable to lose a major potential client, this loss did not significantly change the course of the project. It did not result in the project being reassessed and found to be marginal. By the time cost benefits were radically reassessed in 1977 the whole direction and emphasis of the system had changed.

10.3.8 Internal disaffection

Some members of the project organisation in both branches began to doubt whether sufficient progress could be made to get the system operational. One at least made his fears known to the Acting Secretary of the Board. Another canvassed colleagues about a joint approach to management but unable to convince them decided to act alone. Contrary to normal practice he approached the head of the ADP Division. Receiving no satisfaction, he departed still further from Public Service norms by writing personally to the Board Chairman. The Chairman and one of the Commissioners of the Board took this approach sufficiently seriously that soon afterwards an external project review was announced.

While the approach to the Chairman acted as a trigger for Board action it is not clear that it was a rogue contingent event but for which the whole future of the project might have been different. If it had been just that, there is every likelihood that it would have been largely discounted. In fact, the Board had already been reconsidering its support in May 1976. The ADP Division head had offered the Board four different options with their resource implications. That Mandata would not be implemented in a politically acceptable timescale if it continued at its existing level of resourcing was clear. The Board was also aware that it was likely to receive criticism in the Auditor-General's 1976 report (see section 10.5.3.1). Even if the direct approach to the Chairman had not been made, it is likely that a subsequent press attack on the project in August would have had the same effect. So, the review that followed was triggered but not solely caused by the critic from within.

10.3.9 Summary

The period of initial development from 1974 to mid-1976 was characterised by contingent problems associated with the establishment of the technical infrastructure which in the absence of a full complement of staff both delayed progress in themselves and required effort to overcome. Lacking support from external sources it diverted effort from other problems one of which was the applications system work. By mid-1976 it was clear to the Board that it had to take some action. The action it took was to commission a review of the project.

10.4 REVIEW AND REVISION - 1976

The person invited to review Mandata was an experienced project manager who had worked mostly with large defence projects. His expertise was in project management rather than in software management, though his most recent work had been with a computerised management system for the Government Aircraft

Factories. Though currently with the Department of Industry and Commerce, he had in the past worked at the Department of Supply with the now Chairman of the Public Service Board. On 23rd July 1976 the review was announced to Mandata staff, the announcement indicating that the reviewer had a flexible remit to study the project.

Initially, he had five weeks to review the project with the help of two assistants. The review was conducted relatively informally rather than against precise terms of reference. The task involved extensive reading as well as discussion. He quickly came to the view that the project had not met its objectives. Nor could he see any prospect of its being recovered on the existing plan and rate of progress. In addition, he found team morale low. He concluded that the development of the technological infrastructure should be given a lower priority than getting the application into service with the users.

If a radical change to the project were not already a certainty, it became all the more politically attractive on Saturday, 14th August when *The Canberra Times* led its front page with the headline, '$2.5m PSB computers idle'. There followed a highly critical attack by the paper's Public Service correspondent.

The article in *The Canberra Times* initiated an extended period of press interest, the critical tenor of which was to undermine Mandata seriously. It caused especial offence by openly attacking individuals. But, though the head of the ADP Division wrote to the newspaper alleging inaccuracies in the article, his letter, published on an inside page, could hardly redress the weight of criticism implied by a front page headline. There certainly were inaccuracies in the article, but because there were also grounds for concern that the project was not at that time serving the public interest it had the effect of publicly blowing the whistle on Mandata.

This attack on the project, as much as anything, marked the end of the first phase of the project. Not to have acted decisively would have left the Board open to criticism that it was complacent. In times of economic stringency this would have been very damaging.

The question, then, was what to do about Mandata. Clearly one possibility was to scrap the whole project forthwith. This was an option that had recently been put to the Board but it would surely have been politically unacceptable. For the Board to have abandoned Mandata without a major face saving device would have been interpreted as an admission of incompetence with consequential loss of prestige and influence in the Public Service as a whole.

The actual and potential pressure on the Board meant that the issue was not so much how to achieve the original Mandata goals, but the political one of how to recover appearances. The real question became how to salvage respectability. The answer was provided by a personnel specialist on loan to Mandata from the Department of Productivity. He informed the review team of the existing personnel and establishments system in Productivity. This was not news to Mandata staff who had known about it all along. Neither for that matter was the plan that emerged to implement Mandata using this system a novel concept. Some of those who had been worried about the progress of the project had toyed with ways of implementing some sort of application system as a starter before proceeding to the full automation of the Mandata concept. The difference was that the external reviewer was in a position to persuade the Board to take steps to redirect the project.

The reviewer believed that he could improve the situation by using the Productivity system as a basis for providing a service to users in the short to medium term. He took advantage of both the fear of failure some staff felt and its correlate, their optimism for a new approach. He recruited several of the existing staff who were prepared to work through a rescue plan which would be acceptable to them and which could be offered to the Board. Together they constructed a plan to implement the Department of Productivity's basic personnel and establishments system for twelve of the larger Public Service departments.

The strategy was to use Mandata forms of which many had been designed over the years. The input would be prepared on the minicomputers and then despatched to Melbourne on a tape for update using the Productivity system. The programs for this system would then be run on the Department of Transport's computer which unlike Productivity's own machine had spare capacity. Outputs would then be returned to Canberra to be distributed to the departments. In the next stage of the plan the programs would be converted and ported to the Board's mainframe, and enhanced to achieve the same range of facilities as originally planned for Mandata.

This solution had two main virtues, both of which primarily

Mandata - A Case History

served the interests of good public relations. It minimised the delay in providing some computer support to departments for their personnel and establishments processing. And, it brought the mainframe into applications oriented use sooner than otherwise. In addition, early delivery of applications products was designed to restore internal morale. However, the Productivity system was flawed in a number of ways. The decision to make it the centre of a revised strategy was a clear gamble. The flaws were the price of a working system.

On 27th August the review findings were presented to the Board. The reviewer outlined his view of the project's future if it continued its current path. The solution was then presented to the Board by some of the Mandata staff who had worked on the new plan. In structuring the presentation this way he made it clear that the project had support from at least some of the middle level staff who would be involved in implementing it. The Board, hardly better equipped than in the past to make a critical assessment of such a plan, agreed to it. The prospect of a politically palatable solution which had staff support would have been hard to resist. But the implications of the proposal were not understood. The plan's proponents did not foresee the difficulties that would bedevil the implementation of the plan.

In terms of analysing the provision of support for the project this was an interesting passage for the project. Previously the Board might have been expected to provide its support because it stood to benefit from the system's benefits to the Public Service's functioning. Now, what it stood to lose if it did not continue to support the project became salient.

10.5 REORIENTATION AND CONSOLIDATION - AUGUST 1976 TO JUNE 1980

Although many things changed between August 1976 and June 1980, the strategy agreed to by the Board remained current. The basic personnel and establishments record maintenance application was made operational and several other sub-systems were developed and implemented. But progress was never easy: there were problems in the Productivity system which did not reveal how deep rooted they were until the latter half of 1979; the new Leave system did not impress all its users, requiring considerable amendment after enhancement; and the public scrutiny of the project that commenced in early 1976 continued at more intense levels until the project was scaled back in 1980. By reorienting Mandata in 1976, the Board ensured the project's survival, but along with the name the new strategy also retained the project's reputation which had been damaged by the appearance of *The Canberra Times*' article. That many of the goals implicit in the original concept were also retained as part of the long term strategy meant that high expectations were maintained. All these factors contributed to the almost constant critical attack from a variety of sources which the Mandata project organisation suffered throughout the whole of this period.

Between 1976 and 1980, the project had two directors whose periods of office emphasised reorientation and consolidation respectively. Therefore a sub-section is devoted to each of these two periods. Section 10.5.3 will separately chronicle the investigations of the Auditor-General and the Public Accounts Committee.

10.5.1 Reorientation

The first period which emphasised reorientation lasted from August 1976 to February 1978. The new strategy involved implementation of the Department of Productivity's system (DataStream) on equipment of a quite different manufacturer than that of the Mandata mainframe. The next step was conversion to the Mandata mainframe, and the development of new facilities. All this was scheduled to be implemented in phases as outlined in figure 10.9.

10.5.1.1 Reorganisation

In August 1976 the Board decided to appoint a project manager at a level above that of the branch managers who had previously overseen the development. The Chairman invited the external reviewer to take the job. He reluctantly agreed.

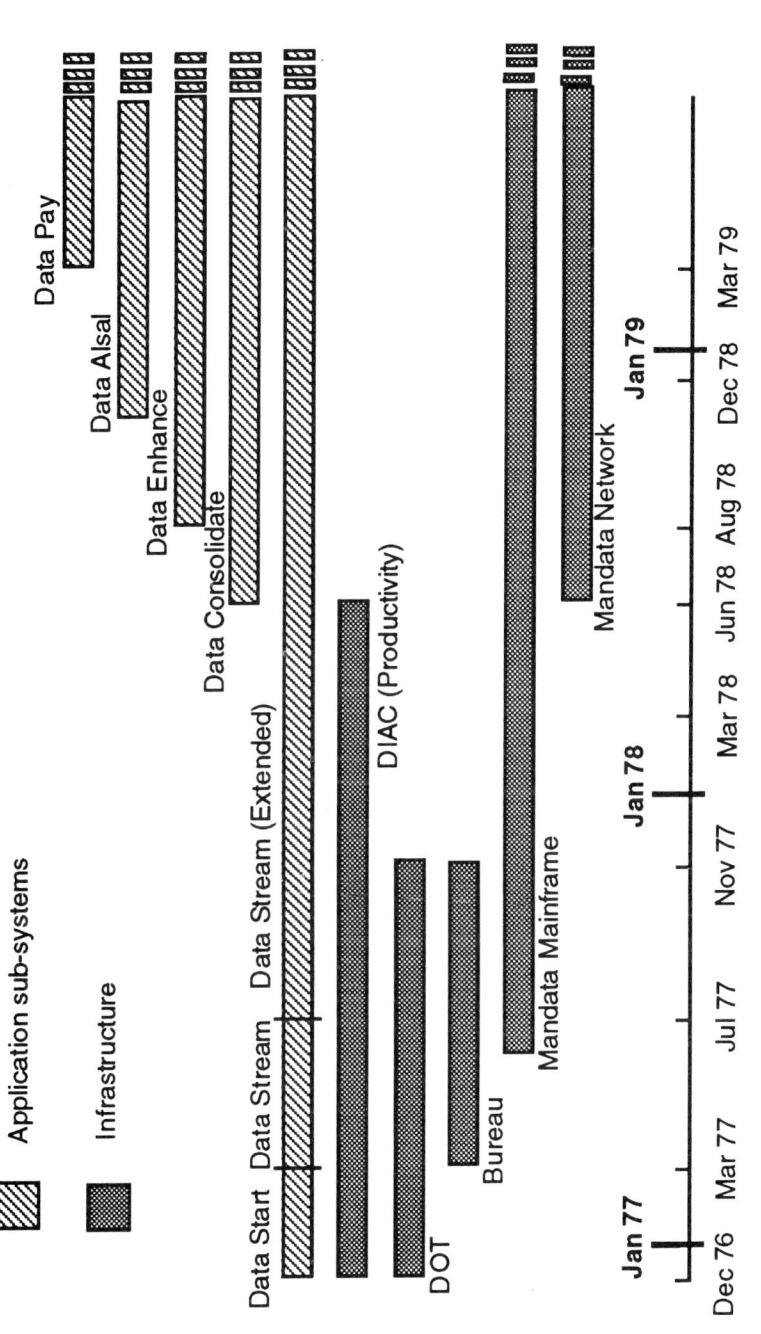

Fig. 10.9. Schedule for the new strategy approved in August 1976

Table 10.2. Organisation and product names arising from reorientation

Product	Description
Data Service/s (Inc)	Pseudo commercial identity for the enterprise of marketing Mandata.
DataStream	Department of Productivity system adopted as the basis for Mandata. Stored personnel and establishments records, produced statutory reports, and basic management information. Maximum of 80,000 records. To be available from March 1977.
DataStream (Extended)	Extension of record base beyond the 80,000 constraint to accommodate the whole Public Service.
Data Consolidate	Provision of on-line enquiry and interrogation. Limited on-line updating. All leave processing. A project control system.
Data Enhance	Educational qualifications recording, automatic gazettal of staff and establishment changes, recording of recruitment/appointment data, person/position matching for selection purposes.
Data Alsal	Upgrading system data relating to designation/occupation and associated salary and allowance conditions sufficient for Data Pay (see below).
Data Pay	Automatic notification to Treasury salaries system of variations to pay.

(This list includes only the major user product names. There were a number of other names for technical products.)

His period of office started in September 1976 in a flurry of activity. He had already started to change the project image and emphasis by focusing on management information benefits rather than clerical staff savings. As part of raising and maintaining motivation he initiated a process of commodifying Mandata. The aim was to instil in the project organisation the idea that they had a product which they would have to use to win and retain customers. Different sub-systems and phases of the project were called products, and were for a time offered by the group called Data Services Inc. The products bore names like DataStream, Data Enhance, Data AlSal and so on. Table 10.2 lists some of the more common names adopted.

At the meeting of the Mandata Coordinating Committee (MCC) on 9th September 1976 user representatives were told that,

'The concept of Data Services developed when it was realised that once Departments became clients they would need to be serviced and provided with additional facilities throughout the life of the Mandata system. This concept was emphasised to the Mandata team by relating it to a commercial type enterprise which sold services to clients. The commercial enterprise would, in turn, contract for software packages from a development team and would apply the software to 'contracted' hardware facilities vis-a-vis the computers and network facilities. This philosophy has been reinforced within the Project by the addition of (Inc) to provide the pseudo commercial identity Data Services (Inc).'

This was a radical departure for the Public Service. It clearly spelled out one side of the exchange in the project organisation-department relationship. It is doubtful that such an approach could have been sustained for any great time without wider acceptance of pseudo commercialisation of services within the public administration. It almost certainly would have required profound change to institutional values. Over time they drifted into disuse, perhaps from institutional embarrassment. The Public Service was not product oriented.

Part of the new strategy involved the establishment of the Mandata Project Office, soon to become the Mandata Program Office (MPO). It was to be organised functionally with organisational sub-units responsible for the equipment facilities management, development of special software, strategic planning, systems development, marketing and promotion, and implementation. Staff would then be assigned to identifiable products. There would be a liaison officer for each client, a project manager for each Mandata application, a pool of development staff to be switched from application to application as needed, and a project management support function including resource scheduling and configuration management. The full proposal was for an executive of 5, a planning group of 4, an integration group of 3, a development pool of 44, client liaison of 5, product services of 20, facilities group of 12, a computer centre of 22, regional cells of 30, and project management and support services of 18.

In August 1977 44 new positions were approved to fill this organisation, with the staff ceiling being raised from 92 to 153. Thus, even with the Board now more actively committed to the project and with a director who had access to the Board, establishment expansion did not occur overnight. And still fewer than half the posts on the Mandata structure chart were filled. The situation was alleviated by the loan of 16 officers from departments. It had taken three-and-a-half years since the Cabinet approval to get authority for a full scale project organisation, but still it remained to fill the positions.

Several other initiatives were taken. Office space was found for the whole MPO at the newly constructed Cameron Offices at Belconnen several miles away from the Board's main office in the centre of Canberra. This helped raise morale because the project organisation's existing office accommodation had been poor. It also had the advantage of giving the project a sense of identity, but the disadvantage of distancing it spatially as well as culturally from the Board. Project planning was instituted with the discipline of Development Cost Plans. The new director also attempted to persuade the Board to establish MPO as a centre of computing excellence for the whole Public Service. His idea was that it should become a proving ground for advanced technologies and thereby become a centre for training staff who could then take their knowledge out into the departments. In terms of winning support and enhancing the power of the project this proposal would have had the virtue of creating greater pervasiveness and hence enhancing departmental dependence on MPO. However, the Board declined to support this proposal.

10.5.1.2 Involving the users

The user departments received their first information about the changes when the seminars to introduce and discuss the contents of Paper 23 were reorganised to form an introduction to the new proposal. The goal was to implement DataStream (ie the core personnel and establishments application in the Productivity system) for twelve large departments in the first instance rather than for all departments. Implementation was to start on 1st March 1977 and proceed to a point where 80,000 records had been set up by 1st July. This would have been full capacity given the equipment available initially. Prior to implementation in departments there was to be a pilot project called Data Start which was to include the Public Service Board itself and the Department of Business and Consumer Affairs. At this stage, the changes were still portrayed as a measure to expedite the automation of the personnel function. The original focal point for the workshops, Paper 23, still defined the long term aim.

At the meeting of MCC on 6th October a different tone was established. The September meeting had 'softened' users by promising rapid support for their personnel and establishments effort, with short term benefits for management as well as a new emphasis on management information reports. Now the other side of the exchange was made clearer. First, the onus was placed on users for planning and resourcing their own implementation and for controlling the rate at which they proceeded. They were then pressured to say when they would start to use Data Services products. Second, departments were asked to formulate their terminal requirements. Third, each department was to nominate an officer at class 9-11 (a middle manager) to be their project co-ordinator. Fourth, they were to nominate people who would be called form sponsors because they were to help with the approval of some 30 Mandata forms over the coming 6-8 weeks. Fifth, a request was made for the loan of 8 to 10 CSOs for 6 to 9 months. All of a sudden the change of direction and the revitalisation of project staff thrust a considerable burden on the users.

This was an intriguing moment in the project's history. It was the point at which the application's clientele first came to have an active role. Previously they had been largely passive. They had been informed and consulted, but little of substance had been asked of them. Before, it would have been easy enough for them to think they were going to receive the benefits of Mandata *gratis*. Now, there were resource issues. What would implementation cost? Where would the co-ordinator come from? Who would assess terminal requirements? Could any CSOs be spared? Moreover, when it appeared a few months later from the pilot implementation that the Board's own office had found that 15% of its records were in error, the prospect of a large scale data purification exercise loomed. (It is interesting to note that data quality appears to be a common problem (Dutton 1981, CGO 1982), and may on occasion be quite crucial (Dickson & Janson 1984).)

Customer commitment was an essential ingredient. It was not a quality exhibited by all departments. As events later showed, some departments made major commitments to implementing the system in their personnel sections, others were uninterested, while yet others were openly resistant. Much depended upon the level of support offered by departmental management and the attitude of the person appointed co-ordinator. But, what no department was prepared to do was to lend its own computing staff though some did lend other classes of personnel. The cost of this refusal to support the project was spelled out at the meeting of MCC on 4th February 1977: initial schedules had assumed the availability of such staff. Therefore, since DataStream (the initial implementation of the Productivity system) had highest priority, other developments would have to be delayed.

10.5.1.3 The consultants' review 1977

In March 1977 MPO completed a new cost-benefit analysis based on the new strategy. Against a background of continuing economic austerity, the project was reviewed by external consultants in response to a request by the Committee of Officials who wanted assurance that the revised strategy represented the best alternative available. A special Inter-Departmental Committee was set up to manage the review. It included representatives of the Board's office, the Department of Prime Minister and Cabinet, and the Department of Finance.

The task of the consultants, a different company from that which had been used in 1972, was to check the cost-benefit analysis and to make a judgement on the MPO strategy. The result was that the cost-benefit ratio was supported, but largely through the

Mandata - A Case History

'discovery' of new savings by the consultants. They also supported the implementation strategy with provisos concerning senior management support and overall project management. Mandata had the go-ahead.

The evaluation is interesting inasmuch as it was again conducted by a third party. This time it was on behalf of a highly influential committee which had the power to recommend that funding be stopped. However, it had no role in the day to day management of the project, and in the absence of any mechanism for ensuring that its recommendations were followed, there was again no constraint on the project organisation to follow them.

This positive evaluation proved a useful resource against the institutional critics. In particular, the Public Accounts Committee accepted the consultants' evaluation. Without it, the Committee would have been more inclined to question the project's worth.

10.5.1.4 Problems with DataStream

The shortcomings of the new strategy emerged in two ways. There were application problems and technical problems. The application problems started to become apparent when the pilot implementation started with the Board's records. The technical problems took longer to fully manifest themselves.

The first application problem concerned the state of the existing records. Many were so inaccurate that they were not easily corrected. The Department of Productivity system required that position records be established prior to recording personal details so that there would be no possibility of records occurring in which individuals held positions about which the system knew nothing. (In passing, it is interesting to observe the way that the bureaucratic primacy of office over office holder is reproduced in computer systems.) Unfortunately for Mandata, the departments had their own methods of recording establishment details, and so there were idiosyncratic as well as common deficiencies. One common problem was that record cards would not include the date when a position was established. This was a necessary detail for DataStream. So clerks would have to turn to the file records, maybe having to work through various papers before finding the required information. Since there was strong pressure to implement quickly, some clerks avoided this delay by entering a false date to serve as a dummy entry on DataStream with a view to correcting it when they had time. Where the necessary time was hard to find, the false data remained on the system.

There were also output problems. The system output was not what managers expected. In the Public Service Board's own offices, for example, they were accustomed to two dimensional diagrams of organisational structures with a variety of annotated information. DataStream did not provide that. The co-ordinator for the Board's own office found herself trading on personal relationships she had built up over many years to encourage the Board's own managers to bear with the new system. At that stage the Mandata implementation staff were better kept away from the management users because they knew so little about personnel and establishments, most having come from the Board's training area. Maintaining enthusiasm was increasingly difficult for users as it became clear that the system did not provide the outputs that had been promised. Moreover it was hard to see that these administrative privations could be justified economically since there was no prospect of the system achieving the savings forecast. Quite the reverse, it cost the Board an extra class 6 clerk to do the co-ordinator's normal job.

After nearly twelve months the Board's own personnel co-ordinator sent the Mandata director a highly critical report outlining the difficulties and limitations of the system. She was immediately co-opted into the project with the offer of a promotion to work as a departmental implementer, thereby quieting a critic and gaining her experience. However, the inherent limitations of the Productivity system could not be avoided. Some problems were immediately apparent, others took time to emerge. Some were specific to particular departments which operated under conditions which had never applied to Productivity.

The user problems had to be experienced to be solved. It took time to gain that experience in the departments. It also took time and experience for MPO to begin to appreciate the difficulties users faced and to staff its user functions with knowledgeable and sympathetic people.

10.5.1.5 Technical problems

The technical problems were also chronic. The first task was to provide an operational service to user departments. This involved providing an interface from the minicomputer based input to the Productivity system. Once that was done there needed to be support for the day to day operations.

The operational strategy was less than straightforward. The Productivity system ran on an altogether different computer from MPO's mainframe. The Productivity machine did not have enough capacity to support the extension of DataStream to 80,000 records. Consequently, capacity was required from other sources including the Department of Transport's centre in Melbourne and a bureau. The medium term strategy was to phase in the use of the MPO mainframe and phase out the other machines over the period to January 1978. This was to mean that for a while data entry was performed in Canberra from forms received from all over Australia, tapes flown to Melbourne for update, further tapes flown back for production of output, and reports redistributed around the continent.

Each department's records were kept on a separate set of main files, so there had to be an operational processing sequence of update and output for each department in turn. The update was not a single sequential pass of the file, but required one pass of both the personnel and establishments files separately followed by a further pass to reset any transactions that had been found to result in inconsistencies. The old sequential technology had never been well suited to the personnel and establishments problem. It was long winded and time consuming. Now as the system was being run over and over again for different departments, this became a serious difficulty. MPO staff found they were hard pressed to complete each week's processing load within a single week. The pressure this placed on the technical side of the project was considerable.

The technical support required for the operational activity leeched effort from development activities whose chief purpose was to enable more processing to be carried out on the mainframe. The first task was to develop suites of programs which could run on the main files generated by DataStream in order to produce printed reports. This proved the main development task for 1977.

10.5.1.6 The LeaveProto sub-system

At the same time as converting the Productivity system, the

Mandata staff were also attempting to demonstrate the value of the original strategy of a unified database with on-line facilities by developing a separate system, Leave. This was to be transaction based. It would use database software supplied by the mainframe manufacturer and the Public Service Board's Processing Framework. The system would not only record leave applied for and taken, but would implement the various rules which governed the calculation of leave balances. It was to provide a service which DataStream did not offer and would automate a clerical process that was error prone and notoriously costly.

The team appointed to develop the leave application set about prototyping the system. A first attempt at the system was to be implemented as LeaveProto in the Board's own central personnel section in October 1977. It was a 'quick and dirty' development with user representatives directing programmers as to the requirements while the programmers entered code at a vdu keyboard. This is an error prone practice because it has no slack in it. As a prototyping tool it is more excusable than when it is used as a conventional construction tool. However, as prototyping is even now only a marginally respectable approach to development, in 1977 the construction of LeaveProto generated internal tensions.

In a review of this system in March 1978 it became apparent that because user requirements had not been systematically collected there were areas of likely requirement not included. The problems that emerged from LeaveProto are more properly a part of the project's consolidation period and will be discussed in section 10.6.2.

10.5.1.7 Bureau operations

One way to respond to the accusation that the MPO mainframe was standing idle was to get other departments to use it. Having agreed to operate it on a bureau basis for both the Department of Capital Territories and for the Department of Immigration and Ethnic Affairs, MPO found itself in June 1978 having to ask the former department to take its operational processing elsewhere because it was delaying development of Mandata. This was less than two months after Capital Territories had completed the transfer of its processing on to the Mandata computer. In August the matter became cause for further adverse comment by *The Canberra Times*.

At just about the same time, negotiations were taking place with the Department of Employment and Industrial Relations (DEIR) to run their SAMIN statistical system on the Mandata network. Despite concerns that such an agreement might further damage progress on Mandata it went ahead, causing a small but recurrent drain on Mandata resources.

The possibility of converting the Board's existing CRP systems to run on the mainframe was also suggested, but this proposal was relatively easily deferred. It would have consumed precious development effort on a non-central activity.

10.5.1.8 A change of directors

Staff turnover was always a problem for Mandata. Even while new staff were being appointed others would resign or be promoted elsewhere. This persistent haemorrhage is no better illustrated than by the case of the new director himself. Appointed in September 1976, he was seen by the Board as the man to put the project on its feet and to see it through to a successful completion. Yet by April 1977 he was only part-time having been invited to join the ex-Chairman who had recently moved to another department. Now, in order to gain access to their project director, senior Mandata staff had to be issued with security passes that would get them into the building in which their director worked. The symbolic importance of this change in arrangements is considerable. It signified that the Board did not consider Mandata to be sufficiently important to warrant the undivided attention of its director.

In November 1977, the director advised the Board to advertise for a new, full-time project director. This time the Board appointed from within its own ranks. The project had by this stage been thoroughly redirected, but users had yet to realise the benefits that would justify continuing support for the project. The task now was to get the operational system implemented on the Board's facilities so as to provide a valued service.

10.5.2 Consolidation - February 1978 to June 1980

In early 1978 the project needed to be advanced on many fronts. DataStream had to be ported to the mainframe and converted to operate under the full range of Mandata facilities. Implementation of departments was under way, but needed to be extended to achieve a much wider record base. The prototype leave system had been implemented in the Public Service Board's own offices, but it awaited far wider implementation. Special purpose software such as the general interrogation package, MIP, was still being developed under contract. In addition, there were other sub-systems to be built such as the designations and salaries table system and the educational qualifications and training sub-system

There remained also the continuing tasks of managing the hardware and software facilities. These were far from routine. Mandata had had to establish its own computer centre from nothing. It was still learning how best to organise its own work. Moreover, much of the software used was unfamiliar, either because staff had little or no experience with the manufacturer's products or because it was original material like the Processing Framework which had been developed by the manufacturer for Mandata. There was a continent wide network to finish installing. There was much documentation to be written both for users and for internal consumption. And most of all, support for the project had to be managed and critics headed off.

The new director's task was to manage all this and thereby consolidate the changes of the previous eighteen months.

10.5.2.1 The new executive

Most recently the new director had not been working in adp. Though he had worked on various projects in the Department of Supply in the 1960s and had run a systems analysis consultancy service for the Public Service Board in the 1970s, he was now working in the Board's division responsible for organisational matters. That he was reputed to be politically aware is suggestive of how the Board itself perceived his task.

In addition to a new director, a new deputy was also appointed. The need for a deputy was clear. The project director would be required to maintain many external contacts and to buffer it wherever possible from environmental pressures. There were user department heads, staff associations, the Auditor-General, the Public Accounts Committee, and the members of the Board all requiring attention. In addition, there were the strategic issues associated with planning the future of the project. The deputy was required to keep the internal processes running smoothly.

The new director's first decision as Director of the Mandata Program Office was to make a clean break with the past. There was no handover from his predecessor. Staff who previously had special security passes to allow them into the building where the old director now worked were asked to give them up. The new director was asserting himself as the controlling influence.

10.5.2.2 Organisational changes in MPO

MPO was reorganised into an operations area responsible for servicing the existing DataStream system users, and a development area to build the replacement for DataStream and the new facilities to be provided in DataConsolidate. The language of commercialism that had been used to reinvigorate the project slipped into disuse. The processes based on the Productivity system came to be referred to as P&E (Personnel and Establishments), while the DataConsolidate processing of leave was referred to simply as Leave.

Regular reporting to the Board was instituted. A formal report was presented every six weeks with interim informal reports in between. The Board at least was now regularly informed even if this did not guarantee its full and unstinting support. The Board was after all likely to view the project with some hesitation after the public embarrassment it had caused. To help improve the quality of the Board's understanding of the project, the new director proposed a series of short papers about Mandata. These were for fortnightly meetings with the Board. The difference between now and the period before the 1976 reorientation was that the director was structurally positioned so as to be able to attempt to influence the Board's view of the project.

A further development in the organisation of the project was the slow formalisation of procedures and documentation. For some time there had been moves to make the production and maintenance of documents a systematic process. A configuration management system was instituted. This provided for a series of drafts of all development documents, followed by a formal proposal and a final, agreed version. Other initiatives in 1978 included Guidelines for Mandata Manuals Production and a proposal for a project control system.

Such disciplines were not always greeted with fulsome support from the staff who were to operate them. The following was attached to one such proposal. It quotes the Duke of Wellington writing to Lord Bradley, British Secretary of War around 1810. According to this anonymous annotator, Wellington wrote, '. . . I shall see that no officer under my command is debarred by attending to the futile drivelling of mere quill-driving in your Lordship's office - from attending to his first duty which is . . . so to train the private men under his command that they may, without question, beat any force opposed to them in the field'. Clearly, the anonymous contributor to the file felt there was too much pen pushing and too little attention to the systems innovation process.

10.5.2.3 The strategy for progress

If a strategy of damage control was to be successful, the project organisation needed to be realistic about what was achievable and what would prove acceptable to Mandata users and to Board management. In a minute tabled to the Mandata Consultative Committee the position was presented concisely. Users had made it clear that they wanted the next phase of development to include at least the same facilities as already available under the initial implementation of the Productivity system. The Board in turn had made it clear that it wanted quick results. It was essential to renew the earlier restriction on system availability: the initial 12 departments would remain the sole users. This immediately took some pressure off the implementation and operational parts of the project. But, in so doing, it postponed indefinitely implementation of Mandata across the whole Service, thereby deferring the benefits to be had from a Service-wide system. At the operational level, this meant that there would be record-keeping difficulties as officers transferred in and out of Mandata departments. There would not be a consistent history maintained for those who left and later returned to a Mandata department but who worked in non-Mandata departments in the interim. At the management level it would mean that there would be no support from Mandata for Service wide manpower planning. At this stage, the importance of reducing pressure on the project and servicing the existing customer base prevailed over the virtues of increasing that base.

The overall strategy proposed was, it was claimed, 'not elegant but worthwhile'. The conversion of the Productivity system to the mainframe would be completed by the end of the year. This would then support updates every two nights instead of every two weeks as in the existing phase 1. Development would proceed on the Leave product so that it would be available with on-line enquiries by February 1979. Further on-line access to personnel data would be provided. This would provide coverage for most of the personal data currently held on SPR cards 53, 54 and 55 as well as establishment data. This would be phase 2. Still further developments were being considered for 1979. These would be phase 3.

10.5.2.4 The Impact Evaluation Study

To help justify the strategy for proceeding, a study was commissioned to determine Mandata's likely effect in departments. The idea of a study of the effect of replacing SPR cards predated the new director. On one interpretation it was an exercise to better understand the personnel function so as to identify what kinds of controls would be required when SPRs were completely replaced. This appears to have changed so that by the time the study got under way in June 1978 it was clearly a study of the likely effects of Mandata phase 2. Ideally, the Impact Evaluation Study would have been a vindication of the development strategy and a resource for defending the project from external criticism and any senior management dissatisfaction. In addition, the evaluation process would function to bring user departments into the project. Participating in the study were representatives of the Auditor-General's Office, Defence, Transport, Health and the Public Service Board in addition to Mandata staff.

As ever, it proved difficult to keep staff who had been loaned. By September the study leaders felt pressured by lack of staff and difficulties they were encountering obtaining reports they needed. In October they were under pressure from the director who stressed that the importance of the report stemmed from statements made to ministers, Cabinet, the Public Accounts Committee, the Auditor-General and staff associations. Furthermore, the Board needed a sound basis on which to make decisions about the structure of personnel record-keeping organisation across the whole Service.

The director wrote, 'I am under increasing pressure at fortnightly meetings with the Board to table documents which provide facts and at least some tentative findings'. In short, he needed some ammunition.

A draft of the Impact Evaluation Study was available by December and a full report was tabled at the Board meeting of 7th March 1979. It did not provide encouragement. Any savings from DataStream (P&E) even in its phase 2 form were more than offset by the costs it incurred in terms of originators of forms, data processing operators, co-ordinators and others. The only net savings to be gained would be from Leave. The estimate here was 70 clerks saved by comparison with a total suggested by consultants who reviewed the project in 1977 of 625. Though it offered a handful of miscellaneous savings, its main conclusion did not provide a resource by which to leverage further support either from the Board or departments. The report argued that considerable staff savings could be made in two ways. One was staff reorganisation in the personnel area, though the benefits to be gained would be tangential to Mandata. The other was for Mandata to penetrate the clerical function more deeply, by automating more of the manual calculation processes. This would involve a substantial redevelopment of either phase 2 P&E processes or pay and allowance recording and calculation. Neither was consistent with a strategy of consolidation, of letting the existing developments bed down and start to bring benefits.

10.5.2.5 Conversion

Prior to full conversion of the Productivity system to the mainframe there was an interim and lesser conversion to make the system run on the Department of Business and Consumer Affairs' computer. This had greater spare capacity than Transport and was expected to greatly improve the overall processing efficiency. The goal was to bring update frequency down to every four nights instead of every fortnight. Like the main conversion this took longer than was expected and started to run behind schedule.

Conversion to the mainframe looked straightforward enough but proved substantially more time consuming than anticipated. One of the problems was that the two manufacturers' implementations of the Cobol language proved infuriatingly different. For example, there were differences in the collation sequences, so that every sorting process had to be checked and many amended in order to retain the correct logic. Another surprise was the discovery that the mainframe's compiler recognised sequences of code ignored by the compiler for the Productivity machine. In addition, there were a number of bugs that turned up simply through the process of converting and testing the programs. For example a difference between the Productivity and Transport machines had resulted in spurious data occurring in some fields.

With any large scale conversion of this sort new errors would also be introduced in the conversion process. The manual amendment of the logical conditions required some thought as well, hence scope for more errors.

In addition, it turned out that the system under conversion was not well constructed in the first place. The Mandata developers discovered all kinds of hidden traps in the Productivity system. Its original developers and maintainers had not documented it well, nor had they maintained the code faultlessly. The Mandata programmers found there were sequences of code that were never called because there had been unexplained bugs in them. To avoid their crashing the system the code had been permanently bypassed. Worse still, the lack of documentation meant that the code had to be deconstructed to ascertain its purpose and operation.

A program graphically named Octopus bore testimony to the limitations of the system. The Productivity programmers had written Octopus to reach into any part of their system and change the records regardless of the Public Service rules the processing was supposed to respect. (It was one of the first programs to be converted!) In thus institutionalising the quick fix, Productivity had apparently acknowledged the ubiquity of bugs.

In addition, enhancements had to be made. The history record for substantive and actual occupancy of a position was extended from 30 to 50 lines. Various other changes were made including rewriting a program that interfaced between the two updates in the update suite to 10% of its original size. The number of error messages was rationalised. Thus, the conversion turned into a more protracted and complicated process than would ever have seemed likely at the time of the decision to adopt the Productivity system as an interim measure. So, it was 11th May 1979 before the announcement was made that it would at last be possible to process all the departmental records not already transferred to the Board's computer in Canberra. This was four months behind schedule.

10.5.2.6 Performance of the technical infrastructure

For the most part the minicomputers and their software appear to have functioned adequately. The central configuration was more problematic. In March 1979, meetings were instituted of a Software and Fault Performance Committee for the mainframe. These proceeded fortnightly and aimed to resolve outstanding problems with special software that the manufacturer had built for Mandata. They documented and discussed the problems, and pursued them to resolution. By June there were 25 unresolved faults and the chairman of the Fault Performance Committee considered that software reliability was now 'almost acceptable'. Ominously though, he suggested that reliability might be related to the machine workload. As one of the outstanding problems was with jobs hanging (ie processes neither progressing nor terminating) requiring a time consuming Halt/Load (ie an operator intervention to restart work on the machine), this possibility did not bode well. Upgrading capacity was an expensive process in the 1970s. It would require special funding to support it. Without it system performance would remain constrained.

There were database problems too. There were still no database recovery procedures documented. Recovery, therefore, could not be undertaken by operators, and so was an unnecessarily time consuming task. Relatively small segments of database would take eight hours to reorganise. A major update of the whole database was a long drawn out and fraught process. Combined with other operational problems it made for very stressful conditions. The reports on system performance make depressing reading. The following is a sample relating to the National Wage Case (NWC) applicable at the end of 1979. (The National Wage Case is a regular industrial process which determines pay levels for large groups of employees in Australia.).

> '. . . The mass change suite was run on 16 December in an attempt to correct records which were unchanged from the July National Wage Case. Numerous hardware faults were encountered. As a result, the mass change was not completed

by start of business on Monday 17 December and the database remained as at the update of 13 December. The P&E update of 20 December was not run due to operational problems.

'2. On Monday 17 December during the prime shift, updates for Leave, Ed. Quals and Des/Sal were processed. No updates were processed on Tuesday due to air conditioning problems all day Monday which prevented the communications system from being available. No Framework updates were run on Wednesday evening. Transactions entered on Wednesday for Leave, Ed. Quals and Des/Sal were processed during prime shift on Thursday. Transactions entered on Thursday were processed on Thursday evening.'

The next report for 28th December to 3rd January read:

'The pre-National Wage Case mass change was again attempted on 3 January. The run failed due to problems with database recovery. It was subsequently re-run successfully on the test system. The intention is to re-attempt the mass change on 8 January.'

They finally completed the mass change for the National Wage Case over 19-20 January, more than one month after they started. The Progress Meeting for 21st January recorded that, 'The Computer Operations section is passing through a rather traumatic period with a number of hardware problems occurring at a time when the workload is increasing and staff are on leave'.

As was noted earlier, it is impossible to say how many of these problems would have arisen if earlier problems associated with siting the equipment and the change of technical strategy had not taken place. The fact is that as at the end of 1979 they were affecting operational performance and requiring considerable attention.

10.5.2.7 Leave and other developments

The major new development of 1978 was the full Leave system. The Board's own personnel section had completed its pick up of data for the prototype system in December 1977. 1978 was spent building from that prototype. It was a particularly complex application incorporating very many conditional rules. There was also a discrepancy between the theory and the practice of leave management. As noted earlier, departmental managers treated as discretionary some regulations which were non-discretionary. Where entitlements were to be calculated automatically according to the rules discretion could no longer be exercised as easily. The development proceeded largely according to plan. However, although there were experienced personnel staff on the development team, no formal systems analysis was performed. The development process itself continued as if it were a prototype with the subject matter staff still specifying processes to programmers at their terminals. By September they had reached a stage where a new version of the Leave system was ready for pilot implementation in Education.

The designation/salary table system (Des/Sal) which was to run on the mainframe was taken from proposal to initial implementation during 1978. Its successful use for the first time late that year also took advantage of the network to make available rates of pay via enquiry transactions and the interrogation system to produce a listing of the changes. The system itself was largely the work of a single computer systems officer. Ten years later it was still in operation in the Public Service Commission, a tangible success for Mandata.

Two further sub-systems were developed. One was to record educational qualifications and any in-service training courses attended. This was a necessary base of information for manpower planning. It was a relatively undemanding information storage and retrieval system. It was only implemented in a few departments before Mandata was terminated. The other system developed was for supporting program planning for staffing. It was called Programs/Forward Staff Estimates (Progs/FSE). It was fully programmed, but never implemented.

10.5.2.8 Implementation and operation

In parallel with these developments there was a continuing push to implement the Productivity system in user departments. Table 10.3 and figure 10.10 display the progress of implementation in terms of records computerised.

The numbers belied the ease of the task. There were complaints from user departments throughout the year. In January 1978, the Department of Defence had written to the Chairman of the Mandata Consultative Committee complaining that 1300 records had gone missing from an update without being flagged by the system. He also noted that the turnaround for ad hoc interrogations using SMILE (the Productivity interrogation system) was, at more than 48 hours, less than satisfactory. The complaint about SMILE was to be echoed many times over the next year by aggrieved departmental representatives. By May the implementation section was faced with a backlog of 1400 errors at Defence and a measure of user resentment. The situation was not good, but some user alienation at the early stages of an implementation is not uncommon.

One locus for expressions of discontent was the operational level coordinating forum called the Mandata User Group (infelicitously abbreviated to MUG) which met approximately monthly. So as to isolate users involved in further development from hearing too many criticisms, MUG was split into two, one addressing development issues, the other operational matters.

Relations between the MPO and departments varied depending upon the individual characteristics of the implementers and coordinators as well as the problems encountered. With some departments it was a running battle. Even the most committed and obliging of departments were affected at times. At the beginning of 1979 Education reported that system downtime had caused staff frustrations and near revolt against the system. In MPO there was a sense of resentment about the more negative users. The following quotation is indicative:

> 'I am concerned and annoyed that [name of departmental officer] felt it necessary to raise these two points in the form of an unanswered complaint when in fact both were discussed and resolved before the MUG meeting. This is not the first occasion of such tactics and I can only assume that he does not conceive of the damage he causes to the spirit of co-operation. . . . A history of such tactics throughout the [department name] implementation process has undermined what would otherwise have been a sympathetic attitude.'

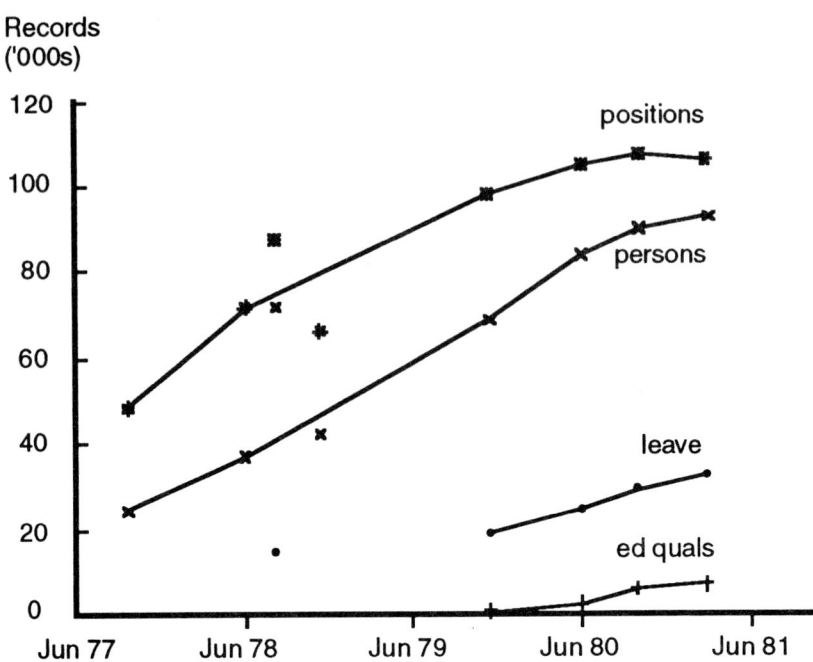

Figure 10.10. Graph of the pick up of records 1977-1981

Table 10.3. The progressive pick up of records 1977-1981

Date	Positions (*)	Persons (x)	Leave (•)	Ed Quals (+)
11/77	47,000	23,000	-	-
6/78	72,000	37,000	-	-
8/78	87,000	72,000	14,000	-
12/78	66,000	43,000	Unknown	-
12/79	98,000	68,000	19,000	1,000
6/80	105,000	83,000	25,000	3,000
10/80	107,000	90,000	29,000	4,000
3/81	106,000	92,000	33,000	5,000

The data in this table are drawn from various sources, and are obviously inconsistent. The data points for 8/78 and 12/78 are marked in the graph but excluded from the curves for this reason.

There was little they could do about it. A marginal note plaintively sums up the adversarial nature of some of these relationships, 'so to round 5'.

10.5.2.9 Decline in '79

The project director's reports to the Board in the first half of 1979 reflect a sense of optimism that progress was good under the circumstances. On 6th April, after a successful run of the update on the MPO mainframe, he wrote to all project staff thanking them for their efforts and indicating that they were satisfactorily placed and would have been better situated but for factors outside the project's control. 'This time next year,' he wrote, 'we should have the 'winning post' in clear view'. Through May, June and July his reports continued to exhibit optimism. It was even proposed to try to convince departments to stop maintaining the SPR cards, thereby eliminating the cost of departments maintaining both Mandata and manual records. By this stage all processing had been moved to the Board's mainframe.

Mid-1979 would have been the highpoint of optimism. Before the end of the year, the mood in MPO had turned to depression because staff simply could not sustain an adequate level of service.

At the beginning of 1979 there had been user complaints about the level of service. The crucial difference from earlier years was that users and MPO had expectations that matters would improve. The presumption was that conversion to the MPO mainframe would achieve this. The introduction of the specialised Mandata Interrogation Package would yield benefits through its flexibility to produce output, while Leave would extend to all Mandata departments facilities that would yield tangible staff savings. But, the complaints persisted throughout the year

The main systems they installed, P&E and Leave, were still seriously flawed. In addition, the Processing Framework software was now in use under conditions that tested it to the full. It proved both to have bugs and to need amendments to accommodate some of the conditions under which it was being used. The mainframe continued to experience hardware faults. The combination of problems meant very inconsistent service.

In early March 1979, the Implementation section

recommended with qualifications that Leave be accepted as a production system. There remained significant problems which it was proving difficult to test because the machine was fully booked two nights per week for testing the conversion process. There were also limited overtime funds available. The most important limitation at this early stage was that the on-line enquiries were not working properly. The release therefore was restricted to Canberra with daily updates of transactions submitted to the Canberra Mandata receipt and distribution point. (Such points in Canberra and other state centres were called 'cells'.) In announcing this, MPO stressed that on-line enquiries were for essential uses only and that the normal mode of enquiry was in batch. The Department of Defence challenged this immediately, noting that this was not what had been advertised in the Leave product description. The impression was that MPO was backing away from the spirit of its commitment.

By July all departments' P&E processing had been transferred to the mainframe. By the 5th of that month there were 440 records showing as out of phase, ie where the establishment record for a position did not match with the record of the person who was supposed to fill it.

In early August, the Board's own personnel staff were complaining of having 57 errors arising from its Mandata processing of which only two were its own mistakes. At just this time, the Mandata Consultative Committee agreed to set up a working group with MPO called the Fault Analysis Task Force. This was to clear all known faults. In September MPO launched an independent initiative to try to bring system reliability for P&E and Leave up to 95%. In view of what the director now called 'the gravity of our situation' he placed seven of his senior staff on call 24 hours a day for Monday to Friday so that snap decisions could be made about how to proceed in the case of operational problems.

In early October, a permanent change was made from two to three computer shifts. At the same time MPO achieved a measure of success. On 12th November it was reported to the Project Progress meeting that since 28th September there had been 26 consecutive successful updates of P&E. The criterion for success was that the update should be completed by 9.00am. However, problems had occurred on 8 of these nights, but the problem had been resolved in time to complete the processing. Thus, though operational success was being achieved, it was still a bumpy course.

Leave's operational performance was also improved. However, its functionality was causing problems. By 4th December the Project Progress meeting recognised that, 'Users are losing confidence in the Leave system which is displaying a number of faults'. For example, it failed to cope with the idiosyncrasies of shift workers. For some departments, like the Board itself, this was a small irritant. Having only 27 shift workers, they could return to card records. Business and Consumer Affairs by contrast had more than 700. They wanted the system to process these records automatically. A problem which affected all users was the fact that the system failed to step through different categories of sick leave available to an officer. What this meant was that if somebody had 6 weeks sick leave credits on full pay and 8 weeks on half pay and they were ill for 9 weeks, the system could not automatically deduct the 6 weeks full pay leave and 3 weeks half-pay leave. Instead, users had to submit one transaction to precisely exhaust the full pay sick credits and then another for the half pay. Since there were many more than two categories of sick leave credit the clerical solution was very time consuming and error prone. In addition, it required that clerks know in advance exactly what credits the officer had prior to submitting the transaction. It was no improvement on the existing manual procedures.

The worry for MPO with these problems was that they were considerably harder than P&E problems to resolve. It subsequently took 41 pages of detailed processing rules to specify step-through sick leave, and over a year to prepare this enhancement for implementation. The introduction of 24 hour clock processing to cover shift workers was likewise an extended process. There were many other problems. The processing for long service leave required to be completely respecified because of the problems it created. And there were omissions such as sick leave for temporary staff in their first year of service. There were also one-off corrections to be made. In one case, a year value had been incorrectly stored. This had been temporarily rectified on the enquiry screen by displaying the year recorded minus one. This made the information displayed correct, but left the error in the record untouched. It needed permanent repair. The list of difficulties thrown up by Leave was discouragingly long.

MIP too gave chronic problems. MIP was the replacement for SMILE, the Productivity interrogation package. It was heavy in machine usage, and there was often a long backlog.

Meetings of the Fault Analysis Task Force were convened weekly, sometimes more often. Faults were recorded and corrected at great speed. For example, between 17th October and 6th December the group met seven times, listing 40 new faults and correcting 33 of them. In view of the fact that each fault had to be diagnosed, a solution specified, the program changed by Applications Development staff or Software staff and then tested and agreed by Implementation, this was an impressive effort. It was not without its tensions though. In mid-October users were back on the attack, accusing the MPO of deleting faults from the list unresolved. The MPO's response was indicative of a difficulty common to implementation and operation. The items removed were not faults, they said, but enhancements and this exercise was strictly intended to clear up faults. The tension manifested itself not just in the accusation but in the MPO's view that the users in question were 'mudslinging'. The episode highlights the difficulties that can occur when there is pressure on a project. MPO was naturally trying to reduce the immediate pressures to an absolute minimum. Defence wanted to get the best it could from MPO. The general issue, whether items are faults or enhancements, is often a matter of perception. If a user office cannot work effectively because the system is inadequately specified, is that a bug to be rectified or an enhancement for future development? Either way it is a flaw. It can be deferred at the cost of goodwill or it can be given attention at some opportunity cost.

1979 had started out promising well for the project organisation. During the second half of the year the implications of the 1976 revised strategy began to become clearer. Matters were exacerbated late in the year by the publication of the Public Accounts Committee's report on Mandata and the critical storm that followed. This is discussed further in section 10.5.3.2 below.

10.5.3 External scrutiny - 1976 to 1980

Neither the extended decision process in the initiation phase nor the Auditor-General's brief notice of Mandata in 1975 prepared the project for the extraordinary level of scrutiny that it was to face from 1976 to 1980. (The consultants' review has already been noted in section 10.4.1.3.) The Auditor-General's Office (AGO) pursued the project for the whole of the period. Picking up on the

Auditor's criticisms, the Public Accounts Committee also investigated. The press amplified the scrutineers' criticisms.

The external scrutiny of Mandata was unparalleled in the Australian Public Service. It was a major contingency which had the effect of imposing considerable constraints which drained resources. The criticisms were made very public with the effect that they were damaging to morale and to the project's ability to raise support. This was to limit subsequent strategic options.

Chronology 10.5. The Auditor-General's investigations 1975-1981

Date	Event
Sep 75	A-G's 1974-75 report first mentions Mandata
Feb 76	AGO advises of intention to review Mandata
Apr 76	AGO review commences
Sep 76	A-G's 1975-76 report tabled criticising Mandata
Sep 77	A-G's 1976-77 report tabled in Parliament
Feb 78	AGO gives notice of new study
Mar 78	Commissioner lunches with the Auditor-General
Apr 78	AGO agrees to review LeaveProto
Jun 78	AGO advises LeaveProto sound
Jul 78	AGO starts 8 week study
Sep 78	A-G's 1977-78 report tabled in Parliament
Oct 78	AGO conducts exit interview
Nov 78	AGO report sent to Board
Mar 79	Board rejects substance of AGO report
May 79	AGO carries out follow up review
Jun 79	Exit interview for follow up review
Sep 79	Further AGO study initiated
Sep 79	A-G's 1978-79 report tabled in Parliament
Jan 80	AGO conducts exit interview
Apr 80	A-G's half-yearly report highly critical of Mandata
Jul 80	Board responds to A-G's 1980 report
Aug 80	A-G agrees to relax the pressure
Nov 80	Treasury minister requests responses to criticisms by February
Mar 81	MPO embarrassed by Board's failure to meet minister's deadline

10.5.3.1 The Auditor-General's investigations 1976-1980

Mandata received its first mention in the Auditor-General's report in 1975. Its existence was noted - no more. In February 1976, the Auditor-General's Office intimated that it would conduct an initial review of Mandata. This was the start of a four year critique which depleted both resources and morale. Chronology 10.5 shows what an extended process it was.

In his 1976 report the Auditor-General devoted one-and-a-half pages to matters his office considered to be of concern (Auditor-General 1976). These included accepting delivery of equipment prior to contracts being signed; potential under-use of equipment; unnecessarily long familiarisation for software contractors; and equipment siting. This was the first time that a computer systems development had figured so large in the Auditor-General's Report.

In 1977 Mandata rated even more space (Auditor-General 1977). Although a good deal of this was merely a follow-up of issues raised before, the inclusion of a section entitled 'Project slippage' set a critical tone.

The 1978 report (Auditor-General 1978), though still extensive, was more a status report and update on matters previously raised than the results of a new study. However, it served to maintain the pressure on MPO.

The 1979 report showed signs of frustration on the part of the Auditor-General's Office (Auditor-General 1979, pp90-92). For example,

> 'My office informed the Board it considered: a number of key organisational control functions either lacked adequate definition or were not recognised and accepted by staff; . . .'

And,

> 'It was represented to the Board that in a project as large and complex as MANDATA, extending over many years and involving considerable resources, a detailed, long-term plan was considered important to the effective and timely completion of the project;'

The report contained further expressions of concern.

In April 1980 the Auditor-General completed his series on Mandata (Auditor-General 1980, pp56-62). He provided an extensive and radical critique of nearly seven pages. The criticism was explicit, larded with normative language. There was reference to 'deficiencies', 'criticisms', 'weaknesses', 'poor level', 'unsuitable', and so on. Most damning of all, recommendations were made for redevelopment of the Personnel and Establishments sub-system. It was an expression of the opinion that the very core of the existing application system was irretrievable.

Relations with the Auditor-General's Office during its investigations were often stressful. In 1978, MPO attempted to disarm the Auditor's staff by coopting them. First, the Auditor-General's Office was asked to lend an officer to the Impact Evaluation Study team. Then it was approached for critical advice on the controls in the LeaveProto system with a view to insuring the full Leave system against criticism. Later in the year the Public Accounts Committee was told that it was MPO's intention to involve the Auditor-General's staff as much as possible.

In the event MPO found itself in a bind requiring further defensive tactics. The request for help with Leave crossed with a notification by the Auditor-General of a further investigation to follow-up his previous criticisms and to carry out a more detailed review of schedules and cost-benefits. Clearly, MPO could not easily resist this because a follow-up was reasonable and having asked for involvement of the Auditor's staff it could not make a principled objection to further reviews. Instead, the director approached his own management with a request for help. The new strategy was simple. A member of the Board would have lunch with the Auditor-General himself and explain the need for relieving the pressure on the project so that it could have a chance to show its worth. There had, as he pointed out, been a lot of investigation over the last twelve months. The outcome of this lunchtime meeting was apparent success. The Auditor-General, it was reported, had said that 'his boys would only be in there to help and would not be overturning the project for another 12 months'.

The relief this brought to the Mandata executive was reinforced when on the last day of the financial year the Auditor's office advised that subject to a number of provisos the LeaveProto system was basically sound. It did, however, sound a note of warning that MPO should watch out for the quality of the data on pick up. A 1973 study had shown that 25% of departmental records were in error. This was unchanged by subsequent amendments to procedures. MPO proposed to pick up the data without 'purifying' them and worry about correcting inaccuracies later. Such an approach was a necessary evil. MPO had hoped that the Auditor-General could be persuaded to back this policy, but was now disappointed.

The relief did not last long. In July 1978 the Auditor-General's staff returned for a further investigation to be conducted by three officers over 8 weeks. However, the terms of reference suggested that the policy of cooption was beginning to work. The review included consideration of computer assisted audit techniques for field auditors, especially in respect of the reconciliation of personnel and pay systems. In other words, it was to be, in part, a developmental exercise for the Auditor-General's staff. Mandata was being used as a testbed. This signalled cooperation rather than criticism. In addition, there was to be an evaluation of existing and proposed audit controls in Mandata. On the 12th October the auditors conducted an exit interview with MPO, sending their report to the Board on 2nd November. The report unexpectedly covered the organisation and management of the project and general control issues. The director noted,

> '. . . a significant discrepancy between the terms of reference and the final report. We share the view that they are 'putting one over us' which is of concern having regard to the discussions between [the Board member and the Auditor-General] earlier this year.'

The MPO's response was for the director and Board Secretary to confront the Assistant Auditor responsible, launching an attack on several fronts. First, they made it clear that while the Auditor-General was soon to have power to conduct efficiency audits in the Public Service, the legislation had not yet been passed. The implication was that the Auditor-General had exceeded his authority. Next, they made the point that after extensive scrutiny in the previous year they had received Cabinet approval for continuing the project. Third, all this scrutiny was acting against the project by deflecting senior management from the task of managing the project. Fourth, they pointed out that they were continuing to work with only 75% of the staff necessary for the

Mandata - A Case History 231

job. It added up to a strong argument that the Auditor-General's staff were aggravating an already difficult situation by exceeding their authority in criticising a project that had support at the highest level. They took the sting from the confrontation by indicating that they would be pleased to see the Auditor's comments in line with the original objectives. (It is worth noting here that they made appeal to Cabinet approval. The very fact of a formal approval over a year earlier still served as a resource to combat criticism.)

The Board responded to the Auditor's report in writing in March 1979, and this was followed up by a further two week investigation in May and June and a second exit interview. The Board in turn made a further response at the end of June so that its position could be included with the Auditor-General's report to Parliament. The whole process had taken a full year and had occupied a considerable amount of time for senior members of the project. Nevertheless, the report presented to Parliament was still critical on a broad front, mentioning operational controls, lack of plans and adequate project control, lack of disaster back-up and project slippage.

Again in July 1979 the Chairman of the Board requested help from the Auditor-General in an attempt to improve Mandata's image. The result was a review lasting from September 1979 until the following January, with tense exchanges reaching a climax in the highly critical report to Parliament of April 1980 and a conclusion in August when the pressure was eventually relieved. The April 1980 report included among others the following comments: '. . . the current P & E sub-system and its basic design were unsuitable for effective control'; 'serious deficiencies in ADP documentation'; and, 'particular concern at the continuing lack of a detailed strategic development plan' (Auditor-General 1980, pp61-62).

Both the investigative process and its critical outcomes were costly. The mutual recriminations were unpleasant. The level of the tension is clear from notes by an apparently senior member of the Board on a letter from the Auditor-General in 1980 where it is recorded that the Auditor-General 'intends to take the pressure off and let (them) get Mandata settled down over the next 2 years'.

The whole process was costly in staff time first dealing with the investigations themselves, and then answering the criticisms. The MPO's response to the April 1980 report by the Auditor-General ran to 43 pages. And, it did the Public Service Board's image and authority no good. At one stage, when attempting to pressurise the Auditor-General via an appeal to Public Service solidarity, the Chairman noted, 'One of the hitherto uncosted 'costs' of Mandata is the damage which continued public criticism is doing to the Board's standing'. It was pressure such as this that forced the Board to continue to support the project.

10.5.3.2 The Public Accounts Committee's investigations - 1977 to 1979

As a result of the general criticisms of the Auditor-General in 1976, the Public Accounts Committee decided to conduct a review of computer acquisition in the Public Service. The particular criticisms directed by the Auditor-General at Mandata then led the Committee to investigate Mandata and report on it separately. Chronology 10.6 notes the major dates.

The Committee gathered its information in several ways. It held hearings at which senior project personnel were examined. The early hearings were distinctly tense, the Committee interpreting the Board's staff's stance as unhelpful. Subsequently, under the second director in 1978, a more cooperative spirit was manifest. But this came too late to alter the tone of the Committee's interim statement to the Parliament in May 1978. This was critical and resulted in a spate of adverse press coverage (see section 10.5.3.3 below).

Chronology 10.6. Relations with the Public Accounts Committee 1977-1980

Date	Event
Jun 77	PAC advises of intention to investigate Mandata
Sep 77	PAC hearings
Oct 77	PAC hearings
May 78	PAC chairman criticises Mandata in the Parliament
Aug 78	PAC visits MPO
Sep 78	PAC hearings
Oct 79	PAC report tabled in Parliament
Sep 80	Finance Minute in response to PAC report tabled

The Committee made a brief visit to the project's offices on 14th August 1978, a visit sufficiently serious for the Chairman to be present to introduce the presentations and to formally state his personal commitment to the project. The strategy adopted was to present a dispassionate review of the situation - there were many difficulties against which the project struggled, progress was less than perfect. The tone struck was not defensive so much as that of a disinterested observer. MPO was now trying to put things right while recognising that not everything could be done at once. It appears to have persuaded the Committee of MPO's good faith.

Behind the formal hearings of the Committee lay the research of its secretariat. The Committee's secretariat requested copies of many documents to assist with the detailed assessment that took place outside the committee room. In addition, they had an independent consultant as technical adviser. He had substantial Canberra experience, and was able to undertake informal investigations through existing contacts as well as guiding the Committee as to what questions it should ask.

Providing documents proved an embarrassment to MPO. Some the Board refused to release on the grounds that they were inter-departmental or were Cabinet submissions. Other requests were irresistible. In the late winter of 1978 a meeting of senior project staff was convened to discuss how to meet the Committee's requirements 'without appearing to have no project documentation at all'. The Committee's files hold many MPO documents bearing the telling legend - draft 1.0. This and requests for time in which to provide them suggest that the solution was to write the documents for the Committee.

The hearings were completed in 1978, but it was not until 9th October 1979 that the full report was tabled in Parliament. It accepted the consultants' conclusion of two years earlier that it was worth persevering with the project, and it emphasised that the benefits should be achieved promptly. It was severely critical of various aspects of the project's history. Its major concerns were with the absence of clearly stated objectives and with the lack of a statement of requirements. This had meant that it was impossible to monitor and control the project because there was no baseline against which to compare progress. The lack of a detailed plan of what needed to be done was also criticised. Many other aspects of the project were singled out including delays in finalising contracts for major items of equipment and the dispute with NCDC over siting the computer. This catalogue of criticisms was taken badly by many in MPO because staff felt it failed to recognise the changes that had taken place in the year since the Committee had completed its hearings.

The Board's response came in a Finance Minute (JCPA 1980), the obligatory form of reply. It rejected most of the Committee's criticisms in detail, but acknowledged some earlier shortcomings. Its concern was to limit the damage to the standing of the Public Service Board. It was by then easy to acknowledge previous shortcomings because most of the major figures from prior stages were no longer associated with the Board.

10.5.3.3 The press

The press had been involved from early in Mandata's life with minor coverage of the proposal and its benefits drawn from press releases. It became a serious influence in 1976 with the article in *The Canberra Times*. From then on the press kept an eye out for Mandata news.

The Public Accounts Committee's interim report to Parliament was picked up and reported in the press thereby further directing attention to the project's shortcomings. Reports appeared the next day in three influential dailies, *The Canberra Times*, *The Melbourne Age*, and *The Australian*. Further articles followed. Almost all were either explicitly or implicitly critical. Only Frank Linton-Simpkins (1978) in an article in *The Australian* on the 6th June gave any support. He asserted that Mandata was at least a good idea. Others were far keener to stress the incompetence of the Public Service and its waste of public money.

The Committee held a press conference on 9th October 1979, the day its report was tabled, which guaranteed a further spate of articles. Most merely reported and reflected the Committee's criticisms. Mandata subsequently even featured in a critical article in *Penthouse* magazine (Newton 1980).

The press's role was to magnify what was already severely undermining criticism. Canberra is a small, one company town, where the company is the state (Hoyle & Thynne 1981). All the people Mandata staff would have mixed with socially and in their work would have read or heard the criticisms. It was an invidious situation for the individual members of the project. The press reports damaged morale, encouraging those with alternative employment options to leave the project, and deterring others from joining it.

10.6 THE DECISION TO SCALE BACK - 1980

It took a comparatively short time for the optimism of early 1979 to evaporate. Not only had MPO's operational systems proved flawed, but the project organisation had been publicly subjected to corrosive criticisms, amplified by unsympathetic press coverage. There was an acute need to achieve something so as to increase the project's standing. The strategy adopted was to scale back the project. Chronology 10.7 details the process.

Chronology 10.7. The decision to scale back Mandata

Date	Event
Oct 79	MCC establishes Sub-Committee on Development Priorities
Nov 79	MPO establishes own Strategic Planning Group
Feb 80	Board acknowledges difficulty of extending P&E
Mar 80	Board announces review of Mandata
Apr 80	MCC Sub-Committee on Development Priorities reports
Apr 80	Board decides to scale back Mandata
May 80	Submission to Cabinet proposing scale back
Jul 80	Cabinet approves scale back

On 17th October the Mandata Consultative Committee agreed to establish a sub-committee to report on development priorities. It met over a six month period and formulated a policy for future development. User confidence was so low that it was easily agreed that what was required was a viable system. The intention was to get P&E and Leave working to specification and then to define what was needed for the total system to be considered viable. However, users' interpretations of 'viable' were constrained by the nature of the existing Mandata systems. They were not being given complete freedom to specify their requirements. It was agreed that the existing system was not capable of extension to provide significant benefits beyond the displacement of SPR cards. The best that could be hoped was the complete replacement of cards by electronic media. The detail was left to be worked out by groups of departmental representatives and officers of the MPO.

At the same time MPO pursued its own planning process, establishing a strategic planning group within MPO in November. This was not altogether a voluntary initiative, the Public Accounts Committee having recommended as critically important that the Board publish a statement of objectives and determine the detailed requirements of the system. There was a mixture of views as to the best strategy to follow. A senior project figure mounted a brief campaign to promote a return to the old Mandata aims. He wanted to try to achieve an integrated P&E and Leave system using the full range of facilities originally envisaged. It was at odds with the political realities. Mandata could not command adequate staff of quality to make this a realistic option. At the same time, discussions within MPO revealed a growing consensus that P&E was not capable of major extension. By February this was clear even to the Board's top management. A briefing note described the Auditor's staff's views about the non-extensibility of the core P&E system as 'independent assessment along similar lines to the thinking which has been emerging from the MPO over the last month or so'.

In April, the Mandata Co-ordinating Committee's sub-committee produced a draft report only to find it pre-empted by the MPO's proposal to revise the project's objectives. The sub-committee redrafted its development priorities in line with the MPO submission to the Board to scale back the objectives of the project. The proposal was to stop extending Mandata facilities to other departments, indeed to offer the Auditor-General's Office and the Department of Prime Minister and Cabinet the option to withdraw. (Both accepted promptly.) The proposal was then to divide further work into two phases. One was scheduled for June 1981, the other for January/March 1982. Within each phase enhancements were divided into P&E, Leave, and Reports. On 30th April MCC received and endorsed the proposal to scale back. On 3rd July the Chairman wrote to departmental heads and to the Mandata Consultative Group advising them of Cabinet's endorsement of the scale back. No doubt the decision was made easier for all parties by the Auditor-General's attacks in his April 1980 report to Parliament. Mandata was ready for its penultimate phase.

10.7 TOWARDS A MINIMUM VIABLE SYSTEM - JUNE 1980 TO APRIL 1981

The period between the end of June 1980 and the end of April 1981 was marked by the reduction in pressure on the project. The Auditor-General agreed to relieve the pressure. Users chastened by their experience and recognising the difficulties of the system were less openly critical. The Mandata Consultative Group proved an exception. Within the project internal tensions were experienced along with a sense of uncertainty as to the future as politico-economic conditions worsened.

10.7.1 The staff associations and the Mandata Consultative Group

Staff representatives made no critical interventions in the Mandata project. From the standpoint of the MPO, MCG was largely a drain on resources. Its meetings often absorbed in the order of 9 Board staff, while providing it with papers and servicing the meetings was time consuming, the more so when the meetings were held in Melbourne.

MCG was initially most concerned to assure itself that the system was secure from interference and from unwarranted access. The various staff associations were keen to assure their members' privacy. Subsequently, there was more serious concern that staff savings would adversely affect manning levels in the Public Service and was therefore a legitimate area of interest.

The Board created a small furore by refusing to release to MCG the Impact Evaluation Report. In April 1979 one of the staff representatives denounced the Board for this lack of candour in an address to a UN Conference on Science and Technology for Development. A subsequent paper for a Royal Institute of Public Administration conference deployed many of the Public Accounts Committee's criticisms to savage the Board. The file copy of this latter is marked, 'The bastards!'. Clearly, the criticisms hurt.

The staff associations appeared to further justify management's suspicions that they were spoiling for a fight when they made a formal complaint to the Board that they had not been consulted about the scale-back decision. Since scale-back was only likely to lessen the threat to jobs it must have seemed a peculiarly perverse response. That such a response had not been expected by MPO is evident from a briefing note which anticipated that 'the staff savings issue would . . . be defused' and that ' an already declining interest in Mandata through MCG will decline further under the scale-back of objectives . . . '. A file note described the staff associations' complaints as an attempt to discredit management.

The staff associations' interventions either through MCG or independent of it did not force the MPO into changes. They merely absorbed resources and amplified the criticisms. From MPO's point of view the staff associations were kicking the project when it was down.

10.7.2 Implementing the Public Accounts Committee's recommendations

In the months that followed the scale-back the project was slowly placed on a sounder footing through a number of changes. First, the agreed reduction and documentation of goals helped reduce uncertainty in MPO. The magnitude of the task was at last defined. The decision had been made to concentrate on the existing departments and on existing sub-systems. The longer term members of the project team saw the objectives as attainable. They now knew enough about the applications to better recognise what the difficulties would be in reaching a minimum viable system.

In October 1980 the project was consolidated into four sections: Applications Development, User Requirements and Implementation, Operations and Systems Software, and Project Co-ordination.

For the longer term, progress was made toward adapting a proprietary methodology for use under Mandata's special circumstances. Its purchase had been agreed in January 1980. The adaptation was performed by MPO with help from the vendor's staff. It was designed to provide a systematic work process for the enhancement and maintenance load which was now Mandata's chief task. The new methodology was gradually introduced into different sections.

Perhaps as a result of the adoption of a formal methodology, this phase of Mandata was characterised by the emergence of its clearest documentation. Functional specifications were prepared in substantial detail showing what each enhancement was required to do. The existence of these documents meant that the development of programs and their testing could be better controlled. Thus Applications Development would write or amend a program for User Requirements who would then test the finished program and return it for further programming if necessary. It would only be added to the live system when formally accepted by User Requirements staff.

Another aspect of documentation was the effort devoted to preparing training manuals and user manuals. Both had been the subject of some criticism in the past. The work prepared in this period was far more obviously user oriented than previous attempts. Experience had enabled the Implementation and Training staff to understand much better what was required from them.

But despite progress there were tensions. One key executive relationship came to a head with the subordinate being transferred from the project. There were other tensions at lower levels, arising from the formal relationship between Applications Development and Implementation as each section blamed the other for delays to work in progress. In view of the criticisms and pressures, and the increasingly precarious position of the project such tensions were hardly surprising.

This penultimate period of Mandata's existence involved a continuing attempt to provide a sound service to the user departments. Complaints were dealt with systematically, and major enhancements to Leave progressed. At the same time, the wider political and economic environment was gloomy. The Liberal administration was re-elected in October 1980. Its policies were austere. The Minister for Industry and Commerce, Phillip Lynch, was given charge of a task force called the Review of Commonwealth Functions whose purpose was to reduce the functions of the Public Service. It was aptly nicknamed 'the Razor Gang'. It would have been clear to all that Mandata was an obvious and easy target. So, for the six months from November 1980 to April 1981 MPO continued its work under the shadow of a possible termination.

10.8 TERMINATION

On 30th April 1981 the Prime Minister of Australia announced to the Parliament that Mandata was to be terminated. The political benefits for the Board were substantial. The Board provided the administrative support to the Review. The termination of Mandata would show that in deciding on its cuts the Board was not unduly influencing the Review to its own advantage. A year earlier it had been noted on the files that the Board would be happy to give up its responsibility for Mandata. (The minutes of the meeting of the Mandata Consultative Committee of 18th June 1980 recorded that a departmental member had recognised that 'the Board was not able to yield its ultimate responsibility for the Mandata project . . . ' against which it was noted, 'It would if it could find someone to take it on!') Termination relieved the Board of a management burden. It also relieved the Board of the continual criticism that had been directed at it since 1976.

Within the Mandata Program Office the consensus was that the decision was mistaken. The accepted wisdom was that the project should have been axed years earlier, but not at this stage. By mid-1981 it was serving a useful function and many departmental users were dependent on it. Most of the faults for which it had been criticised had been corrected. The project had been consolidated. It therefore seemed to them that just as they had completed all the hard work, their achievements were thrown away. There were some who had given seven years of their working lives to the project. For them there was precious little to show for it. Worse still, they feared that their futures might be blighted as a result.

The project was to be closed down by the end of November. This meant that in the following six months 160 staff had to be redeployed. Since staff would leave as soon as they found new appointments in the Public Service, all the Computer Systems Officers were combined into a single, all-purpose, technical section.

The MPO had no future and so had little further interest in servicing its users. Its chief function now was to provide print outs of all the data held on the mainframe so that each department could start again as it saw fit, either clerically or by computer.

Small users would be off the system by 30th June, larger users by 30th September. The cost of this to departments went uncalculated. The project director revealed his view in a minute of a meeting with a journalist. He wrote, 'I tried to duck the question of [mainframe] compatibility (incompatibility more likely) with computers owned by Mandata users.' Further, 'I also tried to duck the question of the number of extra staff needed to run the manual system post-Mandata'.

Mandata - A Case History 241

Meanwhile, the Department of Administrative Services took responsibility for disposing of surplus equipment. The mainframe was given to the Department of Capital Territories, the very department which had been evicted from this same computer in 1978. This meant that the Board was forced to go cap in hand to Capital Territories for processing time to run the systems it was keeping such as the Des/Sal table system. With awful irony they told the Board that the Mandata machine would be too fully utilised. They could have time on a slower machine. The Board's remaining adp staff now found themselves working with a less advanced machine than that to which they had been accustomed in the previous five years. A sad *dénouement* to a story that started with such prospects.

10.9 EPILOGUE

The boundaries of any systems case history are difficult to define. Exactly when Mandata started as a project is unclear. The commencement of the feasibility study serves adequately. Its closedown can equally serve to define its end. But its effects continue to be felt.

In chapter 3, Kling's (1987) recognition of the importance of history was noted. His point is well illustrated here. Mandata's termination not only forced an immediate decentralisation of personnel processing, it also made it next to impossible to get a centralised adp system for personnel back on the agenda. Subsequent to the abandonment of Mandata as a central record of personnel and establishments data the Public Service Board wrote or commissioned two reports into adp in personnel (APSB 1983, APSB 1987). The first noted that there were 38 adp personnel systems in existence in the APS, and 14 new ones under development. There was a real concern that processing would fragment and with it the personnel records. Both reports address the need for a measure of centralisation. It is not hard to read them as somewhat regretful that a fully centralised approach would not be politically acceptable while the memory of Mandata remained.

When it was announced in 1987 that a number of departments would amalgamate into so called mega-departments such as Employment, Education and Training, the problem arose of choosing which department's system to use and then converting the records of the other amalgamating departments. This is a problem that would not have arisen had a centralised strategy been successful. Mandata may now be history but the influence of the project outcome is still felt.

More recently, an Audit Office report (Auditor-General 1991) has severely criticised the Department of Veterans' Affairs' development of a personnel system called PAPAS (Personnel and Pay Administration System) which it would not have needed had there been a central system. The repercussions continue.

Chapter 11
Analysis Of Mandata

The purpose of this chapter is to answer the research questions posed in chapter 9 using the conceptualisation of failure and the model of the process of failure developed in the earlier chapters. In doing this it exemplifies the use of the model for elucidating case studies.

The five research questions posed were:

(A) Was Mandata a failure?
(B) Why did Mandata fail? What were the causes of its failure?
(C) By what process did Mandata come to fail?
(D) What options were there for alternative support management strategies?
(E) Could the Mandata project have avoided failure?

Of these, questions (A) to (D) will be addressed in this chapter while (E) will be discussed in the concluding chapter.

11.1 WAS MANDATA A FAILURE?

Failure requires two conditions to be satisfied. First, it is necessary for all work on a system to have been terminated through lack of support. Second, it requires the system's supporters to be dissatisfied with what the system has done for them.

In the case of Mandata, the first condition was substantially satisfied by the governmental decision to terminate the system in 1981. It is true that some traces of the system remained. The Des/Sal sub-system continued to be operated by the Board for many years thereafter. Other departments continued to operate parts of the system. However, Mandata as an identifiable system ceased to exist after 1981.

In most cases, it is not easy to determine whether the second condition obtains, viz that supporters are dissatisfied with what a system has done for them. Consequently, we look not only for direct evidence in the form of criticisms, but also for surrogates that are indicative of supporter dissatisfaction. Table 11.1 summarises the situation regarding Mandata. It identifies the key supporters and the evidence suggestive of their dissatisfaction.

Table 11.1. Dissatisfaction of Mandata's supporters in 1981

Supporters	Evidence of Dissatisfaction
Cabinet	Termination of funding despite continuation of the application
Public Service Board	Indirect evidence - perceptions of dissatisfaction
Departmental heads	No resistance to termination despite continuation of application
Operational staff in departments	Mandata not 'viable' in 1980. Not yet 'viable' in 1981
Project organisation staff	Concerns for effects on individuals' careers

The Cabinet's dissatisfaction may be inferred from its termination of funding for the project. The Review of Commonwealth Functions was particularly concerned with evaluating the Australian Public Service with respect to the economics of its administration. The Cabinet, advised by the Review, decided to terminate Mandata because it was not yielding economic benefits consistent with government policy. That the same services still had to be provided makes the termination highly suggestive of Cabinet dissatisfaction.

That the Public Service Board was dissatisfied with Mandata can only be inferred indirectly. The system brought it little in the way of direct management benefits. Instead, it exposed it to persistent and damaging criticism over a period of years. The note referred to in chapter 10 which suggested that the Board would be happy to be relieved of responsibility for the project if only it could find someone to take it illustrates the perception that the Board was not satisfied.

It is hard to say how far departmental heads felt the system had failed them. There is no evidence that they made any effort to

Analysis Of Mandata 245

resist the possibility that the project would be axed.

Operational users in the departments were by no means totally dissatisfied with Mandata. Although they had criticised the system over several years, by 1981 it was integrated into the personnel and establishments functions of several departments. However, it had not been deemed 'viable' in 1980, and by April 1981 the improvements to make it 'viable' had not been completed. So, operational users could hardly be described as having been satisfied with the service they had received from Mandata, though it is doubtful that they would have chosen to withdraw support themselves.

Finally, there were the internal supporters, the members of the project organisation. Many of them felt that they had overcome the worst of the difficulties they had faced and to that extent enjoyed a sense of job satisfaction. At the same time, some felt anxiety as to the effect association with the project would have on their careers. Thus, members of the project organisation experienced a mixture of satisfaction and dissatisfaction.

On balance it is fair to say that at the time of its termination Mandata had failed to satisfy the interests of its supporters. To this extent it can be judged a failure. Nevertheless, as analysis of supporters' satisfaction shows, it would be surprising if in a project that survived as long as Mandata no stakeholders had had any of their interests served by the system. The problem for the project was that by 1981 not enough powerful supporters had had their interests satisfied or could see the prospect of their being satisfied. This situation requires further analysis to explain why Mandata failed.

11.2 WHY DID MANDATA FAIL?

The question, why did Mandata fail, is made all the more piquant because it is unclear how far the system's termination was a good business decision. As noted at the beginning of chapter 10, many members of the project organisation thought that termination was a mistake in 1981 because the worst of the problems had been overcome. It was accepted by MPO and the users alike that the system would never meet its original objectives, but it was still serving a number of operational needs for ten departments. A new strategy had been adopted that had not had time to work.

Moreover, the costs of closing down the project and of each department developing its own system appear to have been uncosted. The long term effect was noted at the end of the last chapter - two years after termination there were thirty-eight adp personnel systems in the APS and fourteen new ones under development. The dilemma can be thought of in these terms: Mandata was clearly not going to prove to have been a good financial investment, but on the other hand the cost savings from terminating Mandata in 1981 might well have been less than the costs incurred as a result of termination. It is this situation that makes it particularly interesting to understand why Mandata was terminated.

Table 11.2. Reasons for supporter dissatisfaction in 1981

Supporters	**Interests**	**Reasons for Dissatisfaction**
Cabinet	Reduced cost of APS	System not demonstrating favourable cost-benefit
Public Service Board	Statutory responsibilities Control of APS Corporate image	System not achieving demonstrable efficiencies Limited management benefits Press and institutional criticisms
Departmental heads	Departmental efficiency	No obvious benefits
Operational staff in depts	Ease of operation Ability to serve clientele	Continued use of SPRs Operational flaws
Project organisation	Job satisfaction Career prospects	Limited progress Negative public image of project

Terminal loss of support and supporter dissatisfaction are individually necessary and jointly sufficient conditions for failure. They are linked by the fact that negative evaluations can lead supporters to decide to withdraw support. In asking why Mandata failed, we must ask why it lost crucial support in 1981, why its supporters were dissatisfied, and what links there were between the two.

In view of the possible causal relationship from dissatisfaction to withdrawal of support, it makes sense to consider the question of dissatisfaction first. These matters have already been touched upon in the previous section. Table 11.2 sets out the situation in more detail.

Table 11.2 is not intended to suggest that Mandata had not served any of its supporters' interests. Rather the table shows that there were significant reasons for supporter dissatisfaction in 1981. The federal Cabinet's political agenda included giving high priority to controlling public spending. If Mandata had been able to demonstrate favourable cost-benefit figures then whatever other shortcomings it might have had it would have clearly satisfied Cabinet's interests. However, it had had trouble implementing in whole the features of the system which might have led to the originally projected benefits. The 1980 decision to scale back the project to a minimum viable system was an acknowledgement that Mandata was never going to yield economic benefits which would satisfy a government so concerned with the control of public spending.

The Public Service Board had always stood to make several gains from Mandata if it were to meet a reasonable proportion of its original objectives. The Board had statutory responsibilities for the efficiency of Public Service administration. Mandata promised to streamline personnel and establishments processing, but though it did provide new facilities including on-line access, ad hoc interrogations, and more flexible and up to date management information it did not reduce the staff required. The parallel operation of both Mandata and clerical record systems was continuing evidence that Mandata had not streamlined administrative procedures.

The Board had also stood to gain from the direct central control Mandata would give it over personnel and establishments matters by virtue of the management information it would provide in respect of the whole of the Australian Public Service, and the management tools that sub-systems such as Programs/Forward Staff Estimates would provide. The scale back decision had permanently restricted Mandata's coverage to the ten departments for which it operated. This meant that the service-wide benefits could not be obtained from the current system. That major management tools such as Programs/Forward Staff Estimates had not been implemented further limited management benefits.

The Board's third major interest was its status and position as the authority responsible for the Service as a whole. The public criticisms made by both the press and the institutional authorities such as the Public Accounts Committee and the Auditor-General were severely damaging to the Board's image, a point made by the Chairman to the Auditor-General in 1980, 'One of the hitherto uncosted 'costs' of Mandata is the damage which continued public criticism is doing to the Board's standing'.

Departmental heads had a statutory responsibility for the efficient running of their department, but because Mandata was not central to any department's operations, its importance was limited. For this reason, although Mandata did not deliver many obvious benefits to departmental heads, it is doubtful that they were particularly dissatisfied.

By 1981 Mandata had become integrated into the working procedures of many operational users. The scale back strategy also meant that the position was steadily improving. Nevertheless, there remained the problem of flaws in the system and the continuing operation of the clerical SPR system. Consequently, Mandata did not make it easy to conduct personnel and establishments business, nor did it make it easy to service the operational users' clients - the other officers of the Public Service and managers concerned with staffing.

Finally, as was mentioned in the previous section, although the members of the project organisation felt some satisfaction that they had overcome the worst of their problems, a system which had come closer to meeting its original objectives would have been more satisfying. Moreover, they felt concern that their career prospects might be damaged by association with the project. To this extent, then, the project organisation had reason to feel that the system had not served its interests well. Thus, all the project's main supporters had ground for some degree of dissatisfaction.

In answering the question why Mandata failed, the next stage is to explain why the system lost support and how supporter dissatisfaction affected this. Superficially it might seem that supporter dissatisfaction was sufficient reason for the withdrawal of support. However, the system was performing no worse in 1981

Analysis Of Mandata

than it had been in 1980 when it had been decided to reduce the project's ambitions. Consequently, there is a question to be answered about why the system was terminated after all.

The crucial changes between 1980 and 1981 were the establishment of the Review of Commonwealth Functions and the scale-back decision. The Review was charged with finding areas in which spending could be reduced. Mandata was an obvious target. The scale-back decision had the effect of removing much uncertainty about the project. There was no longer any possibility that Mandata might yield all the benefits to which the Board and the project organisation had aspired and on which it had traded. A major investment incentive had been removed. It would therefore have appeared to the Review that Mandata did not and would not meet the interests against which it was evaluating administrative activities.

However, this alone need not have resulted in termination of the system had the Board felt that it was in its interests to retain the project or had there been strong pressure from departments to keep it. But for departments, even though the operational users were partly dependent on Mandata, the personnel and establishments application was not sufficiently central to their missions for operational users' interests to justify permanent heads fighting for the system. This also meant that the project organisation lacked the power to leverage support either from the departments or the Board. Ultimately, it was not coping sufficiently well with a sufficiently important strategic contingency to be able to exercise the power to demand support.

Since the Board was not benefiting from the system it too lacked a reason to defend it. Indeed, the possibility of a governmental termination of funding was a politically satisfactory solution. It could be represented as *force majeure*. It relieved the Board of its responsibility without the need for an embarrassing admission of defeat. One theory current at the time suggested that the termination saved the Board from having to take any cuts to its core functions. If so, it was a doubly desirable outcome for the Board.

The reason that Mandata finally failed can be summarised as being a combination of the relative dissatisfaction of most supporters, the contingency of the government's policy of austerity together with the establishment of the Review of Commonwealth Functions to pursue that policy, and the prior reduction of the system's objectives which made explicit the limitations of the system and which contributed to the project organisation's limited power.

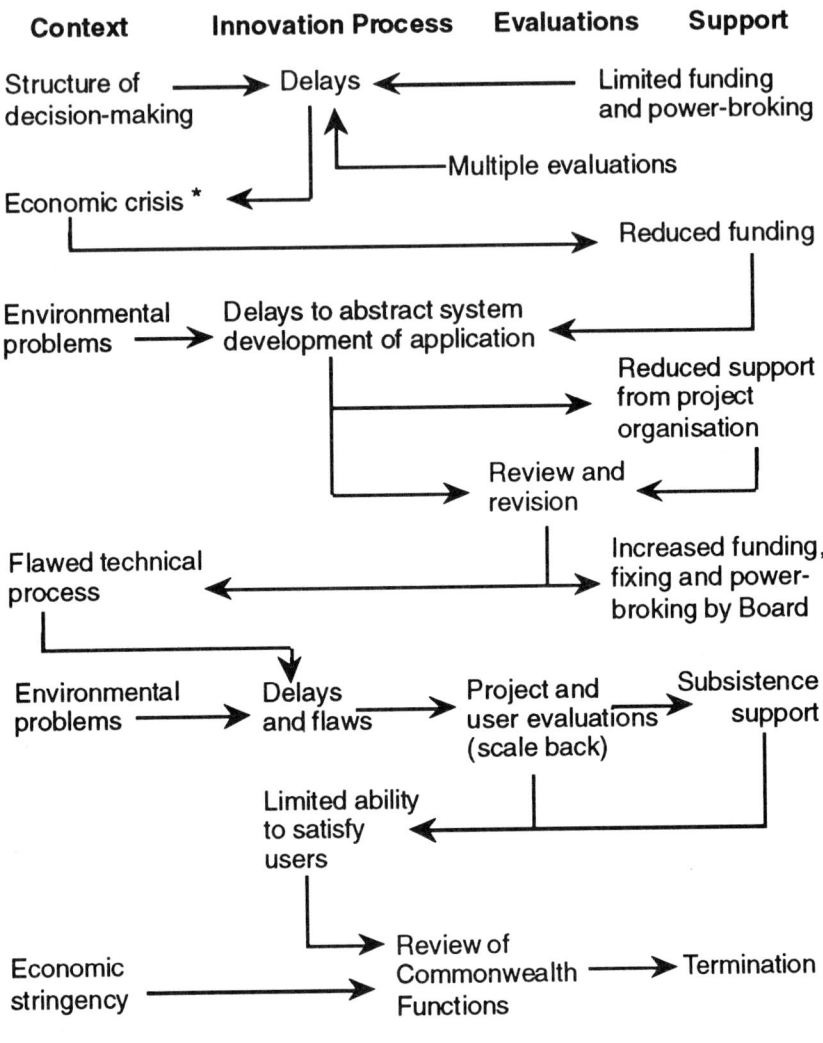

→ = causal links

* The delay in obtaining a strategic decision did not cause the economic crisis but it did cause it to have an important influence on the project.

Figure 11.1. Summary of major influences in the process leading to failure

Although the coincidence of these conditions explains Mandata's failure, it does not explain how these conditions came about. We must therefore consider the third research question posed in chapter 9: by what process did Mandata come to fail?

11.3 BY WHAT PROCESS DID MANDATA COME TO FAIL?

Chapter 8 has shown that information systems failures result from an extended process in which the innovation and support management processes interact leading to a situation in which it is no longer possible for the project organisation to command sufficient support for work to continue on the system in question. The purpose of this section is to examine the interaction of the innovation and the support management processes in Mandata with a view to explaining the project's survival for the period 1970 to 1981 and at the same time explaining the way in which ·this contributed to the situation discussed in section 11.2 which ultimately caused the project's failure.

The model proposed in this book has been based around the triangle of dependences. This has involved emphasising the cyclical influences of the innovation process on the system, the evaluation processes on decisions about support, and the actual flow of support on the project organisation's ability to avoid flaws in the innovation process. It has also involved stressing the role of constraints and contingencies of the organisational context. Figure 11.1 summarises key aspects of the Mandata process in terms of the causal flow of factors encompassed by the four constructs of organisational context, innovation process, evaluation processes and the flow of support. It is inevitably a simplification of a very complex process.

The process described in figure 11.1 is consistent with the division of the Mandata project into phases. In the initiation phase structural constraints on decision-making in the Public Service combined with limited funding and the absence of a fixer who could expedite decision-making to result in the project's being delayed. The delay resulted in Mandata being caught in an economic crisis at just the time when it was seeking to establish its infrastructure in the initial development phase. Funding was therefore harder to obtain. The cost of this limited funding along with environmental contingencies such as those associated with the supply of hardware and software was delay in developing an abstract systems design for the application. This resulted in reduction in support by some members of the project organisation which in turn led to a major reevaluation of the project. The review led to a revision of the applications strategy with twin outcomes.

The first outcome was that under the new strategy the project received greater active support from the Board. The second outcome was that the project organisation adopted a new technical process which yielded political benefits swiftly. However, the technical process was to lead to serious flaws. In addition, the project suffered extensive criticisms which meant that while there was enough support to implement the system and to cope with some of the flaws, there was not enough to overcome these flaws without their having further negative effects on evaluations. The coincidence of three evaluations with a common analysis led to the project being scaled back. It was this that created the situation in which the project was exposed to threats to its support such as that posed by the Review of Commonwealth Functions.

This summary account of the Mandata process can now be expanded taking in turn each of the phases identified in chapter 10 including the decisions to reorient and scale back the project. Each phase will be analysed in terms of the management strategy employed, the progress made, the contextual influences on the innovation process, the important evaluations, and the flow of support. The major decisions will be analysed in terms of the evaluations which affected them.

11.3.1 Initiation

On the surface, the initiation stage achieved what the project's originators and idea champions wanted. Work on the system itself was sufficient to permit progress through the sub-stages of initiation. It also proved enough to win active support from the Board in terms of resource allocation for the latter stages of the decision process involving the IDC, Committee of Officials, staff associations, and Cabinet. The outcome was a strategic decision by Cabinet which endorsed the project and released funds to support it. This automatically generated Board support for the development process. However, in retrospect it can be seen that

Analysis Of Mandata 253

during this phase conditions developed which were to affect the project later. The delays in obtaining the decision to proceed meant that Mandata was unable to establish its infrastructure before an economic crisis broke. The worsened economic situation adversely affected the flow of support subsequently.

The management strategy was essentially to manage the innovation stages according to the bureaucratic norms of the Public Service and to let the proposal win support on its merits. In terms of gaining a favourable strategic decision it was successful because the proposal came at a time when the Public Service itself and public sector spending were both expanding. The costs of the investment detailed in the proposal were less critical to decisions about support prior to 1974 than subsequently.

Progress was made in a number of areas of system innovation. An outline of the system and the technical infrastructure were formally articulated in the feasibility study report. User offices were investigated. Prototype procedures were developed. Progress was made in cooperative ventures with the Treasury and Superannuation Board, especially the successful introduction of the standard AGS number and the initiation of a liaison committee. Substantial progress was also made in the development of a project organisation with the recruitment of new staff after the Board approved the development in March 1973.

All this was possible because the context posed no special constraints at this time. Cognitive limits posed constraints on what problems could be foreseen and how many issues would have to be left open, but these did not create any special difficulties. The technical process was straightforward. Obtaining a favourable strategic decision did not require detailed decisions. It was possible to leave many issues open. The environment was largely favourable. Indeed, to the extent that the Public Service was expanding under the Labour government, this was a good time to initiate a project like Mandata, because attitudes favoured innovative initiatives, because expansion improved the benefit to cost ratio, and because resources were relatively readily available. Admittedly the technology was changing rapidly, but there was enough flexibility during the initiation stage for this to be accommodated in later decisions. Although organisational politics can never be discounted in explaining organisational processes, there were no obvious power plays to create particular difficulties. There were no specific historical constraints. This left the

254   Chapter 11

organisational structures of the Public Service. Here the project organisation did find itself constrained. The Public Service Board was not accustomed to accommodating large technological projects within its structure. It lacked a streamlined process for making the decisions required if technological benefits were to be rapidly grasped. It was largely this that caused the delay of two years from the Board's considering the final Feasibility Report to the Cabinet decision to fund the project. Table 11.3 summarises the role of the context in the initial stage of the innovation process.

Table 11.3. Effects of context on the initiation phase

Contextual Factor	**Effect on Innovation Process**
Cognitive limits	Normal uncertainties in the design
Technical process	Unproblematic
Environment	Relatively favourable. Technology changing rapidly
Politics	No specific power plays
History	No specific precedents
Structure	Lack of streamlined decision process

The decision-making process is summarised in Table 11.4. The table shows the evaluation processes of the initiation stage and the effect they had on support. It can be seen that at this stage the system was widely judged to serve the interests of the various stakeholders. Departments, consultants, the IDC on ADP, and the Committee of Officials all evaluated the proposal in the lead up to two decision processes, one by the Board to support a Cabinet submission and one by the Cabinet. The consultants' review of the feasibility study was conducted by an independent firm. Its team included one consultant who had previously been a prominent and influential proponent of adp developments in the Service. He knew and was known to the people working on Mandata. The project organisation was thus well linked into this corner of the social

Analysis Of Mandata 255

network. The probability of the Board's approval was strongly increased by the consultants' favourable evaluation. This was both a potential defence for the Board and a resource for the project organisation in demonstrating the value of its proposal.

Table 11.4. The effect of evaluations on decisions about support 1971-1974

Evaluations /Decisions	Date	Evaluation	Effect on Support
Feasibility study	Nov 1971	+ve	Led to Board decision to consult further
Public Service Board	Feb 1972	Decision	Decision to consult widely
Consultants	Sep 1972	+ve	Positive effect on Board and IDC on ADP
Departments	May-Dec 1972	Mostly +ve	Encouraged Board to fund Cabinet submission
Public Service Board	Mar 1973	Decision	Board authorises funding for Cabinet submission and initial establishment of project
IDC on ADP	May 1973	+ve	Prerequisite of Cabinet submission
Committee of Officials	Jan 1974	+ve	Prerequisite of Cabinet support
Staff associations	Late 1973	+ve	Little effect. Board proceeds in absence of negative responses
Cabinet	Feb 1974	Decision	Funds approved for hardware and software

Departmental responses were also relevant to the Board's decision. Although there were some doubts raised, the Board's adp staff were well positioned to rebut them. It is, after all, usual that the organisation that has developed a proposal is better positioned in terms of the information available to it than those who raise doubts and objections. The control over information flows is an important resource. Departmental evaluations were also less tightly linked to the Board's decision process than the independent consultants' review which it had commissioned.

As for the other approvals, the project organisation was well positioned to obtain them. The structural relationship between the Board's adp staff and the IDC meant that it was very familiar with what was required to obtain approval, and the staff putting forward the proposal were well known to the IDC. Again, the project organisation was well positioned in the network of important relationships surrounding the project.

The advantage the Mandata submission enjoyed with respect to the Committee of Officials was more circumstantial. The timing for the Committee of Officials' evaluation was favourable. The sequence of submissions meant that Mandata followed several small requests and preceded some larger proposals. Finally, staff associations appear not to have been well sensitised to the issues at this time. As much as anything, it was the absence of opposition from them that was required. In fact, the Board went ahead with the Cabinet submission with only one formal notification of support from staff associations.

Despite the relatively smooth progress of the innovation process at this stage, the actual flow of support to the project organisation did not permit the Feasibility Study schedule to be met. Although there was funding for the Feasibility Study and for the submission to Cabinet, there was no special funding provided to support the consultation process and the revision of the Feasibility Study Report. This meant that the Board's adp staff had to carry out these activities in addition to their normal tasks. This was one of the contributors to the delay in obtaining approval for the hardware and software expenditure. The other factor that influenced the delay was the lack of a power-broker to obtain extra funding and to persuade the Board to expedite the decision process. Up until February 1972 the head of Management Services at the Board had been such a power-broker providing access to the Board's commissioners and chairman, and offering connections to many other constituencies within the Australian Public Service. His replacement did not take over these roles, so this left the project organisation unable to accelerate progress. This was a factor which would also affect the next stage of the project.

There are two other factors that affected the project organisation's ability to command support at subsequent stages. First, the slowness of the decision process may have robbed the project of the chance to establish a powerful alliance with Treasury and the Superannuation Board. The Mandata proposal included supplying the new payroll system with details of payment entitlements. Had the link been made, the organisationally crucial application of payroll would have become dependent on Mandata. This would have increased both immediacy and pervasiveness as well as making the system less substitutable, thereby giving the project organisation some ability to leverage support from departments and Treasury. However, the Treasury started its payroll development ahead of Mandata and the delay in the decision process increased the difference. Though a liaison committee was established, the link to payroll and superannuation was always to be a future prospect rather than a present reality. The Mandata project organisation therefore never had the influence that might have accrued to it through controlling the strategic contingency of pay entitlements for the organisationally central application of payroll.

The second factor was that the support obtained from departments was nominal rather than substantive. The feasibility study indicated that departments would be asked to provide adp and user staff full-time, but how many and from whom was left open. Departments' expressed support was not a guarantee of active support when required. This left it open for them to decide whether or not to offer substantive support when it was requested. It left them room to manoeuvre in the face of changing contextual constraints, specifically economic stringency, at the cost of the Mandata organisation's ability to cope.

It can be seen in retrospect that although the support management process was successful to the extent of keeping the project alive and securing a sizable allocation of resources to pursue it further, the support it secured was not all that it appeared to be. It was open to reinterpretation. This gave supporters room for manoeuvre. Whether they would choose to use it depended on circumstances. In the event, these did not favour Mandata.

The initiation phase of Mandata can be summarised as having achieved its objectives in terms of obtaining a strategic decision to proceed but as having not had the support to do so without delays which were to affect funding in the next stage and hence progress. At the same time other conditions were established, such as the retirement of the power-broker, which would affect support for the project subsequently.

11.3.2 The initial development

The development stage of the information systems innovation process consists of three sub-stages: devising an abstract system, developing a concrete system, and establishing the infra-structure. The development process undertaken between February 1974 and August 1976 mostly addressed the development of the abstract system and the infrastructure.

The management strategy continued to emphasise progress with the innovation process rather than managing support. The flow of support proved to be a major problem throughout the period of initial development. The project organisation's expectation that following the Cabinet decision to fund the equipment all other resources requested would be forthcoming proved misplaced. It showed up the Cabinet's decision as having ambiguous implications, a factor which could be exploited by those who controlled resources at the expense of the project organisation which needed them. The project organisation's response was to make what progress it could on a limited front rather than stretching itself across too many areas thereby creating a flawed product. The cost was delays with the infrastructure and more especially the abstract system, that is the application design.

Nevertheless, just as the initiation stage advanced work on the system itself, so too in this period there were a number of achievements. The central computer and some of the mini computers were acquired, found sites, commissioned, and made operational. The Australian Public Service standard terminal was specified, tested and prototypes delivered. Special software was commissioned and under development, some of it to an advanced stage. There was some progress towards a specification of the abstract system. In addition, considerable efforts were expended on developing procedures and standards for the work of the project

Analysis Of Mandata 259

organisation, and in preparatory work for further development and implementation.

The organisational context became far more constraining in this stage. Table 11.5 summarises its effects.

Table 11.5. Effects of context on the initial development phase

Contextual Factor	Effect on Innovation Process
Cognitive limits	Uncertainties contributed to delays in application design
Technical process	Development of technical procedures in parallel with the innovation process consumed resources
Environment	Supply of equipment, accommodation, special software, and staff all caused problems. Auditor-General's involvement and changing technology also affected progress
Politics	Accommodation provision affected by political factors
History	No specific precedents
Structure	Limited project organisation control over accommodation and maintenance

None of the problems that arose from contextual sources was such that it could not have been suitably solved and the costs absorbed had the project had the right support. As it was, lack of a power-broker meant that necessary support was not immediately forthcoming. This made the context more salient, affecting the innovation process in a number of ways. The NCDC took the opportunity of the economic crisis to make a political point about the decision-making and communication structures associated with computer acquisition. This meant Mandata could not have its central mainframe properly housed. The Public Service structure meant that the project organisation had very little control over the provision of accommodation and the correction of the air conditioning problems. Problems with the manufacturers caused delays in the supply of terminals. Changes to data communication facilities meant that design of the network had to be partly rethought. The whole project was affected by the difficulty of finding suitable staff in a tight labour market which exacerbated the problems which cognitive limits and the establishment of technical procedures caused. Likewise having to cope with the Auditor-General's investigations further put pressure on the innovation process. Shortage of staff combined with uncertainties about the final design of the software Processing Framework and the need to give priority to the infrastructure meant that the applications development work was delayed.

For much of this stage the project was free of evaluations which might affect its support. Its difficulties lay more in the actual flow of support itself. However, prior to the decision to reevaluate the project in mid-1976 there were three evaluations worth noting. They are shown in table 11.6.

The withdrawal of Australia Post and Telecom reduced by half the record base that Mandata would serve. Although this clearly did alter the cost-benefit ratio, it was known that the withdrawal would not change the balance to an unfavourable ratio, and so it did not result in an immediate reevaluation of the project. Australia Post's and Telecom's withdrawal is discussed further in section 11.4 where alternative management strategies are considered.

The Board's decision to commission an external review of the project was triggered by the fact that internal disaffection was brought to its direct notice, although other events had already prepared the way. These included the project organisation's continuing requests for staff funding, the formal presentation of options for the project in May 1976, and the awareness that the Auditor-General's 1976 report would contain criticisms of financial aspects of the project. For the Board, the situation was tantamount to a political crisis. The May review had made it clear that if it did not resource the project better, no date could be given for implementation. If it did not have something to show soon it would risk severe public criticism from the Auditor-General. From the point of view of trying to avoid damage to its interests the Board needed to reconsider the value of the project.

The fundamental problem for the project organisation in this phase of the project was the flow of support. This underlay the delays in development which were the chief reason for the review

Analysis Of Mandata 261

and revision of mid-1976. The principal shortage was of resources for staffing - as section 10.3.3 shows, the ADP Systems Development Branch had to work from mid-1974 to mid-1976 with fewer than half the staff estimated as needed. The project organisation was also dependent on departments and other divisions of the Board's own offices but it had no authority over them and little leverage for persuading them to act as its fixer in matters such as staffing policy and accommodation.

Table 11.6. The effect of evaluations on decisions about support 1974-mid-1976

Evaluations /Decisions	Date	Evaluation	Effect on Support
Australia Post/Telecom	Jan 1975	-ve	Withdrawal resulted in reduced funding for equipment. No other direct effects
Auditor-General	Jun 1976	Focused criticisms	Contributed to pressure to review the project in mid-1976
Project organisation personnel	Early 1976	Criticisms of progress	Triggered decision to review the project in mid-1976

Under conditions of relative abundance of resources the conflict that arose between the Board and NCDC might not have occurred. Scarce resources created conditions in which NCDC's decision to defer work on the agreed site for the Mandata computer also served to make a point it had made over some years to the IDC on ADP to the effect that decision-making about equipment did not adequately respect the problems of siting. The project organisation's close association with the IDC gave added emphasis to NCDC's point about site planning. Thus, while 'networking' may be a means of gaining support, the relationships formed within the network can also be a disadvantage. The effect of limited support was that the project organisation obtained a solution to the accommodation problem which was workable, but only at the cost of the extra effort associated with preparing for operation in a different site.

It was the macro-economic situation which lay behind these difficulties. The Labour government was obliged to rein in its expansionist ambitions. When it was defeated at the polls at the end of 1975, the incoming Liberal administration was not only constrained by the wider economic situation, but was itself politically inclined to public sector restraint.

It was the severity of the economic situation that highlighted the project organisation's lack of power and made it so critical. The application simply was not sufficiently important for the provision of increasingly large resources to be seen to be more important than the government's broader policies of austerity. For the Board, having responsibility for overseeing Public Service establishments policies, it would have been embarrassing for it to be increasing its own establishment while holding back other departments. That the motivation for the project was technology-push started to prove a disadvantage. Lacking direct access to the Board and lacking a power-broker with the ability to influence it, the project organisation was structurally constrained in its ability to manage support. That the Board itself was unlikely to make the running became clear when it instructed the head of the Management Information Branch to give his top priority to the requirements for statistics of the Royal Commission on Australian Government Administration rather than to overseeing the development of the abstract system for the application.

One of the problems for the project organisation was that there were no major evaluation processes built into the project which it could have used to bring home the implications of its lack of resources. It lacked a major process which would have permitted it to overcome the structural barriers to gaining the support it required. It was not until mid-1976 that such an evaluation occurred, and by then the damage had been done.

It should not be thought that the project organisation was without all ability to command support. It obtained sufficient support on the accommodation issue for NCDC to be forced to provide a site for the central computer. Presumably for the Board to have accepted NCDC's decision not to proceed with Anzac Park West would have brought to a head the problem of whether to

Analysis Of Mandata   263

resource the project at all. It was tactically easier to try to partially satisfy both government restraint and its responsibility for Public Service efficiency by supporting the need for a site but not being active in increasing the establishment. It may also be that the economic situation made it all the more important not to waste the resources already invested in the project. However, that the choice of the Trade site was not the project organisation's first preference is an indicator of the relative weakness of the project organisation's position.

The project organisation did make strenuous attempts to improve the staffing situation through the normal channels of making bids for establishment positions, and lobbying for these proposals through officers immediately higher in the formal structure. Ultimately, these efforts bore some fruit but at the cost of significant staff shortages at a critical period which left the project organisation ill equipped to handle all the contextual sources of problems facing it.

In the face of problems with the flow of support and difficulties with the organisational context of the innovation process project management had few choices. This is partly because it did not become apparent that there would be a chronic problem over staffing until the equipment acquisition was well under way. Consequently, the option of delaying the commissioning of the equipment and software was effectively ruled out because by then the Board would have been open to legal action from contractors or would have faced penalty payments. As the application system could not be designed until the detail of the technical system had been decided, there was little choice but for the ADP Systems Development Branch to pursue the development of the technical infrastructure at the expense of working with MIB on developing the abstract system. This situation makes clear that while complex contractual relationships provide the customer with benefits they also impose obligations which then act as a constraint on decision-making and action. The project organisation's relationship with its equipment suppliers was double-edged in just this way.

In fact, it made sense both in terms of the innovation process and the process of maintaining support to pursue acquisition as a higher priority. The sooner the equipment and software were installed, the sooner any unanticipated problems would be discovered. The sooner it was operational, the easier it would be for technical staff to familiarise themselves with the technology. In terms of support, the installation of the network would be a means of improving the project's future by making it more politically costly to terminate because of the sunk capital. Furthermore, the network would serve as a symbol of project progress, and of the importance of the project. From the point of view of the project organisation wanting to continue its effort on Mandata, the disadvantage of this strategy was that it opened up the option of abandoning the application and using the equipment to operate a bureau service.

Thus, the initial development concentrated on the acquisition of the facilities for which Cabinet had provided funds. Lacking the support to satisfactorily solve all the problems it faced, and lacking the power to leverage increased support, the project organisation was forced to accept some sub-optimal solutions which would continue to bedevil the project. The ordering of priorities under conditions of serious staff shortage and in the face of other contingencies was at the expense of delays to the applications development. These pressures and problems left senior officers in the project little time for longer term support management activities. Initially, this was not a source of difficulty because sufficient funds and power-broking were available to sustain some work on the system. It became more important following the events in the first half of 1976 which captured the Board's attention and led to the decision to review the project.

Though much was achieved during the initial development stage the shortage of resources meant that it was not enough to meet the expectations of some internal and external stakeholders. The gradual emergence of a political crisis for the Board established conditions which favoured major change. The evaluation that followed became the focus for that change.

11.3.3 Review and revision

The motivation for the evaluation of Mandata in mid-1976 was the threat of crisis. A number of events had combined to lead the Board to question whether the project as it stood was going to serve its interests. Its response was to commission a third party evaluator who was known to the Chairman through prior ties of work and whose conclusions were thus likely to be influential on the Board's decision-making.

Analysis Of Mandata 265

Table 11.7. Influences on the evaluation July-August 1976

Context	Economic austerity in APS
Situation	Project behind schedule, subject to criticism, internal dissatisfaction
Technique	Informal. Reviewer given flexible brief
Interests	Implicitly the Board's
Evaluator	'Fireman'. Known to Chairman
Prior evaluations	Auditor-General, internal, *Canberra Times*
Time frame	Shorter rather than longer

Table 11.8. Parameters of the evaluation August 1976

Interests	Board, dissatisfied members of the project organisation
Evaluation	-ve immediate short term, +ve short -medium and long term
Accompanying information	Descriptive, prescriptive strategy for achieving beneficial outcome

Table 11.7 summarises the influences on the review in terms of the model developed in chapter 7. Table 11.8 summarises the evaluation outcome.

The influences on the evaluation process as described in table 11.7 largely explain the outcome presented in table 11.8. The situation was that the project was running behind schedule, and had been subject to internal and external critical evaluations. The economic situation for the whole Public Service made the situation particularly embarrassing. The evaluator appreciated the need to consider the short to medium term rather than just the long term interests of the Board and the project organisation.

That the system was not currently serving the Board's interests and was unlikely to do so in the immediate future was clear from the situation. The evaluator's natural inclination to find solutions, *The Canberra Times* called him 'the fireman', and his flexible remit for evaluating the project resulted in the formulation of an alternative strategy which would yield political benefits in the short to medium term - a matter of months rather than years. So, it was possible to present the Board with a more favourable evaluation conditional upon this new strategy. It had the advantage of bringing implementation forward and so getting departments involved sooner. It also satisfied those inside the project organisation who wanted quick results.

The situation and context made the alternative far more immediately attractive. The flexible conduct of the review meant that the internal critics had access to the evaluator. That the review was not precisely defined according to the standards the Board itself promulgated meant that no party could influence the review outcome through the tactic of containing the review to a limited sphere. Moreover, the existing project management team was less able to influence the new strategy because one of the joint de facto project managers was absent seriously ill during this period. Thus, conditions militated against continuation of the existing strategy and in favour of the new.

The particular strategy adopted can be seen to have emerged in part from the contingent circumstances obtaining. The political nature of the situation meant that time was short and this prevented the search for a solution being extended. Little environmental scanning was necessary to discover the new strategy. The presence in the project at that time of an officer who was well acquainted with the Productivity system and the fact that the idea of using it was not new to some members of the project team both contributed to making this the main alternative considered. As a result of time pressures and the obvious benefits of early implementation, the fact that the Productivity system was already flawed and that there would be difficulties implicit in applying it to cases for which it was not designed were accepted as bearable costs. How important this might be it was impossible to say. It was, of necessity, a judgement

Analysis Of Mandata 267

under uncertainty. The short term effect was a system implemented more quickly than otherwise while the longer term effect was a flawed concrete system - the core Productivity P&E system adopted had fundamental flaws which were expensive in effort to correct. In the event, it also proved more difficult than anticipated to convert the system to run on the Mandata mainframe.

The Board's approval of the new strategy was clearly influenced by the close linking of the evaluator to the decision process, but was also influenced by the fact that the evaluator enabled members of the project team to present the revised strategy to the Board immediately following his own presentation of the need for change. In controlling access to the Board, and thereby the flow of information, the evaluator was able to empower the disaffected coalition within the project organisation.

If there was any likelihood that the Board would resist a proposal for change, it was rendered less likely with the publication of *The Canberra Times*' article which made it all the more politically expedient that there be seen to be change. The Board was faced with a situation where the project had been publicly criticised in a newspaper which carried weight nationally in Public Service matters. When this was combined with a negative evaluation of the project by its third party agent, it had no choice but to act radically. To have terminated the project there and then would have caused major embarrassment, further criticism, and a significant loss of influence for the Board in its adp dealings and probably more generally in its responsibilities for administrative efficiency. The damaging implications of this option had been explicitly recognised when the Board was presented with the option in May.

The alternative put to it, to implement the Productivity system as an interim measure, had the obvious political advantages of neutralising the criticism that an expensive machine was lying idle, of heading off any claim that the original strategy was misconceived by retaining the original aims as a long term goal, and of involving departments, making them dependent on an operational system and thereby increasing the likelihood of their support. It also met the demands of those inside the project who wanted change. Whatever its long term effects, change has the short term virtue of neutralising criticisms of the past. They are rendered irrelevant because a new approach is being taken which by implication avoids past mistakes. This in turn buys time while the new approach is followed. What change cannot do is give any guarantees about the new approach.

The events of 1976 brought home the fact that the Board was more dependent on Mandata than it had realised. It had supported the investment of public resources in Mandata. It now needed the system to perform well to justify this support. This illustrates a general point that, to the extent that they are accountable to others and are seen to support a project, supporters harness their own fortunes to those of the project. The reason lies in the lag between support and return. As has been noted previously, support is an investment. It creates supporter dependence on system outcomes as well as project organisation dependence on support.

A looming crisis created the conditions and motivation for the Board to review its support through the vehicle of a third party evaluation. The subsequent increase in support the project received was purchased by a newly empowered coalition within the project organisation in return for a change in strategy which was to have adverse long term implications for the innovation process which would in turn have a subsequent feedback effect on support.

11.3.4 Reorientation and consolidation

The period from September 1976 to June 1980 saw development, implementation and operation stages overlapping. There were two management strategies employed. They both mixed managing the innovation process with managing support.

Under reorientation, the major emphasis was on changing the innovation process from development to implementation. Restructuring and pseudo-commercialisation were directed toward changing the project's image so as to improve morale and increase internal support and to make the project organisation more service oriented. This and other tactics stood to increase demand for Mandata's products. By increasing the system's immediacy it would enhance the project organisation's ability to command support. So, a crucial element of this strategy was the implementation of Mandata products. Other tactics such as representing the system as being more directed toward management information were attempts to achieve greater congruence between the interests served and the project's supporters. Also, under both strategies, Mandata facilities and staff were diverted to provide a bureau service for other departments in order to negate criticisms that the equipment was not being fully utilised and to increase the project's base of support by increasing departmental dependence on it.

Under consolidation, there was also considerable emphasis on achieving innovation targets. This was combined with a number of support management strategies. The project organisation employed a 'networking' tactic in which departmental heads received personal visits from the project director and senior Board officials. It reported directly to the Board on a regular basis thereby ensuring a regular and controlled flow of information to its primary supporter. It also sought to increase its power through evaluations such as the Impact Evaluation Study intended to bolster the perception of its immediacy, and through encouraging the abandonment of the manual SPR system so as to make Mandata less substitutable.

While the reorientation bought the project organisation time, it was at the cost of having to pursue the new strategy. The constraint of the Productivity system meant that the innovation process would encounter a range of problems and at the same time limit the project organisation's room for manoeuvre. In particular, it subsequently restricted the ways in which the system could be used to win support.

The achievements of the period were considerable. They included completion of the work started in the previous phase on the infrastructure including the Processing Framework and other special software, and the installation of the network Australia-wide. Other major achievements included initial implementation of the Productivity system for departments, conversion to the Mandata mainframe, and continuing operation. The Leave, Des/Sal, and Educational Qualifications sub-systems were developed, implemented in a number of departments, and put into regular operation. In addition, the Programs/Forward Staff Estimates subsystem was developed though not implemented.

Mandata's context from 1976 onwards was hostile in a number of ways. These are summarised in Table 11.9. The cognitive limits that affect all problem-solving became the more active as a result of several factors including the relative inexperience of some staff, the fact that there were no well established systematic techniques for conducting technical conversions, the differences between the different machine technologies, and the fact that it took time for the project organisation to acquire detailed knowledge of the Productivity system.

Table 11.9. Effects of context on the reorientation and consolidation phase

Contextual Factor	Effect on Innovation Process
Cognitive limits	Uncertainties associated with the Productivity system made the innovation process harder
Technical process	Problems with technology in conversion, limited hardware facilities, flaws in the Productivity system, and prototyping the Leave system led to delays and flaws in implemented Mandata systems
Environment	Operational user criticisms, some user resistance, extraordinary regulatory intrusion, and conflict with staff associations absorbed resources and damaged morale. Staffing levels hard to achieve because of continuing tight labour market. Culture not oriented to commodification
Politics	User resistance (as above) though not permanently damaging
History	Early project ambitions used as basis for criticisms
Structure	Regulatory bodies pig-a-back on each other

The most fundamental constraint on the project came from the technical process which was now based on an existing system. The Productivity system had been built for the requirements of just the one department, and was not capable of coping with some of the conditions that affected others. It was operationally ponderous as a result of the fact that it had been built for an earlier generation of technology. It incorporated many flaws which required attention from the project organisation. As more departments implemented the system, the operational schedule under the initial processing strategy became very tight.

The other major plank of the Mandata system was the Leave sub-system. This was designed to demonstrate the worth of the long term objectives associated with the original application strategy and to win support by overcoming some of the perennial

Analysis Of Mandata

problems of leave record-keeping thereby controlling an important contingency for users. While it achieved these ends to some degree, prototyping the system unavoidably resulted in flaws which proved to be chronic.

In Mandata's environment, user dissatisfaction became a source of contingent problems. Flaws in the Productivity system, the many errors in the original data holdings, slow operational turnaround, and delays in correcting flaws all created dissatisfaction resulting in criticisms. Furthermore, there was resistance from some departmental implementers. Thus, in addition to technical difficulties, the politics of implementation and operation created problems for the project organisation. This situation was exacerbated by the structural and cultural distance between the development staff and the clerical and administrative staff in the departments - they did not even share a common chief executive. Staff and machine resources were consumed by the bureau service to departments, and there was a significant public dispute which damaged the project's reputation when the MPO terminated this service. In addition, there were the institutional critics, the Auditor-General and the Public Accounts Committee, whose persistent attentions required effort to service and whose criticisms sapped morale among both the project organisation and users. On top of all this, the staff associations became more actively involved. As noted earlier, they started not well attuned to the issues. As their involvement grew, so did their understanding. The Impact Evaluation Study seems to have been pivotal in this relationship. The Board's refusal to release the report to the MCG created suspicion and anger with the result that the hitherto reasonably collaborative relationship became more adversarial. The MCG's bitter complaint that it was not consulted about the 1980 decision to scale the project back even though there was no likelihood that the decision would hurt staff interests demonstrates this. For MPO, the cost was twofold. The continuing relationship with MCG took time and effort, and it was another source of criticisms. Culture played its part too. The decision to commodify Mandata was in contrast to normal Public Service culture. It therefore required a significant effort to engender this new outlook.

The principal cost of the revised strategy was the effort that had to be devoted to the Productivity system, its operation, its conversion and its enhancement. In pursuing the revised strategy, the MPO used up all its slack resources. There was nothing left

Chapter 11

with which to prepare to fulfil the project's longer term ambitions.

There is no doubt that during this period the project organisation was better positioned to command support nor that it was better supported. Positive evaluations of the project reinforced its position and ensured the continuation of support even in the face of other negative evaluations. Towards the end of this phase the latter combined with the continuing difficulties in the innovation process to create conditions for a set of evaluations which would result in the decision to scale back the project. Table 11.10 lists these evaluations.

Table 11.10. The effect of evaluations on decisions about support 1976-1980

Evaluations /Decisions	Date	Eval	Effect on Support
Consultants	Jul 1977	+ve	Resulted in support for revised strategy from Committee of Officials and Cabinet. Resource for combatting criticism from other sources
Public Accounts Committee	Sep 1979	+ve	Precluded immediate abandonment
Auditor-General	1976-1979	-ve	Maintained pressure on the project. Undermined ability to pursue any expansion of the project
Impact Evaluation Study	1978-1979	-ve	Damage to relations with staff associations. Limited MPO's ability to trade on clerical savings

The Board was more actively involved in Mandata throughout this phase. The crisis in mid-1976 had captured the Board's

Analysis Of Mandata 273

attention and had made it realise the project's political importance in terms of its effects on the Board's role within the Public Service if it were to fail. It was the symbolic power of Mandata that was most important because for the Board itself the operational services the system was to provide had very little immediacy whereas as a symbol of the Board's responsibility for efficiency and economic restraint it was central. The fact that a director was appointed at a higher level, with direct access to the Board, was both an effect and a cause of increased support.

The Board's more active support was evident in a variety of forms. The project establishment and staff ceiling were expanded so as to increase staff by over fifty per cent. The project organisation was formed into a single organisational unit with a new director. Brand new office accommodation was provided. At the same time, though, it is worth noting that the flow of support was not consistent. The improved staffing levels for the project were not approved immediately, the accommodation for the central computer remained unchanged, an uninterrupted power supply system was never installed, and for most of 1977 the project director was part occupied working for another department.

Departments also began to contribute. As soon as the system started to be implemented, it gave the project organisation some influence over users. The more sub-systems were implemented and the further integrated they became in departmental work, the more pervasive they became. It took time to create departmental dependence on Mandata sufficient to increase its ability to leverage support. What support departments did provide was administrative and clerical. Some of this was devoted to contributions to project-related committees and working groups. The rest was given to the implementation process. Much needed loans of technical personnel were never made.

One particularly potent resource for the project organisation was the positive third party evaluation made by independent consultants retained by a special, influential Committee of Officials to examine Mandata's cost-benefit under the revised strategy. The evaluators' conclusion was tightly linked into the decision process, being its main component. A negative conclusion would have almost certainly resulted in the Committee's recommending the project be abandoned, and this recommendation would not have been rejected. On the other hand, the positive evaluation made by the consultants served as a powerful argument for the project to obtain continuing support and as a weapon against critics. The formal nature of the evaluation, the fact that it related to cost-benefit, that it had been conducted by independent experts, and was sanctioned by the Cabinet by way of the Committee of Officials all contributed to making this evaluation a powerful resource for the MPO.

The MPO did not achieve more power to command support for several reasons. For users, their involvement was at a net cost, though this was partly because they chose not to rely solely on Mandata. They absorbed the flaws in the system by maintaining in parallel the clerical record system so as to try to provide the customary level of service to their own clients. Despite several efforts, the MPO was unable to convince departments to scrap the old SPR card system. The existence of this substitute system meant that it could not create sufficient dependence on the system by which to leverage more support. And, although initially the revised strategy was represented as emphasising management information benefits rather than staff savings, the shift did not make itself felt in the sub-systems actually implemented. The application therefore never had high immediacy for departmental heads. It was not central to their core tasks. Consequently, though the MPO was better positioned than before, it was far from well positioned to command all the support it would have liked. The problems the MPO had in getting the support it was promised for the Impact Evaluation Study demonstrate how little leverage it had.

The period from 1978 was characterised by extensive efforts to manage support through direct contact with Permanent Heads, commitment to the consultative process through the MCC, MUG, and MCG, and tactics to lessen the damage caused by the institutional critics. MPO's involving the committees in its decision-making and day to day work had the double benefit of giving the Board access to staff resources while also coopting possible critics. But, it was a double-edged tactic in that the different committees served as forums at which critics could gather and act in concert to impose their preferences on MPO. The best that the MPO was able to do to control the negative effects of its use of the committees was to divide the functions of MUG so that the operational MUG meetings, which would sometimes degenerate into sessions in which criticism of MPO was predominant, were held at a separate time and place from the development MUG meetings.

Analysis Of Mandata 275

Table 11.11. Examples of attempts to influence evaluations 1977-1980

Evaluation	Influence Attempt	Category
Impact Evaluation Study	Refusal to grant access to results	Control of effects through control of information
Auditor's investigations	Comment on terms of reference	Influence perceptions by influencing scope of investigations
	Direct appeal to Auditor-General to relax scrutiny	Influence pattern of occurrence of evaluations
	Reference to consultants and Cabinet approval	Influence perceptions
	Confrontation of Auditor's staff	Influence form of expression and interests
	Reference to statutory limitations	Influence interests
	Coopt Auditor's staff	Influence perceptions
	Orchestrated rejection of criticisms	Influence effects by contradiction
Public Accounts Committee	Control of evidence through testimony at hearings, provision of documents, and Committee visit to MPO	Influence perceptions

This more active approach to support management was particularly noticeable in respect to the evaluation processes which were unfavourable to the project. Table 11.11 lists ways in which MPO tried to influence evaluations and their effects.

The most intriguing of the evaluation processes was the Impact Evaluation Study commissioned by the project organisation itself. Its purpose was to establish in a more concrete form than the financial cost-benefit figures of the independent consultants what the benefits would be to user departments and how they would be achieved. The stakeholder interests against which the evaluation was conducted were those of users. Staff were borrowed from other departments including the Auditor-General's to give the evaluation team independent status though the study was controlled from within the MPO. Now that the system was actually implemented in some departments, the use of field studies made it possible to be more realistic about actual as opposed to expected outcomes. The study's conclusion was that Mandata would only realise expected benefits if it satisfied certain conditions, namely that the work organisation of SPR teams be changed - and even then the benefits would chiefly come from that reorganisation not from the computer system. This deprived the MPO of a hoped for resource in seeking continued support. The fact that the study was managed by the project organisation and was not tightly linked into any decision processes meant that its effects could be controlled to avoid adverse effects on support. However, the need to keep its conclusions quiet resulted in damage to the relationship with the staff associations.

The Auditor-General's evaluations were consistently negative after 1975. Initially, it was the public interest in sound financial practices which dominated, but the Auditor's department's own agenda of developing expertise in audit of computer systems and of instituting efficiency audits meant that it took a much broader view of the project over the years. Its interest was far more wide reaching than that of simply getting the system implemented and into continuing operation. It was concerned that this should be achieved by the use of good technical and management practices. This imposed the burden on the project organisation of having to justify the process by which it was working, a process which was to some extent imposed by the constraints of the context and which required unusual and ad hoc problem-solving. The timeframe of evaluation was mostly in the past by virtue of the structural role of

Analysis Of Mandata

the Auditor-General to report on past behaviours and outcomes. Consequently, the evaluations were largely negative in tone, containing diagnostic information though with an implicit conditional that if the sources of criticism were not addressed, further criticism would be forthcoming. The annual publication of reports meant that there was a regular and persistent pattern to the criticism. The Auditor's frustration with the fact that earlier evaluations were not having the effect his department wanted led to a crescendo of criticism. Increased space was devoted to Mandata with each passing year and finally in April 1980 the Auditor-General's report had recourse to what was by bureaucratic standards exceedingly strong language.

It is difficult to assess exactly what effect the project organisation had in its attempts to influence the outcomes of the Auditor's reports. Most, though not all, of its influence attempts were aimed at influencing what the investigators perceived and how they evaluated what they perceived. It would comment on the terms of reference for the studies in an attempt to manage their direction. (It is worth noting that the project organisation had used this tactic in 1976 prior to the Auditor's first investigation.) MPO also strenuously worked on its image as wanting to cooperate to solve its problems. It obtained the Board's support in making direct appeal to the Auditor-General to relax the pressure by reducing the frequency and scope of the investigations. The Board also made appeal to Public Service solidarity. It made reference to prior favourable evaluations and decisions, in particular the consultants' 1977 report and Cabinet's subsequent approval, in an effort to influence the perceptions of the investigators. In 1978 it directly confronted the Auditor's staff over its findings. It appealed to agreed terms of reference and to statutory limitations to constrain the scope of the reports by limiting the interests against which evaluations could be reported. It attempted to coopt the Auditor's staff by asking for their help and assistance in matters such as the design of internal controls. By April 1980 it had sufficient support from users to be able to orchestrate a response from the MCC rejecting the Auditor-General's charges. Seemingly what these influence attempts achieved was to prevent the Auditor's reports from being devastatingly critical until 1980, and then to receive respite for the short time remaining to the project. What they could not achieve was a complete quieting of the criticisms. The one saving feature for the project organisation was that the Auditor's evaluations were not tightly linked to decisions on support. His criticisms were unlikely to lead directly to a Board decision to terminate the project.

There was, however, a tighter linking between the Public Accounts Committee's evaluations and decisions about support by virtue of its status as a powerful parliamentary committee. In addition, since part of its statutory duty was to investigate problems raised by the Auditor, the Public Accounts Committee was bound to compound the earlier public criticisms by virtue of its structural pig-a-backing on the Auditor's work.

The process by which the Public Accounts Committee investigated was to conduct public interrogatory hearings backed up by research by the Committee's secretariat, itself supported by an expert consultant. Unlike the Auditor-General it did not conduct its investigations within the project's premises. This method of proceeding gave the project organisation the opportunity to influence the Committee's perceptions of the project and the people involved. The Board's staff's conduct at hearings clearly affected the outcome. Initially, MPO witnesses were perceived by the Committee as being unhelpful. This contributed to the critical interim statement made to Parliament. A subsequent change of personnel resulted in a shift in strategy toward greater cooperation. The Committee was invited to visit the Mandata installation during which they heard a presentation from senior Board and project staff. At further hearings the Committee chairman was moved to comment on this more cooperative stance.

Another way in which it was possible to influence the Committee's perceptions was through written submissions and the provision of documents. The fact that the investigations were not conducted on site meant that it was possible to cover some omissions by producing documents specially. It also permitted the Board to control which documents the Committee received. In some cases it took refuge behind various accepted privileges to refuse access to documents, a ploy which negated some of the good will built up by the strategy of cooperation.

The timeframe of the Committee's evaluation was, like the Auditor-General's, very much oriented to the past, but unlike the Auditor's it was also directed to the future. In terms of its comment on the project's historical progress it was severely critical. But, in its evaluation of the future it was more positive. Here, the 1977 consultants' report, with its positive evaluation of Mandata's cost-benefit, appears to have assisted the project organisation. The resulting evaluation that the project should be completed came with a number of prescriptive recommendations but the timing of the report's publication in late 1979 meant that events had already to some extent overtaken it. However, the influential status of the Public Accounts Committee as a committee of the joint houses of the Parliament, and the requirement to respond publicly through a Finance Minute meant that the prescriptive elements of its report could not be totally ignored. Along with the flaws in the P&E system and other criticisms, the report contributed to the decision to review the project from within.

Where the Auditor-General's reports were not tightly linked to decisions about support, the Public Accounts Committee's were more so. A recommendation to terminate the project would have been hard to resist. That the Committee recommended continuation was a strong ground for the Board to continue its support. However, the criticisms in the Public Accounts Committee's report were publicly made and strongly worded; they were amplified by the press. The MPO and Board strategy was to lie low and hope that the fuss would die down. Though they monitored press reports, they made no attempt at a public defence, even refusing an invitation from the Australian Computer Society to make a response in its bulletin. As well as damaging project morale, the weight of criticism visited upon MPO helped create a climate in which any increase in the investment of public funds would have been politically ill-advised.

Ultimately, after implementing the first part of the revised strategy, the project had run out of breathing space. Having delivered many products and implemented twelve departments from 1976 to 1979, the project organisation had done sufficient to sustain its support from the Public Service Board. However, it had little success in obtaining funding from the departments and only mixed success in controlling the public criticism of the project. Furthermore, the first few months of operation of the fully converted system exposed its remaining flaws. The combination of having to respond to the Public Accounts Committee, the flaws in the operational system, the difficulty of extending the P&E system and the limited satisfaction of the users all combined to lead to a further reevaluation.

11.3.5 The decision to scale back

Mandata was reevaluated through two parallel processes. The MPO conducted its own internal reevaluation. At the same time a sub-committee of MCC also examined user priorities. Both evaluation processes came to substantially the same conclusion, a conclusion which was further buttressed by the Auditor-General's 1980 analysis.

Table 11.12. Influences on the MPO evaluation late 1979-early 1980

Context	Continuing economic austerity in APS, strong regulatory scrutiny and criticism
Situation	Dissatisfied users, flawed system, problems obtaining/retaining quality staff
Technique	Informal internal
Interests	MPO's, the Board's, and users'
Evaluators	Varied
Prior evaluations	Consultants, Public Accounts Committee: +ve Auditor-General, press: -ve
Time frame	Shorter rather than longer, but any timeframe that would yield a +ve outcome

The internal MPO reevaluation (see tables 11.12 and 11.13) was concerned with the project organisation's interest in retaining continuing support to permit it to proceed with its work on the system. Clearly this involved attending to the Board's and users' interests as well. The situation under evaluation was a system whose flaws were proving costly in terms of the effort required to overcome them during operation and corrective maintenance. They could no longer be written off as the transient problems of implementation, but appeared chronic. They were damaging to user confidence. At the same time, a positive response was required

Analysis Of Mandata

to the Public Accounts Committee. As the reevaluation proceeded, it became more evident that the P&E system was not sufficiently sound to serve as a basis for major development. It needed to be redeveloped itself. It was also made explicit that the project did not have available to it the staff to perform such a redevelopment. This was partly a matter of quality and partly the high turnover rate.

Table 11.13. Parameters of the MPO evaluation early 1980

Interests	MPO, Board, users
Evaluation	-ve long term, +ve medium term
Accompanying information	Prescriptive strategy (minimum viable system) for achieving beneficial outcome
Time of occurrence	Preceded the Review of Commonwealth Functions

The politics of the situation meant that the MPO did not have many options. Its ability to command support was not robust. Internally, there was a perception that the Board continued its support only because it had no acceptable way out. Externally, there was insufficient user satisfaction to act as a platform for more active support than was necessary to service the existing system. The system was not coping with strategic contingencies and it remained highly substitutable because of the continuing clerical back-up system. The project organisation still lacked power.

Limitations on support closed off many options. Broadly speaking there were four possible strategies. These were to redevelop, to continue the 1976 strategy, to stabilise the system, or to terminate it. Of these, the first and last would almost certainly have been unacceptable to the Board. Redevelopment would have required further investment which would have been impossible to obtain from the Treasury under the financial constraints and given the regulators' criticisms. In view of the Public Accounts Committee's enjoinder to complete the project with all haste because it would be valuable to the Public Service, termination would have been seen as an unqualified admission of the MPO's, and hence the Board's, inability to carry out the project. This would have been too damaging to the Board's reputation.

Whether to continue the 1976 strategy or to stabilise the project was a matter for finer judgement. To continue would have been to suggest that all could yet be well. There was some support for this in the project executive, but a number of signs suggested that it was unduly optimistic: the base for further development was fragile; short term flaws would have continued to draw effort from long term developments; it would have been difficult to staff; and it would have required a new injection of resources. By contrast, to stabilise the existing system would create the opportunity for satisfying users in a modest way without taking any new risks. It would be good for internal project morale because it would permit the setting of achievable medium term targets. It could be represented as a response to the Public Accounts Committee's instructions to MPO to define, plan and evaluate the rest of the project. And, this strategy demanded least of the project's main supporter, the Board.

Table 11.14. Influences on the MCC evaluation late 1979-early 1980

Context	Continuing economic austerity in APS, strong regulatory scrutiny and criticism
Situation	Dissatisfied users, flawed system
Technique	Specialist sub-committee of MCC
Interests	Operational users'
Evaluators	Operational user representatives
Prior evaluations	Consultants, Public Accounts Committee: +ve Auditor-General, press: -ve
Time frame	As soon as possible

Analysis Of Mandata 283

The project organisation's own evaluation, then, was that the project was only viable in the long term if it was scaled back. Only if expectations were reduced would it be likely to prove satisfactory. Although this evaluation was less formal than those of external critics, the project director's access to the Board meant that it was likely to be influential. That it coincided both with a similar evaluation by users working through the MCC and with the Auditor-General's most critical report, which also questioned the possibility of extending P&E, reinforced the strength of the MPO's own conclusions. Tables 11.14-11.17 show that despite a number of differences in the processes there was a convergence in the outcomes of their evaluations.

Table 11.15. Parameters of the MCC evaluation early 1980

Interests	Operational users'
Evaluation	-ve short term, +ve (acceptable) medium term
Accompanying information	Prescription - viable system the minimum requirement
Time of occurrence	Preceded the Review of Commonwealth Functions

From tables 11.12 to 11.17 it can be seen that though the MPO, the users, and the Auditor-General were evaluating Mandata in different ways and with respect to different interests, they all concluded that the existing strategy could not be pursued to its conclusion. What the users wanted was a robust system which would meet certain minimum criteria for being acceptable, and this was consistent with the MPO's and Auditor-General's conclusion that the P&E system was not capable of extension.

284   *Chapter 11*

Table 11.16. Influences on the Auditor-General's evaluation late 1979-early 1980

Context	Continuing interest in Mandata, Auditor's commitment to efficiency auditing
Situation	Perception of a badly controlled project
Technique	Limited investigation in situ
Interests	Financial and management issues relevant to the public interest
Evaluators	No special characteristics
Prior evaluations	Consultants, Public Accounts Committee: +ve Auditor-General, press, users: -ve
Time frame	Short, medium and long term
Feedback	Auditor's staff unconvinced that prior criticisms had had their effect

Table 11.17. Parameters of the Auditor-General's evaluation early 1980

Interests	Public interest
Evaluation	-ve evaluation of continuation of existing strategy. Other criticisms of past conduct of project
Accompanying information	Diagnostic: impossible to extend P&E to more financially sensitive functions
Time of occurrence	Last in a sequence of critical reviews, preceded the Review of Commonwealth Functions

Analysis Of Mandata 285

The scale back decision arose of necessity because the project organisation lacked the power to command the support for any alternative strategy. It had no room for manoeuvre. The cost of the scale back decision to the project organisation was to reduce its bargaining power with funders. The minimum viable system was desirable to operational users because it promised to ease the burden of working with a system on which they were now increasingly dependent. But, in abandoning any pretence of yielding net financial savings, the system offered no enticement to those who controlled public spending. It also lost two departments which took up the offer of withdrawing from the system. Worse, though, was the fact that the Board, having enjoyed the nominal support of the Cabinet both in endorsing the original strategy and the 1976 revised strategy, felt obliged once again to seek government approval thereby maintaining a negative image of Mandata. That all this occurred immediately prior to the establishment of the Review of Commonwealth Functions exposed the project to the danger of termination.

The MPO had been forced into a position where it had no room to manoeuvre. It could no longer exert power through the promise of providing a valuable resource to the Public Service at large. Just as important was the public image of the project, already severely damaged by the criticisms, which suffered further in the short term from this decision. Mandata was now very much at the mercy of whatever politics ruled in the straitened economic circumstances obtaining.

11.3.6 Towards a minimum viable system

For the MPO, the scale back decision implied a strategy of retreat into the innovation process. The emphasis was on implementation and operation. There was little prospect of enhancing support beyond the subsistence level required to pursue the newly revised strategy. Where support appeared threatened, it continued to attempt to manage the situation, but it became less proactive in this respect because there was little it could do. Emphasis on stabilising the system and thereby satisfying existing users offered the best hope of reinforcing the project's position.

The decision to scale back, by reducing expectations, relieved some of the day to day pressure on the technical process which allowed it to make some progress during the stage prior to termination. This gave the MPO sufficient slack to attend to internal procedures with renewed vigour: procedures and controls for the production of documentation were followed more scrupulously; a systems development methodology was purchased and tailored to Mandata's special circumstances; and some internal reorganisation took place. At the same time, users were consulted about what they wanted included in the minimum viable system. Extensions to the existing sub-systems were specified and programmed. Effort was allocated to producing better quality user manuals.

Even with the pressure off, the context was far from benign. There were still some user complaints about the system and the service. Nonetheless, it seems clear that scale back had helped to reduce user expectations. Consequently, the relatively conservative innovation strategy now being pursued came much closer to being acceptable at the operational level.

Where possible the project tried to limit further damage to support. MPO reacted to the Auditor-General's April 1980 criticisms with a forty-three page response. In August 1980 the Auditor-General agreed to back off. MPO also produced an extensive response to the Public Accounts Committee which was tabled in Parliament.

None of the above efforts achieved more than to prevent MPO's reputation from suffering further discredit. The conditions which caused Mandata ultimately to fail were beyond its power to change. These have been discussed already in section 11.2.

11.3.7 Summary

The process by which Mandata came to fail was extended over some ten years. The project organisation was clearly hampered by a number of unfavourable contextual factors and by its limited power to command support when it needed it. The project was subject to many different evaluation processes which varied considerably in their effects on support. While there were problems with support and problems in the innovation process, neither alone can be regarded as decisive. Rather, limited support affected the innovation process and flaws in the innovation process affected support. In order to retain support the project organisation had to

Analysis Of Mandata 287

shift its strategy twice. In doing this, it found itself in the position of having no room for manoeuvre when the Review of Commonwealth Functions started to look for cuts.

Having understood both the reasons for failure and the process by which it came to fail, it remains to ask whether the project organisation could have been more successful in its support management during the Mandata process.

11.4 WHAT OPTIONS WERE THERE FOR ALTERNATIVE MANAGEMENT STRATEGIES?

The analysis of Mandata in this chapter has left unaddressed the question of whether the project organisation could have managed support better, and in particular whether this might have left open more options. This question will be considered with respect to the four stages discussed above.

The initiation stage of an information system is principally concerned with support. In Mandata the project staff obtained all the formal approvals and most of the declarations of support they asked for, but subsequently found that not all the support that should have flowed from those approvals did so. What might have been done to improve the chances of being able to leverage that support from the Board or other sources? Accepting that linking Mandata's development to that of the Treasury's new payroll system was not an option once the initiation stage became drawn out, there appear to have been two possibilities.

The first would have been to attempt to woo the Post Office. (No other department would have been as good as the Post Office because of its size.) Merely to have satisfied the Post Office that Mandata would meet all its requirements would not have been enough, it would have been necessary to engage in a cooperative venture. This would have allied Mandata to a very powerful actor in the public sector. It would almost certainly have increased its access to support both through access to Post Office resources and through the interdependence created. However, in view of the Post Office's comments concerning its interest in a personnel and establishments system with lesser functionality, it seems most unlikely that a satisfactory compromise could have been reached without emasculating the Mandata concept. At this stage, there were no special indications that this would have been worth contemplating.

The second option that might have yielded greater leverage was the idea of a pilot project. A successful pilot would have made the potential benefits of the project more tangible. Support for the project would then have been a more certain investment. On the other hand, it is not obvious that anything short of a very extensive pilot system would have shown off these benefits and the infrastructure on which to demonstrate them did not exist. Moreover, the more extensive the pilot, the longer it would be before it was completed, the greater the likelihood the project would be deferred or cancelled altogether. Obtaining the equipment approvals was at least as likely to create the necessary support as a pilot project.

There is one other major alternative which was available during initiation. Its value would have come from reducing the amount of support needed. This would have been to abandon the Processing Framework as recommended by the consultants' report and to try to make do with proprietary software tailored to the project's needs. It is difficult to assess how much work this would have required. The state of the relevant proprietary software at that time was generally unintegrated which is to say that it would have required significant work to link the different software products so as to do what the Processing Framework was intended to do. Tailoring software can be as fraught an exercise as developing it from scratch. In addition, it is possible that had the estimates been lower, then even fewer resources would have been made available. So, while this alternative might have reduced the pressure on the project organisation in 1975 and 1976, it is hard to say whether it actually would have, and if so by how much.

During the stage of initial development, the chronic shortage of staff both demanded support management and militated against it. Moreover, the way that lack of support manifested itself also worked against effective support management. The problem was less that there was a flat refusal to provide staff and more that there were creeping delays - each hurdle might be the last. What was needed was the ability to persuade the Board both as funder and power-broker to intervene to obtain swift decisions and to provide all the staff required. But, the project organisation was structurally distanced from the Board, the relationship mediated by a non-interventionist manager.

Analysis Of Mandata

So, if support could not have been enhanced, could expectations have been lowered in line with the resources available? It certainly seems possible that the expectations of internal supporters, that is the members of the project organisation, could have been addressed with a view to avoiding the internal divisions that arose or overcoming them when they first became visible. However, though these were instrumental in triggering the 1976 project review it is doubtful that the systems innovation process would have been any further advanced. So the appearance of crisis might have been delayed but not altogether avoided by this. It was the Board's expectations that were crucial and managing them at a distance would have been next to impossible.

The only obvious opportunity to influence the Board's expectations and support came in the May 1976 review of options when it might have been possible to obtain a decision for a strategy that would have avoided the political crisis that arose. In fact the paper which the head of the ADP Division presented to the Board offered four options and came without a recommendation. If at that stage there had been a change of strategy or the Board had been persuaded to give its full support then the course of the rest of the project might have been different. However, the project organisation had only limited channels through which to reach and persuade the Board. Moreover, it is far from clear that, without the impetus of a political crisis, a change of strategy would have commanded sufficient support.

During the period of reorientation and consolidation from 1976 to 1980 a lot of effort was devoted to managing support. The Board was briefed regularly, departmental users at all levels were involved or informed, and attention was given to coping with the institutional critics. By the time that the problems arising out of the 1976 strategy became clear there was little that could be done to raise support that would permit the project organisation to transcend the flaws with which it was faced.

Had there been more support available in the form of all the staff requested, the conversion of the Productivity system would have been completed earlier, but the fundamental difficulties would have remained. The economic restraint imposed on the Public Service meant that there was no way the project could raise sufficient support to keep the interim system going and replace it by a better quality, purpose-built system. And, as indicated in section 11.2, there was almost nothing that could be done in 1980 or 1981 to raise enough support to avoid termination.

To conclude, the project organisation was highly constrained in the extent to which it could have acted to raise sufficient support to avoid outcomes that would lead to failure. It is beyond the scope of the current research to consider whether actual or potential supporters might have independently chosen to act in ways that would have saved the project.

11.5 CONCLUSION

In the terms of the conceptualisation of failure developed in chapter 3 Mandata was a failure. Ultimately it was not possible to sustain work on the system in the circumstances obtaining, and its termination came before it had been able to satisfy most of its supporters.

It failed because it reached a position in which the project organisation was unable to manoeuvre at all. It offered limited benefits to the Public Service as a whole and there was no prospect of this improving significantly. The project organisation had little basis for influencing the Board to act to prevent funding being withdrawn.

The process by which this position was reached was a complex set of interactions involving the organisational context, innovation process, various evaluation processes and the actual flow of support. Although alternative strategies for managing support were possible, it is hard to see that any of them would have appeared a better prospect at the time. This leaves the question of whether Mandata's failure could have been avoided. This will be addressed in the concluding chapter.

Chapter 12
Five Case Studies In Failure

Notwithstanding the shared belief among practitioners and researchers alike that failure is widespread, it is difficult to find detailed case histories to which the model developed in this book can be applied. The cases that are described in the literature are used for many different purposes, so they often lack information relevant to this model. However, there are a number of interesting cases which can be used to exemplify parts of the model. Because information is lacking, full analysis is impossible. Instead, commentaries draw attention to interesting facets of each case. References are given so that readers may refer to the original sources if they wish.

Like Mandata, some of these cases date back to the 1970s. They all offer lessons which are as pertinent today as they were years ago. The fact that computing technology has changed in many ways in the last twenty years is largely unimportant. The crucial points do not relate to the particulars of technologies but to the more general relationships between technology and other aspects of organisations. In one of the cases to be discussed a system was not implemented partly because the data processing department proposed to convert an on-line version of the system into batch. This situation may sound old fashioned, but describe it as the data processing department making the system unattractive to users by technical means, and it no longer matters that batch technology is outmoded; the same effect could be achieved as easily today as it could in the mid-1970s. Apart from the technology, project organisations are just as prone to cognitive limits, just as exposed to their environments and just as likely to be embroiled in politics as they ever were. The abstract conceptualisation of the organisational context in relation to information systems processes means that all the cases that follow can help us understand failure.

12.1 THE *USS STARSHIP*

This case concerns the introduction of advanced information

292 Chapter 12

systems for decision support and decision automation into a United States Navy aircraft carrier, the *USS Starship*. The systems were resisted and never fully implemented. Support was limited from the start and it died away altogether as a variety of contextual factors imposed themselves.

The case was originally described and analysed in Sloane (1991). The names are invented but the events are real. No dates were provided in the original.

12.1.1 Description

Each ship in the US Navy is provided with an official manual which details the formal organisational structure of the ship. While the *USS Starship* was being built and commissioned, its *Ship's Organization and Regulations Manual* (SORM) was developed and written by its first captain. According to Sloane (1991), Captain Smart was a thoroughgoing technocrat who wanted to standardise all procedures including expert decision-making, and proposed to automate his organisational design in a computer system, the *Ship's Planning, Plan Implementation, and Evaluation/Maintenance* (PIE) *Procedures for Performing Ship's Mission*. At the core of this was a system called ZOG which facilitated the development of and access to the data structure that reflected Smart's hierarchical organisational design. The idea was that whenever a task needed to be performed, its sub-tasks could be tracked in the data structure. Where human decisions were required, this would be reflected in the information ZOG would provide. Thus, an operational ZOG would provide a means of management control over the ship's activities.

A particularly novel aspect of Smart's proposal was that ZOG's knowledge base would be developed in its operational setting by the officers responsible for running different aspects of the ship. They would provide information about their tasks' structures and the decisions required from which ZOG would build its own knowledge base defining the organisational design. PIE could then use ZOG with its interface to this knowledge base to give the user immediate access to a breakdown of the sub-tasks involved in the completion of any operational task.

ZOG was not the only information system planned by Smart. There was a system to help in running aircraft operations from the

Five Case Studies In Failure 293

ship, another to help manage the stores inventory, and various others. The whole programme of integrating high tech information systems into the ship's normal set of systems was called the Technology Transfer Program (TTP).

The process by which the Technology Transfer Program was initiated was very different from that which is customary in the US Navy. Instead of a slow and detailed process of development and assessment of the technology by Navy R&D specialists, the systems were built by civilian scientists. They were installed in *USS Starship* in time for its maiden voyage, but critical elements of implementation were incomplete. It remained to build the ZOG knowledge base, to test the system in operation and to evaluate it.

Although Smart had negotiated the political hurdles required to obtain approval for TTP, he had not secured any resourcing for its implementation and operation. Consequently he had to establish a special department within the ship's organisation, the Management Department, to run the Program and staff it with personnel originally intended for other roles. However, they were unable to make much progress because of the need to get the ship to a state of full operational readiness - operational objectives being by tradition paramount on US naval ships. Once it became apparent that TTP was impeding progress toward operational readiness, Smart shifted his priorities. As a result, the Program made little further progress during the remainder of Smart's command.

Some elements of TTP were usable by the time Smart's replacement took charge. The usable systems were the aircraft operations management system and a tactical command system which could be operated from the bridge. In fact neither was used. Though the Airplan system for aircraft management could have provided the traffic controllers and their commander with much of the information that they required for planning and controlling operations, they chose to use no computer support. Sloane (1991) cites three reasons. First, there was fear that reliance on a computer system would make them unprepared for manual control in the event of a system malfunction. Second, the personnel in question did not believe that the computer system would help them improve their decision-making. Third, there was a strong shared belief in the essential role of humans as responsible decision-makers, a belief that was deep-rooted in Navy culture. As for the tactical command system, the new captain simply chose not to use it.

Sloane also records that the ship's nuclear reactor officer and its supply officer both rejected computer support for their tasks for the same reason. They had to make decisions more flexibly than they believed a computer system could.

12.1.2 Commentary

TTP failed in that it satisfied nobody, it was not fully implemented, and there was no support to reverse this state of affairs. What can be said about how and why TTP failed?

Clearly, Smart managed the initiation stage successfully, inasmuch as he obtained a favourable strategic decision to proceed. However, though he apparently obtained funds to purchase the TTP systems from civilian suppliers, he obtained no resources for the extra shipboard tasks involved in implementing the Program.

The lack of proper funding for implementing TTP meant that it was exposed to its context without satisfactory means for managing it. The context manifested itself in a number of ways. The Navy's deeply rooted culture was influential in three ways. First, the ship's personnel were not accustomed to being involved in developing innovative systems. In the US Navy it was an expectation that R&D would be carried out and thoroughly tested by the Navy's onshore staff ready for shipboard operation. TTP did not meet this expectation. Second, the task of implementing ZOG conflicted with the traditional top priority of getting the new ship operational. Third, the Navy values the individual as an indispensable component of a ship's organisation. Smart's program appeared to diminish the value of the individual by aiming to give increased decision power to computer systems. Thus TTP was at odds with the Navy's very strong culture and traditions and as a result was at risk from the start.

Other aspects of the context affected implementation. The technical process involved in interacting with the system was constraining. One officer described ZOG as 'worthless because it's so user unfriendly' (Sloane 1991, p89). There were cognitive problems in articulating the details of tasks and the parameters of decisions. Moreover, officers could not see how discretionary decision-making could be easily integrated into ZOG's knowledge base of routine tasks and decisions.

In the face of such deeply rooted resistance and other

Five Case Studies In Failure 295

contingent difficulties, it would have been desirable to call upon a variety of sources of support. Yet, support for TTP appears to have come exclusively from Smart. He was the idea champion, but there is no evidence that he attempted to build any other base of support. It is possible that he believed that his authority as chief executive of the ship would be sufficient. Certainly such a belief would be consistent with the centralisation of decision-making implicit in TTP and with his apparent belief that it would be possible to develop an entirely routinised organisational structure. What is clear is that his support alone was not sufficient to keep both TTP and shipboard operations progressing to schedule. When Smart's priorities shifted away from TTP it lacked the support to keep it moving. Even if his priorities had not shifted, the fact that the Navy rotates its personnel through a variety of tours of duty meant that Smart only ever had a limited timeframe within which to win acceptance for his innovation.

When Smart was replaced, there was no idea champion and no party that perceived itself as standing to gain from the project. Though Smart may have been politically astute in winning authorisation for his proposals from his superiors, he appears to have paid no attention to the politics of winning support from his subordinates. Sloane (1991) records various officers' personal evaluations to the effect that the TTP systems would not improve effectiveness, they would not cope in the cases where humans used intuition or broke the rules, and they would create a risk that humans would not be able to cope when the system broke down. Sloane records no evidence of Smart trying to influence the premises of these evaluations or to rebut their conclusions even though they could only be speculative. The basis for resistance appears to have gone unchallenged.

Even those systems which were usable were not used. Smart's successor personally rejected the technology of the tactical command system thereby demonstrating the legitimacy of rejecting technology and at the same time reinforcing the Navy's cultural norms. It is therefore no surprise that the TTP did not survive the change in command.

In summary, the context of the TTP systems bred resistance which there was insufficient support to combat. The program was clearly intended to serve the captain and not other members of the crew, yet the support of the crew was necessary given the lack of funding for implementation and operation. Higher priorities

296   *Chapter 12*

forced Smart to cut back his own personal support for the programme and when he was relieved by a new commander there was no support remaining.

12.2 THE ENERGY CONSERVATION SYSTEM

Dickson and Janson (1984) describe an attempt to develop and implement a decision support system to assist in energy conservation. The chief interest of the case lies in the authors' contention that the causes of failure were exclusively technical, not behavioural or political. The commentary takes issue with this assessment, using this book's model of failure to show how political factors might have been relevant.

No dates were given in the original paper for the events described.

12.2.1 Description

This case concerns the development and initial implementation of a decision support system by the energy agency of a state in the midwest of the USA. The system was a response to state and federal laws enacted as a result of increasing fuel costs. It was intended that the system would assess the energy consumption of buildings and where necessary recommend changes to building maintenance, operation or structure.

Consultants were contracted to devise the system. Their design was for a two staged system, the core of which would be a deterministic energy consumption model. In the first stage, data would be collected about buildings (their structure, materials, fuel consuming plant etc) so that an analysis could be made of how much energy they should consume. In the second stage, this could be matched against actual consumption for any building. If the discrepancy between predicted and actual fuel consumption were to prove too great then the system would support either of two further audits. The mini audit would require further data collection for the building. This would involve an 'onsite walkthrough by someone designated by the building owner, operator, or administrator' (Dickson & Janson 1984, p72). The alternative was a maxi audit which required more detailed data collection relating to the

Five Case Studies In Failure 297

engineering attributes of the building. The outcome of the mini audit would be relatively low cost recommendations for changes to operational procedures and maintenance. The outcome of the maxi audit would be recommendations relating to operations and building structure which would have capital cost implications. It would be the responsibility of building administrators to provide the data for the model and it would be their decision what to do with its recommendations.

Once the consultants had delivered the energy analysis model they asked the energy agency to institute a data collection activity which yielded a database for 3000 buildings. Having completed this data collection, the model was tested on a few buildings. The energy agency evaluated its output against their expectations and found it wanting. The problem lay in the climatic assumptions made. The model reflected Californian weather conditions instead of those of the midwest. The consultants were asked to amend the model accordingly. When these changes still yielded unsatisfactory results the consultancy arrangement was terminated and another consultant hired.

The new consultant conducted an investigation into the quality of the data used by the model. Finding it to be poor, he set about constructing a relatively simple statistical model which only made use of data which were comparatively accurate or easily corrected. However, this statistical model also proved unsatisfactory. A more detailed investigation of the data revealed that from a sample of nearly 12,000 data items almost 12% were either in error or missing. The main causes for this were errors by building administration staff in filling out the forms and errors in data entry by the energy agency. In the light of this information the consultant decided that the statistical model was useless. The energy agency withdrew staff resources from the project until all support had ceased.

12.2.2 Commentary

Three questions are addressed in this commentary. Was the energy analysis decision support system a failure? How should we understand the process through which it was developed and finally terminated? Is it reasonable to claim that the causes were technical?

Was the system a failure? Dickson and Janson are concerned

in their analysis of this case to explore a distinction among installation, implementation and integration. Their attitude is that it was a failure although they do concede the possibility that it was 'a very, very limited success' (Dickson & Janson 1984, p75) on the ground that some degree of installation and implementation was achieved. This is a generous assessment which reflects the common experience that something is achieved in almost all projects. The system ran out of support before it was in regular operational use and there is no evidence that it satisfied its supporters' expectations. There is perhaps one scenario under which it might not have been a failure. According to this, the energy agency was more concerned to be seen to be attempting to influence energy consumption in public buildings than to make a difference. If this were so, it might be that the system served its purpose politically, though it would presumably have served that purpose rather better had it been used.

Turning to the information systems process, we find we are told relatively little about it. There were energy agency staff allocated to the project so we can infer that there was a project organisation within the agency. We are told of two contextual sources of problems. The first is the technical process which produced the first energy model. This was apparently corrected. The second was an environmental problem - the supply of data was of poor quality. Interestingly, the solution attempted was technical. There was no attempt to correct the data. Rather there was an attempt to make the best of the bad data via a new model which would use those data items which were most accurate or easily corrected. Why did the project organisation not attempt to improve the data by instituting a more rigorous collection process either when the data were first found to be at fault or after the discovery that the second model was unsatisfactory?

Who promoted the project and who supported it we do not know. The project was initiated as a result of the passage of state and federal laws, but whether senior executives used this as an opportunity to pursue a project they favoured independently or whether they were following a directive is unknown. Clearly there were supporters funding the project - consultants were hired as well as agency staff being assigned. Furthermore, when the model was first run and yielded unsatisfactory results there was support for a diagnostic effort which resulted in the consultant doing more work on the model. When this too proved unsatisfactory, rather than scrapping the project a second consultant was hired.

Five Case Studies In Failure 299

What is intriguing about this case is that there was support for two attempts to recover from flaws but not for a third. The initial discovery that the system produced flawed outputs did not result in termination because there was the possibility of retrieving the situation. The change to the climatic assumptions did not yield satisfactory results. The second attempt to recover was no more satisfactory although it appears to have highlighted the problem of data quality. Instead of taking advantage of this knowledge to make a third attempt at retrieving the situation, the project was terminated even though, as Dickson and Janson explicitly note, had the data been corrected the model might have yielded the correct results. So at first there was support in the face of flaws, then there was a withdrawal of support despite the possibility of correcting the flaws. Unfortunately, no information is provided as to the basis on which supporters' decisions were made.

The third question is - was the cause of failure technical? Certainly the system failed to yield plausible predictions of fuel consumption, but whether this was the result of a technical flaw is less obvious. The problem of data quality is an environmental problem of supply. It therefore makes sense to look at the environment for reasons for the problem. Perhaps there were political factors. Perhaps building administrators felt threatened by the energy agency's plans. Or perhaps they saw no benefit in it because nobody had explained the reasons for the initial data collection exercise. If we had some further information on these points it would help to discover why when data quality was first recognised to be a problem, it was treated as if a technical solution would be appropriate. We can speculate that it was a much cheaper solution but this does not explain why, when this cheaper solution failed, the issue of data quality was not addressed. Why was support withdrawn, and why after the failure of the statistical model rather than earlier? The question whether the cause of failure of the energy conservation system was really technical must remain open.

The model presented in this book points to a number of questions which the energy conservation system case leaves unanswered. Without an understanding of the support for the project we cannot come to understand why it was withdrawn. Because flaws can be overcome by support an explanation of failure has to explain the reasons for withdrawal of support. If, in this case, the data quality could have been improved, the reasons the system failed would seem to be more complex and more interesting than that there was a technical failing in obtaining data of suitable quality. Whether these reasons include behavioural and political factors remains an open question.

12.3 THE RETAIL BUYERS' PLANNING SYSTEM

This case relates to a system for supporting the planning process carried out by buyers in a chain of retail stores. It appears to have been developed to order but to have failed in the implementation stage. It is interesting because it shows some of the difficulties associated with traditional prescriptions such as involving users and obtaining top management support. It also shows the importance of support from other sources.

The example is drawn from Rudelius, Dickson and Hartley (1982). The main events described relate to the years 1972 to 1975.

12.3.1 Description

The retail buyers' planning system was developed by a university research team for a retail chain. The initiative came from the firm's Director of Marketing Research and one of the Divisional Merchandising Managers. What was required was an information system which would assist the firm's departmental buyers in their twice yearly planning process.

The application, the buyers' planning process, was moderately complex. It involved each buyer producing a plan which would show how her department would meet the chain's overall management plan. This would involve a breakdown by month, store, and class of goods.

The university R&D team met with buyers to determine how they actually planned. They discovered that there was a variety of approaches and so built their model to support the different buyers' preferences. System operation was interactive, the programs being run from the university's computer installation.

In late 1973 the system was tested on three buyers who were then asked to evaluate it. They appear to have been very pleased. The university team therefore made arrangements to hand over the system to the retail chain's own dp department for implementation.

Five Case Studies In Failure 301

The next the university heard was that the system was to be used more widely in the company but that its usage was to be in batch mode rather than interactive. Buyers would fill out forms for input rather than interacting directly with the system.

When one of the university's researchers attempted to find out the status of the planning system in 1977 there was no trace of it. The Director of Marketing Research and the Divisional Merchandising Manager had both left the company in 1975. The system appeared never to have been operational, nor did many people even recall its existence. At the same time, though, the researcher found that there was a demand for such a system from both buyers and Divisional Merchandising Managers.

12.3.2 Commentary

The retail planning system failed in that it was unable to sustain the support necessary to keep it permanently in operation. This is interesting because the system appears to have worked quite well and the buyers wanted it. Indeed, the demand for such a system was still there years later when the university checked back and found that the system had disappeared. So, although there were no significant difficulties arising from the organisational context during the initiation and development stages, the project appears to have just run out of support. Why?

Rudelius, Dickson and Hartley (1982) analyse this case in terms of four factors which relate to support: management support, user involvement, the implementation process, and the power structure. They argue that management support was only superficial because the managers involved allowed the data processing department to suggest a batch version of the system. They suggest that senior managers saw no need for the system and only approved the project because there were no immediate costs involved. If this is right then we have a case of demand-pull where supporters lacked the power to pursue their idea to full implementation.

As has been noted previously, the appearance of support can be misleading. In a retail chain, the sales, financial and purchasing areas, being the areas on which the organisation as a whole is most dependent, will be the most powerful. So, it would not be surprising if the Director of Marketing Research was not very influential. By contrast, the Divisional Merchandising Manager who supported the project would have come from a more influential area. We can only speculate why he was unable to manage the implementation process satisfactorily. Perhaps he was too low in the hierarchy to be able to command support himself. Perhaps he was personally not respected. Had he enlisted the support of other merchandising managers or of his own superior then it might have been easier to force the issue. Once again, we see that it is one thing for apparently important managers to want a system, but quite another for them to be able to deliver the support needed.

The second factor was user involvement. Rudelius, Dickson and Hartley note that some users were involved. Presumably this contributed to the innovation process producing a system with which the buyers were satisfied. However, as they point out, it was only three buyers, and they appear not to have attempted to inform and influence other buyers. User involvement is not purely a matter of ensuring that a system is built to meet requirements, it is also a support winning process. The support of more than three buyers might have increased the pressure from users on those with the power to fund implementation. So, just as the appearance of top management support may mislead as to the actual support available, so too the fact of user involvement does not demonstrate that all its benefits will be achieved.

The third factor was the non-existence of an implementation process. Rudelius, Dickson and Hartley characterise implementation in terms of attitude formation, demand creation, support management and working with the power structure. They say that there were no implementation strategies devised by the project's supporters. However, it appears that some efforts were made by the system's supporters because the university was notified that a batch version was to be implemented. This suggests that there was some negotiation with the data processing department. Unfortunately, to understand the failure to win support from the data processing department we would need to know more about the negotiation process and the power structure.

The fourth factor cited as contributing to the project outcome was failure to work with the organisational power structure. The data processing department was able to propose a change to the planning system which was at odds with the sub-culture of buyers. The batch system would have bureaucratised their planning process

Five Case Studies In Failure 303

in a way that would probably have been unacceptable to buyers who typically think on their feet and make decisions within very short timeframes. What we do not know is whether the data processing department deliberately tried to destroy the system or whether it was responding to another agenda. Without a fuller analysis of the power structure of the company it is hard to say whether working with the power structure would have made any significant difference.

An interesting feature of this example is that there does not appear to have been any identifiable project organisation within the retail chain responsible for managing the implementation process. This lack of an enduring organisational sub-unit with responsibility for the system would have made it very susceptible to loss of support.

12.4 SWISSAIR

The case described in this section concerns a personnel and payroll system at the airline company, Swissair. It is particularly interesting in comparison with Mandata. There were differences such as more clear-cut organisational arrangements and a well established infrastructure. There were also similarities. As in Mandata, support was constrained by macro-economic factors affecting the host organisation. Another similarity was the importance of the relationship between personnel and payroll systems, though in this case the effect of a break in the relationship is far more obvious.

This case is extracted from Buechi (1982). At the time the paper was published Buechi was Vice President for the Computer and Communications Department at Swissair. The events described took place between 1973 and 1975.

12.4.1 Description

Development of Swissair's Personnel Information and Salary System project (PISA) was approved in May 1973. It was to replace a fifteen year old batch payroll system and develop a sophisticated personnel management system. The payroll was to provide information to a personnel database using IBM's database management system, IMS.

The system developers were required to liaise with two quite separate user departments. Payroll was the responsibility of Finance whereas personnel information was dealt with by Personnel. The two departments had different objectives. The Finance Department was aiming for an economical upgrade of its old system while Personnel wanted a technologically advanced product. The differences in the two departments' perspectives led to conflicting requirements.

In addition to the problems with its clients, the project organisation was constrained by Swissair's limited capacity to run IMS systems. The IMS database software was needed for a system to support a crucial engineering application. If it were used for PISA as well, the performance costs could have been damaging to both systems. PISA, being less important to Swissair's core activities, was the more likely of the two to be sacrificed.

PISA was not well supported by the chair of the Project Policy Board. This would normally have been the Vice President of the user department for whom the system was being developed. Instead the Vice President of Finance delegated this role to his deputy. The deputy was opposed to the project because he did not believe a feasible system could be produced economically. Moreover, he was at the same time head of a task force to establish a programme for combating the effects of recession on the company - essentially a cost-cutting exercise. This was inconsistent with his role as chair of the steering committee for a spending project.

By the middle of 1975, three quarters of the system had been specified, half of this having been programmed. Despite this apparent progress, when recession hit the economy a financial review of all dp projects was undertaken. The review of PISA revealed that in addition to the initial budget of 5.3 million Swiss Francs (SFr) a further 3.6 million were required. This reduced the return on investment from 3% to zero. In June 1975 the Finance Department proposed scrapping the payroll part of the system. The Personnel Department was unable to provide financial justification for continuing alone, so the whole project was terminated.

12.4.2 Commentary

PISA's failure is neatly explained in terms of the model proposed in

Five Case Studies In Failure 305

this book. The innovation process was affected by contextual factors largely in the form of conflicting user objectives. This resulted in a development stage which was more expensive than estimated. Extra support was necessary if the system was to be completed. The chair of the steering committee was potentially a key supporter, but his evaluation of the project was that it would not be cost-effective. Contingently, the economic context imposed priorities on him which were at odds with those of the PISA project organisation. The review generated an evaluation of the whole project which showed it as offering no financial benefit. When the Finance department pulled out of the project, Personnel could not bring forward suitably favourable evaluations for the remainder of the project. Lacking the power to command support in any other way, the project was terminated.

The problem of conflicting user objectives might have been addressed in either of two ways, one structural, the other political. The structural solution would have been to move the payroll function under Personnel. However, this would almost certainly have run counter to the power structure. Personnel departments rarely annex sections of Finance in any organisation. The political solution would have been for the chair of the Project Policy Board to act as broker for negotiations among the project organisation, Finance users and Personnel. However, circumstances were against this option too. The person in question had made a negative evaluation of the project and was responsible for devising economic strategies for dealing with the effects of recession. It is unlikely that he would have been motivated to resolve the problem. Even had he been motivated, it is interesting to note that his own manager, the Vice President, had, in choosing not to chair the Project Policy Board himself, chosen not to give the project his personal support. It is therefore not obvious that the chair would have had the power to resolve the user problems.

The crisis that resulted in the project's termination was precipitated by the environmental contingency of economic recession. All data processing projects were re-evaluated. The recession meant that financial factors would be paramount in deciding on continuing support. Buechi tells us that the Finance Department felt responsible for the whole development but unable to devote enough effort to the personnel side of the application. When the increased estimates became known, they decided to withdraw, leaving Personnel to pursue the development itself if it

306   Chapter 12

could justify it. It is worth noting that this option was easier for Finance because it already had a working payroll system and so was not highly dependent on the new system. It is not made clear why Personnel was unable to produce an evaluation which would have justified its continuation. All we can say is that the system was presumably dependent on the payroll function, and Personnel had no means of leverage over Finance to maintain its interest in the system. Furthermore, the data processing department had made its own negative evaluation of the technical effects of using IMS for both PISA and the more important engineering system. Though this did not trigger termination, it did mean that data processing would not fight for PISA's retention.

A final interesting feature of this case is that the termination of PISA was accompanied by an explicit decision not to make any attempt to revive the project for another five years. Thus, just like Mandata, failure had enduring effects on what could be done subsequently.

12.5 FISCAL IMPACT ANALYSIS SYSTEM

The description and analysis of this case is one of the most detailed in the literature. It relates to a project to introduce a computer-based fiscal impact analysis system into the administration of the City of Tulsa in the USA. The description given here is very abbreviated compared with the original (Dutton 1981, see also Dutton & Kraemer 1985).

Dutton's chief concern is to illustrate the importance of the political environment although he acknowledges the role of technical, organisational and personal issues in the information systems process. This case is of interest in two ways. The first is that the politics of support are clearly revealed. The second is that, like Mandata, it shows how an information systems innovation process can change in character over time. It will not necessarily retain the same form as when initially envisaged.

12.5.1 Description

The City of Tulsa's Fiscal Impact Analysis System (FIAS) was one part of a larger programme, the Growth Guidance System (GGS), designed to manage urban growth. Historically, Tulsa had grown

Five Case Studies In Failure 307

as a result of largely uncontrolled development. A strong development lobby was both a cause and consequence of this. By 1970 when Robert LaFortune was elected mayor, there was an increasing concern among some members of the community that unplanned development was not in the city's best interests. Under LaFortune the city's administration made efforts to promote more balanced growth than would have occurred with unfettered development. GGS was initiated in April 1977 by the Tulsa City Commission. Its proponents were the members of a pro-planning coalition led by LaFortune.

The trigger to initiate GGS was contact with Professor Robert Freilich. Freilich's specialism was the development of legal mechanisms for controlling land use in accordance with formal plans. Freilich was contracted to develop an overall plan for GGS and to carry out legal analyses. Different parties, including other consultants and Tulsa officials would carry out the rest of the work. A central part of the effort was to be the development of different growth strategies and analysis of their financial impacts.

GGS was immediately opposed by the development lobby. One of Tulsa's main newspapers led the public opposition by arguing that GGS was a means to instituting no growth. So, right from the start GGS and later FIAS were public political issues.

Despite this opposition, the planning coalition was able to set its programme in motion. In addition to the principal consultant, two further firms were engaged. After initial resistance because of the political nature of the programme, the Tulsa Metropolitan Area Planning Commission (TMAPC) took responsibility for managing GGS. Data collection and other tasks were allocated to TMAPC and other city officials.

After undertaking a number of preparatory tasks the GGS consultants proposed that a fiscal impact analysis be conducted. Although it was generally supposed by the planning community that balanced growth would be economically advantageous for the city administration because it would permit better control over the use of existing resources, the development lobby did not share this view. LaFortune realised that the city would need fiscal impact evaluations both in establishing the need for growth guidance and in justifying particular policies. So a Fiscal Impact Advisory System Task Force (FIASTF) was established under the supervision of a newly established Growth Guidance Technical Advisory Committee. FIASTF issued a request for proposals for a system the specifications for which were demanding in that the system would be required to assess the direct and indirect costs and revenues of planning options for both public and private sectors. Of all the proposals received, one stood out because it provided both a community model which would project various demographic and economic trends for the city and a fiscal impact model which could evaluate the costs and revenues of the community trends. This proposal looked the more impressive because the provider, Decision Sciences Corporation (DSC), already had a computerised system which they could enhance to meet Tulsa's specifications. The proposal was thoroughly evaluated by the committees responsible and by LaFortune himself. With the full approval of the city commission, DSC was engaged in April 1978 to develop the Fiscal Impact Analysis System.

However, April 1978 was LaFortune's last month as mayor. He was replaced by another Republican, but this time one who was in favour of *laisser-faire* development. The balance of city politics shifted with the emergence of a new dominant coalition. The new mayor replaced supporters of growth guidance on the city planning commission and made a number of other changes at a senior level which indicated to the growth guidance consultants and planners that growth guidance was being discontinued. In practice, it was not as clear-cut. The new Director of City Development, who also became Tulsa's chief administrative officer, had had some involvement with the programme. He supported both the idea of a model and the choice of model, though he had reservations as to how useful it would be. So, in the new political situation which included some support, elements of the programme were wound down but others remained. FIAS was one of those which survived, but the work of the main GGS consultants did not.

Since early 1978 GGS had been under fire from the press because of delays. A major problem was the land related data TMAPC provided for the modelling process. In the first place it was not a preexisting database. Second, when it was collected it proved to be of poor quality. Third, efforts to improve its quality were unsuccessful. A review in August had seen the consultants offering to try to resolve the data quality problems with city officials. This was apparently not sufficient to safeguard the contract. By February 1979 the contracts had been terminated. Dutton notes in his account that though there were criticisms about individuals, organisation, delays, and data quality, these were

Five Case Studies In Failure 309

essentially no more than rationales for a prior political decision.

What remained of LaFortune's growth guidance initiative was a growth planning activity confined to TMAPC. The main plank of this was the fiscal impact modelling based on FIAS. At TMAPC, DSC was assisted by a planner who became a champion for FIAS. By the end of 1978 TMAPC was preparing data collection forms for DSC. Initial tests provided analyses of different growth scenarios which appeared not to support any particular approach but which looked worthwhile because they indicated that some scenarios were simply impracticable. This done, DSC worked on the transfer of FIAS from its PRIME computer to Tulsa's Honeywell. Though there were some technical difficulties these were overcome and by September 1979 FIAS had been installed at Tulsa.

During 1979 the TMAPC champion left, handing over responsibility to two other planners. Though they handled the completion of the DSC contract, the new staff raised doubts about the accuracy of the database both in its land use and its financial components. They also preferred a different modelling philosophy to that implicit in FIAS. They wanted a model that was sufficiently economical in computational resources that it could be run freely, and they wanted a model which they could understand and whose results they could explain and defend. DSC's FIAS was too complex for them on both of these scores. They therefore proceeded to design, develop and implement their own model which they extended to include revenue and expenditure forecasting.

On the face of things, it seems strange that the new staff should have bothered to try to improve TMAPC's modelling capacity when fiscal modelling was off the city commission's political agenda. However, there was a continuing demand for the results of fiscal modelling. Several groups stood to be served by the model. TMAPC itself wanted to evaluate the various main growth scenarios so as to properly inform the city's decision-makers. As part of this, TMAPC planners involved many interested parties in the final scenario preparation, attempting to both include their interests and educate them as to the use of the model. Within TMAPC some of the planners saw FIAS as an aid to short term planning. It could help assess the impact of immediate developments. The Chamber of Commerce, whose support for GGS had been won by LaFortune, continued to support FIAS in the hope that it would be useful in their attempts to promote particular capital developments in the interests of its members. For the Chamber, FIAS had the advantage of providing financial evaluations which were a language the business community understood. It had the further advantage that it looked like an objective method, so it would have legitimacy when used to challenge development. Other interested parties saw FIAS as a means to getting developers to bear more of the cost of development and as a means of persuading the public of the validity of its revenue programmes for capital works. Some city departments even supported FIAS because its data collection activity made available to them a greatly improved database of financial information. Finally, after its association with the GGS débacle TMAPC also stood to gain from an improved corporate image if it could serve some or all of these constituencies.

In the event FIAS and its competitor models did not serve many of these interests. In mid-1980 an increased sales tax to pay for capital improvements was successfully promoted using data from the modelling exercise. But in July the preliminary results of the comparative evaluation of the three main growth strategies was presented to the city commission. The evaluations were mixed, no strategy being clearly better than the others. As a result, and in line with the dominant coalition's preferences, the city commission requested that no particular growth strategy be recommended. The models were then shelved, and three months later TMAPC was dismantled.

12.5.2 Commentary

This case is interesting in two ways. It shows how the politics of support can affect an information systems process. It also shows how contingencies affect the identity of supporters and how this affects the support available. In the light of this, let us review the case, observing how support affected the FIAS innovation process.

FIAS was initiated because LaFortune's support from the top ensured that the project would get through the various consultation and decision processes in Tulsa. LaFortune's commitment is evident from the fact that he personally examined DSC's proposal. Moreover, he had a coalition of supporters of planning in place throughout the political and administrative system. He also had

Five Case Studies In Failure 311

support in the community from the Chamber of Commerce. The problem for subsequent stages of FIAS was that LaFortune retired at the same time as the contract to DSC was let, and his successor favoured development rather than growth guidance. The change of mayor led to the planning coalition being replaced throughout Tulsa's complex system of consultation and decision-making. However, though top management no longer stood to gain from FIAS, other parties gave it sufficient support for the project to be continued for a further two years.

It is unclear why FIAS was not terminated along with all the other GGS contracts. One might speculate that it was because the chief administrative officer supported FIAS even though he was uncertain about how valuable the results would be. There is no evidence in the case description of any interventions being needed to prevent the system's early termination. Dutton argues that FIAS continued because there was no non-political rationale for cancelling the DSC contract, but the fact that GGS was being cancelled would have been good enough reason. Indeed, Dutton himself notes that GGS had been the main rationale for FIAS.

So, the development and innovation stages continued because the system had all the support it needed. DSC was under contract to do the development; and it was supported by a champion in TMAPC who appears to have acted as a fixer for DSC, securing participation of various groups, providing data, and generally facilitating the development and testing of the system. This support helped prevent the technical problems and data supply problems from damaging progress significantly.

When this champion resigned, FIAS became the responsibility of staff with different objectives for the system. Although they did a lot of work on the transfer of the system from DSC to TMAPC, the system did not support their particular interests insofar as it was operationally expensive and its results hard to defend thereby reducing its ability to serve a variety of interests. Thus, the decision to build an alternative made good political sense.

By contrast, it seems to have been far less politically astute to present the model's findings to the city commission since growth guidance was not supported by the dominant coalition. The fact that there was little to choose among the analyses of the different strategies meant that modelling provided no major policy guidance to the commission. This gave them an excuse to scrap fiscal impact modelling.

312   Chapter 12

On the other hand, had TMAPC kept FIAS and the other models for its own use and to serve the various sectional interests, then it might have not have been terminated. After all, it no longer needed any active support at the top level. In the event, the matter is academic because TMAPC was closed shortly after.

It is clear that it required top management support to launch FIAS because it was politically contentious. Change in the political environment resulted in the termination of the GGS contracts which were FIAS's main justification. Once the money had been voted for the contract, the fact that there was support for FIAS within TMAPC meant that the innovation process could be coped with without giving opponents an excuse to intervene. The development of alternative models which might better serve the various interests that still stood to gain from fiscal impact analysis was politically astute. However, once the models' results were made public, the commission had the opportunity to prevent their further use. The system did not serve powerful supporters sufficiently to give the TMAPC team the leverage to ensure its continued operation and use.

12.6 CONCLUSION

It should be clear from the cases presented that there is a variety of ways in which a system can come to be prematurely terminated. It should also be apparent that it is hard to make definitive statements about the causal sequence leading to termination because the original case descriptions do not answer some crucial questions. For example, the retail buyers' planning system was developed and tested, but we know almost nothing about why it was not installed and implemented in its host organisation. Or again, in the energy conservation model we do not know why no attempt was made to correct the data. This is interesting because in the FIAS case a significant effort was made to improve data quality. It is not obvious what distinguishes the two cases in this respect.

One particularly interesting distinction to be noted is that in the cases of the naval TTP, the energy conservation model, and the Swissair PISA system the context created problematic situations which appear to have contributed to flaws in the innovation process - delays, poor data quality, resistance - which in turn influenced decisions about support. By contrast, the loss of support in the cases of the retail buyers' planning system and the FIAS case appears to have been determined by wider political considerations. It is clear therefore that those who seek to promote information systems in particular organisational settings must give their attention to both the systems innovation process and the support management process.

Another factor which is noticeable is that in three of the cases the people who were their systems' chief proponents became dissociated from the project. In the Tulsa case this had a fundamental effect on the availability of support. In the retail planning case it is not known whether the departure of the idea champions was either a cause or effect of the subsequent lack of support. In the naval case, the replacement of the idea champion meant that even the more routine aspects of TTP would not be supported. It is interesting to observe that in the Tulsa and USS Starship examples the departure of the idea champion was predictable. In Tulsa LaFortune had already made public his decision not to stand again. In the US Navy, officers are routinely rotated. The general point to emerge is that where a regular timeframe influences the occupancy of key supporters' positions the project organisation should take careful note because support cannot be guaranteed beyond the end of that timeframe.

It is also important to see that in general the projects' proponents lacked power relative to those whose actual continued substantial support might have made a difference. In the retail planning system the idea champions appear not to have had leverage over the dp department nor over any other organisational power-broker who could have prevailed upon dp to give its support. On USS Starship the captain apparently lacked the power to win sufficient support from his superiors to enable him to overcome internal resistance. At Swissair the Personnel Department lacked representation in the project management structure and lacked the organisational leverage to ensure the project's continuance after the more powerful Finance Department dropped out. In Tulsa a change of dominant coalition meant that FIAS's continued existence would not serve the interests of the most powerful group.

Support for information systems is influenced by the value of the system or its perceived value, and by extrinsic contingencies. If support can be managed then flaws in the innovation process may be overcome. If there is not sufficient support, the flaws will ultimately affect supporters' evaluations. The cases in this chapter reinforce these points.

Suggested Readings

In the early 1980s the journal *Systems, Objectives, Solutions* (SOS) provided a publishing focus for case studies. Though the journal no longer exists, there continues to be an SOS section in *Information and Management*.

Chapter 13
Summary And Conclusions

This book has presented a model of the information systems process which is intended to help us understand the nature and causes of failure. It is a web model (Kling 1987) inasmuch as it makes use of many different elements which interact with each other to produce information systems outcomes. The interaction or feedback in the model means that it does not yield any simple explanations of failure. In this, it respects H.L. Mencken's dictum that, "To every complex question there is a simple answer - and it's always wrong".

The importance of having a web model is borne out when real cases are considered. Actual information systems processes do not always proceed according to well-defined steps or stages. They are influenced by a variety of stakeholders with different, sometimes conflicting, interests, and by numerous other factors. The influences will vary from case to case. Because the reality is complex, so too must be the explanatory model. Application of the model to actual cases therefore serves to highlight the fact that there are no simple answers. This point is especially important for this concluding chapter because it is in drawing conclusions that we typically recommend better ways of handling a problem. The complexity of the problem of information systems failure means that no recommendations can be made which are both simple and certain to succeed. In reminding us of the complexity of the problem, case studies of information systems failure help to keep us honest.

This concluding chapter starts by restating the main points of the book. It proceeds to argue that some information systems processes are so situated that it is impossible for the project organisation to prevent them from failing. A further two sections are devoted to making recommendations for practitioners and for researchers. The final section considers the prospects for the future.

13.1 SUMMARY

Failure occurs when a project organisation is unable to sustain sufficient support to continue work on its system and the cessation of work leaves supporters dissatisfied with what the system has done for them. By comparison with the four types of failure concept discussed in chapter 3 this view of failure is quite conservative. It treats missed deadlines, unmet requirements, dissatisfied customers, unused systems and the like as potential contributors to failure, but not as defining characteristics of it. Nothing specially privileges a particular deadline or stated requirement. When we bear in mind the uncertainties inherent in the information systems innovation process, we can see that there is something arbitrary about fixing on a given standard - be it cost-benefit, development schedule or functionality - and expecting that regardless of what befalls the project that that standard should be achieved. Since many projects continue despite being correspondence, process, interaction or expectation failures, it is clear that such failures are far from being the end of the system's existence - indeed, they are a normal feature of the information systems process. It is therefore pertinent to ask in what way the unmet requirement or the dissatisfied customer affects what happens subsequently. How does the user or supporter respond? What does the project organisation do?

Chapter 3 characterised project organisations as manoeuvring in response to events so as to retain sufficient support to continue their work. In this perspective, failure occurs when a project organisation runs out of support and can no longer work on its information system. Situations which have more traditionally been thought of as failures in themselves are treated as situations in a more enduring process to which the project organisation will respond according to its understanding of their likely effects.

This conception of failure is fruitful in helping us to understand the processes by which failure comes about. In addition, in promoting a more conservative use of 'failure' this approach serves as a valuable counterweight to some of the effects of more promiscuous uses of the term. To use 'failure' as freely as we have in information systems has not been good public relations. It has suggested that information systems professionals have not, in general, done a good job. But, more importantly, it has reinforced a pernicious view of information systems. The liberal use of 'failure' by information systems practitioners and by researchers in

Summary And Conclusions 317

the field has implied that we think we *should have* done better, that all those missed deadlines, budget overruns, flawed systems, flawed developments and so on *could have* been avoided. This has helped encourage a narrow view of the information systems process, a view in which solutions can be simple, and where next time things will be better. It has not encouraged deep thought about the process. By contrast, a more complex view that admits correspondence, process, interaction, and expectation failures as normal problems in the information systems process and that sees the process as beset by a wide variety of constraints and contingencies, not all avoidable, may encourage a correspondingly richer and more complex response.

The model in this book focuses on the relationship between the project organisation and its supporters. It portrays it as an exchange relationship where the information system, or the promise of need satisfaction that it offers, is the project organisation's main bargaining counter. However, the exchange is complicated by the fact that support is required in advance of the system's providing benefits and by the fact that the innovative nature of information systems makes their development, implementation, and continued operation (the innovation process) an uncertain process. The model conceptualises the situation as a triangle of dependences: the system being dependent on the project organisation, the project organisation on supporters, and supporters on the system. Acting upon the innovation process and the process by which support is won and delivered are various contextual factors. Constraints and contingencies of the context act as exogenous factors influencing stakeholders' decisions and behaviours.

The constraints and contingencies that bear on the innovation of the system itself are the sources of problems. These are addressed by systematic problem-solving mechanisms where they are available and by ad hoc problem-solving where they are not. Typically, systematic mechanisms are limited in the extent to which they address contextual sources of problems. Both systematic and ad hoc mechanisms require support in order to be effective. Ad hoc problem-solving is more likely to need ad hoc support and hence may be less systematically effective. Often the support to solve a problem satisfactorily is not available. The upshot is either flawed problem-solving in the form of a sub-optimal decision with problematic consequences or an error, or problem deferral. If the problem is deferred, it may cause problems elsewhere and will eventually require solution anyway. Sometimes the support to solve a problem is only available at the cost of creating some other flaw. The occurrence of flaws is a normal outcome of an uncertain innovation process and of not having all the support necessary to cope.

Thus, the innovation process often does not turn out the way that project organisation and supporters would like, but this is not in itself sufficient for failure. Flaws may result in dissatisfied supporters, but dissatisfied supporters do not necessarily withdraw all or any of their support. The model, therefore, examines the processes of evaluation and decision whereby support is determined. It also pays attention to factors which influence the actual flow of support. What this aspect of the model provides is a basis for the analysis of the strategies by which the project organisation can attempt to manage the support it receives.

Information systems failure, then, is not the simple matter of a flawed innovation process that many have hitherto supposed. The development and implementation of systematic problem-solving mechanisms to the exclusion of all other considerations presupposes either that the context is completely controllable by systematic means or that the systematically uncontrollable aspects are beyond the management of the project organisation. Neither is so. The effects of a flawed innovation process depend on the support available. Support is sometimes manageable independent of the current state of the innovation process. Thus, the management of support is very influential in determining how the problems thrown up by context actually affect the innovation process and what effect they have on the long term existence of the project. But, over the extended duration of an information systems project, it is not sufficient to manage only support. The costs of support management are the reduction in adaptability of the project organisation. In other words, prior manoeuvres constrain the availability of subsequent adaptive options. Ultimately, if an information system cannot be made to deliver benefits satisfactory to supporters it will cease to be possible to manage support, and termination will be unavoidable. Thus, it is the interaction of difficulties in the innovation process and difficulties in managing support that leads to failure. Not the one, nor the other.

The various cases discussed in chapter 12 show that this model raises a number of questions which are frequently not asked in more conventional analyses. By contrast, the case study presented in chapters 10 and 11 aimed to describe an information systems

Summary And Conclusions 319

process according to the model presented and to illustrate the process by which the information system in question came to fail. This case and its analysis according to the model also serves to exemplify the claim that some systems failures cannot be avoided by their project organisation. The next section presents an argument for this claim.

13.2 THE INEVITABILITY OF FAILURES

If methodologists are more inclined these days to stop short of offering guarantees of success, they still rarely acknowledge that there are cases for which their patent remedies are ineffective. While it may be implicit in the work of some writers that they think some systems are inevitable failures, it is a point not often made explicitly. Currently, when practitioners encounter major problems they are encouraged to make a quixotic effort to recover. To acknowledge the inevitability of failure in some cases will result in a more pragmatic approach to information systems. To recognise the possibility that a system might not be recoverable opens up the option of a face-saving wind down. It will not be easy either to recognise unavoidable failure or to respond appropriately but to acknowledge the possibility opens up more options.

Let us be clear about what is being argued. The claim is that in some circumstances a project organisation will be unable to avoid its system being a failure. This is not to say that a project organisation has total freedom to act nor that it has no such freedom. Project organisations have choices, but they are constrained choices. A matching of contextual circumstances and a project organisation's power indicates what scope it has for action. If that scope is so constrained that the project organisation could not reasonably have done other than it did and the system failed, then we may say that it failed unavoidably. On the other hand, if it had open to it a range of options which it chose not to pursue and which were not ruled out by the constraints of the model, then we would say that the system was an avoidable failure.

The core of the argument is that there will be cases where the context imposes problems that cannot be solved satisfactorily with the support available, and where the project organisation is so situated that it cannot reasonably manoeuvre itself into a position of commanding more support. If the contextual problems continue to impose themselves, then the situation may become less and less satisfactory for supporters leading ultimately to a negative evaluation and decision to terminate all support.

For any innovation process it is important to discover the key contextual influences. Is the technical process more than usually complex? Is the application environment very volatile? Are there crucial political factors? How constraining is the past? With any given level of support, some of these factors may be beyond the project organisation's control. For example, a tight labour market may make certain kinds of staff impossible to employ. To take another example, in the case of a highly complex technical development process it may simply be that we lack both the mechanisms and the cognitive skills to impose sufficient order on the complexity. Examples like these show that some level of flaws is often inevitable.

Flaws are most likely to lead to failure when support is lacking. This point is worth emphasising because it appears to be a common assumption among information systems professionals that because senior management has agreed to, even initiated, a project, it therefore wants it enough to support it vigorously. This is a fallacy. Since nothing necessarily links a system's context to the provision of support, it is quite possible for an innovation process to be conducted under a context which is hard to manage yet the system not be of great strategic importance to key supporters. If limited support turns contextual problems into flaws, the difficulties in the innovation process may result in supporters reevaluating the project and reducing or withdrawing their support. Lacking a base of power from which to negotiate, the project organisation will be unable to offer any incentives to supporters. If supporters cannot be substituted, say they have a monopoly on funds, then the project organisation will be unable to resist the effects of decisions to withdraw support. Such a project organisation is so situated that it simply cannot avoid failure.

The analysis in chapter 11 showed how few options were open to the Mandata project organisation. The impetus for the project being technology-push and the system's relative weakness as a source of leverage together suggest that almost any strategic manoeuvring that the project organisation might have attempted after the feasibility study would have run into problems of resource shortage when economic conditions deteriorated. It appeared to require a political crisis to establish conditions for increased

Summary And Conclusions 321

support. However, the political crisis put time pressure on the review which resulted in the adoption of a technical strategy that would be severely constraining. Whether it would have been possible to obtain the necessary extra support to proceed beyond the initial implementation of the system on the Mandata equipment had there not been continuing economic restraint and/or had there not been so much public criticism, it is impossible to say. What can be said is that both these contingencies were substantially beyond the project organisation's control.

To suggest that a particular failure was inevitable is to invite the question - after what point was it inevitable? The earlier the point selected, the harder the case is to argue. In the case of Mandata, the project organisation had no significant room to manoeuvre after 1976. It is a moot question whether the room it had before the decision to reorient could have enhanced its position. With the benefit of hindsight, section 11.7 suggested some options. Without that benefit, it is not obvious that any of them would have appeared a better alternative. In effect, once the nature of the Mandata proposal had been outlined in the feasibility study, circumstances beyond its control overtook the project.

It is another question to ask whether all the circumstances were inevitable. The focus in this book has been on the project organisation. It would need further research to examine *in toto* the behaviour of all relevant supporters. In particular, it is hard to say how much discretion the Public Service Board had to give more support in the period 1974 to 1976 when economic restrictions were first applied. It is much clearer, though, that had it been able and willing to give the project the funding that had been estimated as needed then the course of the project would most likely have been very different.

The conclusion that information systems failure may sometimes be unavoidable by the project organisation highlights the limits to the project organisation's abilities. Extending a point made by Markus (1984) that there are some tasks user managers rather than systems analysts must do, we can say that there are some things a project organisation may not be able do and which must be left to supporters. The failure of supporters to help can be very debilitating.

13.3 RECOMMENDATIONS FOR PRACTICE

To reiterate Mencken's dictum, there are no simple solutions for complex problems. Web models such as that presented here do not offer an easily operationalised structure by which to understand and influence information systems processes. However, a considerable degree of understanding is possible, and the better the understanding, the easier it will be to make informed interventions. It is important to emphasise that this book has focused on the project organisation and that therefore its recommendations will relate to action project organisations can take. The recommendations that follow are divided into those for analysis and those for action. They are not worked out in great detail. Rather, they are indicative of possible ways in which the current model could be used as a basis for practical activities. They do not constitute an integrated approach to successful information systems development.

13.3.1 Practical analysis

The starting point for thinking about the problems involved in the information systems process is the triangle of dependences. Starting with the project organisation, the first question is what problem-solving is needed for the innovation process. Going anti-clockwise round the triangle, this is followed by the question, what support is needed to carry out this problem-solving so that satisfactory solutions are found and flaws overcome. Next, it must be asked, what information systems characteristics must be provided to sustain the support required. And, this leads back to the first question which may be asked again, and so on around the triangle. Proposals for helping practitioners to analyse their situation therefore start with a needs assessment which will define what problems are to be solved and what support would meet this. This is followed by a support-power analysis to determine who has the power to provide the support required. Finally, an information systems impact analysis is required to assess how much leverage the information system will impart to the project organisation. This is based on a resource dependence assessment of the system's effect on supporters.

(1) Needs assessment

The project organisation's assessment of its needs will consist of two parts: analysis of problems, and analysis of the support it needs to solve the problems. Of these, the analysis of the problems faced will also divide into two. The first will include conventional project planning to determine what systematic problem-solving needs to be undertaken. The second will involve a context scanning process. Context scanning will be valuable in two ways. Since context helps define the problems a project organisation faces, a thorough and systematic scan of the context can help make clear the range of likely problems and their nature. That is to say that the constraints and contingencies of the context can make the innovation process specially problematic. Mapping out the constraints it poses can help clarify the actual problems the project organisation will face as opposed to those anticipated in normative theories of system development and maintenance. The second advantage of context scanning is that it can also draw attention to segments of the context which may contingently change within the timeframe of the project. Contingencies by their very nature are hard to anticipate although there are suggestions available for tackling this problem, such as future analysis (Land 1982). What is suggested here is that each component of the context be divided into sub-components and reviewed. Thus, the environment is one component which can be divided into seven sub-components: customers, suppliers, competitors, technology, regulators, representation/interests, and culture/institutions. As indicated when these sub-components were first introduced, they may not all bear upon any single situation. It is part of the purpose of context scanning to discover what is relevant. The analysis can be broken down still further if necessary. Thus, technology is instantiated in hardware, software, ancillary technology, and the technology of problem-solving mechanisms. This analytical decomposition may proceed until a point is reached where it would be most useful to perform the analysis. Contextual scanning should cover the present state of the component under analysis, but should also review its past state and assess its future prospect. At this stage, no particular methods are suggested for doing this.

The second part of needs assessment will help practitioners identify what support they require. Typically, the budget included in a proposal identifies the funding thought to be needed. It does not consider the need for other kinds of support, nor how funding might compensate for lack of other support. The first part of needs assessment having yielded a set of problems, the second part will have to take account of what problem-solving mechanisms are available and applicable to these problems. At present, it is not clear how precisely needs assessment can be done because we do not have a mapping of problem-solving mechanisms to problems. Neither do we have a good theoretical understanding of the relation of support to ad hoc problem-solving. Consequently, in the current state of our knowledge needs assessment will be probabilistic in the same way as other forms of estimating. Nevertheless, it is worth making an assessment of support needed if for no other reason than that it serves as a reminder that the project organisation needs the support of more than just funders.

(2) Support/power analysis

The second proposal for practical analysis of the information systems situation is for a support/power analysis. This is designed to pinpoint who is able to provide the support identified in the needs assessment. So the initial task here is to find relevant sources of funding, fixing and power-broking. Clearly, pre-existing structures will be a good guide to sources of funding. Fixing and power-broking are more likely to be identifiable from examination of historical political alignments in the host organisation. However, having identified potential supporters, it will also pay to scan their context too. What other relationships in the web are likely to affect supporters? What competition will there be for the support the project organisation requires? Which stakeholders might resist support for the project because they stand to lose from the system? The answer to this last will benefit from the third analytical procedure proposed here.

(3) Impact analysis

The third procedure to be advocated is an impact analysis. This involves making an assessment of the impact of the information system in its organisational setting. The purpose of this assessment is largely to determine what power the system will offer the project

Summary And Conclusions   325

organisation and over whom. The crucial thing is to make an estimate of how the system will be perceived by potential supporters since this is what will influence their willingness to give support. This analysis can be conducted using the dimensions of strategic contingencies theory: immediacy, pervasiveness, and non-substitutability. If the outcome is that the project looks as though it might suffer from a shortage of support, then this assessment can be adapted to identify what changes to the project might increase the system's rating on the strategic contingencies variables. But, then the sequence of analyses must start again from the beginning so as to ensure that the changed system will be feasible with the support that it will be able to command.

It is important to bear in mind that we are talking about information systems in process terms. The multiple step procedure sketched above is applicable for an initial analysis but may be applied at any stage. Indeed, it would be desirable to update it regularly to take account of changes in the context and changes in the project organisation's understanding of the process.

It will be apparent to the reader that these proposals are as yet only skeletal. The task of fleshing them out is substantial. I shall say more about how further research can help in the next section. Before that it is worth considering some ideas for action suggested by the model.

13.3.2 Recommendations For Action

What follows is a mixture of recommendations:

- Acknowledge politics and act accordingly
- Manage evaluation processes
- Be guided by prior analysis of the information systems process
- Record and track flaws and their resolution
- Abandon hopeless projects
- Learn from experience through post-project reviews

The first recommendation to practitioners is hardly novel, but it will bear repetition. It is to accept that politics is important and to act with political considerations in mind. Politics affects how different stakeholders behave in the innovation process. Political considerations also affect decisions about how to allocate scarce support. If managing support requires negotiation, bargaining, pressure or other political behaviours, its benefits justify being political. (Some strategies and tactics for managing support were discussed in chapters 7 and 8.) Of course, being political does not mean being political crudely or at any cost. Effective political behaviour is a subtle art acquired through experience. The point is that the traditional view of information systems professionals and software engineers that technology and organisational politics do not mix is profoundly misconceived. The combination is unavoidable. To be politically passive is to fail to attempt to influence an important part of any information systems process. And this applies to all members of a project organisation, not just project management. Even the most isolated software programmer may have formal or informal contacts with external supporters and may thereby contribute to the politics of support.

It follows from this that it is worth trying to plan to manage evaluations wherever possible. This is not so easy when evaluations are unplanned and informal or are controlled by other stakeholders as was seen in Mandata. One strategy therefore would be to develop an evaluation plan which would define when evaluations would occur, who would control them, what techniques they would use, to whom they would report and so forth, all of this with a view to maximising the project organisation's ability to influence both the evaluations and accompanying information, especially conditional antecedents. Designing the structural relationship of such evaluations with supporters' decision processes would be crucial. However, it will not be possible to obtain a controlling grip on the management of evaluations unless the project organisation is already very powerful, it is surely better to plan to have some influence over such a critical process than to treat it as an inaccessible contingency.

For those who are not naturally inclined to organisational politics the above suggestions may be hard to implement. One solution is to formalise a role of support manager within the project organisation executive. In practice, some project executives do include a senior manager whose specialist activity is to manage support, but this is not common. Even where there is such a role, it is not made explicit and it does not have formally defined duties. This may reflect the dubious legitimacy of organisational politics in most organisations, which fact may in turn militate against information systems managers 'coming out' and publicly adopting

Summary And Conclusions 327

a support management role.

The second recommendation for action is to adopt the principle of acting on the basis of prior analysis to anticipate and head off potential flaws. What this implies is that the more volatile and uncertain the innovation context appears on analysis, the more support should be raised so that it may be called upon when necessary. As a hedge against the future the project organisation should also attempt to 'network' to win the support of stakeholders who do not immediately control strategic resources. And, it will be worth continually lobbying supporters to remind them of the value of the system in order to reduce the chance of their backing out when needed.

A third recommendation relates the conduct of the innovation process to the support management process. The idea is to maintain a continuing record of flaws as they are discovered both in the innovation process and in the information system itself. Along with the flaws, a record would be kept of their impact. This would include whether they had been resolved, or absorbed, and in each case at what cost to the innovation process and to supporters' evaluations. This would serve as information for the continued monitoring of the project's situation.

The fourth recommendation concerns the active pursuit of project termination by the project organisation. Clearly, it follows from the conclusion that some systems will fail unavoidably that there will be cases where gathering and servicing support will not be sufficient. The obvious course of action then is to promote project abandonment. However there may be many factors which work against this, the most obvious being the basic commitment that encourages project organisations to pursue their own continued existence. It is certainly not easy for any information systems professional to publicly promote the abandonment of her own project. For anyone convinced of the rightness of such a course of action one approach would be to conduct a political campaign to persuade supporters that their investment would never pay off. If this could not be done explicitly, then it might be achieved through evaluation processes whose outcomes were then made clear to the relevant supporters. But, even were the promotion of project abandonment to be carried out effectively, it would still be hard to prevent the outcome reflecting badly on members of the project organisation. It is therefore far from clear how realistic it is to suggest that information systems professionals themselves promote the termination of a failing project. An alternative is to consider the establishment of a monitoring role independent of the actual systems innovation process. Whoever carries out the role should not be identified with the innovation effort itself, so as to make it easier to recommend abandonment.

If supporters are not prepared to support an independent monitor, they will nonetheless be keen to terminate systems which will not satisfy their interests, and to continue those which will. The problem for supporters is to make the correct evaluations. Procedural advice based on the model of information systems evaluations in chapter 7 is most appropriate. Bearing in mind the assumption that project organisations seek their own survival, supporters would be advised to try to control the evaluation process in such a way as to reduce the possibility of undue influence. Supporters should define their own interests explicitly and specify over what timeframe. They should ensure that whatever evaluation techniques are used are consonant with those interests and that timeframe. They would do well to analyse the information systems process themselves as far as is practically possible, and, where a third party evaluator is unavoidable, to prevent the project organisation from affecting the information flow to and from the evaluator. Clearly it makes good sense to control the occurrence of evaluations so that, for example, evaluations precede a large investment of resources rather than follow it. It will also be worth scanning the environment for other evaluations so as not to miss potentially valuable alternative perspectives. And lastly, it would be worthwhile to examine how effective earlier evaluations have been in influencing the project. In effect, the advice to supporters who wish to protect their interests is to look after the evaluation procedure and the evaluation will look after itself - with the qualification that this will be relative to the effectiveness of the evaluation techniques available.

The final recommendation for action is that post-project reviews be held, especially in the case of failures. The review process serves a number of purposes. It is educational; it helps consolidate experience; and it gives practice in analysing information systems situations. This is not a new recommendation. Others have developed formats and procedures for the conduct of such reviews (Davis & Olson 1985, Boddie 1987, Abdel-Hamid & Madnick 1990). However, they are typically carried out under conditions which do not encourage fruitful retrospection. There

Summary And Conclusions 329

will be pressures to get on with the next job, pressures to forget past failure, and there may be a sense that there is nothing to learn because it is obvious what happened. The post-project review has not been institutionalised as part of the information systems professional's work. It may be, therefore, that where it is performed, it is seen as a mere formality, a last rite to be administered with all speed, rather than the learning experience that it is intended to be. The conduct of a post-project review might usefully take place in several segments corresponding to an initial analysis of the major contextual sources of problems encountered. Thus problems in the programming part of the technical process may reasonably be dealt with separately from, if not entirely independently of, problems in analysts' boundary management activities. Having reviewed parts of the process, a final synthesis would be desirable so as to make explicit to all parties the importance of the interrelations among the activities in the project under review.

It should be clear from the analysis provided in earlier chapters that these recommendations do not come backed by any guarantees. They, and any other intervention derived from the model in this book, will themselves be subject to contextual constraints and contingencies. These will influence how effective they are. Consequently, it is not possible to say in advance how workable any recommendation for action will be. Even where the context is known, the model is not sufficiently detailed for accurate prediction.

Disclaimers aside, this work is predicated on the belief that the better we understand the process by which information systems come to fail, the better prospect we have of avoiding failure. The model developed here provides a number of insights which will help practitioners get a better grasp of the information systems process whether or not these insights are included in specific recommendations.

13.4 RECOMMENDATIONS FOR RESEARCH

There are many areas in which further research could be done. This section discusses those which seem most salient and one or two which have been unduly neglected. The most salient are easily derived from the triangle of dependences and from the recommendations for practice in the previous section. They relate on the one hand to our understanding of the process by which information systems fail and on the other hand to the development of practices. Table 13.1 lists these areas.

Table 13.1. Areas for further research and development

Areas Warranting Further Research	Practices Warranting Development
Innovation process	Practice of politics
Relation of IS to supporters	Support management
Flow of support	Management of evaluation
Management of support	processes
Use of problem-solving mechanisms	Project abandonment
Evaluation processes	Post-project reviews
Project organisation power	
Historical context of IS in host organisation	

The triangle of dependences defines three types of relationship each of which merits further research. The first involves the system's dependence on the project organisation as enacted in the innovation process. The innovation process has received a great deal of attention in the literature, but relatively little of this has been devoted to empirical study (Kwon & Zmud 1987). For example, we know very little about how project organisations use methodologies, what constraints prevent their use, when they are abandoned and why. No studies have explored how project organisations combine ad hoc problem-solving and systematic mechanisms. There is much still to be learned about how project organisations cope in the face of flaws. And, the role of the context warrants further elaboration. What studies such as these would yield is a more detailed account of the innovation process, of its context, its problems, the means available for coping and their effects. The practical value of such knowledge is obvious. It offers the possibility of greater control over a very uncertain process.

The second dependence relation is that of the supporters on the system. Again, we know relatively little about it. How do information systems serve their supporters? What benefits do they really yield? How do supporters evaluate systems? The answers are not obvious. There have been precious few attempts to provide

Summary And Conclusions 331

post hoc evaluations of information systems, consequently we are somewhat in the dark. It is to be hoped that the current upsurge of interest in strategic information systems may yield some further illumination. Chapter 7 outlined a basis for understanding evaluation processes and their role in decisions about support. This aspect of the model would benefit from detailed empirical testing and elaboration.

The third relation depicted in the triangle concerns the actual flow of support. As indicated earlier, expressions of support cannot be taken at face value. Support may be provided in many forms by many different parties. Our understanding of the activities of managing support, of making influence attempts, and of negotiating can all surely be developed further.

In the first instance the best means of making further advances would be the case research method. This would help in a number of ways. For example, more researched cases would be beneficial for testing out the general applicability of the model. They would also yield more case histories which would be helpful for illustrating this model and helping practitioners and researchers understand it better. They would also contribute to the elaboration of the model and the development of its conceptual base. For example, further application of the model may suggest that in describing support there are more useful distinctions to be made than funding, fixing and power-broking. Advances in any of these ways would lead to better analytical techniques for practitioners.

In the previous section, various recommendations for action were given. None is as yet fully worked out. All would benefit from further development and practical testing. Let us take them one at a time.

The first recommendation for action was for practitioners to accept the political nature of information systems and act accordingly. For some this comes naturally, for others it is anathema. It is those in between who are most likely to benefit from some more formal guidance. So far, Robert Block's (1983) *The Politics of Projects* is the only book that attempts to teach information systems professionals about organisational politics. It is largely an informal systematisation of Block's own experience with no theory and no account of the bases of power. Consequently there is plenty of room for developing material that can help raise the awareness of information systems professionals and guide them through the political process. There is nothing like examples from real cases for achieving this. They make abstract points concrete and they illustrate the ways in which politics is enacted. Most of all they show how political interpretations make sense of the information systems process. For those who are not natural organisational politicians this will be a help.

Of course, reading theory does not turn anyone into a successful politician. Practice is essential. However, it would not be realistic to expect information systems departments to send their staff to courses billed as teaching and giving practice in organisational politics. Organisational culture is not yet so liberated. Politics will be best introduced along with technical material in courses such as those introducing and developing the skills of systems analysis. Elements of political behaviour may then be practised within the context of a legitimately technical course. Over the long term organisational culture may change so as to give increased legitimacy to politics, but until then learning about politics will have to be smuggled in under the cover of acquiring more legitimate skills.

The second recommendation for action was the principle that the more volatile and uncertain the innovation context appears the more support should be raised. Research into context scanning should help to develop methods for detecting a volatile context. This leaves the matter of raising support. For the moment it would be useful to have more knowledge of how support is raised in practice so as to provide a catalogue of tactics. Any guidelines will also need an indication of the conditions that must be satisfied before trying each tactic because they will be contingent on circumstances and a failed intervention may be counterproductive.

The third recommendation related to practitioners cutting their losses and abandoning hopeless projects. Clearly, there is scope for research into the role information systems professionals can and do take in project abandonment. Evidence of their actual roles may help us devise ways of facilitating the abandonment process. The suggestion made of an independent monitor, or third party evaluator, requires testing. The difficulty is that there can never be any knowledge of how things would have turned out had the evaluator acted differently. Nevertheless, it might be that an independent evaluator would be able to achieve the distance that the project organisation cannot. If the evaluator were structurally tightly linked to decision processes about support, then the role might be influential in project abandonment decisions. If it were

Summary And Conclusions 333

loosely linked, then it is unclear how effective it might be.

The final recommendation for action was that post project reviews be conducted in all cases, and that they be carried out thoroughly. There is already some literature on reviews in engineering projects (Roman 1983). This work could be extended to the information systems field to incorporate the model presented here. Since the outcomes of such reviews could have considerable influence on the way subsequent developments might be undertaken in a given organisation it would be worthwhile creating a specialist role to be filled by someone with skills in managing review meetings, in exploring and resolving conflict, in breaking stalemates, in ensuring a wide range of people are heard and so forth. It would be worth investigating the advantages and disadvantages of having an internal versus an external person filling this role. Again, for such reviews to be influential it will be important to design the links between the review and decision-makers. In some cases it may be appropriate to have powerful decision-makers involved in the review. In other cases it may be sufficient to feed conclusions into a decision-making arena for further action.

Finally, there are several important areas which have been unjustly neglected by researchers. First, empirical research into the use of methodologies and other problem-solving mechanisms is needed so that we can better understand the contingency factors that apply. Second, conceptual and empirical work can help us match problem-solving mechanisms to problems. Third, study of evaluation processes will yield insights into how support is determined. Fourth, the question of the power of project organisations warrants considerable further investigation particularly since existing research conclusions run counter to expectations. The better we understand the bases of project organisation power, the better we shall be able to assess what support can be won from whom and by what means. Each of these areas deserves further detailed attention.

There is one other area warranting further study. This is the place of information systems projects in the wider historical process of the information systems department and its host organisation. Though history has been included as a contextual variable in this book, the role of past projects in determining the conditions under which future projects are conducted has so far remained unexamined. Yet, it would be unrealistic to suppose that stakeholders avail themselves of the analytic convenience of focusing on a single system in complete disregard of others built and operated in the past. Rather, past failures will surely constrain what can be attempted in the future both technically and support-wise. There is much to be learnt about this aspect of failure.

The message of this section is clear. The current model is no more than a starting point. In capturing some facets of the information systems process, in particular failure, it provides a base for developing useful practices. The descriptions and explanations it offers can be developed further in time with the result that more fine grained and contingently applicable practices can then be developed.

13.5 FINALE

It would be the grossest arrogance to suppose that we have all the answers to the problems of information systems failure. Equally, though, there would be little point in researching, studying and thinking about these problems if we did not believe that this would help to improve the practice of information systems projects. In section 13.3 some practical suggestions were offered. Now it is time to consider the prospects for improvement. Are we likely to see a substantial reduction in the number and magnitude of failures in the foreseeable future? There are five main considerations which deserve attention:

- changes in knowledge
- changes in technology
- changes in perceptions
- the politics of information systems
- the institutionalisation of computing in organisations

Throughout this chapter it has been assumed that knowledge is good and more is better. As our understanding of the information systems process improves over time, we may expect that practitioners will acquire more control over the problems they face. It is fundamental to the model in this book that some uncertainties will remain, but there is still considerable scope for the development of problem-solving mechanisms and political strategies, and for more informed ad hoc problem-solving.

Summary And Conclusions 335

The proposition that greater knowledge will result in improved information systems is empirical and could be tested on various dimensions. It is therefore conceivable that it would prove false. For example, it might be that more politically aware information systems professionals would stir up more conflict and create a more volatile environment. Operational users might use the same knowledge to develop more effective counter-implementation strategies. However, while all this is conceivable, limited cognitive capacities are likely to prevent other stakeholders from taking advantage of specialist knowledge about information systems. On balance, developments in knowledge are likely to favour information systems professionals and to reduce the chances of systems failing.

Only some changes in technology will be significant. Developments in hardware are unlikely to make any major difference to the technical process. The inherent complexities will remain. Developments in software, particularly software tools, will offer increased control over the software development process. But, this will not eradicate all of the problems arising from inherent complexity. Developments in utilities for immediate use by end users may reduce the need for certain kinds of innovation process. Small businesses already buy software off the shelf and adapt their own procedures accordingly. As the product range widens, so the need for the more common application developments will be reduced.

Changes in perceptions could make a big difference. If innovation processes were seen in the fluid form proposed here, it would be much easier to negotiate a system that would satisfy its supporters. However, it is far from obvious that perceptions will change in this way. The widespread availability of computers has not obviously increased public awareness of how difficult it is to develop information systems for organisations. While individual use of microcomputers at home and in the office may have increased public awareness of the ease of making individual errors and hence of the risks of using computers in critical systems, it does not provide the individual with much insight into the difficulties of information systems for organisational applications. If anything the accessibility of computers has encouraged the perception, often promoted in the past by information systems professionals, that information systems can be built systematically and with no real risk. It is doubtful therefore that perceptions of the information systems process will change in line with the approach favoured in this book.

It is most unlikely that information systems will become less political in the foreseeable future. Indeed, as they become more pervasive, control over what information is produced and who receives it is likely to become even more politically charged. As users and other supporters come to understand the implications of information systems, control will become more contested. One factor which may work the other way is the decline in conservatism as people become increasingly familiar with computers in the workplace. This can be expected to result in less resistance to change. Notwithstanding this, the political context is likely to remain at least as volatile as at present.

Finally, computer-based information systems will become increasingly institutionalised. They will become an accepted fact of organisational life in more and more areas. As they do so, more information systems work will involve incremental innovation rather than radical innovation. Existing systems will constitute a well understood and formalised base from which to redevelop. A number of the cognitive problems of building a system for the first time will disappear. The task will remain costly and uncertain but the risks will be fewer. Of course, the extent to which information systems innovations become incremental will depend on factors such as information systems strategies. If there is a move toward greater integration and tighter coupling among the systems within an organisation or even across organisations then the level of newness may continue to be high. In this way institutionalisation may be offset by other changes.

The prospect, then, is that the information systems context will continue to be problematic. Though some parts may become less hazardous for information systems professionals, the outlook is that failures will continue at a level sufficient to justify the continuing study of this problem.

Bibliography

Abdel-Hamid, T.K. & Madnick, S.E. (1990) The elusive silver lining: how we fail to learn from software development failures, *Sloan Management Review*, 39, Fall.
Ackoff, R.L. (1967) Management misinformation systems, *Management Science*, 14, 4, Dec.
APSB (1983) *ADP in Personnel: a Survey and Assessment of ADP Utilisation in the Personnel Function*, Australian Public Service Board and Urwick International Pty Ltd, Canberra, October.
APSB (1987) *ADP in Personnel: Guidelines for Information Standards*, Australian Public Service Board and Koranya Pty Ltd in association with Duesburys, Australian Government Publishing Service, Canberra, May.
Argyris, C. (1971) Management information systems: the challenge to rationality and emotionality, *Management Science*, 17, 6, Feb, B-275-292.
Arthur, C. (1993) Pressurised managers blamed for ambulance failure, *New Scientist*, 6 March, 5.
Auditor-General (1964) *Report of the Auditor-General for the Year 1963/4*, AGPS, Canberra, 1964.
Auditor-General (1976) *Report of the Auditor-General for the Year Ended 30 June 1976*, AGPS, Canberra.
Auditor-General (1977) *Report of the Auditor-General for the Year Ended 30 June 1977*, AGPS, Canberra.
Auditor-General (1978) *Report of the Auditor-General for the Year Ended 30 June 1978*, AGPS, Canberra.
Auditor-General (1979) *Report of the Auditor-General for the Year Ended 30 June 1979*, AGPS, Canberra.
Auditor-General (1980) *Report of the Auditor-General*, AGPS, Canberra, April 1980.
Auditor-General (1991) *Audit Report No 24 1990-1991: Department of Veterans' Affairs - Transport Services - Personnel and Pay Administration System*, Australian Government Publishing Service, Canberra.
Avison, D.E. & Fitzgerald, G. (1988) *Information Systems Development: Methodologies, Techniques and Tools*,

Blackwell Scientific Publications, Oxford.
Avison, D.E., Fitzgerald, G. & Wood-Harper, A.T. (1988) Information systems development: a tool kit is not enough, *The Computer Journal*, 31, 4, 379-380.
Avison, D.E. & Wood-Harper, A.T. (1986) Multiview - an exploration in information systems development, *Australian Computer Journal*, 18, 4, 174-179.
Avison, D.E. & Wood-Harper, A.T. (1990) *Multiview: An Exploration in Information Systems Development*, Blackwell Scientific Publications, Oxford.
Bachrach, P. & Baratz, M.S. (1970) *Power and Poverty: Theory and Practice*, Oxford University Press, New York.
Baker, F.T. (1972) Chief programmer team management of production programming, *IBM Systems*, 1, 56-73.
Bandura, A. (1986) *Social Foundations of Thought and Action: a Social Cognitive Theory*, Prentice-Hall, Englewood Cliffs, NJ.
Bariff, M.L. & Galbraith, J.R. (1978) Intraorganizational power considerations for designing information systems, *Accounting, Organizations and Society*, 3, 1, 15-27.
Benbasat, I., Goldstein, D.K. & Mead, M., (1987) The case research strategy in studies of information systems, *MIS Quarterly*, September.
Benyon, D. & Skidmore, S. (1987), Towards a tool kit for the systems analyst, *The Computer Journal*, 30, 1, 2-7.
Bignell, V. & Fortune, J. (1984) *Understanding Systems Failures*, Manchester University Press, Manchester.
Bjørn-Andersen, N. & Davis, G.B. (eds) (1988) *Information Systems Assessment: Issues and Challenges, Proceedings of the IFIP WG 8.2 Working Conference on Information Systems Assessment*, Noordwijkerhout, The Netherlands, 27-29 August 1986, North-Holland, Amsterdam.
Bjørn-Andersen, N., Eason, K. & Robey, D. (1986) *Managing Computer Impact: An International Study of Management and Organizations*, Ablex, Norwood, NJ.
Blau, P.M. (1964) *Exchange and Power in Social Life*, John Wiley, New York.
Block, R. (1983) *The Politics of Projects*, Yourdon Press, New York.
Boddie, J. (1987) The project postmortem, *Computerworld*, 7 December, 77-82.
Boland, R. & Hirschheim, R.A. (1985) Series foreword in Hirschheim (1985) .

Bibliography 339

Boland, R.J. & Hirschheim, R.A. (eds.) (1987) *Critical Issues in Information Systems Research*, Wiley, Chichester.
Boland, R.J. Jr. & Pondy, L.R. (1983) Accounting in organizations: a union of natural and rational perspectives, *Accounting, Organizations and Society*, 8, 223-234.
Braybrooke, D. & Lindblom, C.E. (1963) *A Strategy of Decision: Policy Evaluation as a Social Process*, Free Press of Glencoe, New York.
Brooks, F.P. jr. (1975) *The Mythical Man Month*, Addison-Wesley, Reading, Mass.
Buchanan, D.A. & Boddy, D. (1983) *Organizations in the Computer Age: Technological Imperatives and Strategic Choice*, Gower, Aldershot.
Buechi, H. (1982) Success and failure in edp project development: two examples, *Systems, Objectives, Solutions*, 2, 39-47.
Burns, T. & Stalker, G.M. (1961) *Management of Innovation*, Tavistock Publications, London.
Burrell, G. & Morgan, G. (1979) *Sociological Paradigms and Organisational Analysis: Elements of the Sociology of Corporate Life*, Heinemann, London.
Campbell-Kelly, M. (1990) Punched-card machinery, in W. Aspray, (ed) (1990) *Computing Before Computers*, Iowa State University Press, Ames, 122-155.
Carey, A. (1967) The Hawthorne studies: a radical criticism, *American Sociological Review*, 32, 3, June, 403-416.
CGO (1982) Air traffic control computer failures, edited version of a report by the Committee of Government Operations, *Systems, Objectives, Solutions*, 2, 89-107.
Child, J., Ganter, H-D. & Kieser, A. (1987) Technological innovation and organizational conservatism, in Pennings and Buitendam (1987).
Child, J. & Loveridge, R. (1990) Information Technology in European Services: Towards a Microelectronic Future, Basil Blackwell, Oxford.
Clegg, S. (1979) *The Theory of Power and Organization*, Routledge and Kegan Paul, London.
Clegg, S. & Dunkerley, D. (1980) *Organization, Class and Control*, Routledge and Kegan Paul, London.
Cohen, M.D., March, J.G. & Olsen, J.P. (1972) A garbage can model of organizational choice, *Administrative Science Quarterly*, 17,1, March, reprinted in March (1988).

340 Bibliography

Colton, K.W. (1972) Computers and police: patterns of success and failure, *Sloan Management Review*, winter, 1972-73, 75-98.
Computer Weekly (1989) Ambulance service switches off system, *Computer Weekly*, 19/10/89.
Computing (Australia) (1990a) Defence Dept owns up to costly DESINE delay, *Computing, Australia*, 10/9/90, pp1 &11.
Computing (Australia) (1990b) System failure: SBS in turmoil, *Computing, Australia*, 5/11/90, p1.
Computing (UK) (1989a) Stock Exchange kills project to focus on Taurus, *Computing, UK*, 2/11/89, p1.
Computing (UK) (1989b) Shape scraps troubled military project, *Computing, UK*, 2/11/89, p3.
Crozier, M. (1964) *The Bureaucratic Phenomenon*, University of Chicago Press, Chicago.
Cyert, R.M. & March, J.G. (1963) *A Behavioral Theory of the Firm*, Prentice-Hall, Englewood Cliffs, NJ.
Daft R.L. & Becker, S.W. (1978) *Innovation in Organizations: Innovation Adoption in School Organizations*, Elsevier North-Holland, New York.
Dahl, R. (1957) The concept of power, *Behavioral Science*, 2, 201-215.
Dalton, M. (1959) *Men Who Manage*, John Wiley, New York.
Davis, D.D. and Associates (1986) *Managing Technological Innovation: Organizational Strategies for Implementing Advanced Manufacturing Technologies*, Jossey-Bass, San Francisco.
Davis, G.B. & Hamann, J.R. (1988) In-context information systems assessment: a proposal and an evaluation, in Bjørn-Andersen & Davis (1988), 283-296.
Davis, G.B. & Olson, M.H. (1985) *Management Information Systems: Conceptual Foundations, Structure, and Development*, McGraw-Hill, New York.
Dean, J.W. jr. (1987) Building the future: the justification process for new technology, in Pennings & Buitendam (eds) (1987), 35-58.
Dearden, J. (1972) MIS is a mirage, *Harvard Business Review*, Jan-Feb, 90-99.
Dickson, G.W. & Janson, M.A. (1984) The failure of a dss for energy conservation: a technical perspective, *Systems, Objectives, Solutions*, 4, 69-79.
Dill, W.R. (1958) Environment as an influence on managerial

autonomy, *Administrative Science Quarterly*, 6, March, 421-442.
Dutton, W.H. (1981) The rejection of an innovation: the political environment of a computer-based model, *Systems, Objectives, Solutions*, 1, 4, 179-201.
Dutton, W.H. & Kraemer, K.L. (1985) *Modeling as Negotiating: the Political Dynamics of Computer Models in the Policy Process*, Ablex, Norwood, New Jersey.
Emerson, R.M. (1962) Power dependence relations, *American Sociological Review*, 27, 31-41.
Ewusi-Mensah, K. & Przasnyski, Z.H. (1991) On information systems project abandonment: an exploratory study of organizational practices, *MIS Quarterly*, March, 67-86.
Fayol, H. (1949) General principles of management, in Pugh (1985).
Feldman, M.S. & March, J.G. (1981) Information in organizations as signal and symbol, *Administrative Science Quarterly*, 26, 171-186, reprinted in March (1988), 409-428.
Fetzer, J.H. (1988) Program verification: the very idea, *Communications of the ACM*, 31, 9, September, 1048-1063.
Feynman, R.P. (1988) Mr Feynman goes to Washington: Investigating the space shuttle *Challenger* disaster, in *What Do You Care What Other People Think?*, Unwin, London, 1990.
Forester, T. & Morrison, P. (1990) *Computer Ethics: Cautionary Tales and Ethical Dilemmas in Computing*, Basil Blackwell, Oxford.
Foster, H.D. (1987) Disaster warning systems, in Wise and Debons 1987.
Franz, C.R. & Robey, D. (1984) An investigation of user-led system design: rational and political perspectives, *Communications of the ACM*, 27, 12, December, 1202-1209.
Friedman, A. L. (1989) *Computer Systems Development: History, Organization and Implementation*, John Wiley, Chichester.
Galbraith, J. (1973) *Designing Complex Organizations*, Addison-Wesley, Reading, Mass.
Galbraith, J. (1977) *Organization Design*, Addison-Wesley, Philippines.
Galliers, R.D. (ed) (1987) *Information Analysis: Selected Readings*, Addison-Wesley, Sydney.
Giddens, A., (1984) *The Constitution of Society: Outline of the Theory of Structuration*, Polity Press, Cambridge.

Ginzberg, M.J. & Zmud, R.W. (1988) Evolving criteria for information systems assessment, in Bjørn-Andersen & Davis (1988), 41-52.
Glasser, J. (1981) Organizational aspects of system failures: a case study at the Los Angeles Police Department, *Proceedings of the Second International Conference on Information Systems*, C.A. Ross (ed), Society for Management Information Systems, 233-245.
Gouldner, A. (1954) *Patterns of Industrial Bureaucracy*, The Free Press, Glencoe, Illinois.
Guardian (1989) £7m computer 'slowed issue of passports', 5th August.
Hage, J. (1980) *Theories of Organization: Form, Process, and Transformation*, John Wiley, New York.
Hage, J. (1987) Reflections on new technology and organisational change, in Pennings and Buitendam (1987), 261-276.
Hall, P. (1981) *Great Planning Disasters*, Penguin, Harmondsworth.
Hamman, H. & Parrott, S. (1987) *Mayday at Chernobyl*, New English Library, Hodder & Stoughton, Sevenoaks.
Hawkes, N., Lean, G., Leigh, D., McKie, R., Pringle, P. & Wilson, A. (1986) *The Worst Accident in the World, Chernobyl: The End of the Nuclear Dream*, Pan and Heinemann, London.
Haynes, V. & Bojcun, M. (1988) *The Chernobyl Disaster*, Hogarth Press, London.
Henderson, E. (1990) Admissions system seizes up, *Times Higher Education Supplement*, 27 July, 10.
Hickson, D.J., Hinings, C.R., Lee, C.A., Schneck, R.E. & Pennings, J.M. (1971) A strategic contingencies' theory of intraorganizational power, *Administrative Science Quarterly*, 216-229.
Hinings, C.R., Hickson, D.J., Pennings, J.M. & Schneck, R.E. (1974) Structural conditions of intraorganizational power, *Administrative Science Quarterly*, 22-44.
Hirschheim, R.A. (1985) *Office Automation: A Social and Organizational Perspective*, John Wiley, Chichester.
Hirschheim, R. & Smithson, S. (1988) A critical analysis of information systems evaluation, in Bjørn-Andersen & Davis (1988), 17-37.
Hoyle, A. & Thynne, I. (1981) Administrative chronicle: federal government, *Australian Journal of Public Administration*, 40, 1, March, 29-34.

Hoyle, A. & Wettenhall, R. (1981) Administrative chronicle: federal government, *Australian Journal of Public Administration*, 40, 4, December, 306-313.
Hunt, J.W. (1972) *The Restless Organization*, Wiley International.
Ince, D. (1988) *Software Development: Fashioning the Baroque*, Oxford University Press, Oxford.
Janis, I.L. (1987) Investigating sources of error in the management of crises: theoretical assumptions and a methodological approach, in Wise and Debons (1987).
JCPA (1966) *86th Report of the Joint Committee of Public Accounts of the Parliament of the Commonwealth of Australia: Automatic Data Processing (The Bureau of Census and Statistics Network)*, A.J. Arthur, Australian Government Printer, Canberra, 26 October.
JCPA (1978a) *174th Report of the Joint Committee of Public Accounts of the Parliament of the Commonwealth of Australia: Use of ADP in the Commonwealth Public Sector - Acquisition of Systems in the Public Service*, Australian Government Publishing Service, Canberra, 24 November.
JCPA (1978b) *Use of ADP in the Commonwealth Public Sector - Stage 1, Minutes of Evidence, Joint Committee of Public Accounts*, Australian Government Publishing Service, Canberra
JCPA (1979) *175th Report of the Joint Committee of Public Accounts of the Parliament of the Commonwealth of Australia: Use of ADP in the Commonwealth Public Sector - The MANDATA Project*, Australian Government Publishing Service, Canberra, September.
JCPA (1980) *183rd Report of the Joint Committee of Public Accounts of the Parliament of the Commonwealth of Australia: Finance Minutes on the One Hundred and Seventy-fourth and One Hundred and Seventy-fifth Reports*, Australian Government Publishing Service, Canberra, September.
Johnson-Laird, P.N. (1983) *Mental Models: Towards a Cognitive Science of Language, Inference, and Consciousness*, Cambridge University Press, Cambridge.
Juddery, B. (1974) *At the Centre: the Australian Bureaucracy in the 1970s*, Cheshire, Melbourne.
Kane, F. & Whitebloom, S. (1993) Stock Exchange boss resigns over computer fiasco, *Guardian Weekly*, 21 March, 4.
Kling, R. (1980) Social analyses of computing: theoretical

perspectives in recent empirical research, *Computing Surveys*, 12, 1, March, 61-110.

Kling, R. (1987) Defining the boundaries of computing across complex organizations, in Boland & Hirschheim 1987, 307-362.

Kling, R. & Scacchi, W. (1982) The web of computing: computer technology as social organization, in Yovits, M., (ed), *Advances in Computing*, 21, Academic Press, New York.

Kraemer, K.L., Dutton, W.H. & Northrop, A. (1981) *The Management of Information Systems*, Columbia University Press, New York.

Kraemer, K.L., King, J.L., Dunkle, D.E. & Lane, J.P. (1989) *Managing Information Systems: Change and Control in Organizational Computing*, Jossey-Bass, San Francisco.

Kwon, T.H. & Zmud, R.W. (1987) Unifying the fragmented models of information systems implementation, in Boland & Hirschheim 1987, 227-251.

Land, F. (1982) Adapting to changing user requirements, *Information and Management*, 5, 59-75, reprinted in Galliers (1987), 203-229.

Lawrence, P.R. & Lorsch, J.W. (1967) *Organization and Environment: Managing Differentiation and Integration*, Graduate School of Business Administration, Harvard University, Boston.

Lehman, J.H. (1979) How software projects are really managed, *Datamation*, Jan, 119-129.

Lindblom, C.E. (1959) The science of 'muddling through', *Public Administration Review*, 19, 2, reprinted in Pugh 1985.

Linton-Simpkins, F. (1978), Mandata was a good idea, *The Australian*, 6 June 1978.

Little, S.E. (1987) The role of time frames in design decision-making, *Design Studies*, 8, 3, July, 170-182.

Little, S.E. (1990) Task environment versus institutional environment: understanding the context of design decision-making, *Design Studies*, 11, 1, Jan, 29-42.

Lucas, H.C. Jr (1975) *Why Information Systems Fail*, Columbia University Press, New York.

Lucas, H.C. Jr (1984) Organizational power and the information services department, *Communications of the ACM*, 27, 1, January, 58-65.

Lukes, S. (1974) *Power: a Radical View*, Macmillan, London.

Bibliography 345

Lyytinen, K. & Hirschheim, R. (1987) Information systems failures: a survey and classification of the empirical literature, *Oxford Surveys in Information Technology*, Vol 4, 257-309.

March, J.G. (ed) (1965) *Handbook of Organizations*, Rand McNally, Chicago.

March, J.G. (1988) *Decisions and Organizations*, Basil Blackwell, Oxford.

March, J.G. & Simon, H.A. (1958) *Organizations*, John Wiley, New York.

Markus M.L. (1984) *Systems in Organizations: Bugs and Features*, Pitman, Marshfield, Mass.

Markus, M.L. & Bjørn-Andersen, N. (1987) Power over users: its exercise by system professionals, *Communications of the ACM*, 30, 6, June, 498-504.

Markus, M.L. & Pfeffer, J. (1983) Power and the design and implementation of accounting and control systems, *Accounting, Organizations and Society*, 8, 2/3, 205-218.

Mason, R.O. & Mitroff, I.I. (1973) A program for research on management information systems, *Management Science*, 19, 5, January, 475-487.

Merton, R.K. (1936) The unanticipated consequences of purposive social action, *American Sociological Review*, 1, 894-904.

Meyer, J.W. & Rowan, B. (1977) Institutionalized organizations: formal structure as myth and ceremony, *American Journal of Sociology*, 83, 340-363.

Miller, C.L. (1983) How to successfully resist a computer system and avoid its benefits: a victory for the bureaucracy?, *Systems, Objectives, Solutions*, 3, 3-12.

Mintzberg, H. (1973) *The Nature of Managerial Work*, Harper and Row, New York.

Mintzberg, H. (1979) *The Structuring of Organizations: A Synthesis of the Research*, Prentice-Hall, Englewood Cliffs, NJ.

Mintzberg, H., Raisinghani, D., & Théorêt, A. (1976) The structure of "unstructured" decision processes, *Administrative Science Quarterly*, 21, 2, June.

Mohr, L.B. (1985) The reliability of the case study as a source of information, *Advances in Information Processing in Organizations*, 2, 65-93.

Morgan, H.L. & Soden, J.V. (1973) Understanding MIS failures, *Data Base*, 5, Winter.

Newman, M. & Rosenberg, D. (1985) Systems analysts and the

politics of organizational control, *Omega International Journal of Management Science*, 13, 5, 393-406.

Newton, M. (1980) Bureaucratic outrages, *Penthouse Australia*, July.

Office of Charles and Ray Eames (1990) *A Computer Perspective: Background To The Computer Age*, Harvard University Press, Cambridge, Mass.

Pedersen, P.H. (1986a) Organizational power systems, ch 8 in Bjørn-Andersen, Eason, & Robey (1986), 150-167.

Pedersen, P.H. (1986b) Influence and discretion of different user types, ch 9 in Bjørn-Andersen, Eason, & Robey (1986), 168-185.

Pennings, J.M. & Buitendam, A. (eds) (1987) *New Technology as Organizational Innovation: The Development and Diffusion of Microelectronics*, Ballinger, Cambridge, Mass.

Perrow, C. (1967) A framework for the comparative analysis of organizations, *American Sociological Review*, 32, April, 194-208.

Perrow, C. (1970), *Organizational Analysis: a Sociological View*, Tavistock Publications, London.

Perrow, C. (1979) *Complex Organizations: A Critical Essay*, Scott, Foresman & Co, Glenview, Illinois.

Perrow, C. (1984) *Normal Accidents: Living with High Risk Technologies*, Basic Books, New York.

Pettigrew, A.M. (1973) *The Politics of Organizational Decision-making*, Tavistock, London.

Pfeffer, J. (1981) *Power in Organizations*, Pitman, Marshfield, Mass.

Pfeffer, J. & Salancik, G.R. (1978) *The External Control of Organizations: a Resource Dependence Perspective*, Harper & Row, New York.

Public Service Board (1964) *39th Report On The Public Service Of The Commonwealth By The Public Service Board: 1962-63*, Commonwealth Government Printer, Canberra.

Public Service Board (1974) *50th Annual Report*, AGPS, Canberra.

Pugh, D.S. (1985) *Organization Theory: Selected Readings*, 2nd ed., Penguin, Harmondsworth.

Reason, J. (1987) An interactionist's view of system pathology, in Wise and Debons 1987.

Rogers, W. (1986) *Report of the Presidential Commission on the Space Shuttle Challenger Accident*, US Government Printing

Bibliography 347

Office, Washington, DC.
Roman, D.D. (1983) A proposed project termination audit model, *IEEE Transactions on Engineering Management*, 3, August, 123-127.
Rudelius, W., Dickson, G.W. & Hartley, S.W. (1982) The little model that couldn't: how a decision support system for retail buyers found limbo, *Systems, Objectives, Solutions*, 2, 115-124.
Sapolsky, H.M. (1972) *The Polaris System Development: Bureaucratic and Programmatic Success in Government*, Harvard University Press, Cambridge, Mass.
Saunders, C.S. (1981) Management information systems, communications, and departmental power: an integrative model, *Academy of Management Review*, 6, 3, 431-442.
Saunders, C.S. & Scamell, R.W. (1986) Organizational power and the information services department: a re-examination, *Communications of the ACM*, 29, 2, February, 142-147. .
Schmitt, J.W. & Kozar, K.A. (1978) Management's role in information systems development failures: a case study, *MIS Quarterly*, 22,2, June, 7-16.
Schon, D.A. (1967) *Technology and Change: the New Heraclitus*, Delarcorte Press, New York.
Scott, W.R. (1981) *Organizations: Rational, Natural and Open Systems*, Prentice-Hall, Englewood Cliffs, NJ.
Scott, W.R. (1987) The adolescence of institutional theory, *Administrative Science Quarterly*, 32, 493-511.
Selznick, P. (1949) *TVA and the Grass Roots*, University of California Press, Berkeley.
Shrvastava, P. (1987) *Bhopal: Anatomy of a Crisis*, Ballinger, Cambridge, Mass.
Simon, H.A. (1957) *Administrative Behavior: A Study of Decision-Making Processes in Administrative Organization*, Macmillan, New York.
Simon, H.A. (1981) *Sciences of the Artificial*, MIT Press, Cambridge, Mass.
Sloane, S.B. (1991) The use of artificial intelligence by the United States Navy: Case study of a failure, *AI Magazine*, Spring, 80-92.
Srinivasan, A. (1988) Discussant note on: Information systems assessment as a learning process by Preben Etzerodt and Kim

Halskov Madsen, in Bjørn-Andersen & Davis, (1988), 346-347.
Stamper, R. (1973) *Information in Business and Administrative Systems*, Halsted Press, John Wiley, New York.
Strauss, A. (1978) *Negotiations: Varieties, Contexts, Processes, and Social Order*, Jossey-Bass, San Francisco.
Taylor, F.W. (1947) *Scientific management*, in Pugh (1985).
Thompson, J.D. (1967) *Organizations in Action*, McGraw Hill, NJ.
Turner, B.A. (1976) The organizational and inter-organizational development of disasters, *Administrative Science Quarterly*, 21, September, 378-397.
Wason, P.C. & Johnson-Laird, P.N. (1972) *Psychology of Reasoning: Structure and Content*, Batsford, London.
Weick, K.E. (1979) *The Social Psychology of Organizing*, Addison-Wesley, Reading, Mass.
Wilkinson, B. (1983) *The Shopfloor Politics of New Technology*, Heinemann, London.
Wiltshire, K. (1974) *An Introduction to Australian Public Administration*, Cassell Australia, N. Melbourne.
Wise, J.A. & Debons, A. (eds) (1987) *Information Systems: Failure Analysis*, NATO Advanced Science Institute, Series F: Computer and Systems Sciences, vol 32, Springer-Verlag, Berlin/Heidelberg.
Wood-Harper, A.T., Antill, L. & Avison, D.E. (1985) *Information Systems Definition: The Multiview Approach*, Blackwell Scientific Publications, Oxford.
Woodward, J. (1965) *Industrial Organization: Theory and Practice*, Oxford University Press, Oxford.
Yin, R.K. (1989) *Case Study Research: Design and Methods*, Sage, Newbury Park.
Yuchtman, E. & Seashore, S.E., (1967) A system resource approach to organizational effectiveness, *American Sociological Review*, 32, 891-903.
Zammuto, R.F. (1982) *Assessing Organizational Effectiveness: Systems Change, Adaptation, and Strategy*, State University Press of New York, Albany.
Zammuto, R.F. (1984) A comparison of multiple constituency models of organizational effectiveness, *Academy of Management Review*, 9, 4, 606-616.

Glossary Of Terms Associated With The Mandata Case

adp: Automatic data processing.

AGO: Auditor-General's Office

AGRBO: Australian Government Retirement Benefits Office. Previously the Superannuation Board.

AGSTB: Australian Government Supply and Tender Board.

Anzac Park West: Offices initially agreed as the permanent home of the Mandata central computer. Situated about a mile to a mile-and-a-half from the Public Service Board's offices.

APO: Australian Post Office.

APS: Australian Public Service

Auditor-General: Chief officer of the Auditor-General's Office. Reports findings to the Parliament.

Auditor-General's Office: Agency within the Australian Public Service responsible for auditing departments' financial transactions and for auditing the efficient working of departmental operations.

Australia Post: After 1974, an independent authority responsible for postal services.

Australian Government Supply and Tender Board: Public Service purchasing and contracting authority.

Australian Post Office: Prior to 1974 the Director-General directed a combination of postal and telecommunications services in a single agency.

Automatic data processing: A now slightly outdated term for computing.

ccu: Central computer unit.

Cell: See Mandata cell.

Committee of Officials: A special committee established by the government to examine bids for computing equipment in the light of overall government priorities.

Commonwealth Scientific and Industrial Research Organisation: A public sector research organisation.

Continuous Record of Personnel: Computer system operated by the Public Service Board. Recorded data on permanently appointed officers of the Public Service to enable the Board to provide statistical reports to the Parliament on the state of the Australian Public Service.

CRP: Continuous Record of Personnel.

CSIRO: Commonwealth Scientific and Industrial Research Organisation.

CSO: Computer Systems Officer.

Data Alsal: Intended to upgrade system data relating to designation/occupation and associated salary and allowance conditions sufficient for Data Pay.

Data concentrator unit: A mini computer dedicated to acting as a multiplexer to make efficient use of expensive data communications lines.

Data Consolidate Provision of on-line enquiry and interrogation. Limited on-line updating. All leave processing. A project control system.

Data Enhance: Educational qualifications recording, automatic gazettal of staff and establishment changes, recording of

Glossary Of Terms 351

recruitment/appointment data, person/position matching for selection purposes.

Data Pay: Automatic notification to Treasury salaries system of variations to pay.

Data Service/s (Inc): Pseudo commercial identity for the enterprise of marketing Mandata.

Data Stream (Extended): Extension of record base beyond the 80,000 constraint to accommodate the whole Public Service.

Data Stream: Department of Productivity system adopted as the basis for Mandata. Stored personnel and establishments records, produced statutory reports, and basic management information. Maximum of 80,000 records. Also the name of a similar system operated by the Canadian Public Service.

dcu: Data concentrator unit.

DEIR: Department of Employment and Industrial Relations

Department: Ministerial department. Here used to include statutory public authorities as well.

Department of Supply: Earlier name for Department of Productivity.

Des/Sal: Mandata name for a sub-system which automated the Designation/Salary translation.

Designation/Salary: A formal translation table for mapping salary to class (designation) of position.

DMI: Department of Manufacturing Industry.

Document 23: See Paper 23

EXCO: Executive Council. The Public Service council responsible for approving the establishment of new positions prior to formal approval by the Governor-General.

Framework: See Processing Framework.

IDC: Inter-Departmental Committee

IDC on ADP: Inter-Departmental Committee on Automatic Data Processing

JCPA: Joint Committee of Public Accounts

Joint Committee of Public Accounts: Committee of the Joint Houses of the Australian Parliament (House of Representatives and Senate) acts on behalf of and reports to both Houses. Responsible for overseeing public accounts, following up audits, and recommending changes to financial reporting.

Leave: A Mandata sub-system designed to record and automatically maintain leave balances.

LeaveProto: A prototype version of Leave.

Management Information Branch: Branch responsible for user requirements and user implementation 1974-1976.

Mandata: A computer system for automating personnel and establishments processing in the Australian Public Service.

Mandata cell: State and territory based data centre. Performed data entry and hard copy distribution. Based in offices of the Public Service Inspector.

Mandata Consultative Group: A consultative forum including representatives of the staff associations (unions) and the Public Service Board.

Mandata Coordinating Committee: High level consultative committee of Public Service Board and user Department officials.

Mandata Interrogation Package: A query language purpose built for use with the Mandata system.

Glossary Of Terms 353

Mandata User Group: MPO and user committee for operational level consultation and problem resolution.

MCC: Mandata Coordinating Committee.

MCG: Mandata Consultative Group.

mcu: Mini computer unit.

MIB: Management Information Branch.

Minute: Internal memorandum.

MIP: Mandata Interrogation Package.

MPO: Briefly Mandata Project Office. Subsequently Mandata Program Office.

MUG: Mandata User Group.

National Capital Development Commission: Authority responsible for overseeing and managing the development of office sites in Canberra.

National Wage Case: Feature of Australian industrial relations system providing wage adjustments in response to economic conditions such as inflation.

NCDC: National Capital Development Commission.

NWC: National Wage Case.

Octopus: A program in the Productivity system designed to permit changes to records regardless of applicable regulations. Intended for correcting errors caused by incorrect programs.

P&E: Personnel and Establishments. The name by which Data Stream came to be known.

PAC: Public Accounts Committee

Glossary Of Terms

Paper 23: Strategic Plan - Activities in Phase 1 Mandata. A high level statement of the functions and boundaries of the original Mandata concept.

Permanent Head: Permanent administrative head of a government department.

Post Office: Australian Post Office.

Processing Framework: The software system specially built for Mandata which managed the transaction and batch processing environment of the central computer. Provided privacy and security protection.

PSI: Public Service Inspector.

Public Accounts Committee: See Joint Committee of Public Accounts.

Public Service Board: An independent authority within the Australian Public Service responsible for overseeing the organisation and effective running of the Public Service.

Public Service Inspector: The state and territory based representative of the Public Service Board.

SMILE: Interrogation system provided with the Department of Productivity system.

SPR: Standard Personnel Record

Standard Personnel Record: Data recorded about officers of the Australian Public Service.

Telecom: Post 1974, an independent authority responsible for telecommunication services.

Appendix
Chronology Of The Mandata Project

Date	Event
1970	
Sep	Feasibility study commences
1971	
Jan	Initial feasibility study report presented
Nov	Full feasibility report completed
1972	
Feb	Board considers report
Feb	ADP Division created
Apr	Report circulated to departments and IDC on ADP
Jul	Board asks staff associations for comments
Jul	Consultants commence review of proposal
Sep	First draft accommodation specifications for equipment
Sep	Consultants support feasibility study findings
Oct	Treasury backs Mandata
1973	
Jan	NCDC complains to Treasury about inadequate consideration of site costs
Mar	Revised feasibility study approved by Board
Mar	Mandata allocated 28 positions
Apr	Information papers written for staff associations
May	IDC on ADP endorses Mandata
Jul	Mandata Liaison Committee with Treasury and Superannuation Board starts
Aug	Mandata Consultative Group established
Aug	Board agrees on no staff redundancies
Aug/Sep	Recruiting undertaken overseas
Dec	Board approves submission to Cabinet for funds

1974

Jan	Committee of Officials approves equipment bid
Feb	Cabinet approves funding
Mar	Board announces equipment funding
Jun	Common staff numbering scheme announced
Aug	NCDC complains to IDC about lack of concern for site issues
Aug	IDC on ADP approves tender specifications
Aug	Staffing restrictions advised
Aug	Call for tenders issued
Sep	Mandata applications definition committee established
Sep	Mandata Coordinating Committee's first meeting
Sep	Board suggests use of Trade Offices for equipment
Oct	NCDC again complains to IDC
Nov	Tenders close
Nov	Board's proposal to use Trade Offices rejected by NCDC

1975

Jan	Australia Post and Telecom withdraw
Jan	Anzac Park West under discussion as Mandata site
Feb	Tender evaluation completed
Mar	IDC on ADP endorses equipment selection
Apr	Planning commences with mini computer supplier
Apr	Letter of intent to terminal supplier
Apr	Agreement to use Anzac Park West
Jun	NCDC warns Board of financial problems with site alteration
Jun	Steering committee with central computer manufacturer established
Jun	Letters of intent issued to successful tenderers
Jul	Project manager for central computer and software installed
Aug	NCDC advises of site delay
Aug	Agreement to use Trade as an interim site
Sep	A-G's report first mentions Mandata
Oct	Software producer concerned about Processing Framework requirements
Nov	NCDC stops work on Anzac Park West
Nov	Early version of Paper 23
Dec	First minicomputers accepted
Dec	New Liberal government stresses need for austerity

Chronology Of The Mandata Project

1976

Jan	Reassurance that Mandata will not be cut back
Feb	Trade site finished and mainframe delivered
Feb	Manufacturer finds central computer site below specification
Feb	AGO announces initial audit review
Mar	Computer room conditions stop work
Apr	AGO review commences
May	Bid to Board for more staff
May	Building work problems in computer room
Jun	Computer room environment improves
Jun	Anzac Park West project cancelled
Jul	Project review commences
Jul	Revised version of paper 23
Aug	*Canberra Times* criticises Mandata
Aug	Review findings presented to the Board
Sep	New project director appointed
Sep	Mainframe accepted
Sep	Presentations on Mandata for selected departments
Sep	Proposal to use mainframe for bureau services
Sep	A-G's report critical of Mandata
Oct	Users asked for help at MCC
Dec	Mandata commences pick-up of records for Productivity system

1977

Jan	Attempt to broaden MPO remit
Mar	New cost-benefit analysis completed
Apr	DataStream effectively operational
May	Consultants engaged to review Mandata
Jun	DataStream officially operational
Jun	PAC announces its intention to investigate
Jul	Consultants support Mandata
Aug	Mandata staff ceiling raised from 92 to 153
Aug	Mainframe has 95% uptime
Sep	A-G's 1977 report tabled
Sep/Oct	PAC hearings
Oct	MPO prints reports on central mainframe
Oct	Pick up of records on mainframe
Oct	Leave Proto implemented

1978

Feb	AGO announces new study of Mandata
Feb	New project director appointed
Mar	Board approaches A-G to relieve the pressure
Mar	Leave Proto reviewed
Apr	Decision not to extend implementation beyond existing 12 departments
Apr/May	Dept of Capital Territory processing operational on mainframe
May	Chairman of PAC criticises Mandata in Parliament
May/Jun	Press echoes the criticisms
Jun	Impact Evaluation Study commences
Jun	Dept of Capital Territory asked to remove its work from the mainframe
Jul	AGO starts new study of Mandata
Aug	PAC visits Mandata offices
Aug	Full Leave system replaces Leave Proto
Sep	PAC hearings
Sep	A-G's 1978 report tabled in Parliament
Nov	Des/Sal system implemented

1979

Jan	MUG users express discontent
Mar	Leave system accepted by implementation staff
Mar	Impact Evaluation Study submitted to Board
Mar	Major effort to clean up software commences
Apr	Optimism after first successful run on central computer
Apr	Staff association representative critical of Board
Apr	Hardware problems, slow processing
May	Transfer of all departmental computer records to central computer
May	AGO commences follow up review
Jul/Aug	Errors emerging on the records
Sep	A-G's 1979 report tabled in Parliament
Sep	AGO initiates further review
Oct	Three shift operation instituted
Oct	PAC report tabled in Parliament
Oct	Extended press criticism
Oct	MCC Sub-Committee on Development Priorities established
Nov	Strategic Planning Group established

Nov   Investigation of development methodologies starts

1980
Jan   Ed Quals processing goes into production
Jan   Board agrees to purchase systems development methodology
Feb   Board acknowledges Mandata's limits
Mar   Board announces it will review Mandata's future
Mar   Some problems with Ed Quals
Mar   Chairman complains to A-G that his criticisms damage the Board
Apr   MCC Sub-Committee on Development Priorities reports
Apr   Board decides to scale back
Apr   MCC rejects A-G's 1979 criticisms
Apr   A-G's interim report severely criticises Mandata
May   Submission to Cabinet to scale back Mandata
Jul   Cabinet approves scale back
Jul   Board rejects A-G's criticisms
Aug   A-G agrees to 'cool it'
Sep   Finance Minute in response to PAC report tabled in Parliament
Oct   Internal MPO reorganisation
Oct   Liberal government reelected
Nov   MCG complains about lack of consultation

1981
Mar   Implementation of methodology commences
Apr   PM announces termination of Mandata
Nov   Mandata closes

Index

abandonment 27, 124
Abdel-Hamid, T.K. 328
Aberfan 20
acceptance 67, 85
accidents 19
Ackoff, R.L. 21
adaptation 67
adoption 67
Administrative Services
  Dept of 241
administrative theory 36
adoption 67
ADP Development Branch
  159
ADP Systems Development
  Branch 261, 263
agenda
  control of 52
AGSTB 181
Antill, L. 87
Anzac Park West 262
approaches 78, 79
APSB 241
Argyris, C. 21
asymmetric dependence 48
attitude formation 68, 129
Auditor-General's Office 138,
  141, 142, 143, 148, 155,
  172, 196, 228, 229, 231-
  232, 242, 248, 260, 271,
  276, 280, 283, 286
Australia Post 195, 260
Australian Computer Society
  279
Australian Public Service 138,
  143, 146-149, 154, 157,
  162, 203, 241, 244

Avison, D.E. 78, 87

Bachrach, P. 48
Baker, F.T. 79
Bandura, A. 113
Baratz, M.S. 48
Bariff, M.L. 115
Bay of Pigs 19
Becker, S.W. 120
Benbasat, I. 134, 144
Benyon, D. 86
Bhopal 19
Bignell, V. 19, 20, 33
Bjørn-Andersen, N. 91, 111,
  114
Blau, P.M. 48, 49
Block, R. 331
Boddie, J. 328
Boddy, D. 34
Bojcun, M. 19
Boland, R. 3, 22, 105
bounded rationality 38, 73,
  112
Braybrooke, D. 39
Brooks, F.P. 23, 31
Buchanan, D.A. 34
Buechi, H. 23, 303, 305
bug 63, 64
Bureau of Census and
  Statistics 154, 155
Burns, T. 45
Burrell, G. 35
Business and Consumer
  Affairs
  Dept of 205, 216

Cabinet 180, 244, 247, 252, 254
Campbell-Kelly, M. 154
Canberra 140
Canberra Times 197, 266, 267
Capital Territories
 Dept of 210, 241
Carey, A. 36
Carnegie school 37
case approach 3, 8, 133-144
case history 133
case studies
 value of 133-134
CGO 206
Challenger 19
Checkland, P. 89
Chernobyl 19
Child, J. 34, 68
Classical Theory 36
Clegg, S. 46, 48
coalition building 52, 105
cognitive limits 5, 38, 47, 58, 59, 61, 72, 73, 83, 253, 269
Cohen, M.D. 13, 37, 39, 54
Colton, K.W. 22
Committee of Officials 179, 206, 252, 254, 256
competitors 45
complexity 73, 74, 83
Computer Weekly 1
Computing (Australia) 1
Computing (UK) 1
Concorde 19
conflict 76
conservatism 68, 120
constraints 42, 43, 45, 46, 58, 64, 71, 73, 74, 75, 76, 77, 100, 103, 119, 123, 129, 137
context 5, 35, 42, 58, 59, 60, 66, 68, 69, 70, 80-84, 85, 86, 87, 88, 90, 91, 97, 98, 103, 106, 108, 113, 114, 116, 120, 126, 133, 137, 251, 259, 286
contingencies 30, 42, 58, 64, 69, 73, 75, 76, 82, 100, 103, 119, 121, 123, 137, 252
contingency model 35
contingency theory 87
Continuous Record of Personnel 151, 165
coopting 52, 105, 109
criticism 28, 106, 107, 108, 109, 243, 252, 274
Crozier, M. 49
CRP 211
CSIRO 154, 155
culture 46, 271
customers 45, 75
Cyert, R.M. 37, 39

Daft, R.L. 120
Dahl, R. 48
Dalton, M. 36
Darwin cyclone 19
Data Alsal 202
Data Consolidate 202
Data Enhance 202
Data Pay 202
Data Service/s 202
DataStream (Extended) 202
Davis, D.D. 34,
Davis, G.B. 67, 88, 91, 111, 328
Dean, J.W. jr 40, 68
Dearden, J. 21
decision-making 37-42, 47, 97, 98
 affective factors 40, 41
 fallible 40-41
Defence
 Dept of 155, 221

definition 67
Des/Sal 220, 243, 269
development 56, 58, 60, 67,
  68, 70, 71, 77, 84, 85, 129,
  130, 251, 258
Dickson, G.W. 206, 296, 297,
  298, 300, 301, 302
Dill, W.R. 45
disjointed incrementalism 39
dissatisfaction 27, 28, 31, 55,
  93, 105, 244, 245, 247, 271
division of labour 48, 76
documentation 71, 83
dominant coalition 39
Dunkerley, D. 46
Dunkle, D.E. 118
Dutton, W.H. 116, 206, 306,
  311

Eames
  Office of C. and R. 154
Education 221
Educational Qualifications
  269
Emerson, R.M. 48
Employment and Industrial
  Relations
  Dept of 211
Energy Conservation System
  296-300
enhancement 69, 86, 130
environment 5, 42, 43, 45-46,
  47, 58, 59, 60, 61, 69, 74-76,
  77, 82, 98, 252, 253, 271
evaluation 5, 31, 41, 60, 62,
  65, 91, 99, 124, 128, 130,
  246, 251, 252, 254, 260, 272
  descriptive information 94
  diagnostic information 92,
    94
  effect on support 96-99

first party 97, 110
form of expression 93
formative 91
influences on 95-96, 265
management of 104-109
nature of 92-94
prescriptive information 94
scale 93
summative 92
techniques 106
third party 97, 108, 110,
  264, 273
time of occurrence 92
timeframe 93, 95, 104, 105
Ewusi-Mensah, K. 27, 124
expectation failure 24-26, 28,
  30
expectations 24, 31, 106, 129

failure
  approaches to 3, 21
  causes 3, 21, 22, 134, 135
  concepts 22-23
  correspondence 22
  costs of 1
  definition 27
  expectation 23
  inevitability of 319-321
  interaction 23
  level of 1
  model of process of 55-65,
    134
  nature of 4, 5, 18-33, 55,
    63, 134
  process 23, 134
failure as termination 27, 28,
  30
Fayol, H. 36
feasibility study 71
Feldman, M.S. 122
Fetzer, J.H. 74

Feynman, R.P. 19
Finance
  Dept of 206
Fiscal Impact Analysis System 306-312
Fitzgerald, G. 78, 87
fixers 57, 61, 81, 82, 100-103, 111, 123, 126, 128, 251
fixing 14
flaws 4, 5, 40, 63, 64, 65, 66, 69, 70, 74, 80, 81, 82, 83, 84, 85, 86, 87, 88, 112, 114, 120, 121, 122, 126, 127, 128, 130, 248, 251, 252, 270
Forester, T. 1
Fortune. J. 19, 20, 33
Foster, H.D. 20
Franz, C.R. 105
Friedman, A.L. 42, 68, 87
funders 57, 81, 100-103, 111, 123, 251
funding 14

Galbraith, J.R. 37, 79, 115
Ganter, H-D. 68
garbage can 40
Giddens, A. 35, 93
Ginzberg, M.J. 91, 92
Glasser, J. 127
Goldstein, D.K. 134, 144
Gorry, G.A. 16
Gouldner, A. 36
Guardian 1

Hage, J. 43, 68
Hall, P. 19
Hamann, J.R. 91
Hamman, H. 19
Hartley, S.W. 300, 301, 302
Hawkes, N. 19
Haynes, V. 19

Health
  Dept of 155
Henderson, E. 1
Herald Of Free Enterprise 19
Hickson, D.J. 49, 115, 132
Hinings, C.R. 49, 115, 132
Hirschheim, R.A. 3, 22, 23, 30, 32, 33, 35, 36, 91, 92
history 5, 42, 46-47, 77, 253
Hixon 20
Hollerith, H 154
Hoyle, A. 139, 234
Human Relations 36
Hunt, J.W. 43

IDC on ADP 155, 175, 183, 252, 254, 256, 261
idea champion 120, 252
Immigration and Ethnic Affairs
  Dept of 210
impact analysis 324-325
Impact Evaluation Study 215
implementation 67, 68, 69, 77, 85, 130
Ince, D. 23
incorporation 67
influence attempts
  costs of 109
information flows
  control of 48, 104
information systems
  abstract form 11, 56, 68, 73, 84, 129
  concrete form 11, 56, 68, 70, 73, 84, 104
  department/organisation 115-119
  innovation process 5, 12-13, 14, 28, 31, 34, 57, 63, 66-88, 98, 103, 106, 112,

114, 119, 120, 121, 123, 124, 128, 251
methodologies 74, 86, 88
nature of 4, 10, 11, 12
information systems process 10-16, 26, 30, 40, 58, 61, 64, 91, 93, 112, 113, 119, 125, 133
infrastructure
  development of 251
  establishment of 68, 85
initiation 67, 68, 70, 77, 84, 129, 251, 252, 258
innovation 38
installation and operation 67
institutional environment 45
integration 67, 69
interests 23, 24, 26, 55, 57, 60, 62, 91, 92, 93, 95, 96, 104, 105, 118, 130, 247

Janis, I.L. 19
Janson, M.A. 206, 296, 297, 298
JCPA 135, 153, 154, 155, 175, 176, 182, 184, 191, 234
Johnson-Laird, P.N. 45
Juddery, B. 149

Kieser, A. 68
King, J.L. 118
Kling, R. 46, 53, 113, 132, 241, 315
Kozar, K.A. 127
Kraemer, K.L. 116, 117, 118, 123
Kwon, T.H. 67, 330

Lane, J.P. 118
Laudon, K.C. 33
Lawrence, P.R. 36

Leave 220, 223, 225, 269, 270
LeaveProto 209
Lee, C.A. 132
legitimacy 49, 52, 57, 96
Lehman, J.H. 23
Lindblom, C.E. 37, 39
Linton-Simpkins, F. 234
Little, S.E. 46, 93
Lorsch, J.W. 36
Loveridge, R. 34
Lucas, H.C. jr 3, 22, 33, 115, 132
Lukes, S. 48
Lyytinen, K. 22, 23, 30, 32, 33, 92

Madnick, S.E. 328
maintenance 56, 58, 69, 86, 130
management
  departmental 118
  information systems 115, 116, 118
  top 4, 5, 90, 102, 115, 118
Management Information Branch 262, 263
management states
  theory of 118, 119
management strategies 120-125, 252, 258, 266, 268, 285, 287-290
Mandata 145-290
  research method 134-144
Manufacturing Industry Dept of 191
March 13, 37, 38, 39, 54, 73, 122
Markus, M.L. 17, 32, 59, 76, 114, 321
Mason, R.O. 21
MCC 194, 203, 206, 214, 221,

224, 235, 236, 240, 274, 277, 280, 283
MCG 176, 237, 271, 274
Mead, M. 134, 144
Mencken, H.L. 315
Merton, R.K. 36
methods 3, 66, 78, 85, 105
Meyer, J.W. 45
Miller, C.L. 23
Mintzberg, H. 37, 42, 43, 53
Mitroff, I.I. 21
Mohr, L.B. 139
Morgan, G. 35, 53
Morgan, H.C. 21
Morrison, P. 1
MPO 141, 203, 213
MUG 221, 274

natural disasters 19
NCDC 189, 259, 261, 262
needs assessment 323-324
negotiation 50, 57, 62, 93, 113, 124, 128, 129, 130
networking 129, 261, 269
Newman, M. 79
Newton, M. 234
Northrop 116

Olsen, J.P. 13, 37, 39, 54
Olson, M.H. 67, 88, 328
operation 56, 58, 67, 69, 77, 85, 86, 112, 130
organisation theory 34-53
organisational structure 12, 42, 59, 60, 72, 79, 98, 104, 107, 108
organising devices 78, 79

P&E 213, 223, 281, 283
Parrott, S. 19
Pedersen, P.H. 115, 116

Pennings, J.M. 132
performance gap
  detection of 67, 68
Perrow, C. 20, 36, 44, 45, 73
Pettigrew, A.M. 39, 48, 104, 114
Pfeffer, J. 11, 48, 49, 50, 52, 54, 76
planning disasters 19
Polaris 105
political process 51-52
political tactics 52
politico-military failure 19
politics 5, 7, 31, 39, 41, 47-52, 59, 61, 72, 76, 84, 91, 99, 103, 104, 105, 108, 112, 116, 121, 122, 133, 138, 139, 249, 252, 253, 264, 271
politics of evaluation 60
politics of innovation process 59
politics of support 59
Pondy, L.R. 105
Post Office 153, 172, 178, 195, 287
Postmaster-General's Department 155
power 30, 39, 47-52, 76, 82, 97, 100, 109, 121, 126, 128
  nature of 48
  of project organisation 114-119, 125-131
  sources of 48-51
power-brokers 57, 62, 81, 82, 100-103, 109, 111, 116, 128, 258
power-broking 14
Prime Minister and Cabinet Dept of 206
problem-solving 38, 59, 66, 67, 70-84, 85, 126, 128

ad hoc 5, 77-80, 82, 85, 87, 126
  mechanisms 5, 70, 71, 78, 80, 81, 84, 85, 86, 87, 126, 134
  strategies 86
  systematic 5, 77-80, 82, 84, 87, 126
problems 63, 66, 67, 85
process failure 30
Processing Framework 260, 269, 288
production lattice 113
Productivity
  Dept of 198, 209
programming 68
programming constructs 45, 73
Progs/FSE 220, 247, 269
project organisation 4, 10, 11-12, 16, 27, 43, 55, 56, 57, 58, 60, 61, 66, 70, 77, 90, 111
Project Services Branch 159
Przasnyski, Z.H. 27, 124
Public Accounts Committee 135, 140, 141, 142, 175, 180, 207, 232-234, 271, 278, 281, 286
Public Service Act 1922 165
Public Service Board 140, 141, 142, 143, 149-151, 159, 205

Raisinghani, D. 37
Reason, J. 20
reciprocal causation 113
reciprocal interdependence 44, 73
regulators 45, 74
representative/interest groups 46

research
  suggestions for 329-334
research method
  choice of site 138-140
  database 143-144
  design 135-138
  process 140-143
resistance 21, 48, 69, 85, 130
resource dependence 49, 113, 114
resources
  financial 101
  information 49, 56
  material 49, 56
  monetary 49, 56
Retail Buyers' Planning System 300-303
Review of Commonwealth Functions 239, 244, 249, 252
Robey, D. 105
Rogers, W. 19
Roman, D.D. 333
Rosenberg, D. 79
Rowan, B. 45
Royal Commission on Australian Government Administration 262
Rudelius, W. 300, 301, 302

Salancik, G.R. 11, 49
SAMIN 211
San Francisco earthquake 19
Sapolsky, H.M. 105
satisficing 38
Saunders, C.S. 115
Scacchi, W. 113
Scammell, R.W. 115
Schmitt, J.W. 127
Schneck, R.E. 132
Scholes, J. 89

Schon, D.A. 120
scientific management 36
Scott, W.R. 4, 46
Scott-Morton, M.S. 16
Seashore, S.E. 100
Selznick, P. 36
Services and Property
  Dept of 191
Shrvastava, P. 19
Simon, H.A. 37, 38, 73
Skidmore, S. 86
Sloane, S.B. 1, 23, 292, 293, 294, 295
Smithson, S. 91
Soden, J.V. 21
software complexity 45
software decay 86
software medium 45
solutions 70-84
SPR 215, 223
Srinivasan, A. 91
stage model of innovation 66, 67
stages of innovation 67-70, 84, 104
stakeholders 24, 25
Stalker, G.M. 45
Stamper, R. 34
Standard Personnel Record 152, 164
strategic contingencies
  control of 49, 57, 115, 122, 126, 249
strategic decision 68, 70, 84, 129, 253
Strauss, A. 113
structure 5, 42, 43, 47, 51, 60, 61, 62, 77, 251
Summerland 20
sunk costs 105
Superannuation and
  Retirement Benefits Boards 155
Superannuation Board 178, 253, 257
suppliers 45, 75
Supply
  Dept of 175
support 5, 14, 29, 52, 55, 56, 57, 59, 60, 61, 65, 66, 70-84, 86, 90, 99, 100-111, 112, 114, 116, 119, 121, 122, 123, 128
  flow of 90, 91, 99-103, 110, 119, 124, 251, 258, 260, 273
  loss of 5, 57, 62, 64, 87, 88, 112, 125, 126, 247
  management of 5, 13-14, 15, 34, 52, 62, 83, 103-109, 112, 120, 121, 122, 123, 125, 136, 251, 257, 274, 287-290
  timeframe of 103
support/power analysis 324
supporters 4, 5, 14, 16, 27, 31, 56, 57, 60, 61, 65, 90, 97, 99, 102, 121, 122, 124, 126, 130
  external 57
  internal 57
Swissair 303-306
Sydney Opera House 19
systems analysis 68
systems definition 67
systems design 68
systems failure 19-21
systems proposal 67, 68, 84

Taxation
  Dept of 155, 173
Taylor, F.W. 36
technical process 5, 42, 43-45,

47, 59, 60, 73, 74, 84, 252, 253, 270
techniques 2, 71, 72, 74, 78, 79, 104
technology 42, 43, 46, 75, 139, 253
technology-push 40, 262
Teheran hostages 19
Telecom 195, 260
terminal failure 27, 28
termination 27, 29, 31, 55, 99, 121, 244, 245, 246
testing 68
Théorêt, A. 37
Thompson, J.D. 37, 39, 42, 44, 45, 73
Three Mile Island 20
Thynne, I. 234
toolkits 86, 87, 88
tools 2, 66, 78, 79, 105
Trade and Industry Dept of 172
Transport Dept of 198, 209
Treasury 155, 173, 178, 253, 257, 281
triangle of dependences 4, 30, 55-58, 61, 62, 66, 99, 113, 114, 118, 122, 125, 251
Turner, B.A. 20

uncertainty 12, 28, 38, 49, 60, 66, 84, 85, 88, 102, 112, 115, 119, 249
unit production 44
US Bureau of Census 154
use
  innovation sub-stage 67
users 11, 58, 63, 75, 104, 121, 130
USS Starship 291-296

Veterans' Affairs Dept of 242

Walton, R.E. 17, 89
Wason, P.C. 45
Watergate 19
Weapons Research Establishment 154
web models 113-114, 117, 129
Weick, K.E. 47, 54
Wettenhall, R. 139
Wilenski, P. 140
Wilkinson, B. 34
Willcocks, L. 111
Wiltshire, K. 149
Wood-Harper, A.T. 87
Woodward, J. 36, 43

Yin, R.K. 135, 137, 138, 139, 143, 144
Yuchtman, E. 100

Zammuto, R.F. 92, 124
Zmud, R.W. 67, 91, 92, 330